Marxist Literary and Cultural Theories

transitions

General Editor: Julian Wolfreys

Published Titles

NEW HISTORICISM AND CULTURAL MATERIALISM John Brannigan
POSTMODERN NARRATIVE THEORY Mark Currie
MARXIST LITERARY AND CULTURAL THEORIES Moyra Haslett
DECONSTRUCTION•DERRIDA Julian Wolfreys

Forthcoming Titles

NATIONAL IDENTITY John Brannigan
GENDER Alison Chapman
IDEOLOGY James Decker
QUEER THEORY Donald E. Hall
POSTCOLONIAL THEORY Claire Jones
RACE Brian G. Niro
LITERARY FEMINISMS Ruth Robbins
SUBJECTIVITY Ruth Robbins
PSYCHOANALYSIS AND LITERATURE Andrew Roberts
TRANSGRESSIONS Julian Wolfreys
FORMALIST CRITICISM AND READER-RESPONSE THEORY
   Kenneth Womack

Transitions
Series Standing Order
 ISBN 0–333–73684–6
(*outside North America only*)

You can receive future titles in this series as they are published by
placing a standing order. Please contact your bookseller or, in case of
difficulty, write to us at the address below with your name and address,
the title of the series and the ISBN quoted above.

Customer Services Department, Macmillan Distribution Ltd
Houndmills, Basingstoke, Hampshire RG21 6XS, England

transitions

Marxist Literary and Cultural Theories

Moyra Haslett

First published 2000 by
MACMILLAN PRESS LTD
Houndmills, Basingstoke, Hampshire RG21 6XS
and London
Companies and representatives
throughout the world

ISBN 0–333–69213–6 hardcover
ISBN 0–333–69214–4 paperback

A catalogue record for this book is available
from the British Library.

This book is printed on paper suitable for recycling and
made from fully managed and sustained forest sources

10   9   8   7   6   5   4   3   2   1
09   08   07   06   05   04   03   02   01   00

Printed in Hong Kong

 Published in the United States of America by
ST. MARTIN'S PRESS, INC.,
Scholarly and Reference Division
175 Fifth Avenue, New York, N.Y. 10010

ISBN 0–312–22673–X (cloth)
ISBN 0–312–22674–8 (paper)

Contents

General Editor's Preface

Transitions: *transition–em*, n. of action. 1. A passing or passage from one condition, action or (rarely) place, to another. 2. Passage in thought, speech, or writing, from one subject to another. 3. **a.** The passing from one note to another. **b.** The passing from one key to another, modulation. 4. The passage from an earlier to a later stage of development or formation ... change from an earlier style to a later; a style of intermediate or mixed character ... the historical passage of language from one well-defined stage to another.

The aim of *Transitions* is to explore passages and movements in critical thought, and in the development of literary and cultural interpretation. This series also seeks to examine the possibilities for reading, analysis and other critical engagements which the very idea of transition makes possible. The writers in this series unfold the movements and modulations of critical thinking over the last generation, from the first emergences of what is now recognised as literary theory. They examine as well how the transitional nature of theoretical and critical thinking is still very much in operation, guaranteed by the hybridity and heterogeneity of the field of literary studies. The authors in the series share the common understanding that, now more than ever, critical thought is both in a state of transition and can best be defined by developing for the student reader an understanding of this protean quality.

This series desires, then, to enable the reader to transform her/his own reading and writing transactions by comprehending past developments. Each book in the series offers a guide to the poetics and politics of interpretative paradigms, schools and bodies of thought, while transforming these, if not into tools or methodologies, then into conduits for directing and channelling thought. As well as transforming the critical past by interpreting it from the perspective of the present day, each study enacts transitional readings of a number of well-known literary texts, all of which are themselves conceivable as having been transitional texts at the moments of their first appearance. The readings offered in these books seek, through close critical reading and theoretical engagement, to demonstrate certain possibilities in critical thinking to the student reader.

It is hoped that the student will find this series liberating because rigid methodologies are not being put into place. As all the dictionary definitions of the idea of transition above suggest, what is important is the action, the passage: of thought, of analysis, of critical response. Rather than seeking to help you locate yourself in relation to any particular school or discipline, this series aims to put you into action, as readers and writers, travellers between positions, where the movement between poles comes to be seen as of more importance than the locations themselves.

Julian Wolfreys

Acknowledgements

A book of this sort always contains many debts. Principal thanks must go to Julian Wolfreys, who, as general editor of this *Transitions* series, offered constant, transatlantic encouragement and was patient when the original deadline was exceeded. I am especially grateful for the many helpful comments he made on successive drafts and for his generosity of spirit and intelligence. I'd also like to thank Margaret Bartley, commissioning editor for this series, for her faith in the series, and in this book in particular; and my copy editor, Keith Povey, for his care in reading and correcting the manuscript. Ruth Robbins read and discussed many of the ideas and interpretations presented here, particularly the chapters on Jane Austen and Oscar Wilde, and gave of her time – and library – generously. Students of 'Introduction to Literary Theory' at the University of Luton were unwitting guinea pigs for some of the material contained herein and so perhaps need apologies as well as thanks. Thanks also to my mother, Maisie Haslett, for her willingness to be an impromptu research assistant whenever I needed one. But the greatest debt of all is, as always, to John Brannigan, whose commitment to this book was equal to that of his own contribution to the *Transitions* series. The strengths of the book, such as they may be, are largely due to his continuing love and support and to our shared commitments, political and otherwise.

Introduction:
The Politics of
Intellectual Work

Marx: 'All I know is that I am not a Marxist.'
(Marx and Engels 1965, 415)

'... virtually all of [these various Marxisms] include within themselves
a crucial denunciation of bad or "vulgar materialist" Marxisms: ... it
has seemed impossible for any Marxism to define itself or to assert its
identity without this internal exorcism of the "frère ennemi" or
ghostly double which would be this bad or vulgar Marxism, the
reductive one, what "Marxism" is for everybody else, for the non-
Marxists; and this from Marx himself onward (whose "I am not a
Marxist" probably no longer needs to be quoted).'
(Jameson 1995, 104)

'Marxism ... can best be thought of as a *problematic*; that is to say, it
can be identified, not by specific positions (whether of a political,
economic or philosophical type), but rather by the allegiance to a
specific complex of problems, whose formulations are always in
movement and in historic rearrangement and restructuration, along
with their object of study (capitalism itself).'
(Jameson in Makdisi 1996, 19)

There are possibly more preconceptions and casual definitions of
marxist literary theory than of any other theoretical approach. The
marxist critic is largely perceived as obsessed with the economic
context of the literary text, a context which he – and it usually is 'he' –
understands only in a rigidly prescriptive manner. And because, it is
thought, each individual is rigidly determined by the economic mode
of production, the author becomes an anonymous class-representa-
tive who programmatically rehearses the ideas of his or her own class.

I

But this caricature hugely oversimplifies Marx's argument that men and women make their own history on the basis of anterior conditions, or the inextricably *social* dimension of the economic in marxist analysis.[1] Marxist theories are frequently criticised as reductive, deterministic, and suffused with a grand-narrative privileging of revolutionary class struggle. For example, in a recent attack on marxist aesthetic theories, Dmitry Khanin argues that the 'major underlying assumption' of marxism is that 'every utterance is related to the political interests of certain classes and is eventually relevant to the overriding cause of class struggle' (1992, 270). And because such perceptions have become almost commonplace, marxist theories frequently denounce those features others assume are intrinsically part of marxism. The shame is that those who caricature marxism in this way do not usually read marxist texts in any detail, if indeed they do at all.[2]

The perception of marxism as a monolithic theory is partly because the terminology 'marxist' implies rigid adherence to a founding father, Karl Marx, and a prescriptive political code which determines literary readings. In fact, marxist literary theories are diverse and marxist literary and cultural debate is marked by a considerable degree of contestation, not least of which are the debates as to how we should read Marx himself. Many marxist thinkers have argued over ways in which we might interpret Marx, while others claim that perceived differences with Marx's own writings are not inhibiting.[3] In *History and Class Consciousness* (1922), for example, Lukács defined marxism as a method, rather than an uncritical acceptance of Marx's arguments, however those might be interpreted (xxv). And while Lukács argued for the primacy of history over economics as the most significant element in the methodology of marxism, drawing inspiration from the 'early' work of Marx, Althusser, in his rereading of Marx, repudiated the early writings as 'not Marxist' and adhered only to the 'scientific' Marx of the later works (see Althusser 1984, 32).[4] One of my aims in writing this book is thus to argue that marxism itself is a text, not a code. For this reason I have chosen to refer to 'marxist' theories throughout this book, since the use of lower case illustrates diversity from any 'original' model and reminds us that we cannot fix marxist theories as easily as we might think.

Many predict the demise of marxist approaches in the wake of the collapse of communist regimes in the former USSR and Eastern Europe (1989), yet they forget that Western left disillusionment with the Soviet Union occurred as early as the 1930s with the intense repression of the Stalinist years and became even more pronounced after the Soviet intervention in Hungary in 1956, in Czechoslovakia in 1968 and with the rise of the Solidarity movement in Poland. Certainly the relationship between marxism and communism has always been problematic: marxist theories have been more complex and nuanced than the monolithic orthodoxy of Stalinism but this has been obscured by the misidentification of marxism with communist regimes. Many of the stereotypes of marxist theorists aptly describe 'orthodox' figures like Zhdanov, who infamously championed a propagandist 'social realism' as the only permissible form for socialist art. But Zhdanov never influenced or was part of Western marxism. Indeed 'Western marxism' is defined by its opposition to 'scientific', official Communist marxism. So while many commentators prophecy the death of marxism as a theory with the apparent demise of the Soviet revolution, there is no intrinsic reason, from within the theo ries which this volume considers, why this should be so. Western marxism is characterised by a turn to culture which itself has been interpreted as a consequence of political disappointment. After the First World War, the conditions for revolution among the working classes in Europe were perfect, according to all 'orthodox' marxist predictions. When revolution failed to materialise anywhere outside Tsarist Russia, itself not particularly auspicious as a site of revolutionary change according to orthodox marxist analysis, the incomplete nature of economic analysis was all too clear. This is the history which Perry Anderson sketches in explaining why Western marxism has consistently focused on culture rather than economics or politics (Anderson 1979) and why Lukács and Gramsci turned to cultural analysis in order to understand why revolution had failed to arise in Hungary or Italy. As Francis Mulhern argues: 'The long reign of party dogmatism, through the decades of Stalinism proper and beyond, was also a golden age of Marxist aesthetics' (Mulhern 1992, 9).

The fall of statist regimes is potentially a moment of 'liberation' for marxist theories too, in that it provides an opportunity for the many other varieties of marxism to disassociate themselves from the kinds of thinking which have been mistakenly attributed to them. Indeed, marxism as an allegiance is now more necessary than ever, at a time when capitalism's alleged triumph is global, and no alternative economic systems seem possible.[5] The nature of contemporary capitalism has certainly changed enormously since the work of the first

marxists in the nineteenth and early twentieth centuries: the dominance of finance capital, for example, means that speculation is a
more appropriate term than production, and culture becomes
increasingly significant as commodification penetrates throughout a
global market. Culture has become a business while the economic
and commercial spheres have become cultural. Marxist critiques of
postmodernism point to the ironies in contemporary culture's
refusal of marxism, for marxist theories are accused of totalising at a
time when advanced capitalism penetrates into culture, nature and
social life. While the crisis of marxism is invoked as a commonplace
topic of discussion, the recurrent structural crises of capitalism are
overlooked, or make no theoretical impression. (With the stock
market crash in Asia in 1998, we can see that predictions that Japan
would be the centre of capitalism in the twenty-first century may
have been mistaken.) And while marxism's strengths are underestimated, we are losing the opportunity, not just of opposing, but of
understanding capitalism. Ellen Meiksins Wood mimics the political
defeatism of current commentators when she argues that: ' ... if we
can't really change or even understand the [capitalist] system (or
even think about it as a system at all), and if we don't, and can't, have
a vantage point from which to criticize the system, let alone oppose
it, we might as well lie back and enjoy it – or better still, go shopping'
(Wood 1997, 9).

One of the saddest ironies is the disappearance of class as an issue
from contemporary commentaries. Social class continues to be relevant to the structures of advanced capitalism and yet it has been
eclipsed as a category from all but marxist theories. Among the most
exciting theories currently practised are those which define and read
difference, including, and in diverse ways, feminist, postcolonial, and
poststructuralist readings. It is hardly surprising that marxism has
contributed greatly to these approaches, since it has always been
concerned with the difference of social class, but despite this
antecedent, many of these theories have countered marxism's legacy
in such a way that class itself is in danger of being forgotten (see Coole
1996). The current occlusion of class as an issue is partly due to
marxism's own blindness to other categories in the past. While
marxism, feminism and postcolonialism share many of the same
approaches and ideals, they have also developed as competing theoretical and political claims. Co-operative work has been hampered in
the past by often rather futile arguments about the prioritisation of

categories, so that debates have centred around 'which-comes-first' (class, race, gender or sex). And marxist theories have largely been responsible for these missed opportunities. One of the most significant problems with marxist theories has been their insistence on the primacy of socio-economic class at the expense of other forms of social division.[6] In too many marxist theories this has led to an omission of other categories of social differentiation such as ethnicity, race, gender and sexuality. Many of the marxist theorists I discuss and esteem *did* ignore issues of gender and race and this is comprehensible – though not justifiable – when we recall the periods in which they lived and wrote. To repeat their errors today would be inexcusable. But it would also be wrong to deny that their work has any value for us, despite these absences.

While many marxist theories are not nearly so intolerant of other approaches as this criticism would imply, most marxist theorists do believe that their approach is more comprehensive than others, and thus is the more explanatory. This is a matter of firmly held political belief: that marxism as a theory has a political priority in that its aim is to change the world, not interpret it (here paraphrasing Marx's famous argument concerning the role of the philosopher) and that its transformative ambitions must be defended. While few marxist theories today would claim to reveal absolute truths, they do assert a *situated* argument of what is true or false, for that specific historical moment. For example, marxism argues that all viewpoints are socially determined, but that does not entail that all viewpoints are equal in value. A prisoner is more likely to recognise the oppressive nature of a particular juridical system than a judge. (In classical marxist terms, the working classes will recognise the injustices of capitalism rather than the capitalists.) All marxist theories continue to assert that certain inequities – such as class exploitation and poverty – will always be 'wrong', and marxist literary theories continue to assert that these issues are not unrelated to literature. Marxist approaches to culture believe that they have a commitment to argue on behalf of those social classes which suffer under capitalism: not only the working classes, but those non-working classes, the unemployed, travellers, single parents, the elderly poor whose place in capitalist society is far from comfortable. While this commitment makes marxism appear pious and humourless to its detractors, it is also a necessary reminder that there is a world beyond the academy to which we are inescapably connected:

> Men and women do not live by culture alone, the vast majority of
> them throughout history have been deprived of the chance of living
> by it at all, and those few who are fortunate enough to live by it now
> are able to do so because of the labour of those who do not. Any
> cultural or critical theory which does not begin from this single most
> important fact, and hold it steadily in mind in its activities, is in my
> view unlikely to be worth very much. (Eagleton 1983, 214)

There is a grim irony in the fact that, while class begins to be seen as
an 'outmoded' category for current cultural analysis, simultaneously
we have witnessed considerable growth in the numbers of working
poor, unemployed and homeless and in slave labour, insecure and
part-time labour. The international structure of capitalism has esca-
lated and has put most 'developing' countries into permanent poverty
so that the direct exploitation of the labour forces has moved from the
West into the Third World. Contemporary capitalism relies upon the
structurally unemployed. (André Gorz, 1982, for example, has theorised the ways in which the 'non-class of non-workers' has taken the
place of the proletariat, despite their absence from rather than their
situation within relations of production.) So, while class relations in
the 'West' have certainly become more and more complex, this does
not mean that they no longer exist. Most commentators today –
marxist and non-marxist – would agree that the end of the twentieth
century has been marked in the West as a time of political quietism.
Marxist commentators warn that we are in danger of forgetting not
just to act but to think in resistance to capitalism.

A book on 'marxist literary and cultural theories' justifies its incorporation into a series like *Transitions* because of the enormous influence they have exercised over the growth and development of a range
of other theories. Marxist concepts and arguments have certainly
influenced other theoretical approaches to an unprecedented degree,
whether we think of Freud as a materialist thinker or trace the origins
of new historicism and cultural materialism or the very discipline of
cultural studies. Indeed, many writers who would refuse the title and
precise commitments of marxism still work in close affinity with it.
But to think of marxism in these terms is to reduce marxism to historical interest only. At the heart of this book, then, resides my own
continuing commitment to marxism as a current practice. Marxism
will always be a political rather than a literary choice, so that my

choice of marxist literary theories is both a conviction that the historicist and materialist perspectives involved in studying literature are the most worthwhile, but also the most politically enabling and ultimately self-aware. For one of the most appealing, and disarming aspects of a politicised criticism – marxism, black studies, feminism, queer studies, postcolonialism – is its openness. These approaches do not attempt to hide or deny the ideological nature of what they do, they do not pretend to an 'impartiality' or 'objectivity' which is increasingly seen as impossible. My own work attempts to marry marxist approaches with those of feminism and postcolonialism, especially as my research includes special interests in women writers and Irish writing.

Thus because marxism is an obviously political philosophy and activity, it is not vulnerable to charges of self-deception which might be levelled at other, ostensibly 'neutral' readings. Is an ideologically 'neutral' or 'impartial' mode of reading possible? In *Formalism and Marxism*, Tony Bennett argues that reading is inevitably a positioning:

> The literary text has no single or uniquely privileged meaning, no single or uniquely privileged effect that can be abstracted from the ways in which criticism itself works upon and mediates the reception of that text. In this sense, literature is not something to be studied; it is an area to be occupied. The question is not what literature's political effects *are* but what they might be *made to be*. (Bennett 1979, 137)

Marxism and literary and cultural studies

While diversity is true of all marxist theories, it is especially so of marxist literary and cultural theories. While Marx and Engels frequently refer to literature in their writings, and Marx intended to devote himself to a study of Balzac once *Capital* was completed, their brief discussions do not form a comprehensive system of literary theory. Additionally, marxist approaches to culture have always dissented from orthodox, or 'vulgar' marxisms by virtue of their interest in literature, art and music alone. Unlike deterministic marxisms, marxist cultural theories are rarely in danger of ignoring the non-economic. Despite their own diversity, however, marxist cultural theories share important characteristics and commitments. First and most fundamental of these is the refusal to separate art from society. Even those aestheticist artworks which attempt or claim to resist context – abstract painting, a Mills and Boon or Harlequin romance, Lewis Carroll's 'nonsense' poem 'Jabberwocky', the aestheticism associated with Walter Pater and Oscar Wilde, improvisatory jazz – are social, for they are all created and received in concrete contexts. In all marxist readings, art is interpreted as a material practice, perhaps because it relies upon a 'technology' (the pen, the printing press), is concretely realised in situations which themselves are material (the folk ballad sung in a bar or courtly masque performed for royalty) or is bought and sold like other commodities (and is thus subject to such factors as sponsorship, marketing, financing, production and distribution). One marxist reading of ostensibly aestheticist artworks, such as those suggested above, argues that aestheticism is itself an attempt to disguise its very implication in the kinds of commercial concerns which it so disdains. At the level of the producer of art – the novelist, folk singer, cartoonist – art is also already social, since the artwork is created by an individual with a class, gender and racial identity, and whose fashioning of the artwork is determined by such factors as education and affluence. In place of the author as expressive genius, whose intrinsic talents mean that she transcends her own time and place, we have the author as producer who is inevitably part of her own context. At the level of the word too, art is social, since language is a social convention rather than a merely individual one (as Vološinov argues contra Saussure).[7] Marxist literary theories thus attempt to situate the artwork within a total context, an ambitious project which will always be an aspiration rather than a necessarily completed task.

Marxist theories are then distinguished from other approaches in the way in which they prioritise the materiality of culture, the way in which it is produced, distributed and received as a concrete and social practice. For marxist theorists the economic mode of society is crucial here because it is the economic system which frequently, though not always, determines how art will be so constructed. The relationship between the economic and the literary is both the central concern of marxism and the subject of its most heated debates. Williams wrote of how the economic determines a 'whole way of life' and that non-economic (in marxist terms superstructural) forces, such as literature, should be related to this rather than to the economic element alone.

In practice, indeed, no separation between spheres is possible: the 'economic' sphere includes the social relations of people, and the 'literary' is marketed and bought like any other product. The theoretical persistence with which marxist theories situate the art work within society is also a political resistance to the ways in which capitalism separates the social and the individual, culminates in the division of labour and specialises spheres of human activity. So that while marxist approaches to literature attempt to describe and understand this splitting of aesthetics and society, they are also attempts to rectify this splitting, to change it.

Within these parameters, marxist approaches to literature are surprisingly varied, and there is no programmatic way of 'applying' marxist ideas. Of course, marxist critics will continue to discuss such issues as class struggle, commodification, the alienation of labour and so on, but these shared concerns have not entailed that marxist readings are always identical in approach, or even that their conclusions will be the same. Literature might be seen to reflect life under capitalism: for example in arguing that modernist art portrays and even exacerbates the individual's solipsism and isolation (Lukács) or that art is split between elitist 'high' art and popular 'low' art (cultural studies theorists, such as Bourdieu). Alternatively however, literature might be seen as opposing the ill-effects of capitalism: that specifically artistic traditions may be relatively free of economic determination so that this relative autonomy permits art to critique capitalist relations (Adorno), or that art alone resists appropriation by the market (Bürger on Cubism and avant-garde art); or that new technologies make a collective imagination possible (Benjamin on photography, newspapers and cinema). Some marxists celebrate realism as a mode by which we can understand society through its faithful portrayal (Lukács), while others deny that 'realism' can ever be anything other than a distorted or selected representation (Heath and MacCabe); some focus on the context of culture's production, others on its reception (cultural materialism), and some attempt to marry both these approaches (Williams); some examine the aesthetic and formal dimensions of art (Adorno), others concentrate on the material and educational production of art-works (Bourdieu). But all these marxist approaches to literature attempt both to articulate the relationship between literature and society and to call the separation which this implies into question. Pragmatically, we may have to separate art and society in order to explain their relation, but simultaneously we need to resist this separation by remembering that art is *part of* society, and vice versa. Contemporary marxist approaches to literature thus situate literary study within the wider parameters of social, economic and cultural history, and in doing so they erase the distinction between 'literary' and 'cultural' theory which is implied in this volume's title. Cultural studies grew out of marxist traditions of literary study, but it has also influenced literary theory in turn, so that all marxist literary theories are properly cultural theories too. (See Easthope 1991.) In the growth of cultural studies as a discipline, marxism has had to confront the possible elitism of its own practices, in a self-reflexivity which continues in the debates between marxism and 'post-marxism'.

I work within marxist paradigms of cultural study because of this self-reflexivity, but also because of their historicist and materialist approaches and their sense of political commitment. As a consequence of situating culture within society, marxist literary and cultural theories ask the most challenging questions. Within literary studies, for example, marxism asks: what is the relation between literature and society? Does literary value exist, and if so in what? What is the relation between my study and the lives of others outside of the academy? Can my study make anything of a difference, and if not, why not? Ultimately it would be arrogant – and foolish – to believe that studying literature or culture might change the world. Stuart Hall stresses the importance of intellectual modesty, often lacking in the ambitious sweep and aims of marxist approaches, and draws a careful distinction between 'the politics of intellectual work and substituting intellectual work for politics' (in Morley and Chen 1996, 275). But any marxist perspective will always engage with the world beyond itself, will attempt to speak for those who have been silenced, or permit those voices which have been ignored to be heard. While our social and economic systems continue to 'succeed' by crushing and inhibiting the potential of others, marxism will continue to remind us of their various forms of oppression, whether that is the slave labour exacted of the Third World or the structural inequalities in the British and American educational systems (which is not to say that such diverse forms of injustice are equivalent). Whether we listen to music on Walkmans, mass-manufactured through cheap labour in Asia, or praise the current renaissance in British painting or literature, we need to remember that the Asian worker or the young school-leaver whose parents could neither afford private schooling nor college fees is a part of what we do and value. This may be 'bleeding-heart liberalism' to critics of this book and of these theories, but making such arguments is the least we can do.

Notes

1. The marxist definition of the 'economic' modes of production includes both the forces and relations of production, and because the forces of production include not only raw materials and technologies, but also the skills of men and women, the economic itself is thoroughly social.

2. Khanin's strong denunciation of Western marxisms is interesting because he is writing from within the former Soviet Union. For the different Russian and Western interpretations of Bakhtin, see Emerson (1997). For marxist responses to such caricaturing, see the epigraphs at the head of this chapter and Jameson (1995, 93, 104–5).

3. In an essay entitled 'You're a Marxist, Aren't You?' (1975), Williams argued that there is something 'fundamentally wrong' about a whole tradition being reduced to a 'single name', 'a single thinker' – even one as 'great' as Marx, who is 'incomparably the greatest thinker in the socialist tradition' (1989, 66). Drew Milne discusses the differences between Macherey's early work, *A Theory of Literary Production*, and his most recent, *The Object of Literature*, in terms of the differences between formal – but coercive – recognition of Marx and explicit refutations of Marx: 'Whereas previously a specific Communist Party register involved reference to Marx and Lenin to legitimate unorthodox readings, here Marx is cited to legitimate readings which mark their agility by arguing against Marx' (Milne 1996, 203).

4. See Belsey (1980) on Lacan's reading of Freud and Althusser's of Marx: 'The contradictions have been suppressed by orthodox (ideological and recuperative) Marxism and Freudianism, which have sought to extract in each case a single, coherent and univocal reading *authorized* by Marx or Freud. Althusser's Marxism makes no pretence of being "what Marx thought", but offers itself as the product of Marx's work, a product which there is no guarantee that Marx himself would have acknowledged' (151–2).

5. Corredor poses the question of marxism after the fall of communism to her interviewees (1997). See especially Eagleton's reply (147–8) for how marxist theory contains within itself an understanding and critique of Stalinism. The most notorious defence of capitalism's triumph as 'the end of history' is Fukuyama's book of that name (1992).

6. As always, however, this is not true of all marxist approaches. In the work of Adorno, for example, there is no class judgement.
7. For a discussion of Saussure's theories, see Currie (1998, *passim*).

Part I

Key Theories

1   Culture and Society

'We have got into the habit, since we realized how deeply works or values could be determined by the whole situation in which they are expressed, of asking about these relationships in a standard form: "what is the relationship of this art to this society?" But "society" in this question, is a specious whole. If the art is part of the society, there is no solid whole, outside it, to which, by the form of our question, we concede priority. The art is there, as an activity, with the production, the trading, the politics, the raising of families. ... It is then not a ques- tion of relating the art to the society, but of studying all the activities and their interrelations, without any concession of priority to any one of them we may choose to abstract. ... I would then define the theory of culture as the study of relationships between elements in a whole way of life.' (Williams 1965, 61–3)

'Culture is not reducible to those processes that Marxist political economy studies for its own purposes, but culture *is* embedded in those processes.'
(Ahmad in Wood and Foster 1997, 97)

Despite the diversity of marxist literary and cultural theories there are some general characteristics which all such theories share. The intro- duction has already discussed the emancipatory ideal of marxist theo- ries, the hope and belief that they can make a difference to what they study, that they might transform both themselves and their subjects. But most fundamental of all is the shared focus on the relationship between literature and society, a relationship which is so interwoven that it almost makes no sense to speak of a relationship at all. Literature and other artistic forms are inevitably social. Art cannot exist outside society. And marxist interpretations believe that the splitting of realms, so that a novel or oil painting, for example, is viewed as autonomous of society, is itself a symptom of capitalist or industrial modern societies. In *Ways of Seeing* (1972), for example,

John Berger argues with Kenneth Clark's reading of Gainsborough's portrait, 'Mr and Mrs Andrews'. For Clarke, this is a painting in which Mr and Mrs Andrews philosophically contemplate the natural beauty of their park; for Berger, a large part of this natural beauty is Mr and Mrs Andrews' ownership of it. Berger does not deny that such landowners found philosophic enjoyment in nature, but he reminds us that such enjoyment was primarily to be found among landowners, who could 'afford' the leisure needed for such contemplation and who actually owned increasingly large swathes of the countryside. Berger has been accused of being obsessed with property: here he intrusively brings issues of wealth and class to bear on an oil painting which expresses a delight in nature which transcends class and history. But class and history cannot be so removed from this painting's meaning: Berger's history of oil painting shows that the vast majority of oil paintings were demonstrations of what money could buy. And, in the composition of Gainsborough's painting, Mr and Mrs Andrews look at *us* rather than at 'nature', so that the land, and they as owners of it, are both on display. Concluding his discussion of this painting, Berger argues:

> ... among the pleasures their portrait gave to Mr and Mrs Andrews, was the pleasure of seeing themselves depicted as landowners and this pleasure was enhanced by the ability of oil paint to render their land in all its substantiality. And this is an observation which needs to be made, precisely because the cultural history we are normally taught pretends that it is an unworthy one. (Berger 1972, 108)

Marxist critics such as John Berger, Raymond Williams and Terry Eagleton have argued that art began to perceive and represent itself as 'outside' society only in the late eighteenth century, the very time at which art was becoming increasingly commodified. Art's pretence of its separation from society might then be seen as an attempt to disguise its very implication in the kinds of commercial concerns which it so disdained. But the attempt to escape from commercialism is still a response to that same commercialism, as marxists as diverse as Williams, Eagleton and Adorno have recognised.

Once we begin to think of literature as a cultural form, this kind of division becomes less meaningful. In a marxist vocabulary, 'culture' represents a whole way of life and could incorporate a novel and a comic book, a trade union movement and a Sunday school, the way in which families raise their children and the way in which society treats its prisoners. In this almost anthropological definition, 'culture' retains something of its original sense of cultivation or development. At its worst, this definition becomes so broad it is difficult to see what it could possibly exclude (and thus how effective it might be as an explanatory concept). At its best, this definition allows us to think of all things as connected and to prevent the kinds of separations between different aspects of human practice which have often become commonplace. (What has contemporary fiction got to do with the stock market? Quite a lot, actually.) This definition also positions itself against that narrower meaning of 'culture' – as a specialised form of art, or that 'high' art which embodies the 'best which has been thought and said' – which was created in the nineteenth century and here expressed by Matthew Arnold.[1] This definition is narrower in both subject ('high' art defined by its poise, ambiguity, complexity, elitism) and its application (those who produce or enjoy such art are almost invariably 'well educated'). We still retain this narrower sense when we speak of someone as 'cultured', certainly not a term which we would expect to see *The Daily Telegraph* apply to a striking miner. Thus the marxist challenge to this narrow concept of culture is to recognise the ways of living of whole peoples, to acknowledge the cultures of the uneducated, of slaves and factory-hands. And by revising the very term which has marked the separation of art and society, it radically opposes this separation, while still permitting studies of the specific nature of art, or indeed, the way in which art has become autonomous through transformations in society.

Base and superstructure

Marxist approaches to literature are thus attempts both to articulate the relationship between literature and society and to call the separation which this implies into question. Pragmatically, we may have to separate art and society in order to explain their relation, but simultaneously we need to resist this separation by remembering that art is *part of* society. The theoretical complexity involved in this double manoeuvre has often been overlooked, as marxist theorists have been accused of 'reducing' literature to a passive reflection of society, rather than seeing literature as fully implicated within it.[2] These debates have been most notoriously articulated around the marxist concepts of 'base' and 'superstructure' and the relationship between them.

The 'base' of society is the infrastructure or the mode of production which characterises the society. In medieval England, for example, the economic mode of feudalism entails a relation of obligations between the lord and his serf, in which the serf pays his landlord a feudal rent while remaining largely self-subsistent. In nineteenth-century England, the economic mode is capitalist, a system by which the capitalist class owns the means of production, as it not only owns the necessary raw materials, buildings, capital to invest and so on, but also buys the labour of those it employs. The 'base', in marxist analysis, is primarily economic because it is our economic status which determines our status within society and indeed our ability to buy aesthetic commodities such as books. (Thus the Victorian beggar would never have the 'culture' of the nineteenth-century middle or upper classes, since access to adequate food, let alone the works of Shakespeare or the price of a theatre ticket, could not be guaranteed.)

The 'superstructure' of society incorporates non-economic forms of production: legal, political, philosophical, religious, aesthetic formations which are defined by the economic structure of the base. This analysis of society is most usually traced to Marx's preface to *A Contribution to the Critique of Political Economy* (1859):

> In the social production of their existence, men inevitably enter into definite relations, which are independent of their will, namely relations of production appropriate to a given stage in the development of their material forces of production. The totality of these relations of production constitutes the economic structure of society, the real foundation, on which arises a legal and political superstructure and to which correspond definite forms of social consciousness. The mode of production of material life conditions the general process of social, political and intellectual life. It is not the consciousness of men that determines their existence, but, their social existence that determines their consciousness. (Marx and Engels 1991, 173)

This passage is frequently quoted and variously interpreted in marxist debates. It seems to legitimate the priority of the economic over any other mode, to suggest that all forms of experience will be determined by the prevailing economic mode of production. This permits a revolutionary politics: change the social conditions under which people live and you will change their ways of thinking. However the priority of the economic is also problematic because it does not permit the possibility of differences within this principle, it does not recognise that there are moments in which the legal, political, aesthetic, religious (all superstructural forms) will escape the apparent priority of the economic. (For example, the Cultural Revolution in China in the late 1960s was ideological rather than economic in nature.) If this priority of the economic is held to be absolute, then literature or culture will only reflect the economic 'base' and will never be able to alter the economic mode itself. Even though total determination of this kind is wholly opposed by most marxist literary approaches, communist marxism has largely followed a deterministic model of the base/superstructure relationship. This has been true too of many early or 'classical' marxist literary theorists, such as the English critic Christopher Caudwell. In *Illusion and Reality* (1937), for example, Caudwell's view of poetry is highly 'reflectionist', that is, English poetry is measured against the prevailing economic mode and judged to 'reflect' this base. Thus for Caudwell, the characteristic heroic couplet of eighteenth-century poetry is explained in terms of contemporary mercantilism and the limited possibilities of the middle classes in this period (1946, 86) and English poetry since the fifteenth century is deemed 'capitalist' (55), a statement which ignores the ways in which poetry has resisted, as well as celebrated, capitalism. Caudwell's 'readings' of poetry scarcely look at the texts themselves as the chronological drive of changing social and economic conditions races him through the centuries. The following 'reading' of Byron is typical in this regard: 'Byron is an aristocrat – but he is one who is conscious of the break-up of his class as a force, and the necessity to go over to the bourgeoisie. Hence his mixture of cynicism and romanticism' (1946, 90). While I think this is a fair comment on Byron's writing, the casual assumption that the class status and political opinions of the author solely determine the political nature of the text is much too reductive.[3] The belief that this economism is a doctrine of marxist literary theory has been instrumental in creating the stereotypical idea of the marxist theorist or the 'vulgar' marxist, but the stereotype has tended to obscure the many marxist theories which have attempted a more nuanced interpretation of the base/superstructure relationship.

Firstly, most contemporary marxist theorists recognise that these categories – 'feudalism', 'industrial capitalism', 'late capitalism' and so on – are convenient fictions by which we might theorise. As Jameson has argued in *The Political Unconscious*, 'no historical society has ever "embodied" a mode of production in any pure state' (Jameson 1983, 94), and thus we ought to think of the ways in which any one society will consist of *several* modes of production which co-exist, some increasingly anachronistic, some potentially anticipatory.[4] Indeed, Jameson argues, Marx's *Capital* attempts to construct the abstract concept of capitalism, rather than an empirical description of any one society. Thus any 'superstructural' forces will be criss-crossed by conflicting economic modes, rather than mechanically reflecting just one, and these multiple impulses will affect superstructural forms to different degrees and in different ways. Secondly, Marx's language in describing the relationship between the base and the superstructure itself varies: the verb used may be 'determine', 'condition', or the much more neutral 'correspond to'; yet the very terms 'base' and 'superstructure', with their metaphorical suggestions of a foundation and its structures, do seem to imply a degree of causality. As such, the words themselves inadequately express the complexity of the relation. But we need to remember that Marx did not use 'base' or 'superstructure' because this passage, quoted above, is itself a translation from Marx's German text. Fredric Jameson returns to Marx's sentences and translates them in a way which reveals a greater complexity:

> ... we must initially separate the figuration of the terms base and superstructure – only the initial shape of the problem – from the type of efficacity or causal law it is supposed to imply. *Uberbau* and *Basis*, for example, which so often suggest to people a house and its foundations, seem in fact to have been railroad terminology and to have designated the rolling stock and the rails respectively, something which suddenly jolts us into a rather different picture of ideology and its effects. (Jameson 1996, 46)

In the metaphor of the house and its foundation, we have an image of absolute determination: a house cannot exist without its foundations. In the metaphor of the railroad, however, both the trains and the tracks are impotent without each other. It is this image of mutual determination, rather than prior determination, which is crucial to most marxist literary and cultural theorists. Jameson himself replaces the concept of deterministic causality with that of the 'conditions of possibility' (Jameson 1994, xv). Even in Marx's expression of the problematic, we can see simultaneously depictions of a social whole in which everything is interconnected and a social totality which is divided into a number of seemingly separate spheres.

Jameson published his comments above in 1990. But the debate concerning the 'base/superstructure' model begins at least a century earlier. In a letter to Joseph Bloch in 1890, Engels distinguishes his and Marx's thinking on this issue from that of the 'vulgar' marxist interpretations:

> According to the materialist view of history, the determining factor in history is, *in the final analysis*, the production and reproduction of actual life. More than that was never maintained either by Marx or myself. Now if someone distorts this by declaring the economic to be the *only* determining factor, he changes that proposition into a meaningless, abstract, ridiculous piece of jargon. (Marx and Engels 1991, 651)

Engels continues by situating his and Marx's work in the context of its time, namely their opposition to those Hegelian philosophers who maintained the autonomy of ideas from economic production, if not their priority. Thus, Engels suggests, the importance of the 'base' was somewhat deliberately overemphasised, a strategic manoeuvre in the debate with the Young Hegelians. Engels's argument is supported by Marx's most notorious consideration of art, that 'superstructural' form. In the notebooks entitled *Grundrisse* (c.1857–8; first published 1939), Marx questions why we continue to find pleasure in ancient Greek art, a significant question because it raises the 'unequal development of material production and e.g. that of art' (reprinted in Eagleton 1996, 34–5). Marx's own reply to this is exceedingly problematic: he suggests that such pleasure is nostalgic in that we respond to ancient Greek art as the childhood productions of our civilisation. This answer may have more to do with nineteenth-century idealisations of Greek and Roman antiquity than with marxist analysis. But the question he poses – as to the persistence of art, irrespective of changing economic modes – suggests that the base/superstructure or economy/literature relationship was never viewed as one of unilateral influence, in which the superstructure can only ever reflect the base.[5]

In the classical Marxist tradition, therefore, there are two theories which need to be balanced: the determination by the economic mode of production *in the last instance,* and the relative autonomy of the superstructures. In *For Marx* (1965), Althusser analysed how these two principles might permit a non-reductionist treatment of the superstructures which would nevertheless be grounded in a properly materialist analysis. Althusser suggested that we might categorise three practices within society: the economic, the political and the ideological. (We might see this as a reading of Marx's distinction in the above quotation between 'economic structure', the 'legal and political superstructure' and 'social consciousness'.) Each of these spheres would both interact and operate within its own specific autonomy, its own effectivity. And because of their interaction, any individual human practice would be influenced both by internal contradictions and by a complexity and diversity of others. The idea of 'determination' is thus revised as a complex system of 'overdetermination'.[6] (At one point Althusser explains his adoption of the term 'overdetermination' as a neater substitution for a causality which is 'complexly-structurally-unevenly' determined; 1990, 209.) While one structure may be dominant, this does not reduce the others to 'secondary' status, as they will have already influenced the dominant. Thus within this complex model, the economic may be the 'ultimate' determinant, or the dominant structure, but that 'ultimate' stage will never be evident, because the economic can never operate in isolation from the political and ideological. To an extent, Williams had already formulated this problem in *The Long Revolution* (1961), as the epigraph above suggests. In Althusser's terms, the economic is productive of the real rather than merely reflective of a reality which is already given. Althusser sketches this important theory humorously, mocking the pretensions of rigid determinism:

> ... the economic dialectic is never active *in the pure state*; in History, these instances, the superstructures, etc. – are never seen to step respectfully aside when their work is done, or, when the Time comes, as his pure phenomena, to scatter before His Majesty the Economy as he strides along the royal road of the Dialectic. From the first moment to the last, the lonely hour of the 'last instance' never comes. (Althusser 1990, 113)

While in theory the economic is the ultimate determinant, historically the economic has never been (and never will be) the sole determinant and the 'final instance' can never be seen or experienced, only conceived.

It is significant that one of Althusser's most vigorous opponents shared his opposition to the determinism of 'orthodox' marxism. The English historian E.P. Thompson wrote an impassioned attack on Althusser and his influence on marxist thinking in *The Poverty of Theory* (1978). Although they differed in their arguments, Althusser stressing structures within social formations, Thompson stressing human practice, both in their own ways exploded the myth of a deterministic base/superstructure relationship. Thompson continually wrote of class as a cultural as much as an economic phenomenon. In *The Making of the English Working Class* (1968), he discussed how the working class was 'made' only once it became conscious of itself as a class: 'class happens when some men, as a result of common experiences (inherited or shared), feel and articulate the identity of their interests as between themselves, and as against other men whose interests are different from (and usually opposed to) theirs' (Thompson 1968, 9–10). This self-consciousness was forged through such 'superstructural' forms as popular culture, religion, trade unionism, and political struggle.[7] Throughout his writings, Thompson's historical explorations embodied his opposition to structural determinism and its 'belittling [of] ... conscious human agency in the making of history' (Thompson 1957, 114). For Thompson, such structural determinism was as characteristic of Althusser, as it was of Soviet communism, but Althusser and Thompson share the attempt to escape the iron logic of absolute economism.

This opposition to economic determinism is characteristic of western marxism, even if it is not always achieved. Williams, in *Problems in Materialism and Culture* (1980), redefined determinism as a matter of setting limits and exerting pressures. Lucien Goldman changed the terminology of 'base/superstructure' to that of 'social totality' and conceived of correspondences between social modes which he theorised as 'homologies', thus asserting parallelisms and analogies between disparate levels (a theory which was in turn accused of wilful linking). In Benjamin's theory of 'correspondences', cultural effects are viewed as equivalents to forces of production, without the hierarchy implied in theories of 'reflection'. (Although Adorno criticised Benjamin's correspondences, for the apparently casual linking of elements of culture with significant aspects of the material base. See Adorno et al. 1980, Presentation III.) Althusser's opposition to economic determinism was influenced by Gramsci's earlier analyses of the ways in which the economic, the political and the ideological are mutually determining forces. (Yet Laclau and Mouffe later charge Gramsci with failing to escape the determination of class analysis.)

Given these debates, the only resolution we might find is Jameson's insistence that the base-superstructure problematic is not a fully-fledged theory but the name for a problem, a theoretical crux with which we must continue to struggle.[8] Certainly, theoretical debates and difficulty with the use of such terms ought not to prevent the attempt to think of the relationship between text and context, since the 'fact of sheer interrelationship is prior to any of the conceptual categories, such as causality, reflection, or analogy, subsequently evolved to explain it' (Jameson 1974, 6). Strategically we might need to think in terms of these – always problematic – categories. But abandoning these categories would prohibit our attempts to theorise the relationships between art and that which is not-art, or the network of relations in which the art work is inevitably situated.

The materiality of culture

The arguments concerning the relationship between 'base' and 'superstructure' and the intrinsic problems with this very model are especially significant for marxist approaches to literature. Because the materiality of literature and culture is always an assumption of any marxist literary criticism, marxist literary theory has been especially vociferous against the kinds of rigid distinctions which other marxist theories (economic, sociological, political) might make. Such distinctions include 'base', as opposed to 'superstructure', and 'material' as opposed to 'ideal'. Most simply, we might think of materialism as the contention that everything which exists either is, or depends upon, matter or physicality, as distinguished from ideas. In reality, just as in the case of 'base' and 'superstructure', we can never separate the two quite so simply. (And, as we shall see, dialectics is the term which describes the attempt to negotiate such 'oppositions', to think of them in ways other than pure oppositionality.) If we think of literature only in terms of a narrow definition of 'superstructure', of belonging only to the sphere of thought and relationships, and then compound this by neglecting to situate literature within the economic and political contexts of production, distribution and reception, we will forget that art works are material productions.

For the most part, literature is printed matter, that which relies upon a 'technology', whether that is the pen, the printing press or the computer. The emergence of new media, such as the hypertexts of information technology, has to an extent reawakened this sense. Oral forms of literature – ballads, storytelling, drama – are also material in that they are concretely realised in situations which themselves are material (for example, in such buildings as the court, the bar, the theatre). Novels, sculptures, films and comics are not only structures of meaning, but also commodities, and like other commodities, cultural artefacts are made by and for people and are subject to social and economic laws. Literary production, for example, is shaped by social, economic and technological factors such as the histories of printing, publishing and the reading public. If we study the ways in which horror fiction has been published, for example, we can see many of these changes and the shifting conceptions of the relationship between creativity and the market which accompany them. When Horace Walpole published *The Castle of Otranto* (1764), traditionally thought to be the first gothic fiction, he did so in a limited edition print run, produced by his own 'cottage industry', the Strawberry Hill Press. But by the 1790s, Gothic tales published by William Lane's Minerva Press were read by thousands (Lane's was both a printing company and a lending library), and especially by women, so that by the Victorian period, an audience for horror fiction had already begun to define itself, and be defined by the marketing strategies of Victorian publishers, who advertised the sensational effects of Bram Stoker, Le Fanu and Marsh accordingly, targeting a discrete, but mass, audience. Not only are the practices of reading and writing historically determined, but so too is the writer herself, insofar as she has the requisite education to write, or to compose in recitation. Only half of labouring men, and a proportionately smaller number of labouring women were literate in the eighteenth century, at a time when the index of literacy was being able to spell one's own name and the price of a book was greater than the average labourer's weekly wage (Porter 1982, 183). This context is important when we study, not just eighteenth-century peasant poets like Stephen Duck (the 'thresher' poet), John Bryant (tobacco-pipe maker) or Ann Yearsley (milkmaid), but all writing. Marxist theories urge that we remember that literary texts and writers operate within complex economic systems which include those of sponsorship, financing, production and distribution.

Interpreting literature in its institutional and material contexts is not an exclusively marxist approach: sociological studies of culture and cultural materialism also investigate the production and reproduction of texts and artefacts and many of these critics would resist 'marxist' as a category for their practice. But attending to the production of art always necessitates an economic dimension which is marxist in its insistence in the determination 'in the last instance' of the economic base. Critics of marxism often accuse the linking of the aesthetic and the economic of being 'vulgar', which we might read as a neatly suggestive pun (coarse, heavy-handed *and* unmannerly, rude or without 'taste'). But the economic determination cannot be denied, though it is often forgotten: writing or reading literary texts requires certain levels of literacy (which will always be an economic issue when education is not fully equitable), material affluence (to buy books, writing materials and other resources), leisure-time, shelter, lighting and privacy. Artistic works are always implicated within economic and symbolic economies, even when they ostensibly resist it.[9] In the eighteenth century, for example, Lady Mary Wortley Montagu wrote poetry, prose, periodical essays and a play, but nothing she wrote ever appeared with her name on the title-page and some works were never published in her own lifetime (for example her play, *Simplicity,* was never performed or published). As an aristocratic lady, Montagu was timid of the 'taint' of publication, that which might expose her to charges either of being 'unfeminine' or of desiring to sell her works for a profit. In 1716 Edmund Curll produced an unauthorised edition of her poems from, he claimed, a manuscript which she had dropped in the street. In the context of eighteenth-century society, it is not entirely fanciful to speculate that this was an elaborate ruse to justify such publicity. The embarrassment surrounding an aristocratic female author submitting literary works for sale is an important part of her texts' reception.[10]

Terry Eagleton has analysed the materiality of literary production by adapting a marxist literary theory of the 'literary mode of production' (Eagleton 1976a, 45). In Marx's writings, the mode of production is the economic structure of society, comprising *relations* of production (economic relations between groups of people, most obvious in the class structure) and *forces* of production (forms of available production, which include not only obviously 'material' forms, such as raw materials and technology, but also the skills and abilities of the workers). In suggesting that literature is produced in a manner which is comparable to the economic system, Eagleton's theory can imagine both what literary and economic modes of production share and the ways in which literary production has its own autonomous history. In some ways, then, this is a theory which articulates the 'uneven development' which puzzled Marx's attempt to understand why we still enjoy Homer. Economic and literary modes of production overlap in the very materiality of literature: the book, for example, is produced, distributed, exchanged and 'consumed' in a way analogous to any other commodity. Literary production requires social relations of production, the relations between publishers, writers and readers, for example, but also forces of production: cultural forms (the Victorian three-volume novel, the newspaper, the balladeer's broadsheet) and such material technologies as paper manufacture and printing. The idea of the book has become so naturalised that we need to remember that print culture is a technology: the invention of printing with movable types by Gutenberg, Fust and Schoeffer between 1450 and 1460 in Mainz, Germany enabled the development of the book. It is thus also a form of production, of labour. Indeed, it has been suggested that the book was 'the first modern-style mass-produced industrial commodity' (Anderson 1991, 34).[11] But print culture was also a product of social developments: the demand for texts from a new reading audience preceded the invention of print. A new bourgeois class, and especially merchants and lawyers, required a considerably greater number of texts than any manual scribe could produce. In their history of the origins of print, *The Coming of the Book* (1958), Lucien Febvre and Henri-Jean Martin discuss literature as both commodity and aesthetic artefact: the typographer worked with his hands, like other workers, but he was also an 'intellectual', since he could read and would frequently know a little Latin (Febvre and Martin 1997, 128): ' ... the book was a piece of merchandise which men produced before anything else to earn a living, even when they were ... scholars and humanists at the same time' (109). It is commonly accepted that the book represents creative or scholarly endeavour, but only marxist approaches remind us that the early bookseller was also a financier. Printers needed to be backed by capital: 'the backer, the capitalist ... was the one who took the risks, the one who took a chance on the sale of the product, and very often it was he who chose the texts for publication. Sometimes he even started a workshop on a big scale, more like an industrial plant than the old craftsman's shop. There were many capitalists ready to finance such operations' (116). Even though capitalist relations existed before the advent of print (vernacular manuscripts were also copied and sold as early as the end of the twelfth century in France), there is a special fusion between print production and capitalist commodity exchange. This fusion is neatly expressed in Benedict Anderson's term 'print-capitalism'.

By the late seventeenth century England had become an important producer of paper, type and publications, in part due to the abolition of printing restrictions in 1695. In the eighteenth century the selling and buying of books became a recognisable industry, flourishing with the rise of a sizeable middle-class readership and its desire for novels, newspapers and periodicals and satirised by Pope and Swift in the image of 'Grub Street', a street in London frequented by hack writers, those authors who could be hired for little money, to write whatever the hirer pleased. Writing, in Daniel Defoe's words, had now become 'a very considerable Branch of the English Commerce' (*Applebee's Journal*, 31 July 1725). The eighteenth century witnessed rises in capitalism (the dominant economic mode, although aspects of feudal artisan activity continued), in the middle classes (a political, ideological and cultural phenomenon), in the demand for and production of texts (novels, newspapers, engravings) and the 'ideological' and 'aesthetic' concepts of literary originality and property. For the first time, authors were viewed as the 'owners' of their works; their works were viewed as 'original' to them, and thus they were entitled to expect financial remuneration and security from their 'property'.[12]

We might compare this system with that of the production of Shakespeare's plays within the Elizabethan context, where plays were produced by the company as much as by one author, they were not published by 'Shakespeare himself' and were openly adapted from other sources, classical and modern history, tales popular in the late Middle Ages and Renaissance. (*King Lear*, for example, is adapted from a range of other texts which includes an earlier play 'The True Chronicle History of King Leir'; extracts from the Elizabethan historian Holinshed, from Edmund Spenser's poem *Faerie Queene* and from Sir Philip Sidney's poem *Arcadia*.) It is only in the eighteenth century that the identification of the plays with one man – William Shakespeare – is made. And it is made because of the new demand that great works of literature should be original, the product of one writer who owns that work. (In his history of copyright, David Saunders suggests that because Shakespeare stole from authors whom the cultivated public of the eighteenth century did not read, it was possible for them to imagine him as the great original; 1992, 42.) As early as the 1740s pilgrims began to visit Stratford on Avon in quest of Shakespearean relics. (The rather appropriately named Thomas Sharpe, for example, sold pieces of an old mulberry tree that Shakespeare was supposed to have planted.) But the real instance of the creation of Shakespeare as a canonical figure came in 1769 when the actor David Garrick organised a jubilee at Stratford in his honour. There was pageantry, feasting and dancing, but not a single one of Shakespeare's plays was performed. It would appear that the crowds gathered to canonise the personality, not the plays (see Rose 1993, 121–2). By the middle of the eighteenth century, Shakespeare had become in England the standard by which literary value was measured, the great writer of originality and genius against whom every other writer was measured and their works priced accordingly. With this interest in the author went an increasing tendency to read the works of authors in the context of their biographies (evident in, for example, Samuel Johnson's *Lives of the Poets*, 1779–81) and the rise of the novel, a form explicitly devoted to the display of character.

The study of the origin of the legal laws concerning copyright thus raises a range of elements: economic and technological in the rise of the publishing industry; ideological in the importance of individualism and its philosophical underpinning of capitalism; aesthetic(-ideological) in the genre of the novel and the concept of authorship. Copyright legislation was fought first between publishers, between those London publishers who wished to retain a monopoly over 'bestselling' authors and ambitious publishers in Edinburgh and Dublin, keen to undercut metropolitan prices. But the battle in the courts influenced the ways in which 'literature' itself was considered, particularly in the concurrent privileging of originality. The eighteenth century ended the idea that writing was not properly a profession, something for which you would or ought not to be paid. Catherine Macaulay, for example, in *A Modest Plea for the Property of Copyright*, argued that Shakespeare was more concerned with filling the theatre than with instructing mankind (see Rose 1993, 106). By the early nineteenth century, it was authors themselves who were petitioning for extended copyright terms, led by Wordsworth, concerned that he should leave an estate for his family. Yet at the same time that the artist was becoming a merchant, selling his/her labour and the products of that labour just like any other manufacturer, the idea of the writer as inspired, as an original genius, was being consciously created in order to counter the contamination which the market seemed to represent. The cultural fears of the 'contamination' of the market can be seen in Lord Camden's outburst:

> It was not for Gain, that *Bacon, Newton, Milton, Locke*, instructed and delighted the World; it would be unworthy such Men to traffic with a dirty Bookseller for so much as a Sheet of Letter-press. When the Bookseller offered *Milton* Five Pounds for his Paradise Lost, he did not reject it, and commit his Poem to the Flames, nor did he accept the miserable Pittance as the Reward of his Labor; he knew that the real price of his Work was Immortality, and that Posterity would pay it. (Quoted in Rose 1993, 105)[13]

There was thus considerable anxiety among authors in the middle years of the century about the commodification of writing. Authors such as Johnson, Goldsmith and Fielding responded to this by dismissing the mass of writers as 'mere Mechanics' and developing the notion of the literary profession as a canonical group of 'legitimate' authors. Thus, as Eagleton has argued in *The Ideology of the Aesthetic*, the representation of the artist as a transcendent genius is born 'just when the artist is becoming debased to a petty commodity producer' and this mystification can be understood in part as 'spiritual compensation for this degradation' (Eagleton 1990, 65).

The continued expansion of printing thereafter illustrates Benjamin's theory of 'mechanical reproduction' ('The work of art in the age of mechanical reproduction' 1936; reprinted in 1992). In the late nineteenth century, mass production of texts was achieved due to technical developments in printing such as the steam-powered press, the web press which printed on continuous rolls of paper, and typesetting machinery. All of these innovations allowed texts to be produced at lower prices. Once cultural production is characterised by a relatively large-scale replication of artefacts by means of machine technologies, the work of art can no longer be thought of as 'original' or 'authentic'. This is true of prints, lithographs, woodcuts, books, photographs, film, radio, television. In Benjamin's terms, the work of art is stripped of its 'aura' and this has implications for the way in which the work of art is received. Commensurate with its 'aura' is the authority which the work exercises. The mechanical reproduction of art reflects the logic of capitalist repetition, commodities are mass-produced. For Adorno and Horkheimer in *Dialectic of Enlightenment* (first published 1944), this is depressingly symptomatic of how capitalism destroys 'art'.[14] But for Benjamin mechanical reproduction alters reception in a way which is liberatory: the mass-produced work makes a genuinely popular culture possible.[15]

Benjamin's argument is also that the truly 'revolutionary' work of art must be revolutionary in its form, or its medium. He traced potential emancipation, for example, in the newspaper, that art form which many claimed would debase language. Benjamin saw instead the possibility of a reciprocal relationship between writer and reader. Every newspaper reader had the potential to become a news writer. The newspaper broke down the authority of writing, by which a writer required a specialist training. Thus the loss of the 'aura' of the work of art was matched by that of the 'artist'. Benjamin's manifesto for revolutionary techniques was first articulated in his essay 'The Author as Producer' (1934; reprinted in Benjamin 1977). Although Benjamin only sketched the idea which is suggested by this title, the consideration of the author as producer rather than creator was later explored by Pierre Macherey and Terry Eagleton. All these marxist thinkers opposed the post-Romantic idea of the artist as divinely inspired, as endowed with special powers, as privileged.

Marx wrote of all human labour as ideally creative practice and as one of the most significant ways in which we mark human capacity. He compared the activity of the spider and the weaver, the bee and the architect. While their activities share many features (for example, the bee constructs an intricate structure of cells in the hive, as the architect designs a complex structure which uses all her knowledge of engineering and structure to complete), the weaver and the architect are distinguished from the spider and the bee by the human capacity to imagine the process before beginning it. Human labour takes a characteristic form because '[m]ore than merely working an *alteration* in the form of nature, he also *knowingly works his own purposes into* nature; and these purposes are the law determining the ways and means of his activity, so that his will must be adjusted to them' (quoted in Wolff 1993, 14–15). But labour is only ideally creative because under capitalist modes of production, men and women are alienated from their labour. This is most attenuated in the factory-line: each worker produces only a fragment of the whole product, she is unlikely to see the completed product and will certainly not own it. In the large shirt factories of the late nineteenth and early twentieth centuries, for example, female workers were assigned to cuffs, borders or collars, and so on. Each worker owns only her own labour which she 'freely' sells in return for wages. This is relevant to literature and culture once literary texts and cultural artefacts are also recognised as social products. Like the factory-line worker, those involved in making cinema films have only a very specialised function to play in the complete and complex process: camera-operators, director, producers, stars, scriptwriters, sound and lighting engineers, set mechanics, promoters, distributors, cinema managers and so on. Even the director may feel that she has little 'ownership' or control over the ultimate film: screen tests, for example, frequently dictate that the endings of blockbuster Hollywood films must be altered to suit the tastes of the sample audience. The writer who is commissioned by a patron or sponsor may feel similarly inhibited. The constraints on artists are often forgotten when literature and culture are treated as creative practices rather than modes of production. However, there are cases in which the literary text or cultural artefact is freely created and the artist is a figure who escapes the constraints typical of other forms of labour in capitalist societies. (For example, the production of a novel is different from that of other commodities in that the author is more like an artisan, selling her 'product' rather than labour.) But this freedom does not prevent the artist from being a producer and creativity is then no less social.

The French marxist Pierre Macherey refuses the term 'creator' because it suggests that the author invokes an absolutely chosen form from nothing, as if the materials with which she works never existed before. But Macherey does not speak of material instances such as technologies, institutions, economic conditions for production, distribution or consumption, but of the self-production of the text from pre-existing conventions and traditions:

> The writer, as the producer of a text, does not manufacture the materials with which he works. Neither does he stumble across them as spontaneously available wandering fragments, useful in the building of any sort of edifice; they are not neutral, transparent components which have the grace to vanish, to disappear into the totality they contribute to, giving it substance and adopting its forms. The causes

that determine the existence of the work are not free implements, useful to elaborate any meaning: ... they have a sort of specific weight, a peculiar power, which means that even when they are used and blended into a totality they retain a certain autonomy; and may, in some cases, resume their particular life. Not because there is some absolute and transcendent logic of aesthetic facts, but because their real inscription in a history of forms means that they cannot be defined exclusively by their immediate function in a specific work. (Macherey 1978, 41–2)[16]

The 'materials' of which Macherey speaks in this section might include language itself, literary conventions, ideas, all of which contain a 'weight', their own autonomous connotations, which are altered but not deleted by their incorporation into the work. In a later example, Macherey notes how it would be 'astonishing' if the hero vanished after the opening pages, unless the novel was playing with the convention itself, parodying and subverting our expectations (48). Thus the author does not 'invent' so much as 'discover' the conditions under which her narrative will be written. The first reader of a work is thus its own author. These already created materials, however, are not just conventions, forms, genres; the writer is also adapting materials which include ways of speaking and behaving, social practices, institutional structures, contemporary beliefs and attitudes and widespread ideological discourses. These might impose constraints on the author too, who cannot be the ultimate guarantor of meaning in the text because s/he is shaped by society or the historical context, just as she might in turn shape it. Because of the multiplicity of elements in any one literary text, the text is not seamless, unified, complete; it is always fractured. All texts are internally contradictory because of the diversity of elements from which they are constituted.

Texts and cultural artefacts are not only 'produced' at their moment of composition or publication. They are also 're-produced' in their readings. Marx argued that the process of production is completed only with consumption. In this sense, literature is never 'completed' but endlessly re-produced. One school of marxist literary criticism in contemporary Britain is that of cultural materialism. Cultural materialists such as Alan Sinfield, Jonathon Dollimore and Catherine Belsey focus on the reproduction of canonical texts in contemporary readings and interpretations. For example, Alan Sinfield's reading of Tennyson's *In Memoriam* consciously takes a poem thought to be

quintessentially Victorian, with all its associated morality and prud-
ishness, and reads the very poem which made Tennyson poet laureate
as a coded expression of homosexual love (Sinfield 1986). Sinfield has
also examined how 'we' are constantly involved in re-inventing and
re-producing Shakespeare to suit the interests and needs of contemporary culture and society (Sinfield 1992).[17] Once literary criticism is
viewed as a form of 're-production', literary debates must shift from
positions of 'intrinsic' meaning to considerations of their own modes
of working. And in the question of reception, as with all other categories of literary production, the relationships between art and
economic structures, politics and ideologies, were always reciprocal.
In the sixteenth to eighteenth centuries, those who bought books
were themselves products of the relatively modern print culture: the
invention of the press had raised the levels of literacy in England, as
elsewhere. In this way literature, and specifically newspapers and
novels, reflected the demands of new reading publics as it also
created them.

   While these kinds of studies of literary production are central to
many marxist analyses, the relationships between literature and
society remain highly specific and not always synchronous. However,
general trends can be perceived, and among the most significant of
these is the growing autonomy of literature from society in the nineteenth century. This separation can be traced to such material conditions as the eighteenth-century shift from patronage to the market, as
authors became more independent of external constraints (the
patron's demands for flattery or political propaganda). Literature
continues to be intrinsically social, but its conventions, forms and
content may also be partly produced by specifically artistic traditions
of which they form a part. In this way, literature might be said to be
'relatively' free of economic determination. But such 'relative autonomy' does not contradict the arguments that literature is inevitably a
product of its times, since this autonomy is created as a result of a
splitting of spheres which is itself thoroughly indebted to the structural logic of capitalism. If literature comes to enjoy an autonomous
status, this autonomy is itself a product of the economic, political and
ideological conditions of nineteenth-century society. For this reason,
Williams preferred to think in terms of literature's 'specificity' rather
than its 'autonomy'. The most sustained studies of the relative autonomy of literature include those of Theodor Adorno and Peter Bürger,
whose theories enable marxist readings of even the most apparently

anti- or non-materialist writing, as epitomised in the aestheticist ideals of 'art-for-art's sake' associated with Walter Pater and Oscar Wilde.

Materialism and dialectics

These kinds of approaches to literature and culture, in which, for example, the book is read as a product and special attention is paid to publication, printing, bookselling and audience, have been adopted by both marxist and feminist critics. But, given the shared approaches, it makes little sense to speak of 'marxism' and 'feminism' as discrete approaches. When Norman Feltes (1986) studies the determining influence of magazine publication on Hardy's novel *Tess of the D'Urbervilles* or Gaye Tuchman (1989) writes of the way in which George Eliot's dramatic poem *The Spanish Gypsy* was unfavourably reviewed on the basis of her gender, both might more usefully be described as 'materialist' critics. The importance of materialism to both marxist and feminist theories of culture thus demands that I look more closely at the implications of 'materialism'.

As we have seen from the previous section, literature itself is both material and abstract because it takes material forms (the book, the money which is exchanged in return for the purchase of the volume of poetry, the audience at the theatre) and obviously mental forms too (the experiences of reading, watching, listening). This is to define 'material' as that which is tangible, embodied, or 'real'. 'Materialism' might thus be defined as a philosophy which is grounded in material reality, insofar as it does not explain concepts by ideal constructions. To define materialist in this way is to keep the sense of a binary opposition (between ideal and material or subjective and objective) firmly in place. But in marxist terms, this is a mechanical definition of materialism which dooms the ideal and the material to mutual exclusion, instead of seeing the ways in which they interact. Thus marxist philosophical or historical materialism attempts to hold this opposition in tension, to ground its thinking in material reality but also to include human activity as a primary force. People work on physical things but the ways in which they do this and the relations they enter into as they do this in turn work upon their own 'human nature' (see Williams 1983, 197–201). Marx's critique of 'mechanical materialism' can be seen in the following excerpt from *Theses on Feuerbach*:

> The materialist doctrine that men are products of circumstances and
> upbringing, and that, therefore, changed men are products of other
> circumstances and changed upbringing, forgets that it is men who
> change circumstances and that the educator must himself be
> educated. (Marx and Engels 1991, 28)

If people were always determined by their context alone, by the material circumstances in which they find themselves, then no change
would be possible, and the system would merely keep replicating
itself. People are formed and constructed by their environment, but
they also in turn form and construct that environment by their own
interaction within it. We might say that people are determined by
structures, and that they in turn alter structures through their own
activity, or 'agency'; or that literary texts are determined by the institutional contexts of economic modes of production, distribution and
reception, but they also work upon and transform these 'contexts'.
This is an articulation of a key issue in marxist debates: the relationship between structure and agency. When Shelley wrote in the preface
to *Prometheus Unbound* that 'Poets, not otherwise than philosophers,
painters, sculptors and musicians, are in one sense the creators, and
in another the creations, of their age', he anticipated a key mode of
thinking in marxist theories: that of the dialectic.

Once the relationship between human subject and history, or
cultural artefact and society, is thought of in terms of mutual reciproc-
ity, the materialist grounding of subjectivity or aesthetics in material
reality becomes dialectical: humans are not solely determined by
society, but also in turn determine and shape their society; the literary
text is not merely a product of its context, but also in turn influences
that context. Dialectical thinking is an attempt to keep these mutually
interacting forces continually in play. Engels defined marxist dialectics in 'Socialism: Utopian and Scientific' in the following way:

> To the metaphysician, things and their mental reflexes, ideas, are
> isolated, are to be considered one after the other and apart from each
> other, are objects of investigation fixed, rigid, given once for all. He
> thinks in absolutely irreconcilable antitheses. ... For him a thing
> either exists or does not exist; a thing cannot at the same time be
> itself and something else. Positive and negative absolutely exclude
> one another; cause and effect stand in a rigid antithesis one to the
> other.

At first sight this mode of thinking seems to us very luminous, because it is that of so-called sound commonsense. ... [But] we find upon closer investigation that the two poles of an antithesis, positive and negative, e.g. are as inseparable as they are opposed, and that despite all their opposition, they mutually interpenetrate. And we find, in like manner, that cause and effect are conceptions which only hold good in their application to individual cases; but as soon as we consider the individual cases in their general connection with the universe as a whole, they run into each other, and they become confounded when we contemplate that universal action and reaction in which causes and effects are eternally changing places, so that what is effect here and now will be cause there and then, and *vice versa*. (Marx and Engels 1991, 389)

For Engels, dialectics is a mode of understanding 'things and their representations, ideas, in their essential connection, concatenation, origin, and ending'. His attempt to negotiate the material and the ideal, or 'things' and 'ideas' is to keep the possibilities of their placing in relation to each other continually open. Thus while dialectics is generally held to mean the interactions between contradictory or opposite forces (see Williams 1983, 108), it is also crucially a consideration of process, the constant change, motion, transformation which characterise history and society, and a tracing of the internal connections that make a coherent whole of this process.

Some marxist thinkers have been criticial of the idea of dialectics as the resolution of social contradictions becomes dangerously like 'transcendence', suggesting some ultimate, final resolution to every kind of struggle (often, in marxist analyses, the class struggle). But, as Simon Dentith has argued of the Russian marxist thinkers Vološinov and Medvedev: 'without any anticipated transcendence, ... [dialectics] becomes a means of discussing social process and interaction, the vastly complex ways in which words, voices, people and social groups act and react upon each other and are transformed in the process' (Dentith 1995, 15). Dialectical thinking is thus an open way of considering elements which appear to be in opposition, such as the individual versus society, art as subjective versus science as objective, theory versus practice, things versus processes, parts versus wholes and other oppositions which later chapters will consider such as exchange-value versus use-value; science versus ideology. But it is able to consider these elements not as monolithic entities, unchanging objects which are irreducibly in opposition, but as elements which are always continually in transition, not the least of these elements the relationship between them. A dialectical synthesis of these elements is not a matter of a compromise between thesis and antithesis, not an averaging of their effects or a resolution into a new unity but, in a negation or critique of both thesis and antithesis, a formation which lies beyond them while also incorporating them. Many key marxist phrases have thus, appropriately, been seemingly paradoxical, contradictory or oxymoronic (for example, Williams's 'structures of feeling', Wolff's 'situated choices'). *The Communist Manifesto* traces the historical development of capitalism in which the reader is encouraged to think of this development as simultaneously positive and negative. (This dynamic underpins Jameson's refusal to identify postmodern culture as either progressive or regressive, although he does also question the consequences of this balancing, fearing that it is tantamount to a surrender of position. See Jameson 1992, 47.)

Dialectical thinking attempts to refuse an ultimate prioritising of the terms or structures which it views in relationship. But for many recent marxist theorists, dialectics continues to keep binary structures in place, however it might avoid either deterministic relationships or isolation between them. A new thinking of dialectics has been enabled by translations of the theorists of the Russian circle of the 1920s, whom we might name as Bakhtin, Vološinov and Medvedev (although there is a great deal of uncertainty concerning specific authorship, given the extent of collaboration, and even perhaps the use of pseudonyms among the group).[18] All were first translated into English only in the late 60s and 70s and have subsequently influenced a wide range of theoretical perspectives (narratological, poststructuralist as well as marxist). Amongst this body of work is the central concept of 'dialogics', a reconceptualisation of dialectics in which the relationships between structures or voices are permanently open-ended, and the potentially systematic nature of dialectics is refused. Bakhtin's theory of 'polyphony', for example, celebrated those novels in which there was constant dialogue between voices without any hierarchical arrangement of these voices. (His exemplar here was Dostoevsky.)[19] His study of Rabelais rediscovered the 'carnival' spirit of popular-festive life in medieval and Renaissance France, as portrayed in his novels of Gargantua and Pantagruel (1532–51). Here 'carnival' permits the expression of anti-authoritarianism in the free pleasures of corporeality and subversive inversions of hierarchies (such as the dominance of the pieties of Church and State over the scatalogical pleasures of popular entertainment, or the classical as opposed to the grotesque form). Bakhtin's analyses both of polyphony and carnival are always situated within precise historical and cultural contexts, a material grounding which is forgotten when his ideas are subsumed into generalised principles of textual 'play' (as in many versions of poststructuralism). And these contexts open polyphony and carnival onto the dialectics of class opposition. But contemporary marxist uses of Bakhtin's ideas have tended to shift this metaphor to the adjacent and overlapping one of the 'dialogics of multiaccentuality', in which there is always something unaccounted for or left over by the idea of antagonism implied in dialectics.[20] This supercession of binary opposition by multiaccentuality, of dialectics by dialogism, however, can be seen much earlier in Vološinov's (possibly Bakhtin's) work on the materiality of language.

The materiality of language

In *Marxism and the Philosophy of Language* (1929; trans. 1973), Vološinov sees a proper consideration of the materiality of the word as a way in which naively simplistic and abrupt links between base and superstructure, the worst excesses of mechanistic causality, can be avoided. In his example, to 'explain' Turgenev's character of Rudin (*Rudin* 1856), the 'superfluous man' with no role in society, by pointing to the ways in which the gentry class was degenerating, is to make an absurdly wide claim from the evidence of isolated examples. The novelistic 'superfluous man' exists in contexts other than that of the contemporary status of the gentry class: he is also a literary convention, performing a role within the structure of the novel, itself a genre implicated within changes in the whole field of literature and within social life as well. Thus the links between elements of the base and superstructure are always implicated within infinitely multiplying contexts. Given the plurality of these interrelations, and their continual transformations, how could we ever begin to analyse them? Thus far, Vološinov's argument mirrors to an extent many of the positions we have encountered already in this chapter: the opposition to a rigid causality typical of 'Western Marxism', the importance of prior literary conventions as 'material' constraints on the present work (Macherey), of economic and social structures in the production

(Febvre and Martin, Benjamin, Eagleton, Wolff) and reception (cultural materialism) of literary texts.

But in Vološinov's argument, it is only in the micro-level of the word that these links can be significantly traced: 'The problem of the interrelationship of the basis and superstructures – a problem of exceptional complexity, requiring enormous amounts of preliminary data for its productive treatment – can be elucidated to a significant degree through the material of the word' (Vološinov 1986, 18–19). This is because the word is both a social sign and the medium of consciousness. Language is a form of social communication which occurs between people. As a social sign, it is 'the most sensitive *index of social changes*' (19), changes both past and imminent. As the medium of consciousness, language is the predominant signifying system, which mediates and translates our understanding of non-verbal arts: music, pictures, dance. Indeed, understanding itself is seen as a form of inner speech: '*Consciousness itself can arise and become a viable fact only in the material embodiment of signs*' (11; Vološinov's emphasis). Vološinov's work is important to our study at this stage because it reveals that even in that most private and apparently individualised of all places – human consciousness – we are already thoroughly socialised. There in the most 'immaterial' of all settings is the material, social sign of the word, that which cannot be divorced from the concrete forms of social intercourse. (However, it is important to recognise that the word is 'material' only in the sense that it originates in material practices and appears as concrete when embodied in a particular text. Language as a system of signification is not, in itself, material. Eagleton, for example, argues that 'meaning is not material in the sense that bleeding or bellowing are'; 1991, 149.)[21] Vološinov's theory of language is reached through a criticism of existing modes of language analysis, characterised by Vološinov as 'abstract objectivism' (epitomised by Saussure and structuralist accounts of language) and 'individualistic subjectivism'. In Vološinov's account, language is both inescapably social and produced by individual speakers. What people say is determined in advance by the existing historicity and structures of language, but this determination is not final: people also mould and adapt language as they use it.

Language is also the site of class struggle: because people of different classes use one language, differently 'accented' words are interchanged. This is what Vološinov calls the 'multiaccentuality' of the word, the ways in which different social groups use language differently, with different accents and inflections, even different meanings. The meaning of a word is not fixed indefinitely, but can mean differently according to context, speaker, addressee and so on. It is this multiaccentuality which embodies its vitality and capacity for development: 'Any current curse word can become a word of praise, any current truth must inevitably sound to many other people as the greatest lie. This *inner dialectic quality* of the sign comes out fully in the open only in times of social crises or revolutionary changes' (23). At times of stability, dominant forces in society can stabilise the sign, so that yesterday's meaning is made to seem today's.

We can see the ways in which language is socially inflected in the following excerpt from Byron's *Don Juan* (1819–24). The narrator of this epic poem is frequently the urbane man-about-town, *au fait* with the latest poetic similes, but also contemptuously dismissive of them (the narrator opens Canto III, for example, with 'Hail Muse! et cetera ...'). In this excerpt from Canto XI, the narrator describes how the Spanish Don Juan first arrives on the outskirts of London, singing the praises of English freedom, only to be interrupted by a group of highwaymen.

13
Juan yet quickly understood their gesture
And being somewhat choleric and sudden,
Drew forth a pocket pistol from his vesture
And fired it into one assailant's pudding,
Who fell, as rolls an ox o'er in his pasture,
And roared out, as he writhed his native mud in,
Unto his nearest follower or henchman,
'Oh Jack! I'm floored by that 'ere bloody Frenchman!'

14
On which Jack and his train set off at speed,
And Juan's suite, late scattered at a distance,
Came up, all marvelling at such a deed
And offering as usual late assistance.
Juan, who saw the moon's late minion bleed
As if his veins would pour out his existence,
Stood calling out for bandages and lint
And wished he had been less hasty with his flint.

17

The cravat stained with bloody drops fell down
Before Don Juan's feet. He could not tell
Exactly why it was before him thrown,
Nor what the meaning of the man's farewell.
Poor Tom was once a kiddy upon town,
A thorough varmint and a real swell,
Full flash, all fancy until fairly diddled,
His pockets first and then his body riddled.

18

Don Juan, having done the best he could
In all the circumstances of the case,
As soon as 'crowner's 'quest' allowed, pursued
His travels to the capital apace,
Esteeming it a little hard he should
In twelve hours' time and very little space
Have been obliged to slay a freeborn native
In self-defence. This made him meditative.

19

He from the world had cut off a great man,
Who in his time had made heroic bustle.
Who in a row like Tom could lead the van,
Booze in the ken or at the spellken hustle?
Who queer a flat? Who (spite of Bow Street's ban)
On the high toby spice so flash the muzzle?
Who on a lark with black-eyed Sal (his blowing)
So prime, so swell, so nutty, and so knowing?

20

But Tom's no more, and so no more of Tom.
Heroes must die; and by God's blessing 'tis
Not long before the most of them go home.
Hail, Thamis, hail! Upon thy verge it is
That Juan's chariot, rolling like a drum
In thunder, holds the way it can't well miss,
Through Kennington and all the other 'tons',
Which make us wish ourselves in town at once;

21
Through groves, so called as being void of trees
(Like *lucus* from no light); through prospects named
Mount Pleasant, as containing nought to please
Nor much to climb; through little boxes framed
Of bricks, to let the dust in at your ease,
With 'To be let' upon their doors proclaimed;
Through 'Rows' most modestly called 'Paradise'.
Which Eve might quit without much sacrifice. (Byron 1982, 400–1)

In this excerpt, the text illustrates the disparity between differently inflected words. There is the poetic sophistication of the narrator, who can casually refer to Shakespeare: the phrase 'the moon's late minion' is already anachronistic in the Regency period, an archaic trace of Elizabethan poetry, and an evocative allusion to Falstaff.[22] This narrator is obviously distinguished from the highwaymen by social class, here represented by their language as much as their behaviour. While the narrator speaks rather pompously of 'vesture' and refers to the Thames by the Latinate 'Thamis', the highwayman Tom not only cannot tell the difference between a Spaniard and a Frenchman but drops the 'h' of 'here' in obvious allusion to his Cockney dialect. But this narrator is also chameleon-like; he begins to mimic the voice of the lower classes as he describes the encounter between the foreign nobleman and the Cockney criminals: Don Juan fires his pistol into one assailant's 'pudding', a Scottish or dialect word for the bowels or guts, and certainly not a word familiar to the 'ton', or upper class London society. And in stanzas 17 and 19, the narrator parodies or parrots a veritable lexicon of street-life: *kiddy*, young thief; *varmint*, dashing; *flash*, knowing ('the swell was flash, so I could not draw his fogle [or] The gentleman saw what I was about, and therefore I could not pick his pocket of his silk handkerchief'); *ken*, a house that harbours thieves; *spellken*, the playhouse; *queer a flat*, to puzzle a gull or silly fellow; *high toby spice*, robbery on horseback; *flash the muzzle*, to swagger openly; *lark*, fun or sport of any kind; *his blowing*, a pickpocket's mistress; *so swell*, so gentlemanly; *so nutty*, so strongly inclined.[23] Many of these slang terms are so far removed from received English (both Regency and late twentieth-century English), that they constitute another language, a 'flash' language spoken by pickpockets, thieves and harlots which needs to be translated for the 'proper' reader of 1823 (when Canto XI was first published) and of today. Here then is an embodiment of the way in which language is socially inflected.

This section also epitomises Vološinov's theory of the way in which language is continually in flux. 'Flash' language is also cultivated by a class of Regency society which does not belong to the criminal underworld: it is becoming popular among sportsmen and then mimicked as fashionable by urbane gentlemen such as the narrator of *Don Juan*. This is evident in the popularity and even the titles of slang dictionaries in the Regency period: 'Captain' Grose's *The 1811 Dictionary of the Vulgar Tongue: Buckish Slang, University Wit and Pickpocket Eloquence* and, included in James Hardy Vaux's *Memoirs* (1819), 'Vocabulary of the Flash Language'. In Byron's poem too it is the educated narrator who speaks this flash language and in the process continues the 'embourgeoisment' of these words, perpetuating their 'chicness'. Despite the apparent education, sophistication and urbanity of the poem's narrator, his language is also one of frequent colloquialisms, ungrammatical expressions, popular phrases, the mocking of polite speech (see stanza 21 above) and innumerable examples of slang and bawdy word-play. The upper classes had long enjoyed a sexual libertinism which would have allowed them to comprehend and enjoy the kind of bawdy humour and sexual word-play which might otherwise be characterised as decidedly 'low-brow'. That bawdiness was seen as typical of both upper- and working-class cultures is an indication of the cultural stratification of class sexualities and the peculiar allegiance which it created of an equivalence in sexual behaviour between such socially and economically disparate sections of Regency society. But this almost-equivalency does not mean that flash language is used in exactly the same ways: slang uttered by the highwayman and the cultured gentleman 'mean' differently. Indeed, such language is the index both of the highwayman's lack of education and of the educated gentleman's fashionable up-to-dateness.

Language is thus always socially marked and in flux, never neutral or static. It is always used in a context. Only if we were learning a new language might we study vocabulary as a formal system, divorced from a context of meaning (and Vološinov argues that the formation of linguistics as a discipline through philology and the teaching of foreign languages lies at the heart of its problematic systemisation of language-use). Vološinov's theory is thus also, though it is never named as such, a criticism of Saussure's theory of language, and in particular the highly influential argument that the relationship between signifier (word) and signified is arbitrary.[24] In Vološinov's theory, this relationship is thoroughly conventional rather than arbitrary, but this conventionality does not entail that the relationship is immutably fixed.

Vološinov's argument is that the word is thoroughly 'ideological' and in the following chapter's discussion of literature and ideology, we will see how Vološinov's theory of language is paralleled in the work of later marxists, interested in language as a site of ideological struggle.[25] But this interest in, and anger with, the way in which language is transversed by issues of taste and literacy is also found in many contemporary writers. The anger at the divisions so evident in language itself is most notably found in the poetry of Tony Harrison. Two poems, entitled 'Them & [uz]', rage against Received Pronunciation, the way in which, for example, the young poet was made to play the part of the porter in *Macbeth* at school, because, as his teacher argues: '"Poetry's the speech of kings. You're one of those / Shakespeare gives the comic bits to: prose!"' (1984, 122). And in *V.*, the cultured, erudite poet confronts the skinhead who has sprayed graffiti on his parents' tombstone and who speaks the northern, working-class language which poetry disdains and which Harrison believed he had left behind. For as they harangue each other, Harrison begins to mimic the skinhead's expletive slang, while just about containing this angry working-class dialect within the poem's strict neo-classical form:

'The only reason why I write this poem at all
on yobs like you who do the dirt on death
's to give some higher meaning to your scrawl.'
Don't fucking bother, cunt! Don't waste your breath!

'You piss-artist skinhead cunt, you wouldn't know
and it doesn't fucking matter if you do,
the skin and poet united fucking Rimbaud
but the *autre* that *je est* is fucking you.'

Ah've told yer, no more Greek ... That's yer last warning!
Ah'll boot yer fucking balls to Kingdom Come.
They'll find yer cold on t'grave tomorrer morning.
So don't speak Greek. Don't treat me like I'm dumb.

(Harrison 1985, 19)

Harrison's poem speaks to its cultured audience – like the one sipping

wine in Richard Eyre's television film of the poem (1987) – with its
inter-textual allusions to Gray's 'Elegy in a Country Churchyard',
Wordsworth's manifesto on behalf of the 'language of ordinary men',
the French symbolist poet Rimbaud's 'Je est autre'. But it also
reminds us that, in a capitalist society, 'verses' have become synonymous with 'versus', that the language of poetry is ultimately an exclu-
sivist and elite taste, and that our social divisions are most apparent,
and deep, in the very language we speak.

Notes

1. Arnold, *Culture and Anarchy*, quoted in Storey (1994, 6).
2. Misunderstandings have often been due to different uses of the concept
   of 'mediation'. In a literal sense, mediation refers to an intermediary by
   which connections between two discrete entities can be made, and as
   such it is frequently used in logics and epistemology. But the marxist
   category of (always complex) 'mediation' needs to be understood in
   relation to dialectics (see below). Here no such autonomy – neither of
   the 'parts' or of mediation itself – is possible since all are integral to a
   study of social being.
3. It is easy to mock Caudwell's 'grand narratives', especially when represented in tabular form (see 117–122), and Marxist theorists have been
   repudiating Caudwell since Williams's attack in *Culture and Society*
   (1958). However, Caudwell deserves to be judged in terms of his own
   historicity, his writings as a response to the 'close reading' of the New
   Critics which ignored social context completely as an irrelevance.
   Caudwell has recently been defended by Leonard Jackson, in a book
   which attacks the tradition of 'Western marxism' (including its anti-
   economism) from a 'non-marxist' perspective. See Jackson (1994,
   127–141).
4. Jameson's discussion draws upon Nico Poulantzas, but echoes of
   Williams's discussion of ideology as 'dominant, residual and emergent'
   are also apparent in the following: 'the overlay and structural coexis-
   tence of *several* modes of production all at once, including vestiges and
   survivals of older modes of production, now relegated to structurally
   dependent positions within the new, as well as anticipatory tendencies
   which are potentially inconsistent with the existing system but have not
   yet generated an autonomous space of their own' (95). For Williams,
   see the following chapter.
5. McKeon (1983) discusses Marx's question concerning ancient Greek art

as illustrating how Marx, like other nineteenth- and twentieth-century critics, naturalised concepts of aesthetic value.

6. Althusser adapts this term from Freud. See entry for 'overdetermination' in the glossary of the English translation of *For Marx* (Althusser 1990, 252–3).

7. This makes Thompson's definition of culture seem equivalent to Williams's, but there is an important distinction to be made. Thompson felt that Williams's conception of culture as a 'whole way of life' was tainted by its original context (T.S. Eliot's *Notes Towards a Definition of Culture*) and argued instead for a view of culture as a 'whole way of struggle'. Thompson preferred this usage because it acknowledged that culture is also a terrain of hierarchical power relations, inequality and exploitation, aspects which Williams's definition seemed to ignore. Williams replied to these criticisms insofar as he later conceptualised society as an arena of competing ideologies. See Chapter 2.

8. See Jameson (1992, 409; 1996, 46, 48). Stuart Hall has also argued that only concrete, empirical studies might satisfy the base-superstructure model and that we ought to learn from Marx's historical procedures rather than attempting to make of the distinction a once-and-for-all principle, in other words, a theory (Hall in Bloomfield 1977).

9. For his theory of 'symbolic' value, see Bourdieu (1993).

10. For the particular relationships between women writers and the market, see Tuchman and Fortin (1989) and Lovell (1987). Tuchman documents how men gradually supplanted women as novelists once novel-writing was perceived as potentially profitable, in part because of the changes in the system of publishing and rewarding authors. Lovell traces the ways in which the novel as commodity was seen as dangerously 'feminine' until its absorption into 'high' cultural form as the Victorian realist novel, and argues that this transformation (from debased commodity to literature) was largely achieved by countering women's dominance of the genre.

11. Anderson's claim is based partly on the role which print-capitalism played in the dissemination of ideas and thus the development of modern Europe. Andrew Milner (1996, 64) also claims that Febvre and Martin's work suggests that 'the book trade was almost certainly the historical prototype for modern capitalist industry in general'.

12. Defoe, *Review*, 6 December 1709: 'Why have we Laws against House-breakers, High-way Robbers, Pick-Pockets, Ravishers of Women, and all Kinds of open Violence [and yet not protection for the author?] When in this Case a Man has his Goods stollen, his Pocket pick'd, his Estate ruin'd, his Prospect of Advantage ravish'd from him, after infinite Labour, Study, and Expence.' Quoted in Rose (1993, 37).

13. The desire for fame can itself be interpreted in 'economic' terms. See Pierre Bourdieu's discussion of 'symbolic' or 'cultural' capital (1984).
14. Adorno's essay 'On the Fetish Character in Music and the Regression of Listening' (1938; reprinted in Adorno 1991), was written as if in response to Benjamin's essay. It argues that Benjamin's theory of the possibilities of film is not true of modern, mass-reproduced music. See also Benjamin's response to this essay (in Adorno et al. 1980, 139–41). The exchanges between Benjamin and Adorno are further discussed in Chapter 3. Williams, in his essay 'Cinema and Socialism', also questioned Benjamin's thesis that new cultural technologies are *inherently* radical or populist (in Williams 1996, 107–18).
15. Benjamin himself confined his discussion to late nineteenth- and early twentieth-century technological forms. See Adorno et al. (1980, 108n.) for a discussion of 'originary' modes of technical reproduction in antiquity. Benjamin's theory is strongly critiqued by Peter Bürger who, in arguing that the loss of 'aura' was first expressed by dadaism rather than by film, negates the determinism by technology which is implicit in Benjamin's argument (Bürger 1984, 27–34).
16. Cf. Macherey (1978, 197–8): ' ... there is also all that "material variety", the repertoire of images and fables, without which nothing could be done, and which would not exist if it had to be invented afresh each time. The way in which the conditions of its possibility *precede* the work (a fact which is so obvious but which centuries of criticism have ignored) systematically censures in advance any psychology of inspiration ... Against these metaphysical and supernatural representations must be advanced a coherent conception of the business of the writer, which is not the same as the business of writing. (It is absolutely not a question of describing a literary or artistic work as pure technique.)'
17. Cultural materialism is discussed in more detail in Brannigan (1998).
18. For a summary of some of these debates, see Hall in Morley and Chen (1996, 297–8) and Dentith (1995, Introduction).
19. For a critique of Bakhtin's choice of Dostoevsky, and indeed of his theory of the polyphonic novel in general, see Dentith (1995, 41–64).
20. Stuart Hall argues that this transformation of the metaphorical way of thinking dialectics is evident in the work of Allon White and Peter Stallybrass, *The Politics and Poetics of Transgression* (1988). See Hall in Morley and Chen (1996, 287–305; 'For Allon White: metaphors of transformation'). Many of these definitions of dialogism, however, rely on 'vulgar' reductions of dialectics. In a proper consideration of marxist dialectics, the distinction between dialectics and dialogics is scarcely meaningful, other than as a reminder of the ways in which some marxist uses of dialectics have tended to collapse dialectics into

Hegelian forms in which there is an ultimate synthesis of the oppositional terms.

21. This point is made by Wolff (1993, 64–5), who refers to other marxist
critiques of the 'idealist' nature of semiotic theories which discuss the
'materiality of the signifier' (164 n.69).

22. See *Henry IV Part I* I ii 25–6: Falstaff uses this phrase as a metaphor for a
thief: 'let us be Diana's foresters, gentlemen of the shade, minions
[favourites] of the moon'.

23. Definitions taken from *The 1811 Dictionary of the Vulgar Tongue*
(London: Senate, 1994) and from James Hardy Vaux, 'Vocabulary of the
Flash Language' (1819) quoted in Byron (1984, 693).

24. The 'arbitrary' relationship between signifier and signified was originally defined in distinction to the idea that the word and thing signified
were immediately, transparently, iconically linked. Vološinov's criticism of the theory of 'arbitrariness' is oriented rather towards those
adjacent meanings of a casual, random relationship which had subsequently developed. See Williams (1977, 35).

25. Eagleton includes language as a factor in the 'literary mode of production'. See Eagleton (1976a, 54–58). For other marxist accounts of
language, see the work of Williams (1977, 165–72; 'Signs and
Notations'); Michel Pecheux (1982) and Bourdieu (1991).

2 Culture and Ideology

'... one is ... tempted to dispose the multitude of notions associated with the term "ideology" around these three axes: ideology as a complex of ideas (theories, convictions, beliefs, argumentative procedures); ideology in its externality, that is the materiality of ideology, Ideological State Apparatuses; and finally, the most elusive domain, the "spontaneous" ideology at work at the heart of social "reality" itself.' (Žižek 1994, 9)[1]

The influence of Marxist approaches on contemporary literary theories is greatest in the analysis and significance of ideology. There have been several recent full-length studies of ideology: Terry Eagleton, *Ideology* (1991), Michèle Barrett, *The Politics of Truth* (1991), David Hawkes, *Ideology* (1996) and several 'readers' of significant theories of ideology: Terry Eagleton, *Ideology* (1994) and Slavoj Žižek, *Mapping Ideology* (1994). Both Eagleton (1991) and Hawkes (1996) trace the history of the use of the term, from the Enlightenment definition of ideology as the scientific study of human ideas to the postmodernist discrediting of ideology as an outmoded concept (a reading which is equally 'ideological'). Although definitions of ideology are extremely diverse, two important tendencies can be broadly identified. One associates ideology with a sense of illusion or distortion, an 'epistemological' definition insofar as it suggests that this falsity can be recognised and thus, perhaps, countered by knowledge, science or argument. The second approach treats ideology more neutrally in the sense of values or beliefs which are shared by groups of people. In the writings of such marxists as Lenin and Lukács, ideology is the consciousness or world-view of historical social classes. This treatment of ideology has been challenged by post-marxist approaches which, having witnessed the conflicting loyalties of the working class in the second half of the twentieth century, believe that we can no longer assume political allegiances or a sense of 'class belonging' (see Laclau 1977).

This chapter will follow Žižek's consideration of ideology outlined above, although simultaneously remembering the merely convenient use of this categorisation: Žižek writes of his categorisation only that 'one is tempted' to analyse ideology in this way and subtitles his section 'the Spectral Analysis of a Concept'. Žižek's threefold treatment of ideology parallels Hegel's consideration of religion as doctrine, ritual and belief. This is an appropriate parallel – not least because religion, the 'opium of the masses' (Marx) might itself be described as 'ideological' – but also because of the interconnections of materiality and interiority which are characteristic of many ideologies, not least religion. Religious faith is both a private and public experience, private in its public manifestations, communal in its individual re-enactments. The congregation prays silently and collectively and the individual's absorption into the Church is conducted through the rituals of baptism, confirmation, marriage and funeral. The activity of kneeling in prayer itself epitomises some of these paradoxes, since it is both an expression and an effect of inner belief. Thus while the three axes are discussed separately, they never operate alone.

Ideology as doctrine

Ideology is most commonly used to denote an illusory belief, a dogma which people believe irrespective of its falsity and, within classical marxism, one which serves to mystify or occlude class interests. In this sense ideology is wholly pejorative and it is applied only to a contrary way of thinking from one's own. Marx and Engels used ideology in this sense of 'false consciousness' when they attacked their adversaries, the 'Young Hegelian' philosophers (e.g. Feuerbach, Bauer, Stirner), in *The German Ideology* (1845–7). Whereas the Young Hegelians had emphasised the importance of ideas in the formation of society, Marx and Engels argued that any true transformation of society would be created primarily through changing its material conditions. The 'German ideology' which they expose is the illusory belief that correct ideas can 'liberate' people from subjection to erroneous ideas and that this critique of illusion can itself be made within the realm of ideas. However, since those who control material production also control mental ideas – because they have the power to impose their own ideas upon others – change will only be possible through a change in the material powers which determine power and legitimation: 'Nor shall we explain to them [the Young Hegelians] that it is possible to achieve real liberation only in the real world and by real means, that slavery cannot be abolished without the steam-engine and the mule jenny, serfdom cannot be abolished without improved agriculture, and that, in general, people cannot be liberated as long as they are unable to obtain food and drink, housing and clothing in adequate quality and quantity' (quoted in Jerome McGann 1983, 154).[2] The ruling classes are able to promote their own ideas, to censor those ideas which are oppositional or do not conform to their own, to represent society in ways which flatter their own interests. As Marx and Engels argue in *The German Ideology*: 'Each class which puts itself in the place of the one ruling before it, is compelled, merely in order to carry through its aim, to represent its interests as the common interests of all members of society, that is, expressed in an ideal form: it has to give its ideas the form of universality, and represent them as the only rational, universally valid ones' (1970, 64). Something of this definition was retained in Marx's later work, the *Eighteenth Brumaire of Louis Bonaparte* (1852). In this text, Marx examined the ways in which the bourgeoisie of 1848 dressed its revolution in the costumes and rhetoric of classical Rome, to legitimate and flatter their enthusiasm as creating a great historical tragedy and to conceal from themselves the tawdry limitations of the content of their struggle. This also marks a significant shift, however, since now 'ideology' is not related to the economic base in the mechanistic way in which the abolition of slavery is a 'reflection' of new technologies such as the steam engine. Instead, the 'superstructural' effects of ideological beliefs and practices are related to material reality in complex ways, and may even be semi-autonomous of the 'base'.

Already we can see that Marx's own writings on ideology were highly diverse. Michèle Barrett (1991) sets out six different treatments of the concept in Marx as a prelude to the conflicting definitions of later marxist theorists. In neither *The German Ideology*, nor *The Eighteenth Brumaire*, however, does Marx suggest that ideology is 'false'. David McLellan argues that 'false consciousness' was never used by Marx and was popularised rather by Engels in a letter to Franz Mehring in 1893 (McLellan 1986, 18). In Marx's writing, ideology is used to describe that which conceals a contradictory and inverted reality (see Bottomore 1991, 248–9). The mistaken ideas of the Young Hegelians, for example, are themselves symptomatic of social, material problems. So long as people are unable to resolve contradictions in practice, they will project these contradictions into ideological forms of consciousness and thus resolve them with mental or discursive solutions. This self-deception may ultimately serve the interests of the ruling class if, for example, it fosters political quietism. However Marx's theory of ideology here has frequently, if inaccurately, been interpreted so as to apply to all kinds of error, but principally to the kinds of false arguments which are deliberately disseminated by the ruling classes. This view of ideology is often referred to as the 'dominant ideology thesis' (or, in Williams's phrase, the 'inherent dominative mode'). The ideas which are favourable to the ruling classes will appear as objective facts, so as to disguise their self-interest. The beliefs of the ruling classes may not be recognised as 'ideological' since strategies, often characteristic of ideology itself, are deployed to disguise the partiality of these beliefs: they are presented as universal or are naturalised, made to appear inevitable. In these ways, people accept the beliefs of the ruling class, perhaps as that which is unalterable ('Obviously, with mass third level education, the government will be unable to afford maintenance grants ...') or that which is in their own interests ('It's clear that we need ...'). Žižek writes of the ways in which apparently 'commonsensical' comments are saturated with unseen political and economic motives when he writes: '"Let the facts speak for themselves" is perhaps the arch-statement of ideology – the point being, precisely, that facts *never* "speak for themselves" but are always *made to speak* by a network of discursive practices' (Žižek 1994, 11).

However, there have been many marxist objections to this 'dominant ideology thesis'. Even if we could define what the dominant ideology is, it is not necessarily the case that people will be 'dominated' by it. This kind of critique has largely come from within cultural studies and its explorations of popular culture. Feminist work on such cultural forms as soap opera, the royal family and romantic fiction, for example, suggests that many women enjoy and are not necessarily exploited by these forms.[3] In *The Dominant Ideology Thesis* (1980), Abercrombie, Hill and Turner argued that people are kept in place primarily by the dull compulsion of economic necessity (by having to work to earn a living, having few choices available to them and so on) rather than by any ideology, dominant or not. And Williams argued that no dominant ideology will ever be exhaustive: '*no mode of production and therefore no dominant social order and therefore no dominant culture ever in reality includes or exhausts all forms of human practice, human energy, and human intention'* (Williams 1977, 125; original emphasis). Williams's objections to the reductive tendency of the dominant ideology thesis – in which there are few possibilities of an escape from ideology – form an important part of his own thinking about ideology, as we shall see shortly.

Despite these criticisms however, the dominant ideology thesis can be a useful one for literary study, once we recognise that its usefulness will be specific and not true of all literary texts, in all periods. There are certainly occasions in which the power of the ruling classes to perpetuate their own value system can affect the ways in which litera-ture and culture is produced. The most obvious examples of this would be in the domain of censorship legislation. During the reign of Charles I (1625–49), publishers might be in danger of losing their ears if their publications were seen to criticise the political or religious authorities. And because printing was monopolised by the Stationers' Company, whose charter might be withdrawn by the Crown, a consid-erable degree of self-regulation operated. During the civil war of the seventeenth century, any book had to be licensed by parliament. (This is the context for Milton's defence of the liberty of the press in *Areopagitica*, 1644). In 1695 the House of Commons allowed the Licensing Act to lapse, thus ending pre-publication censorship, and thereafter Britain was honoured and celebrated for the freedom of its press.[4] However, these obvious restrictions are paralleled in the production of art in democratic capitalist societies: the publisher, for example, becomes a modern form of legislator, since while publishers may not affect what authors choose to write, they certainly control which writing is distributed and how widely. Marxist approaches to culture remind us of the ideological control which the economic, social-institutional and technological spheres continue to exercise.

Many literary historians have suggested that patronage as a way of funding the arts began to disappear in the eighteenth century. But they ignore the ways in which patronage of the arts adapted to a capi-talist age, perhaps disguised in the form of, for example, Arts Council subsidies, tax policies, foundation grants, art collectors and theatre subscribers. Many of these versions of patronage are controlled by the ruling classes who will distribute grants and sponsorship according to their own 'value' judgements. One of the best known examples of a marxist approach to patronage, and the way in which it exercised a kind of self-censorship over what poets might say, is Raymond Williams's reading of the English country-house poems, a poetic genre popular in the seventeenth century. Williams's reading of these poems (Ben Jonson's 'Penshurst' and 'To Sir Robert Wroth', and Thomas Carew's 'To Saxham') reveals the ways in which these poems idealise English country life and sanitise its social and economic realities. Before *The Country and the City* (1973), the English country-house poem had been interpreted as a record of England's 'arcadian' past, of its status as an organic rural society, later destroyed by capitalism. Williams traced the ways in which this is a comforting self-delusion: even the use of the term 'arcadia' to describe English pastoral contains a political deception, for Williams reminds us that the park in which Sir Philip Sidney's *Arcadia* (1590–3) was written was created by enclosing a village and evicting the tenants (Williams 1973, 22). These poems praise their gentry families hyperbolically:

> The Pheasant, Partiridge, and the Larke,
> Flew to thy house, as to the Arke.
> The willing Oxe, of himselfe came
> Home to the slaughter, with the Lambe,
> And every beast did thither bring
> Himselfe, to be an offering.   ('To Saxham', ll. 21–6)

Hospitality is organised around the dinner-table, but a dinner-table which is never seen as being actively prepared by domestic servants and field-labourers. Rather it is as if nature bountifully gives of itself. No portrayal of labour is possible within the rural idyll, and this in turn falsifies the presentation of those 'poor' who are hospitably and charitably fed at Saxham or Penshurst, eating what 'now and somehow, not they but the natural order has given for food, into the lord's hands' (Williams 1973, 32).[5]

Because these country seats of the aristocracy are also well documented in other discourses, these poetic representations of the estates can be measured as representations: ' ... some of them are interested lies, some of them are ways of seeing which are related not to mendacity but to privilege, some of them are much deeper and less conscious limitations of the vision of an inherited or class position, some of them are partial breakthroughs, others are relatively complete insights' (Williams 1981, 304–5). Here we can see Williams attempt to distance himself from an overly reductive treatment of these poems. He is reluctant to dismiss these poems as ideological in the sense of 'false' and thus, perhaps, as worthless. Instead of outright dismissal, he argues that these poems might also be productive in the ways in which they expose ideology. That literature performs as much as it represents ideology has been an influential way of reading in marxist literary theories and will be discussed in more detail later in this chapter. But Williams's resistance to an exclusive focus on dominant ideology is also evident in his own theorisation of ideology. For Williams (1977), the dominant ideology is never static or total, but in continuous opposition with alternative, even oppositional forces. These might be 'residual' cultural forms from earlier periods, or 'emergent' in the sense of new practices and experiences. But both are 'alternative' as much as 'oppositional' since they might be incorporated within dominant culture or might resist it. Here Williams was largely reworking a theory of ideology and hegemony which he adapted from the Italian marxist thinker, Antonio Gramsci. And it is to this enormously influential theorist of ideology that I will now turn.

Gramsci most famously argued that people may collude or invest in ideas and beliefs which are detrimental to themselves. To adopt the religious metaphor which Žižek uses for ideology, doctrine is most successful when it blurs the distinction with belief, when that which is taught becomes accepted as something which does not even require teaching. The ruling classes achieve and maintain their power not only through domination but also through intellectual and moral leadership. Gramsci's theory is an attempt to unite the orthodox marxist emphasis on the economic base with the liberal philosophy of the role of ideas. Any successful ruling body, Gramsci argues, will need both forms of power, economic and ideological. Both will operate through 'political' and 'civil' society, the apparatus of government and such 'civil' institutions as the family, school, church, court and trade union. (This distinction, Gramsci urges, is 'methodological' rather than 'organic', that is, permanent or 'essential'.) Gramsci identifies two fundamental ways in which the ruling body governs, although its power needs to extend to the supposedly 'private' or non-political spheres of civil society (the first of Gramsci's categories below), if its domination is to be seen as 'democratic':

> 1. The 'spontaneous' consent given by the great masses of the population to the general direction imposed on social life by the dominant fundamental group; this consent is 'historically' caused by the prestige (and consequent confidence) which the dominant group enjoys because of its position and function in the world of production.

2. The apparatus of state coercive power which 'legally' enforces discipline on those groups who do not 'consent' either actively or passively. This apparatus is, however, constituted for the whole of society in anticipation of moments of crisis of command and direction when spontaneous consent has failed. (Gramsci 1971, 12)[6]

Coercive and consensual power are thus both necessary powers for the State but their importance is usually divided depending on whether the State must seize power or maintain it. Physical force and aggressive laws will be necessary to seize power: consent is necessary if power is to be maintained. Once the ruling class manages to win the active consent of those over whom it rules, then it will be powerful indeed. Its relations of domination will dominate most when they are not even visible as such. In the late twentieth century, capitalism has become the almost exclusive mode of production, not only because of its system of production, but because of its social organisation. Capitalism is a way of life as well as a mode of economic production. The fall of the communist regimes in the USSR and Eastern Europe, for example, was partly due to their people's desire for the consumerism so evident in images of American society. Post-1990, many conservative and liberal commentators have argued that history and ideology have ended, with the 'triumph' of capitalism as the only serious economic mode of production for the twenty-first century. Capitalism's dominance is thus more ideological than ever. One of the most ideological of contemporary ideas is that of the 'free' market, when the global market is dominated by multinational companies and 'oligopolies', in which a small number of competitive firms control the market. To the family-run hamburger business, the arrival of McDonald's on their doorstep has little to do with *its* freedom, and everything to do with *theirs*.

Thus for Gramsci, ideology refers to the ideas, beliefs, representations and practices which bind people together. Related to this is the term 'hegemony', which refers to the relationship between classes, sections, political groupings, and the state of social and political unity existing between them. Both concepts suggest that individuals are actively involved in their own conditioning but also that ideology is therefore diverse, embodied in material practices rather than unified monolithically according to class. Indeed, Gramsci's example of successful hegemony was that of the French Jacobins who encouraged the bourgeoisie to widen its class interests, to discover what it shared with the lower classes, and enabled it to lead a coalition of classes to triumph in the French Revolution. Gramsci's theory of hegemony thus allowed political struggle to be interpreted as complex relations of forces rather than a simple confrontation between antagonistic classes. And because of this too, hegemony is never absolute or static. To consider ideology only as a form of 'false consciousness' would be to ignore the complexity of ideology and the ways in which people actively invest in it. If we re-read the quotation from *The German Ideology* given above, we might now interpret it, in Gramscian manner, as suggesting not that the dominant class simply imposes their ideas upon subordinate classes, but that it must 'represent' its interests as universal. The uncertainty which this formulation permits suggests that ideological struggle will be inevitable.

Stuart Hall's analysis of 'Thatcherism' as an ideology was largely influenced by Gramscian theory. Hall sought to explain and understand why Margaret Thatcher's policies were so popular among the working classes in Britain in the 1980s, and recognised that the attraction of her particular brand of politics – what Hall called 'authoritarian populism' – could not be explained only in economic terms. Thatcher's populism was based on ideologies of patriotism and national identity (the Falklands War in particular), 'family values', 'traditionalism', 'authority' (standing up to the miners), all of which are consonant with traditional 'one nation' Toryism. But it coupled these with 'the aggressive themes of neo-liberalism – self-interest, competitive individualism, anti-statism' (Hall 1988, 48) and material social relations, including the use of new media forms (such as the marketing strategies of Saatchi and Saatchi and the dominance of the tabloids).[7] Caryl Churchill's portrayal of Marlene in *Top Girls* (1982) allowed her to voice the multiple, and often contradictory, reasons why people supported Thatcherism: 'Get the economy back on its feet and whoosh. She's a tough lady, Maggie. I'd give her a job. She just needs to hang in there. This country needs to stop whining. ... First woman prime minister. Terrifico. Aces. Right on. ... I believe in the individual. ... I hate the working class which is what you're going to go on about now, it doesn't exist any more, it means lazy and stupid. I don't like beer guts and football vomit and saucy tits and brothers and sisters ... and I will not be pulled down to their level by a flying picket and I won't be sent to Siberia or a loony bin just because I'm original. And I support Reagan even if he is a lousy movie star because the reds are swarming up his map and I want to be free in a free world'

(Churchill 1990, 137–40). Marlene's allegiance towards Thatcherism thus springs from a way of seeing the world in which the working class is simultaneously threatening (the 'flying picket') and does not exist. But these inconsistencies are what Marlene believes in, as Thatcherism appeals to her desires (for social aspiration and material betterment) and fears and anxieties (of being prevented from realising these desires by the demands of others). Those who supported Thatcherism subscribed to and thus sustained and renewed its ideological power. They are unlikely to have recognised its contradictory nature in the way which Churchill suggests in her portrayal of Marlene. As a socialist writer working in the largely bourgeois medium of the theatre, Churchill herself may have been well placed to recognise the ambivalences and complications of the way we live our relations to society.

Ideology as ritual

Žižek's second category of ideological formations as that of 'ritual' plays with the metaphors not only of ceremony and performance but also with that which is habitual. Rituals are only so constituted by being repeated. Thus the first part of this section is concerned with how ideology is lived, rather than thought. The French marxist philosopher Louis Althusser will be discussed at this point, because in his theory, ideology not only shapes how we live our lives, but constitutes us as 'subjects'.

Althusser's essay 'Ideology and Ideological State Apparatuses' is subtitled '(Notes towards an Investigation)', and Althusser added that the ideas of the essay were merely introductory. But despite this tentativeness, Althusser's theory of ideology has been one of the most influential of twentieth-century marxist literary and cultural theories. (First published in 1970, it was quickly translated into English in 1971.) Althusser's discussion of ideology is influenced by the theories of hegemony and ideology sketched in Gramsci's *Prison Writings* as it too is an attempt to explain how and why capitalism is a self-perpetuating system, why, in effect, the citizens of capitalist countries, including and especially those whose labour is exploited by the system, continue to support its workings in a consent that is scarcely recognised. The continuous reproduction of labour power requires not only the reproduction of skills by teaching apprentices and schoolchildren, but also the reproduction of submission to the rules of the established order.

Althusser argues that the State exerts power over its citizens in various ways which can be categorised as either 'repressive' or 'ideological'. The Repressive State Apparatus (RSA) functions by a form of violence or coercion and operates through such forms as the government, the administration, the army, the police, the courts, the prisons. All of these operate together, as a single form of power, in a way which is obviously apparent to the state's citizens, for the RSA conducts its business in public. The ideological power of the State, however, works in diverse ways, and thus the unity of ideological apparatuses is not immediately apparent. Ideological State Apparatuses might include such formations as the Church, the educational system, the family, culture, communications (radio, newspapers etc.), the political system (in political parties) and other forms of organisation (e.g. trade union movement), sport (in the way in which it encourages nationalist pride) and, a formation which the ISAs share with the RSA, the legal system. Many of these 'institutions' belong to what we would consider the 'private' sphere and map onto Gramsci's definition of 'civil' society and the way in which the State continues to wield its power there too. And, paralleling Gramsci's discussion of both coercion and consent, the most important distinction between RSA and ISA is the ways in which they function: although both operate by means of both repression and ideology, the RSA primarily operates by repression, the ISA by ideology. For example, the running of the prison service, its values and rules are ideologically decided, but its effects on its inmates are primarily those of force. Conversely, at school, pupils are often disciplined, but ideological teaching is more prevalent; literature may be the subject of state repression in the form of censorship, for example, but in its realisation in reading, the literary text will work predominantly through ideology.[8]

In Althusser's analysis, the State requires both the Repressive State Apparatus and the Ideological State Apparatuses to ensure that its mode of production (whether ancient, feudal, capitalist) continues to function smoothly. For example, in capitalism ownership is private, factories and manufacturing are in the hands of the comparative few, property is bought by private wealth and so on. Thus in a capitalist state, the police, courts and prisons must punish severely those who trespass or steal. When the development of agricultural capitalism led to increasing parliamentary Enclosure Acts in the late eighteenth century, those who picked sticks by the roadside or poached a hare might be transported to a penal colony in Australia, under new legislation designed to enforce the ideology of land as property. In 1690, Locke had argued in *The Second Treatise of Government* that 'Government has no other end but the preservation of property' and the 'rights of property' were so stressed throughout the eighteenth century that increasingly they were claimed to be 'natural' and their ideological nature – that they served the interests of the propertied classes – was obscured. By 1793, William Blackstone could write of 'that law of property, which nature herself has written upon the hearts of mankind' and capital statutes concerning offences against property grew from about fifty to over two hundred between 1688 and 1820. Among Wordsworth's *Lyrical Ballads* (1798) is the song of Goody Blake's affirmation of her right to gather wood against Harry Gill. The farmer Gill is cursed by Goody Blake when he prevents her from 'stealing' from his hedge in a cold winter, and is condemned to a life of shivering and chattering teeth, irrespective of the weather. But the sympathy of the poem is entirely with the old woman, who cannot afford coal, who profits where she can from those pieces of wood which the wind splinters from houses or trees, who works as best she can for a living, but can never afford to keep warm:

> Now, when the frost was past enduring,
> And made her poor old bones to ache,
> Could any thing be more alluring,
> Than an old hedge to Goody Blake? (ll.57–60)

That Goody's 'curse' is spoken as an appeal to God ('God! Who art never out of hearing, / O may he never more be warm!'; ll.99–100), and that the poem is written in the popular ballad form associated with folk traditions, both reinforce the sympathy with Goody Blake and question the ideology by which her desperation to keep warm is a 'crime'. Later in the Romantic period, those 'Luddites' who broke the frames of machines were protesting against the mechanisation which threatened their livelihoods, and were supported by many local businessmen and farmers, who often left out their machines deliberately for rioters to destroy. Byron's first speech to the House of Lords was in defence of the framebreakers (1812) and he wrote a scandalously rebellious poem in support of their actions, 'Song of the Luddites' (1816). But the growth of capitalism required such mechanisation and, in 1830, the government had to send a sharply worded circular, reiterating that 'machines are as entitled to the protection of the law as any other description of property' (see Hobsbawm 1977, 24). In such ways capitalist relations of production are also maintained by ideological means: the Church teaches that it is immoral to covet that which belongs to others, children are taught that to be hardworking is to be virtuous. Thus Althusser argues that: 'All ideological State apparatuses ... contribute to the same result: the reproduction of the relations of production, i.e. of capitalist relations of exploitation' (see Althusser 1984, 22–31).[9]

In modern society therefore, ideology is crucially concerned with guaranteeing the maintenance of the capitalist mode of production. Capitalism's continued existence requires that as members of capitalist society we contribute to this continuity, by our acceptance of the mode of production. But this acceptance is achieved at an unconscious level: capitalism encourages each one of us to think of ourselves as individual, even when the functions which capitalism requires of us are always exceedingly and necessarily replaceable and, ultimately, dispensable. Thus there is a crucial difference between how we perceive our function in, and relationship to society and what that 'function' or 'relationship' really is. And this difference is necessarily unknown or unrecognised by us. This is what Althusser means when he argues in the first of two theses on ideology that: 'Ideology represents the imaginary relationship of individuals to their real conditions of existence' (36).[10] We might say that those who work for a low wage are being exploited, and that this is the 'real condition of their existence', but they themselves might be convinced that their being there is a matter of 'choice'. That they take the job out of their free choice appears obvious to them. However, in this case the argument of 'choice' is an imaginary, not a real relationship because 'choice' can be only partially accurate when the alternatives (such as unemployment) are not truly equivalent. Although Althusser speaks only of capitalism, we might think too of human experience in relation to nationalism: people imagine a relationship between themselves and others of the same 'nationality', that they share similar characteristics, speak the same language, have similar experiences, even though they will never have met the vast majority of their compatriots. Thus when Benedict Anderson defines a nation as an 'imagined community', his theory of national identity is similar to Althusser's formulation of capitalist society.

The second of Althusser's theses on ideology is related to the first, in referring to the way in which ideology is performed in our experiences. Althusser argues that 'Ideology has a material existence' (39). For example, if, as a committed socialist, I took out private medical insurance, then despite my own beliefs (socialist 'ideology' in the sense of a system of beliefs and values), I would be living the ideology of capitalism. In this example, my beliefs would be literally and metaphorically 'immaterial', because the practice of paying privately would have a greater impact in supporting, materially, private medicine. We can see here that Althusser's theory of ideology displays the same kind of doubling which was a feature of the study of culture and society in the first chapter: ideology is both material and imaginary. Catherine Belsey articulates this clearly when she explains Althusser's two theses in this way: ' ... ideology is both a real and an imaginary relation to the world – real in that it is the way in which people really live their relationship to the social relations which govern their conditions of existence, but imaginary in that it discourages a full understanding of these conditions of existence and the ways in which people are socially constituted within them. ... Althusser talks of ideology as a "material practice" in this sense: it exists in the behaviour of people acting according to their beliefs' (Belsey 1980, 57).[11]

But in Althusser's theory, ideology is not only a matter of performing but also of living in ideology. Ideology is inescapable because our very selves are constituted by it: there is no subject outside of ideology (except in 'science', a point I will return to). Althusser's central thesis is that 'ideology hails or interpellates concrete individuals as concrete subjects' (47). That we are concrete, free, individual, irreplaceable and distinguishable subjects is the 'elementary ideological effect' (46). And because we are born as subjects (even before we are born our subject-hood is already 'hailed' in the determination of a surname, for example), ideology has always-already hailed us as subjects. In interpellation, the subject comes to recognise itself as hailed in language. In this way Althusser locates ideology within consciousness itself, and it is this always pre-existing working of ideology which guarantees its effectiveness. In Althusser's terms, it would be quite exceptional for any one of us to say: 'I am in ideology' (the exceptional case being a scientific marxist), since there is no position 'outside' of ideology from which we could make such a statement. As in Gramsci's theory of hegemony, Althusser's definition of ideology attempts to explain why we freely accept subjection. As in Freud's theories, it is our unconscious which shapes our subject-hood. We are unconscious of the way in which ideology determines our behaviour and thinking, a theory which is radically opposed to the humanist belief that we command our thinking. Ultimately, for Althusser, ideology reproduces the relations of production (as Marx argued that production reproduces the forces of production): through ideology, we live capitalist relations.

Althusser's own concrete examples of his theories are most frequently drawn from religion as an ideological apparatus. But even though Althusser is not a literary theorist, his ideas have been influential in literary and cultural studies. For example, his theory of the interpellation of subjects has influenced the ways in which we might read and consider autobiographical writing. Felicity Nussbaum in her work on eighteenth-century autobiography, writes, following the suggestions of Althusser's work, that 'the autobiographical subject would believe in its agency to express and know and regulate itself without discerning the economic and political powers that limit its expression' (Nussbaum 1995, 34). Althusser's theory of interpellation has also been influential in feminist work: not only is a baby born with a (usually patrilineal) name and status, and will be judged according to prevailing ideologies of 'human nature', but each baby is also gendered, a gender which is always already socially defined. Normative prescriptions for 'correct' gender behaviour are evident everywhere: in tabloid reporting on the behaviour of the female royals, in contemporary women's magazines with their advice to women on how to be successfully careerist, sexy and good mothers – simultaneously. These contemporary images have antecedents in those conduct manuals especially popular and influential in the eighteenth century.[12] These conduct manuals are clearly ideological: they attempted to teach women of the middle and upper classes that they ought to be modest, chaste, self-deprecating, passive, restrained, timid. They thus constructed an ideal of proper femininity. But they also blurred their own ideological aims when they professed that they were not prescribing rules for feminine conduct, but describing what femaleness was like – 'naturally'. We might think of women in the eighteenth century then as explicit examples of the ways in which identity formation is bound up with and constituted by ideology, and these conduct manuals as exemplifying ideology in their internal contradictions (femininity is 'natural' yet it needs to be learned from such manuals).

The relationship between subjectivity and Catholicism in Kate O'Brien's novels is one which can be easily read in Althusserian terms. In a characteristic plot, her heroines chafe against the moral codes of Irish or Spanish society. In *The Ante-room* (1934), for example, Agnes Mulqueen organises her family's rituals, playing hostess to her guests and arranging the family mass while her mother lies dying in an upstairs room. And while she attempts to control the household during the religious devotions of the Eve and Feast of All Saints and the Feast of All Souls, she must tussle with her own conscience and desires, torn between pity for her dying mother, intense loyalty to her sister, Marie-Rose, and an illicit passion for her sister's husband, Vincent. But for Agnes, as for other O'Brien heroines, there is no simple way of renouncing conventional pieties and moral codes. And her renunciation is complex, not because these codes take the powerful form of 1880s Irish, respectable, Catholic upper-middle-class life, in which divorce is forbidden by Church and State, but because her own subjectivity is so deeply formed through Catholicism and through love for her sister, so that the choice she must make is not between 'internal' and 'external' impulses but within her own selfhood. *The Ante-room* does not permit us to read Agnes's character as a passive woman, cowed by the pressures of her society, but as a heroine whose subjectivity is 'interpellated' through the very forces which refuse her desire. And this is mirrored in Kate O'Brien's own combination of psychoanalytical radicalism with relatively orthodox Catholicism.

Althusser's greatest influence in literary and cultural theories has been in the ways in which his own practices of reading and thinking about literature were developed by others, principally by Pierre Macherey (*A Theory of Literary Production,* first published 1966) and Terry Eagleton (*Criticism and Ideology,* 1976). Althusser's theory suggests that those elements which are apparently most 'non-ideological' are where ideology deeply resides. How then can we know or recognise ideology? For Althusser, a scientific, theoretical knowledge of ideology is possible, a knowledge which, unlike empiricism, does not assume that knowledge is guaranteed by a direct encounter with reality, by an unmediated vision of the object of study. In an essay on the playwrights Bertolazzi and Brecht, Althusser argues that no dialectic of consciousness is possible: 'consciousness does not accede to the real through its own internal development, but by the radical discovery of what is *other than itself*' (Althusser 1990, 143; original emphasis). Theoretical knowledge locates itself outside of ideology, thinks by concepts and is 'scientific' insofar as it is subjectless. The confidence in this 'objectivity' is unlikely to be shared with non-marxist thinkers, however, and Althusser's concept of 'science' as true knowledge is exceedingly problematic when post-Saussurean theories of epistemology (the grounds of knowledge) argue that no such distinction between language and the object of that language is possible.[13] In addition, Althusser's concept of total ideology, an ideology which not only always-already exists but always-will, has disquieted almost all of his commentators. If ideology is so deeply implicated in our subject-formation, how can an 'outside' of ideology be possible?[14] And this in turn asks how any change might be possible. How can we step outside of ideology in order to question it? Thus Althusser's concept of 'science' is necessary, however theoretically unconvincing, if he is to retain the crucial marxist belief in the possibility of change. Here Althusser's positioning of 'Literature' as initiating a knowledge between ideology and science has been significant in that 'Literature' becomes the agent which can mediate between being-in-ideology and knowledge-of-ideology. This in turn is made (theoretically) possible by Althusser's argument of the 'relative autonomy' of the super-structure (see Chapter 1).

Althusser's clearest statement on literature came as a result of a letter from André Daspre in *La Nouvelle Critique* (1966) which inferred from Althusser's silence on art that he ranked art among other ideologies. Althusser's reply to Daspre is that art neither constitutes knowledge nor ideology, but has a special relationship to both. Art gives us a knowledge of ideology and it permits us to know ideology because it remains within ideology, not because it transcends it. But this knowledge is of a special kind:

> I believe that the peculiarity of art is to 'make us see' (*nous donner à voir*), 'make us perceive', 'make us feel' something which *alludes* to reality. ... What art makes us *see*, and therefore gives to us in the form of '*seeing*', '*perceiving*' and '*feeling*' (which is not the form of *knowing*), is the *ideology* from which it is born, in which it bathes, from which it detaches itself as art, and to which it *alludes*. ... Balzac and Solzhenitsyn give us a 'view' of the ideology to which their work alludes and with which it is constantly fed, a view which presupposes a *retreat*, an *internal distantiation* from the very ideology from which their novels emerged. They make us 'perceive' (but not know) in

some sense *from the inside*, by an *internal distance*, the very ideology in which they are held. (Althusser 1984, 174–5)

Art and science both permit us to recognise ideology, but they differ in the specific form of this recognition: art permits us to see, perceive or feel ideology, science to 'know' it (in the strict sense of scientific, theoretical or conceptual knowledge). This theory resolves a question which has concerned many marxist thinkers, including Marx himself: why authors with known political views write works which appear to contradict these views. (Marx asked this of Balzac, Lukács of Sir Walter Scott and Macherey of Tolstoy.) This literary theory was fully developed by Pierre Macherey in *A Theory of Literary Production* (1966; first English translation 1978).[15] In Chapter 1 I considered some aspects of Macherey's work – namely the argument that the artist is a producer rather than a creator, and that the literary text is necessarily fragmented and decentred, because it is constituted by elements which precede the text and impinge upon it in diverse ways. But Macherey does not lament the lack of unity in the literary text. Instead this 'decentredness', this lack of organic wholeness, is the text's most significant aspect. As a reader, Macherey is not attempting to 'complete' the text, not trying to unify the text, reconcile its contradictions, or to make it harmonious. For this reason it is better to speak of the text as 'decentred' than 'incomplete' (because to say that it is incomplete assumes that it needs to be completed). Macherey's argument is that we should seek to read the text's internal contradictions, fragments and gaps in 'productive' ways. Reading the contradictions and fractures of the text is productive because it is in the gaps and indeterminacies of the text that ideology can be known.

For Macherey (and Althusser) ideology is a discourse which is contradictory and illusory: thus it can never be embodied. But because the literary text is made up of a multiplicity of parts, it is able to make ideology visible. Thus Macherey would argue that ideology is hollowed out or made visible in a text. What is significant in a text is thus what it does *not* say or is unable to say, just as the author is unable to know the gaps of her knowledge and why the text does not 'say' or 'know'. Ideology is insubstantial, illusory and because one of ideology's effects is to eradicate contradiction, ideology itself cannot 'show' contradiction. But its self-contradiction can be seen elsewhere: literary texts put ideology into contradiction by giving it a *form* which highlights or foregrounds this contradiction (rather than, say, reflect-

ing this contradiction in its content). It shows the limits, the gaps of
the text and thus forces its silences to 'speak' as it were; texts unconsciously 'stage' the limits of knowledge. Here Macherey's theory
alludes to Freud's analysis of dreams and *parapraxes*, or slips of the
tongue, and the way in which these can be read as 'symptoms'.
(Indeed both Althusser and Macherey describe their mode of reading
as 'symptomatic'.)[16] Dreams represent a reality by condensing,
displacing, eliding, transferring affects, and by representing them
symbolically. Literary texts embody reality in a way which is similar to
this. A further analogy with Freudian theory is that of the unconscious:
in order to live in a certain way (often defined as the 'normal') the
subject must repress particular desires which do not actually disappear but which could be said, paradoxically, to be the preconditions of
'normality'. Thus one of the effects of writing – and the function of
criticism – is to articulate ideology's repressed preconditions, to articulate its unconsciousness, the things it cannot say in order to exist.
Eagleton neatly summarises Macherey's theory in *Against the Grain*:

> The work does not 'reproduce' ideology, in a way which would make
> its own contradictions reflective of historical contradictions. On the
> contrary: the contradictions within the text are the product of an
> ideologically determined *absence* of such a reflection of real contra-
> dictions. It is the work's problematical *relationship* to ideology which
> produces its internal dissonances. Rather than 'reproducing' ideol-
> ogy, the text *produces* it, setting it in motion, endowing it with a form,
> and in so doing reveals in its own internal dislocations the gaps and
> limits which signify that ideology's contradictory relation to real
> history ... in transforming rather than merely reproducing ideology,
> the text necessarily illuminates the 'not-said' which is the significant
> structure of the 'said'. (Eagleton 1986, 15–16)[17]

An example of the way in which literature can be said to 'perform'
ideology can be demonstrated in a reading of William Watson's poem
'England and her Colonies'. Written in 1890, this poem can be read as
illustrating something of the ideology of its historical and political
context, namely the 'scramble for Africa' of the 1880s and 1890s.

> She stands a thousand-wintered tree,
>   By countless morns impearled;
> Her broad roots coil beneath the sea,
>   Her branches sweep the world;

Her seeds, by careless winds conveyed,
  Clothe the remotest strand
With forests from her scatterings made,
New nations fostered in her shade,
  And linking land with land.

O ye by wandering tempest sown
  'Neath every alien star,
Forget not whence the breath was blown
  That wafted you afar!
For ye are still her ancient seed
  On younger soil let fall –
Children of Britain's island-breed,
To whom the Mother in her need
  Perchance may one day call. (Brooks 1996, 275)

This poem can be read as 'performing' the ideology of empire, for here we can trace the contradictions which undermine the confidence of the poem's gestures. Britain is depicted as a vast tree, whose roots coil beneath the sea and whose branches sweep the world. Yet despite this image of overarching presence, the 'seeds' of British culture or colonisation are conveyed by 'careless winds' to the 'remotest strand' and her colonies are made from its 'scatterings'. These images appear contradictory: Britain is an overarching presence, yet the colonies are remote. Colonisation is benevolently determined, yet the scattering of seeds suggests that the colonial project is arbitrary. The suggestion of contradictions continues in the second stanza: despite the apparent bond between empire and colony, the act of colonisation is depicted as alien in the juxtaposition of 'ancient seed' on 'younger soil'. This stanza continues the mother empire-colonial children analogy of the first stanza, although here, instead of the colonies depending upon the 'motherland' ('New nations fostered in her shade'), it is the mother who is dependent upon her children. Britain of course in the late nineteenth century could be said to have 'depended' on its colonies for trade and military power, but this is something which the poem does not 'wish' to say, but nevertheless allows us to suggest. The poem is written as a ballad form with its closely rhyming stanzas, yet it uses this popular, even 'working-class' form for a political message of state importance.

Most ideological of all, however, is the poem's anxious reassertion of a self-evident truth: that the empire is a great and benevolent project. The poem is ostensibly addressed to the colonised, a reminder of Britain's goodness ('Forget not whence the breath was blown ...'), but the repetition of this might also be read as a reassurance addressed to the coloniser and colonised alike, of the fitness of its colonising project. Thus on the one hand, colonisation is addressed as self-evidently beneficial for the colonised country, yet on the other, it needs to be constantly reasserted, evident in the many texts justifying colonisation which have accompanied any imperial expansion.[18] The above phrase – 'the anxious reassertion of a self-evident truth' – is adopted from Homi Bhabha's discussion of colonial stereotypes ('The Other Question' in Bhabha, 1994).[19] That a Machereyan analysis has here been demonstrated in a reading which could just as easily be categorised as 'postcolonial' indicates how marxist analyses have influenced postcolonial (and feminist) theories. Indeed, Macherey's reading of *The Mysterious Island* is an exposure of the colonialist ideology which informs the novel.

Macherey's ways of reading are opposed to traditional Anglo-American criticism, which seeks to read the text so as to reveal its unity, to articulate what the text is saying, indeed to imitate and complete the text by tracing its outline. The text's meaning is thus intrinsic, waiting to be discovered and revealed by the critic. Macherey calls this reading 'a penetration of appearances in order to appropriate some secret' (Macherey 1976, 51). It limits itself to seizing hold of something already given, and confines the process of understanding the work to the search for a single meaning. Macherey's reading however is not the *reproduction* of an organic, inherent meaning, but a *production* of meaning. It does not strive to 'complete' the work, since the text's incompleteness is determinate, it is this way and no other. Indeed, we might say, following Macherey, that the text is complete in its incompleteness. But marxist readings do intervene in the sense that they read this incompleteness as revealing, they put the text into a position of self-contradiction, they make it reveal its silences, what it does not wish to say. Marxist readings (like feminist and postcolonial approaches) make a difference to the text but, unlike other readings, in 'reading against the grain', they do not pretend to be ideologically neutral themselves.

However, despite this obvious opposition to traditional humanist readings, formalist, new critical, and Leavisite, Macherey's theory has been accused of latent formalism by Eagleton (in an essay originally published in 1975 and later collected in 1986) and Bennett (1979). Macherey argues that literature reveals ideology in giving a 'determinate representation' (64) of it. While the content of literature might itself be ideological, it is its form that permits this ideology to be read. Eagleton and Bennett argue that this is to fetishise the ways in which texts represent, or their form, as non-ideological. Indeed, this splitting of form and content is typical of many humanist approaches to literature, and, it could be argued, is itself ideological. Macherey does not quite essentialise content and form in this way, his theory includes the possibility that form itself might be thoroughly 'ideological': 'Even if this form is itself ideological there is an internal displacement of ideology by virtue of this *redoubling*' (133). (The following chapter considers marxist approaches to realism as an ideological form, for example.) But in viewing this displacement as achieved always and only through literary form, even here Macherey suggests, as Frow argues, that 'formal structures are in some sense a neutral tool applied from outside ideology' (Frow 1988, 26). Thus all literary texts will be subversive, insofar as they reveal ideology and thus permit political readings to interpret them as radically opposed to ideology, even where they ostensibly support it. Both Bennett and Eagleton argue that Althusser and Macherey forget the materialist practices of marxist theory when they define 'science', 'ideology' and 'literature' (Althusser) or 'theory', 'illusion' and 'fiction' (Macherey) as essences, as forms of practice which are unchanging and permanent. The literary text, instead of being considered in its particularity (in its historical, social, economic, ideological, technological or institutional matrices), becomes a manifestation of the invariant structure which is 'Literature'. In reifying an idea of 'Literature' in this way, they merely duplicate such non-marxist readings as those of the formalists, and the literary text is measured against, instead of being itself situated within, ideology.

This residual formalism can certainly be traced in the ways in which both Althusser and Macherey implicitly support a canonical view of 'Literature'. (This is why I have capitalised 'Literature' in the preceding paragraphs.) Althusser in 'A Letter on Art in Reply to André Daspre' (1966) defines 'art' in obviously elitist terms: 'Art (I mean authentic art, not works of an average or mediocre level) ...' (Althusser 1984, 174). And Macherey, despite references to gothic and detective fiction, his profession of defending 'popular literature', and his reading of Verne, a writer peripheral to the canon of 'great' French

writers, still talks in terms of 'minor literature' and 'great literature'
(Macherey 1978, 28). This distinction sits oddly with Macherey's
attack on the 'empiricist fallacy' in criticism which deems that it need
only *receive* its object of study and his assertion that '... in theoretical
practice ... the object is never given but is progressively discovered'
(Macherey 1978, 5). And Macherey did quickly begin to revise his writings on literature: in a 1977 interview in *Red Letters*, the literature
journal of the British Communist Party, Macherey questioned an
automatic, 'natural' (i.e. ideological) assumption of 'Literature',
arguing that to ask 'What is literature?' is a false question: 'Because it
is a question which already contains an answer. It implies that literature is *something*, that *literature* exists as a *thing*, as an eternal and
unchangeable *thing* with an essence' (Macherey 1977, 3).

This interview appeared before the first English translation of *A
Theory of Literary Production*, and was followed by further revisionary
work, an essay on the 'Problems of Reflection' (1977; reprinted in
Barker 1977), and collaborative work with Etienne Balibar, 'On
Literature as an Ideological Form: Some Marxist Propositions' (1978;
reprinted in Eagleton 1996). This latter project developed Althusser's
idea that ideologies in contemporary mature capitalist formations are
dominated by the Ideological State Apparatus of education (Althusser
1984, 27–31) and was originally written as an introduction to Renée
Balibar's study of the use of literature in the French educational
system, *Les français fictifs* (1974). Thus, influenced by Althusser's
emphasis on the material nature of ideology, Etienne Balibar and
Macherey argue that 'Literature' must be understood as an object
which is determined by the moment of its reproduction, defined only
in relation to those social practices which in turn define what it is, and
how its own ideological nature is inflected. In particular, 'Literature'
in nineteenth- and twentieth-century France is defined according to
how it is constructed within the classroom and there moulded
according to the ways in which language itself is taught. Balibar and
Macherey differentiate between vernacular and institutional
languages, or 'basic' and 'literary' French and see these differences as
constructed out of class difference. Those children who are educated
only to primary school level speak a vernacular language which
stamps them as lower class. Successful and predominantly middle-
class children, who progress to secondary and tertiary levels of education, are equipped to speak and read a 'literary' language which in
turn reflects their status. Renée Balibar, in *Les français fictifs*,

compares two text-books which ostensibly transcribe the same excerpt from George Sand's novel, *The Devil's Pool*. One is a language-primer for children, the other a 'critical edition' for secondary school and university students. The differences between the two transcripts reveal that literature is 'produced' in different forms, and that we receive it in a predetermined way, overlayered by material and institutional matrices such as the uses to which it is put, the apparatus which surrounds it (editor's preface, notes, annotations), even, perhaps most obviously, the design of the cover. The language and grammar of the primer's version were simplified and stripped of 'cultural/cultured' references to painters such as Holbein, Michelangelo, Goya and so on. The technical presentation of ploughing in the primary level primer became an aestheticised image of rural life in the 'critical edition' (see Bennett 1979, 156–68). These differences reveal a linguistic division which is perpetuated by, as it itself perpetuates, class division.

Many commentators on Balibar's work have argued that his highly specific model of the French educational system does not translate exactly to a British system.[20] While this is undoubtedly the case, Balibar's analysis is paralleled in the studies of British cultural materialists who have analysed the ways in which Shakespeare is institutionalised in such diverse forms as holograms for bank-cards, set-texts for school pupils and advertisements for military weapons (see Dollimore and Sinfield 1985; Sinfield 1992).[21] There have also been several interesting explorations of the ways in which the canon of 'great' British writers was formed in collusion with ideological interests in education. For example, in an article entitled 'Education, ideology and literature' (1978), Tony Davies argues that 'standard English', with its formal specifications, its prescriptions for spelling, grammar and pronunciation, defined a 'literary' language in which 'literariness' is itself defined according to class prescriptions embedded in the linguistic practice of 'standard English'. 'Standard English' passes itself off as a national language, but it is the language which defines the ruling classes, just as, in a tautological movement, their language defines what is judged to be the 'national' or 'standard' language. Davies reads Eliot's *The Mill on the Floss* as, in Macherey's terms, permitting us to 'see' the ideology of linguistic 'competence', because it itself is 'an outstanding exemplar of the very formation that it "criticises"'. *The Mill on the Floss* is a 'novel about the educational and sexual exploitation of lower-middle-class children written – how could it not be? – in the "literary" language of the educated classes; written, furthermore, by a woman *disguised as a man'* (in Bennett et al. 1981, 260). The contradictions of this novel are produced by such Victorian ideologies as the necessary embourgeoisement of the writer, the removal of 'working-class' identity in the expression of that identity, and the properly masculine activity of writing. But the novel also participates in the production of such ideologies. It too is enmeshed in the very ideologies which it permits us to see. Davies's article thus comes to the same theoretical conclusion that Balibar and Macherey propose: 'Dialectically, literature is simultaneously product and material condition of the linguistic division in education, term and effect of its own contradictions' (Eagleton 1996, 282).[22] Definitions of 'English', as much as 'French Literature' can be interpreted as ideological in their attempts to smooth over the class and ideological contradictions embedded within language itself. These analyses intersect in important ways with Vološinov's theories of language. Indeed, Vološinov argued that the *'word is the ideological phenomenon par excellence'* (Vološinov 1973, 13) and the section on the 'materiality of language' in Chapter 1 might now be reread in the light of this discussion.[23]

Eagleton argues that Macherey's writings on literature in these articles are too sociological. Here, it seems, Macherey stops reading literary texts in an exclusive interest in situating them within their material matrices.[24] Eagleton's *Criticism and Ideology* (1976) attempts to revise and supplement Macherey, to revisit *A Theory of Literary Production* in the light of the later work on 'literature' as itself ideological. Eagleton situates the production of the literary text within a range of contexts: the general mode of production (the dominant form, such as late capitalism); the literary mode of production (such as print-capitalism, distributing cheap broadsides in the streets); general ideology; authorial ideology (not an 'expression' of the author's beliefs, but that which is produced by a combination of the general ideology and biographical factors); and aesthetic ideology (the specific, aesthetic region of the general ideology). The literary text is produced by an interaction of these structures, but it is not the passive product of such formations, since the text also 'determines its own determinants' (Eagleton 1976a, 63). Eagleton's work here is extremely theoreticist and the listing of these determinants makes his 'science of the text' appear overly schematic. In his discussion of each of these categories, however, Eagleton's attention to the specificity of different formations, and the many individual examples cited in support, are more nuanced than might have been anticipated from the scheme. Eagleton discusses a range of possibilities in the relationship between literary text and ideology. Not all texts, for example, work 'against' ideology, in being able to reveal it just by nature of their 'literariness' (68). And the relationship between literary text and ideology can be dialectical once the 'literary' is itself analysed as ideological. Eagleton's 'science', in distinction to Macherey's, is an examination both of 'the nature of the ideology worked by the text and the aesthetic modes of that working' (85). But this has not meant that it has been immune from criticism, as we shall see when we consider those theories of 'popular culture' developed through cultural studies (Chapter 4).

Ideology as belief

After *The German Ideology* and its central focus on ideology as illusion, Marx rarely used the term 'ideology'. But in his later critiques of political economy, particularly in *Capital,* Marx identified a chimera, or we might say, an ideological distortion at work in the very heart of the actual process of social production, in the commodity form itself. Our misperceptions are then not the product of a 'false consciousness' but caused by contradictions in the material structure of capitalism itself.

Jorge Larrain traces the continuity between the early and later writings of Marx in his discussion of ideology in *A Dictionary of Marxist Thought* (Bottomore et al. 1991, 247–52). Larrain's argument is that, even in *The German Ideology,* Marx linked distorted, ideological ideas with the contradictions in and inverted nature of the material base itself. Ideology is produced by, but also in turn disguises, those real contradictions. In his later analyses of advanced capitalist social relations, Marx develops the way in which 'inverted consciousness' and 'inverted reality' are related. The relationship is not a direct one, but mediated by the 'phenomenal forms' of reality itself, the operation of the market and competition in capitalist societies. The exchange of commodities in capitalist markets appears as an image of freedom and equality: one trader sells, the other buys, so the total value exchanged remains the same and there is an equivalence between what both gained (the commodity/the money exchanged for the commodity). But commodity exchange is only apparently equal and free within capitalism. For when the worker sells his or her labour, there is no equivalence between labour and the product of that labour, the commodity. The commodity is sold for more than its 'cost' (in wages, raw materials, distribution). The owner of the means of production recuperates the cost of the commodity plus a surplus value. Thus there is a fundamental inequality in the production and exchange of commodities. As for 'freedom', it might be said that the worker 'freely' sells her own labour but in doing so she loses her freedom. Marx appropriately speaks of this operation ironically, that rhetorical device which itself operates on two levels, that which is said and that which is understood: 'The sphere of circulation or commodity exchange within whose boundaries the sale and purchase of labour-power goes on, is in fact a very Eden of the innate rights of man. It is the exclusive realm of Freedom, Equality, Property and Bentham' (Marx 1995, 113).

In this exchange, social relations become alienated, as the determining principle is always the abstract and reified one of the exchange of labour for surplus value. Social relations take on the form of a relationship between things and relations between persons become material. Marx terms this commodity fetishism, in which the economic forms of capitalism conceal underlying social relations: 'A commodity is therefore a mysterious thing, simply because in it the social character of men's labour appears to them as an objective character stamped upon the product of their labour; because the relation of the producers to the sum total of their own labour is presented to them as a social relation, existing not between themselves, but between the products of their labour' (Marx 1995, 43). A commodity is valued in terms of money, rather than the network of social relations between the producers of diverse commodities. But this is also a misrecognition of complexity, relations and process. The labourer is valued in terms of her labour power, one reified part of her being, and the product is valued in terms of only one exchange, money. Adorno's example of such commodity fetishism is in the way in which mass culture is thoroughly commodified, and nowhere more so than where it least appears to be 'commercial': 'The consumer is really worshipping the money that he himself has paid for the ticket to the Toscanini concert. He has literally "made" the success which he reifies and accepts as an objective criterion, without recognizing himself in it. But he has not "made" it by liking the concert, but rather by buying the ticket' (Adorno 1991, 34). Adorno's point would seem to be vindicated by the policy at Covent Garden opera house in the 1980s and 1990s, in which most of the best and very expensive seats are filled by corporate bookings.

Marx's exploration of commodity fetishism appears to rely upon a dichotomy between appearance and concealed reality. This is read by Jameson as paralleling the focus in aesthetics on the strategic distinction between content and form of the art work. Marxist conceptions of both the capitalist formation and the discourse of aesthetics rehearse an idea of form and content, appearance and essence, manner and substance. Thus, in Jameson's reading, there is a particular analogy between marxist economic analyses of the commodity and aesthetic theories (Jameson 1991, ch.8). But there is a danger here that the marxist distinction between appearance and the 'real' is essentialised. In Marx's writings appearance is not necessarily false, it is not only that relations between people are disguised as relations between things. It is also that elements from a complex structure of interrelations are isolated and the focus on process, on the diversity of elements, is lost. The juxtaposition of the two spheres is not so that the 'content' can be revealed by unveiling it as if from under the concealment of form; rather, marxist analysis attempts to unveil the secret of the form itself. This is discussed by Žižek in his comparison of the interpretative procedures of Marx and Freud:

> The theoretical intelligence of the form of dreams does not consist in penetrating from the manifest content to its 'hidden kernel', to the latent dream-thoughts; it consists in the answer to the question: why have the latent dream-thoughts assumed such a form, why were they transposed into the form of a dream? It is the same with commodities: the real problem is not to penetrate to the 'hidden kernel' of the commodity – the determination of its value by the quantity of the work consumed in its production – but to explain why work assumed the form of the value of a commodity, why it can affirm its social character only in the commodity-form of its product. (Žižek 1989, 11)

This continues the revision of Marx's concept of ideology. Ideology in Marx's writings is not theorised as a form of 'false consciousness' (as it is by, for example, Lukács). There is no simple dichotomy of falsity obscuring truth. As Eagleton argues in *Criticism and Ideology*, '...in *deformatively* "producing" the real, [ideology] nevertheless carries elements of reality within itself' (Eagleton 1976a, 69). It is not a matter of looking behind a veil to discover the real which lies hidden there: 'The real is by necessity empirically imperceptible, concealing itself in the phenomenal categories (commodity, wage-relation, exchange-value and so on) it offers spontaneously for inspection' (69).[25] Illusion cannot be straightforwardly counterposed to reality because reality itself contains the illusional, in Žižek's words, 'ideological distortion is written into its very essence' (Žižek 1989, 28). Our postmodern age is characterised by cynicism, in which we can recognise and even know ideology, but, Žižek argues, this does not eradicate ideology. If ideology is at the heart of the social, or the real, then ideology will continue in our practices, irrespective of whether we 'recognise' it or not. What we do not know is the illusion which structures reality, our real social activity. Žižek thus revises Marx's consideration of ideology in *Capital* ('they do not know it, but they are doing it') as 'they know that, in their activity, they are following an illusion, but still, they are doing it' (33). Ideology thus operates in the same way as fantasy imbues the real in Lacanian analysis. Ideology is not an illusion into which we can escape from an insupportable reality; it is a fantasy which structures reality itself: 'The function of ideology is not to offer us a point of escape from our reality but to offer us the social reality itself as an escape from some traumatic, real kernel' (45). Žižek chooses as an example of this theory the ideology of anti-Semitism:

> It is not enough to say that we must liberate ourselves of so-called 'anti-Semitic prejudices' and learn to see Jews as they really are – in this way we will certainly remain victims of these so-called prejudices. We must confront ourselves with how the ideological figure of the 'Jew' is invested with our unconscious desire, with how we have constructed this figure to escape a certain deadlock of our desire. ... The proper answer to anti-Semitism is therefore not 'Jews are really not like that' but 'the anti-Semitic idea of Jew has nothing to do with Jews; the ideological figure of a Jew is a way to stitch up the inconsistency of our own ideological system'. (Žižek 1989, 48)

Žižek continues by depicting a scenario: a 'good anti-Semite' in Germany in the late 1930s is bombarded with anti-Semite propaganda but he has friendly relations with his neighbour, the Jewish Mr Stern. This everyday experience however does not annul his anti-Semitic ideology, because ideology cannot be simply resisted by experience in this way: 'An ideology is really "holding us" only when we do not feel any opposition between it and reality – that is, when the ideology succeeds in determining the mode of our everyday experience of reality itself'. This man, confronted with this discrepancy, only turns this 'gap', this discrepancy into further corroboration for anti-Semitism. He replies: '"You see how dangerous they really are? It is difficult to recognize their real nature. They hide it behind the mask of everyday appearance – and it is exactly this hiding of one's real nature, this duplicity, that is a basic feature of the Jewish nature."' Žižek adds that 'An ideology really succeeds when even the facts which at first sight contradict it start to function as arguments in its favour' (49).

In many ways, this kind of indistinction between the 'real' and the 'imaginary' is more obvious now, in our 'postmodern', 'post-marxist' age than ever before. In an early text of 'postmodernism', *The Society of the Spectacle* (1967), Guy Debord argued that the 'real' cannot be known as such since the media structure our perception of reality in advance. In a 'hyperreal' age of live television coverage, media manipulation, information technology and virtual reality, it becomes more difficult than ever to know the difference between the simulated and real. And these debates are important for contemporary cultural studies: how should we address and understand the power of Hollywood film, television advertising, contemporary practices of news-reporting? In the 1990s, the media's images of war are visually and aurally equivalent to the computer games we play at home or in arcades. (Thus, for Baudrillard, the 1991 Gulf War 'did not happen'.)[26] Our sense of value, our aspirations and hopes, our ways of living, are refracted through fashion, through advertising images and collective fantasies which are manipulated by powerful corporate interests which we cannot, or do not wish to, refuse. For Debord, as for his theoretical successor, Jean Baudrillard, it is in the image that we see a form of commodity reification in late capitalism. Slick, glossy advertising means that when we buy a car, for example, we buy not just the car itself, but the image which is associated with that car through its advertising. Some cars are sold through appeals to their safety and reliability, some through their sexiness or chicness. To an extent then, we buy an image which other people will have of us.

Peter Weir's film *The Truman Show* (1998) illustrates not only the degree to which the media now dominate public perception of 'reality', but also suggests that 'reality' itself, its normative beliefs and ways of living, may themselves be constructions. Truman Burbank has been raised as the star of a television drama, relayed live twenty-four hours a day around the world. He remains unaware that his life is constantly on television, and that his 'wife' and 'best friend' are merely simulating those roles. Thus the film demonstrates the potential power of corporations, to manipulate us totally, and might be thought of as an illustration of Adorno's 'manufactured society'. But the film also explores the boundaries between the 'real' and the 'simulated': Truman's creator, the show's director, Kristof, argues that in leaving the show's fictional world of 'Seahaven' and venturing out into the 'real' world, Truman is merely exchanging one fabrication for another. In the postmodern context, distinguishing 'truth' from 'falsity' becomes problematic.

For Eagleton, the arguments of such postmodernists as Baudrillard breed a political pessimism, in which the attempt to critique ideology is doomed from the outset. But many contemporary theorists, including Žižek, argue that, even though we cannot separate ideology from reality clearly because ideology is already at work in everything we experience as 'reality', we must not abandon the attempt to critique ideology. He argues that 'it all hinges on our persisting in this impossible position' (1994, 17). Post-marxism attempts to continue the critiques of exploitation, oppression, injustice and inequalities which marxism has always sought to maintain, but under a 'weakening' which entails that we can no longer confidently or complacently assume our own position from which we might effect this, for our own assumption of the role of ideology-critic masks the ways in which we may collude with, or even fail to recognise an aspect of, ideology. But this is an argument which I will discuss more fully in the context of post-marxism.

Notes

1. Žižek's own work, its synthesis of Hegel, Lacan and poststructuralism, is discussed in more detail in Roberts's forthcoming book on psychoanalytical theories for the *Transitions* series. A Žižekian reading could be demonstrated through a reading of Wordsworth's poem, 'The Thorn', in which the narrator's obsessive pursuit of the truth of Martha Rey and her illegitimate child is constantly revisited in his return to the thorn tree, metonymic sign of her possible infanticide. For Žižek the inaccessibility of the thing confronted is displaced by focusing on the object which stands in for it.

2. Marx's uses of the term 'ideology' are various and frequently more neutral: in *Contribution to the Critique of Political Philosophy* (1859), for example, 'ideological' is used in the sense of any system of belief: 'the legal, political, religious, aesthetic or philosophic – in short ideological – forms'.

3. Examples might include Ien Ang, *Watching Dallas* (1985); Janice Radway, *Reading the Romance* (1984). For a more detailed discussion of the study of popular culture see Chapter 4.

4. At times of crisis (as in times of war in the twentieth and early nineteenth centuries), an indirect form of censorship was exercised by imposing a tax on periodicals which restricted their sale among the poor.

5. See Mary Leapor, 'Crumble-Hall' (1748), for a satirical 'country-house poem' written by a labouring woman. This poem is discussed in Chapter 5, and reprinted as an appendix to this volume. Williams's reading of the country-house poems is paralleled to an extent in Marjorie Levinson's reading of Wordsworth's 'Tintern Abbey' against historical accounts of the scene (1986).

6. Because they were written in prison, Gramsci's theories are fragments rather than sustained, developed arguments. There have therefore been diverse interpretations of his work: for example, as to whether by 'hegemony' Gramsci means the non-coercive aspects of class rule, or rather the relationship between both coercive and non-coercive means of securing consent. (See Barrett 1991, 54–5.) And Laclau and Mouffe's reading of Gramsci leads to a post-marxism which transcends as much as it interrogates marxist theories.

7. In a famous series of articles in the *New Left Review*, Jessop et al. argued that Hall's analysis of Thatcherism failed to grasp the real economic shifts and social reconstructions it effected. (See Jessop et al. 1984, 1985, 1987, 1990.) However, as Thatcherism continued without serious ideological challenge, Jessop and his colleagues began to admit the importance of ideology. (See Leys 1990 and Hall's reply to Jessop et al. 1985.)

8. Eagleton criticises the totalisation of these ISAs, since schools, churches, families, media are not *sheerly* ideological structures but teach and disseminate other ideas too (1991, 147). Eagleton's discussion of Althusser in *Ideology* is highly recommended (see 136–53).

9. We can see in Althusser's conception of ideology as generating State Apparatuses an extension of his theory of the 'relative autonomy of the superstructure', discussed in Chapter 1.

10. This theory continues Althusser's argument with the early writings of Marx: in distinction to *The German Ideology*, Althusser here argues that

ideology is not intrinsically false or illusory but a system of representations concerning the real relations in which people live.

11. See Tony Bennett's criticism of this conjunction of 'materialism' and
'idealism' in which he argues that Althusser's concept of ideology is
made to do 'too much' (Bennett 1979, 118).

12. For excerpts from these conduct manuals, see Vivien Jones (1990). Here
the example of 'interpellation' is in gender-formation. See Jameson for
the way in which Althusser's theory anticipates the 'group identity'
theories pervasive in contemporary (feminist, postcolonial)
approaches: '"interpellation" ... was already a group-oriented theory to
begin with, since class as such can never be a mode of interpellation,
but rather only race, gender, ethnic culture and the like .... class
consciousness as such – something infrequently achieved and only
laboriously conquered throughout social history – marks the moment
in which the group in question masters the interpellative process in a
new way ... such that it becomes, however momentarily, capable of
interpellating itself and dictating the terms of its own specular image'
(1992, 345–6).

13. Most commentators have read the distinction between Althusser's
concepts of 'science' and 'ideology' as that between 'truth' and 'falsity'.
However see the glossary definition of 'ideology' in Althusser (1990,
252): 'It is distinguished from a science not by its falsity, for it can be
coherent and logical (for instance, theology), but by the fact that the
pratico-social predominates in it over the theoretical, over knowledge.
Historically, it precedes the science that is produced by making an epistemological break with it, but it survives alongside science as an essential element of every social formation ...'. This glossary is written by
Althusser's translator, Ben Brewster, but corrected and agreed by
Althusser. Eagleton makes this distinction when he reprimands
commentators who have misinterpreted Althusser's definition of ideology as 'false' as meaning 'untrue' rather than 'unreal' (see Eagleton
1991, 21).

14. Belsey has attempted to defend the possibility of agency within
Althusser's theory with two arguments: that since ideology, despite its
apparently 'obvious' status, is also self-contradictory, incoherent, and
non-explanatory, a knowledge which recognises this, whatever the
scrutiny of its own claims might later reveal, is possible (Belsey 1980,
63–4) and since, using Lacan's theory of identity-formation, the subject
is constructed as a site of contradiction, perpetually in the process of
construction, there is always the possibility of change in the ways in
which the subject resolves these contradictions (1980, 64–6). Because
Lacan's theory of subject-formation is constructed through language,

Belsey also justifies Althusser's apparent privileging of literature as a site where the perception of ideology is possible. See criticisms of this privileging below. The first of Belsey's defences is similar to that of Eagleton who has argued that Althusser's concept of ideology is not a knowledge and therefore not truly comparable with 'science' as a knowledge. The difference between ideology and science is thus epistemological rather than sociological, and since they are of different orders, they cannot be arranged hierarchically. (See Eagleton 1991, 139.) However, contrary to Belsey, Eagleton argues that Althusser misreads Lacan by making the subject equivalent to the ego of Lacan's theory, that already unified and stable identity, rather than Lacan's split and lacking subject, which might allow the possibility of transformation (144–6). Eagleton reads this as part of a political pessimism which Althusser shares with Foucault, as if subjectivity is a form of self-incarceration.

15. Althusser and Macherey collaborated on *Reading Capital* (1965) and Macherey's *A Theory of Literary Production* includes an essay on 'Lenin, critic of Tolstoy', first written in December 1964 and referred to by Althusser in his reply to Daspre of 1966. Althusser's essay 'Ideology and Ideological State Apparatuses' was first published in 1970 and influenced subsequent work by Macherey. Influences between the two thinkers have been obscured somewhat by the chronology of their first English translations.

16. Picking up on a comment by Lacan, Žižek discusses how Marx 'invented' the notion of the symptom. See Žižek (1989, ch.1). Žižek quotes Lacan's comment on page 23.

17. Macherey illustrates his theory in readings of Jules Verne, *The Mysterious Island*; Defoe, *Robinson Crusoe*; Borges's short fiction and Balzac's *Les Paysans* and in an analysis of Lenin's reading of Tolstoy (Macherey 1978). Terry Eagleton applies these ideas to Conrad's *The Secret Agent* (1978; reprinted in Eagleton 1986), Catherine Belsey to the Sherlock Holmes stories and to Matthew Arnold's poem 'The Scholar-Gipsy' (Belsey 1980) and Fredric Jameson to *Paradise Lost* (Barker et al. 1986, 35–56).

18. We might compare this particular reading with a section from Macherey's theory: ' ... we can only describe, only remain within the work, if we also decide to go beyond it: to bring out, for example, what the work is *compelled* to say in order to say what it *wants* to say, because not only would the work have wanted not to say it ... but certainly the work did not want to say it. Thus, it is not a question of introducing a historical explanation which is stuck on to the work from the outside. On the contrary, we must show a sort of splitting with the

work: this division is *its* unconscious, in so far as it possesses one – the unconscious which is history, the play of history beyond its edges, encroaching on those edges: this is why it is possible to trace the path which leads from the haunted work to that which haunts it. Once again, it is not a question of redoubling the work with an unconscious, but a question of revealing in the very gestures of expression that which it is not' (Macherey 1976, 94). The contradictions of the work are not necessarily a reflection of historical contradictions, but consequences of the absence of this reflection (128).

19. Bhabha (1994, 66): the stereotype 'is a form of knowledge and identification that vacillates between what is always "in place", already known, and something that must be anxiously repeated ... as if the essential duplicity of the Asiatic or the bestial sexual licence of the African that needs no proof, can never really, in discourse, be proved'.

20. See for example Eagleton (1986, 20): ' ... an argument which is considerably too narrow, homogenizing and specific to the history of France'.

21. See for example Sinfield's essay 'Give an account of Shakespeare and Education, showing why you think they are effective and what you have appreciated about them. Support your comments with precise references', Holderness's essay 'Radical potentiality and institutional closure: Shakespeare in film and television' (Dollimore and Sinfield 1985) and Sinfield's essay 'Heritage and the market, regulation and desublimation' (added in 1994 edition).

22. See also Eagleton's reading of Thomas Hardy in terms which parallel those of Balibar and Macherey (1981, 126–30 and 1986, 42–4).

23. For an application of Vološinov's linguistic theories to those of ideology, see Barker (1989), 262–78.

24. Michael Sprinker, who detects a return to 'formalist' interests in Macherey's most recent publication, *The Object of Literature*, denies that there is a contradiction within his literary theories: 'The task of formal analysis is to expose the contradictions in a text's linguistic practices that sociological investigation demonstrates to be constitutive of literature as an ideological apparatus' (Macherey 1995, foreword xi).

25. Žižek usefully summarises the differences between Althusser's concept of the ISAs and commodity fetishism as that between 'the *materiality that always-already pertains to ideology as such* (material, effective apparatuses which give body to ideology) and *ideology that always-already pertains to materiality as such* (to the social actuality of production)' and argues that these formations can be mapped onto State and Market respectively: the State as 'the external superior agency that organizes society "from above"' and the Market as 'society's "self-organization"' (1994, 18).

26. Like the Vietnam War, the Gulf War was perhaps only 'a psychotropic dream in which the issue was not politics or victory but the sacrificial, excessive deployment of a power already filming itself as it unfolds, perhaps expecting nothing more than consecration by a superfilm which perfects the war's function as a mass spectacle' (Baudrillard 1987, 17).

3 A Question of Form: the Realism/Modernism Debates

'What we have, if I may use the reductive terminology suitable to such schemas, is: an idealist realist (Lukács); two idealist modernists (Bloch, Adorno); a materialist modernist (Brecht); and a modernist who blends elements of both idealism and materialism (Benjamin). The unoccupied location, then, is a "materialist realist" ... .'
(Eagleton 1981, 159)

One of the most common attacks on 'vulgar' marxist literary theories is that, in examining literature in its ideological, historical and social contexts, all considerations of specifically literary modes are forgotten. Yet marxist theories have, since their inception, been preoccupied by the nature of literary form, and this is especially apparent in the debates concerning realism and modernism. Realism as a literary mode is both aesthetic and cognitive, since it demands to be read against the context of what it is representing. Realism implies the possibility of 'knowledge'. It is not surprising therefore that realism has always had an intrinsic interest for marxist theorists. Realism is the form in which the interaction between literature and society appears to be most obvious. In realist texts, literature might be seen to reflect society, or history. The marxist critic therefore need only 'read' the contents of the text to see an image of society, and from there pursue the more interesting topic of society itself. This is rather unfair to such early marxists as Engels, who expressed a strong preference for literary realism. Engels knew that literary texts could not straightforwardly 'reflect', but needed to be made to do so. This would necessitate choices, selections, deliberation. We can see something of Engels's consideration of realism in a letter he wrote to Margaret Harkness concerning her novel, *A City Girl*: 'If I have any criticism to make, it is perhaps that your novel is not quite realistic enough. Realism, to my mind, implies, besides truth of detail, the truthful rendering of typical characters under typical circumstances' (April 1888).[1] The idea of 'typicality' would later be explored by Georg Lukács.

The legacy of Engels's preference was, however, much less nuanced. Communist marxism adopted this preference for realism as a prescriptive formula, and constructed an extremely narrow definition of it which lasted for several decades. At the Soviet Writers' Congress in 1934, Andrey Zhdanov (then Secretary of the Central Committee of the Soviet Communist Party) opened the congress with a speech in which he contrasted 'socialist' realism with the literary decadence of bourgeois art.[2] The early twentieth century had witnessed the flourishing of 'modernism', a term which came to describe an international artistic movement which encompassed a range of experimental and anti-realist aesthetic movements, including symbolism, expressionism, imagism, vorticism, dada, cubism, futurism, constructivism, and surrealism.[3] Modernism is often understood as a reaction to the urbanisation, the bureaucratisation and the rapid social change associated with modernity. In specifically aesthetic terms, modernism appeared to embody this in its reaction against realism and naturalism, denying the representationalism which characterised the dominant nineteenth-century modes. In contrast, socialist realism would 'express' the social reality of the new political system, a 'reality' which would be narrowly defined as a roseate portrayal of communism. Zhdanov urged Soviet writers to combine such realism with 'revolutionary romanticism': 'Soviet literature should be able to portray our heroes; it should be able to glimpse our tomorrow. This will be no utopian dream, for our tomorrow is already being prepared for today by dint of conscious planned work'. Thus Zhdanov was able to redefine 'romanticism' as a form of 'realism'.[4] Such debates found few adherents outside of communist administrations. Adorno, for example, dismissed the official communist doctrine of socialist realism as the 'imbecility of the boy-meets-tractor literature' (Adorno et al. 1980, 173). But it did, of course, powerfully impact on those within communist parties and states, such as Brecht in East Germany, who devised his 'dialectical' theatre as a marxist rejection of the naturalist theatre of realism, officially sanctioned by the Soviet Union. Throughout his career Georg Lukács defended a 'critical realism' which, rather more cautiously, rebuked the programmatic definitions of realism by the Communist Party of which he was a member.

Lukács's realism

> 'The decisive ideological weakness of the writers of the descriptive method [or naturalism] is in their passive capitulation to these conse-quences, to these phenomena of fully-developed capitalism, and in their seeing the result but not the struggles of the opposing forces. And even when they apparently do describe a process – in the novel of disillusion – the final victory of capitalist inhumanity is always anticipated. In the course of the novel they do not recount how a stunted individual had been gradually adjusted to the capitalist order; instead they present a character who at the very outset reveals traits that should have emerged only as a result of the entire process.'
> (Lukács 1970, 146)

Lukács, the most consistent defender of literary realism, was an extremely prolific writer of marxist aesthetics, largely because his political writings were denounced by the Hungarian Communist Party. His 'Blum theses' (1928) argued that communist attacks on all democratic-capitalist and reformist moves were ill-advised (see Anderson 1979, 30) and, although he published a recantation of this draft, his literary criticism and philosophy suggest that he did not change his private views. Like Marx, Lukács did not believe that all 'bourgeois' elements needed to be eliminated in socialism, and thus his championing of the novel, that ostensibly 'bourgeois' form, and specifically of 'critical realism', its appropriate mode, was of a piece with his earliest, 'unorthodox' communism.[5] Lukács's celebration of critical realism was opposed both to the modernism of many contem-porary aesthetic movements and (if a little more obliquely) to socialist realism. He was opposed to the mechanistic form of reflection theory first espoused by Plekhanov and later adopted by Zhdanov, which viewed literature as the passive recorder of social trends and events. In its most extreme form, this argued that, in a politically decadent society, art would itself inevitably be decadent. Lukács countered this determinism in proposing a renewal of the classical realist novel of the nineteenth century, in a form appropriate to an epoch of socialist revolution.

Lukács's defence of realism is as a genre in which human existence can be portrayed as resolutely social. In 'The Ideology of Modernism' (1957), Lukács argues that, while modernism portrays humans as essentially solitary and asocial, with only accidental or superficial contact with others, realism portrays individuals in their social and historical environment. Lukács traced the impulse of aesthetic modernism to philosophers such as Kierkegaard and Heidegger. As Heidegger, for example, wrote of human existence as 'thrown-into-being', so too the hero of modernist literature is portrayed as without purpose or design, as if his existence and experiences are merely accidental. With no pre-existent reality beyond him, he is confined within the limits of his own experience. The modernist hero is also confined within the moment, since his personal history is not portrayed. He does not develop through contact with the world. Lukács conceded that modernist writers, such as Joyce, Kafka and Musil, are rarely as abstract as this. But, he argued, the social, historical context against which they portray their characters (Dublin or the Hapsburg Monarchy) is merely a background. And the isolation of the characters is only compounded by the pervasive use of interior monologue.

Underpinning Lukács's aesthetic theories is a philosophy of society and consciousness. He believes that, even in the fragmentary, disruptive context of capitalism, society is a unity and that it is the task of the marxist critic to recognise this unity. Under capitalism, the economy achieves unprecedented autonomy, and this is obvious when financial crises can arise directly from the circulation of money. Consequently, capitalism itself appears to 'disintegrate' into a series of elements all driven towards independence. The underlying unity of capitalism, the interrelatedness of all these seemingly autonomous elements, is then visible only in times of crisis. Knowledge of capitalism thus requires a dialectical grasp of both surface and depth, appearance and essence. Knowledge requires a recognition of 'surface' autonomies, separations, disunity and the 'essential' unity below. This philosophy explains why Lukács wanted to sketch a particular kind of 'critical' realism:

> If literature is a particular form by means of which objective reality is reflected, then it becomes of crucial importance for it to grasp that reality as it truly is, and not merely confine itself to reproducing whatever manifests itself immediately and on the surface. (Adorno et al. 1980, 33)

Thus critical realism is distinguished from 'naturalism', which, in confining itself to surface details, accepts that 'reality' is equivalent to the immediacy of appearances. Naturalism arose in the second half of the nineteenth century and is most often associated with the novels of Zola. For Lukács the popularity of naturalism at this time is itself a reflection of the alienation which people experience under capitalism. (Although his criticisms of naturalism also need to be read as covert criticisms of socialist realism, which Lukács could not attack openly.)

Lukács's clearest expression of the distinctions between naturalism and critical realism is an essay entitled 'Narrate or describe?'. Whereas naturalism describes events from the standpoint of an observer, critical realism narrates such events from the standpoint of a participant. Naturalism frequently presents abstract, schematic characters, instead of realism's focus on action as the moment in which 'typical characters with a richly developed inner life are tested in practice' (Lukács 1970, 124). Naturalist writers overprivilege detail and, in aspiring to ever greater precision, tend to replicate the divisions of specialised labour by using 'correct', professional jargon. (Lukács's example here is Zola's confident discussion of 'flats' in the theatre; 136.) Realist writers aspire to the omniscience and comprehensive vision of ancient epic writers. Naturalism might portray social problems, as indeed Zola's novel *Nana* describes the state of theatre under capitalism and the capitalist connections between the life of the actress and that of the prostitute, but, Lukács argues, these problems are stated as facts, rather than seen, or 'narrated', in the process of becoming social problems.[6] In order to avoid the excessive detail of such techniques as naturalism, Lukács's definition of critical realism requires that it does not portray those aspects of reality which are immediately obvious, but those which are 'permanent and objectively more significant', those which will 'outlast mere fashion' (Adorno et al. 1980, 48). Critical realism will capture the tendencies of development, the lasting features of society, if it can achieve both generality and singularity. This it can do through the mediation of particularity ('besonderheit'), and its embodiment in the creation of characters as types. These types must embody both the typical and the particular. In Dickens's *Little Dorrit* (1855–7), for example, Merdle is the financier of reputedly enormous wealth, but is 'imprisoned' by the falsity of his status, and by the trappings of that false wealth, a spendthrift wife and an arrogant butler. For Leonard Jackson, Merdle is an example of Lukács's type, since he figures both as an individual and as a symbol of capitalism itself: 'Merdle ... would not be an allegory of capitalism, a mere embodied generalisation about it; but nor would he be a mere individual with some interesting personal idiosyncrasies, such as being a fraud with thousands of financial victims; rather, he is a type, and general truths about capitalism inhere in him' (Jackson 1994, 155). Thus for Lukács, critical realism is the genre which accommodates the dialectical relationships between essence and appearance, general principle and individual case, concept and immediacy.

Lukács's warmest praise was thus for 'historical novels' in which the hero is caught between two factions, whose conflict both defines the hero's character and produces the emergent nation for which he comes to stand. In Sir Walter Scott's novel *Waverley* (1814), for example, Bonnie Prince Charles, who represents one side of the Scottish-English conflict of the mid-eighteenth century, is an ostentatiously minor character within the narrative, while Edward Waverley, a character invented by Scott and designed to play the role of someone caught between the two sides, is presented as an 'ordinary' and 'typical' character. His typicality is defined precisely by his having experienced two sides of the conflict (not, as in vulgar marxist use, in being a mere symbol of a class).[7] This is dramatised in the first chapters of the novel in the opposition between Waverley's father and uncle. His uncle (Sir Everard) is politically Tory, a 'High Church' Anglican and sympathetic to the exiled House of Stuart and is thus sympathetic to the cause of the Scottish rebellion. Waverley's father, in contrast, is Whig and supports the Hanoverian succession. Waverley is formed by both of these men, as his father elects to share his upbringing with Sir Everard. In order to be representative, such heroes as Waverley are also necessarily portrayed as passive, rather than active, played on by events rather than mastering them. Lukács's typical hero is a 'middle-of-the-road hero' (Lukács 1962, 71) in the sense that the action of the novel revolves around him as a passive 'hub'. And in other ways Waverley might appear rather 'un-average'. With his poetic fantasies he often appears as much of a 'literary' character as 'lifelike'. But in Lukács's terms, Waverley is located in a precise way within the form of the novel, in such a way that he draws together and reveals the conflicts between three historically significant social groups (his Tory uncle on the land, his Whig father in town and the Jacobite-rebel life of adventure epitomised by the Highlanders). Waverley goes to Scotland with a commission from the English Whig government which his father procures for him. But his association with his uncle secures him an invitation to the Baron of Bradwardine, who is a Lowland Jacobite, and through him he meets the Highlanders, led by Fergus MacIvor. Throughout the novel Waverley's loyalty is split between such rival factions. For example, even though he fights for the Jacobite cause at Prestonpans, he retains some feeling for the army of which he was once part (see Scott 1906, 331). Waverley, like all Scott's central characters, has the function of bringing into contact with each other the extremes whose struggle fills the novel and the clash of these extremes expresses artistically a great crisis in society. The character of Waverley is thus not a historically significant type in himself but a vehicle for presenting typicality, the fusion between the individual and the general in history. Lukács found Scott's heroes interesting because they made history visible, even though, or rather because, by their 'middling' nature, they really did not participate in history. Rather, the great struggles and contradictions waged around them while they stood on 'neutral ground'. Thus while the relationship between the part (the 'typical' hero) and the whole (the social and historical context) is not that of pure reflection, the part does mirror the whole, if in mediated fashion. It is this formal mediation which differentiates his theory of realism from Zhdanovian socialist realism.

Lukács argued that the historical consciousness in literature, initiated by Sir Walter Scott, declined after 1848, when the bourgeoisie, having abandoned its conflict with the nobility for a struggle against the proletariat, turned decadent. Thereafter the bourgeoisie entered a phase of ideological decadence, in which the primary aesthetic expression is at first naturalism, before developing into twentieth-century modernism. For Lukács, modernism, like naturalism, is also a reflection of alienation under capitalism. Modernism accurately portrays modern consciousness as disintegrating, with discontinuities, ruptures, 'crevices'. But, he argues, modernism cannot know or reveal the extent of distortion because such distortion can be known only by comparing it with reality. Thus the consciousness of characters must be contrasted with a reality independent of them. (This explains why Lukács can praise the use of interior monologue only when this technique is set into relief by other perspectives.) Unaware of the limits of immediacy, the expressionists, for example, portray human existence as one-dimensional. This is the context for Lukács's advocacy of contemporary realism (especially the novels of Thomas Mann) and his argument that critical realism should renew the tradition of Scott and his nineteenth-century followers (identified as Fenimore Cooper, Manzoni, Pushkin, Balzac and Tolstoy).

In the late twentieth century, critical realism continues to be theorised by feminist literary theories, theories of film and popular fiction. Rita Felski reads contemporary feminist debates as re-enacting the marxist aesthetic debates of the 1930s (Felski 1989, 3), in which Felski, in her readings of autobiographical realist fiction, and Elaine Showalter in her criticisms of the modernist aesthetic of Virginia Woolf, continue in the tradition of Lukács (see Moi 1985, 4–8). Lukács's concept of the 'typical' is still present, though redefined, in black women's writing of the later twentieth century: instead of the 'middling' character Lukács identifies in the novels of Walter Scott, black women's fiction develops protagonists whose 'typicality' (the quality that best allows them to understand and represent a particular era) is their marginality. There is an important parallel here too with the positioning of the working classes in Lukács, what Jameson has called his 'standpoint theory' (in Corredor 1997, 92). In *History and Class Consciousness* (1922), the proletariat is a privileged site for dialectics: this class alone is able to view society from the 'centre' as it were, as a coherent whole because of their 'standpoint'. Because the proletariat is simultaneously, and uniquely, the subject and the object of the socio-historical process, the proletariat 'know' capitalism in a way which the bosses and administrators never can. Thus Jameson redefines realism as the coming-to-articulacy of an emergent group. The influence of Lukács, and the 'Hegelian marxism' we associate with his work upon Jameson means that he continues to exert an influence upon marxist debates today. But before turning to these contemporary debates, I need to sketch other marxist voices: those of Bloch, Adorno, Brecht and Benjamin.

The modernist response

> 'It is only with the second or monopoly stage of capitalism, and the emergence of a classical imperialist system beyond the confines of the various national experiences, that a radical aesthetic and epistemological doubt about the possibility of grasping society as a whole begins to be felt: and it is precisely this radical doubt that inaugurates modernism as such and constitutes the representational drama specific to it.' (Jameson 1990, 244)

Lukács was opposed by many contemporary marxists who defended modernism from the censures of both Lukács and orthodox marxism. These debates were particularly vigorous in the 1930s. The most famous of these interventions are Ernst Bloch's defence of expressionism and Lukács's subsequent reply, both published in 1938 in *Das Wort* (a Paris-based literary journal for writers in exile and a forum for anti-fascist writers and critics); and a series of essays by Brecht attacking Lukács's theories (first published posthumously in 1967, though written also in 1938).[8] Lukács's attack on expressionism was because, he argued, its fragmentary style obscured society's true interconnections which form a 'totality'. In his view, the world only seems chaotic, but beneath this surface level is an underlying totality which makes surface appearance ideological. When expressionist works replicated this fragmentation, they thus colluded in perpetuating this ideological illusion. Bloch's reply was to ask: 'What if authentic reality is also discontinuity?' For Bloch, the experience of capitalism is an experience thoroughly characterised by confusion and fragmentariness.[9] Expressionist art explores the real fissures in society, an experiment which might be 'in demolition' but is not necessarily, as Lukács would argue, a 'condition of decadence' (Adorno et al. 1980, 22).[10]

Brecht's most trenchant criticism was that Lukács's theory was insufficiently historicist. He questioned how bourgeois artists of the nineteenth century could be appropriate models for a new age. By denying the historicity of genres, Lukács had fallen into exactly the kind of empty formalism of which he accused modernist writers and their defenders. Brecht did not disagree that art ought to explore and reflect reality. With the rise of fascism in 1930s Germany, it seemed that the ruling classes were more able than ever before to disseminate their own ideas as 'the truth'. The importance of art as a vehicle for countering those ideas was now urgent. But Brecht argued that writers and theoreticians could not afford to be rigidly prescriptive about kinds of realism, they needed to use whatever means suited the particular moment: 'Reality changes; in order to represent it, modes of representation must also change' (in Adorno et al. 1980, 82).

Brecht also criticised Lukács's exclusive interest in the novel as narrowly prescriptive. Brecht himself of course was primarily a poet and dramatist. Speaking from his experiences as an experimental director and playwright, he questioned that realism was the more 'popular' form. Lukács's definitions of 'popular' were conceived in the same way as those for 'realism': in both cases contemporary models were compared with previous models. But like realism, the nature of 'popularity' would and *could* change too: 'There is not only such a thing as *being popular*, there is also the process of *becoming popular*' (Brecht in Adorno et al. 1980, 85). Brecht's arguments are certainly significant but he did not reply to Lukács with a comparable theory. Today this might be seen as a potential strength in Brecht's own argument, but it did prevent him from really engaging with the terms of Lukács's own theory and from providing his own comparable philosophy of aesthetics and the relationship between literature and society.

In an interesting discussion of the Brecht-Lukács debate, Terry Eagleton suggests that Brecht's most significant manoeuvre was in shifting the terms of Lukács's fixation with the 'reflection' of the 'real' (Eagleton 1981, 84–90). In criticising Lukács's theory as ahistorical, Brecht also argued that 'realism' could only be judged retrospectively. Realism was not intrinsic in a particular form, what was 'realistic' for one period would not necessarily be so for another. Eagleton argues that: '[a] text may well "potentialize" realism, but it can never coincide with it; to speak in this way of "text" and "realism" is in an important sense a category mistake. Texts are no more than the enabling or disabling occasions for realist effectivity' (88). Similarly the audience of the play is just as qualified to judge its 'realism' as the playwright, and if its response is that the play is not suitably 'realistic', then perhaps it is the audience itself, not the formal properties of the text, which needs to be altered. Brecht thus altered Lukács's definitions of realism, which were aesthetic and ontological, to the political and philosophical definitions raised by his own artistic practice.

Brecht's theatre was inspired by Erwin Piscator and the new workers' groups, who turned their backs on the proscenium-arch theatres of bourgeois drama and performed instead in the street, at factory gates or in workers' clubs. Brecht, like them, created a theatre which would radically oppose the prevailing naturalism. For Brecht, the effect of naturalism was to naturalise the unacceptable and this it did by persuading its audiences to identify so fully with the characters and situation that they unquestioningly accepted what they perceived. Brecht wanted his audiences not to suspend all disbelief, but rather to recognise the constructed nature of the stage's representations, to recognise that all things could have been and might be otherwise. His theatre attempted, not to absorb its spectators, but to 'estrange' them. Actors might change into costume on-stage, or switch roles midway through performances, no curtain would screen scene-changes, conflicting arguments might be displayed on film simultaneously with the stage action – all of these were common devices which Brecht used to create the estrangement (*verfremdung*) by which the audience would be roused to think rather than passively consume the 'meaning' of the play.[11] Brecht outlined the differences between his own 'epic' or 'dialectical' theatre and the traditional 'dramatic' theatre explicitly:

> The dramatic theatre's spectator says: Yes, I have felt like that too – Just like me – It's only natural – It'll never change – The sufferings of this man appal me, because they are inescapable – That's great art; it all seems the most obvious thing in the world – I weep when they weep, I laugh when they laugh.
>
> The epic theatre's spectator says: I'd never have thought it – That's not the way – That's extraordinary, hardly believable – It's got to stop – The sufferings of this man appal me, because they are unnecessary – That's great art: nothing obvious in it – I laugh when they weep, I weep when they laugh. ... (Brecht 1990, 71)

By making the everyday seem strange, Brecht's theatre would expose assumptions of inevitability as ideological. Brecht's theoretical writings are a necessary corrective to the ways in which 'Brechtian' techniques have subsequently become de-politicised. 'Brechtian' has become a cliché, applied to any production which shocks the audience, allows its actors to perform half of the performance in casual, rehearsal clothes, or changes scenery in view of the audience. Peter Brook's production of *King Lear* starring Paul Scofield (1962) was widely received by the critics as 'Brechtian' because it alienated sympathy for Lear. But, as Margot Heinemann notes, this production was *anti*-Brechtian in its simplification of the play's message: the servants who resisted Cornwall and Regan and tried to help the blinded Gloucester were cut from this production because Brook did not want the audience to be given the 'reassurance' that goodness existed. '[T]he crucial turning point, when the oppressed common people begin to resist the bullies and torturers, has to go ... ' (Heinemann in Dollimore and Sinfield 1994, 247).

This detail in *King Lear* is one which Brecht would have fastened on, not just because it provides a marxist opportunity to demonstrate the possibility of revolution, but because it is in such details that Shakespeare's plays display their 'realism'. For Brecht, realism was not a matter of verisimilitude so much as the embodiment of contradictory material: 'True realism has to do more than just make reality visible on the stage ... One has to be able to see the laws that decide how the processes of life develop' (Brecht 1977, 27). In this, Brecht begins to resemble Lukács, insofar as his definition of realism is not reflectionist. In contrast to Eagleton, I would view Brecht as the 'materialist realist' which Eagleton considers as lacking from twentieth-century marxist theories. Brecht's theatre company, the Berliner Ensemble, performed not just avant-gardist and expressionist plays (often Brecht's own) but also adaptations of classical, even 'realist' plays such as Kleist's *Zerbrochener Krug*, Molière's *Don Juan*, Farquhar's *The Recruiting Officer*, Goethe's *Urfaust*, Lenz's *Der Hofmeister* and Shakespeare's *Coriolanus*. This last adaptation is the most interesting for us because the company recorded the discussions they had before rehearsing the first scene (see Brecht 1990, 252–65).

Coriolanus opens with a group of mutinous citizens (the plebeians) who complain that the Roman nobility feed plentifully and profit from corn while they starve. Particular hostility is directed towards the patrician Coriolanus, a successful leader, puffed up with his own pride and patriotism. Their revolt is suppressed by the news of imminent war against the Volscians, for which they will provide cannon-fodder, their loyalty bought by the granting of plebeian commissars. The Berliner Ensemble celebrate the complexity and realism with which this scene interweaves class and nationalist struggles and discuss how they might perform the scene so that a marxist interpretation (here, sympathy towards and understanding of the plebeians) is true to the text itself. For example, the senator Agrippa tells the plebeians a parable of the 'belly' to justify patrician extravagance, but the Ensemble note that there is no textual evidence that the plebeians are convinced by this parable. No edition of Shakespeare included stage directions, and those accepted by traditional productions use merely those directions which were added later, when the plays were first transcribed. Thus one of the Ensemble suggests that the legionaries could come on stage slightly earlier than in usual performances: their silent presence on stage would suggest that the union between patricians and plebeians is not an ideological one (produced by Agrippa's persuasive rhetoric), but because, more expediently, war is imminent and the legionaries themselves are better armed than the plebeians (258). Other elements of theatrical production permit similar interpretations: costume (the second citizen who hesitates about revolution could be dressed slightly more prosperously, 257) and props (if the plebeians are armed with improvised weapons which display their inventiveness and craftsmanship, they will win respect and suggest that they are a real threat rather than comic 'low-lifes'). These interpretations are in marked contrast to performances in the bourgeois theatre, in which the scene is performed as an exposition of Coriolanus's character and the production identifies itself with the patricians' cause, not the plebeians' (255). But the Ensemble do not present their version as straying from the text. At one point, one of the actors protests: '*Coriolanus* is written for us to enjoy the hero!'. But the answer to Brecht's project is given by another: 'The play is written realistically, and includes sufficient material of a contradictory sort' (257).[12] The Ensemble also situate the production within their own context: rehearsing in 1953, they consider the ways in which the play will be received by an East German audience after the Second World War: 'Spectators many of whom were still under the influence of Nazi myth and glamour, brought up in SA or Hitler Youth, could all too easily see the story in terms of the true patriot and military hero, stabbed in the back by the cowardly masses under Red labour leaders. The production must show that no leader, however talented, is indispensable' (Heinemann in Sinfield and Dollimore 1994, 245).

Heinemann's essay on 'How Brecht read Shakespeare' notes how Brecht viewed Shakespearean theatre as prefiguring 'epic' theatre, its staging full of such estranging effects as daylight performances, boys playing girls, direct addresses to the audience (e.g. the choruses in *Henry V*), the collective nature of constructing the play, the Elizabethan audience with its mixture of classes, and the ways in which the groundlings participated in the play (heckling, hissing, laughing), rather than the 'eavesdropping' which characterises bourgeois audiences (in Sinfield and Dollimore 1994, 232). Classical performances of Shakespeare had fostered a tradition of concentrating on the psychology of the hero and encouraging the audience to identify emotionally with his plight: Brecht argued that empathy was only ever intermittent in Shakespeare's theatre and that the plays' focus was on storytelling. This made Shakespeare closer to, say, Piscator's 'epic' theatre, in which the 'hero' was not the individual but the epoch itself, than so-called 'traditional' productions in which the impressive naturalism of the leading roles was the defining feature of the production.

(The psychological impersonation which we associate with 'traditional' productions was only instituted in 1741, when David Garrick played Richard III in a way which he described as 'bringing [acting] down to Nature', in opposition to the more 'stilted' declamations of earlier acting modes.)[13] When political theatre in the early twentieth century (Piscator, agit-prop, Tairov, Vakhtangov) began to practise anti-naturalistic techniques, their 'estrangement' techniques thus remind us of the historicity of stage-practice itself. The Russian director Tairov recalled that in the 'stylized theatre' launched in 1905–6, actors strove 'not to experience emotional suffering, anger, love, hate, or joy, but only coldly and calmly to *represent* them'. And one actor who worked with Vakhtangov in 1922 wrote: 'It should appear as if the actor were saying to the spectator: "Now I am crying, but I, the actor, know about it. Look, I'm wiping my tears, and look, I'm not only wiping my tears, but notice how I'm doing it. ... One must ... *feel one's attitude to the character and to history as a whole*' (Drain 1995, 79). This kind of theatre is not anti-representational; instead it saves representation for dialectics, it is a kind of reflexive realism. Brecht's most significant response to Lukács is therefore not to be found in the reply which he intended for *Das Wort* but in the more radical definition of realism which his own dramaturgy implied.

While Bloch defended expressionist practice and Brecht defended the experimental techniques of his own theatre and poetry, the most sustained opposition to Lukács's critical realism came later, with Adorno's defence of modernism, an artistic movement which was only identified as such in the 1950s. Many of the modernist forms were non-representational, so that traditional theories of 'reflection' were inadequate in accounting for their particular ways of expression. And Lukács's analysis of realist fiction was unable to read those experimental works which foregrounded the process of literary production rather than communicating an unambiguous content. It is significant therefore that Adorno's aesthetic theories drew so often on music. (After completing his doctorate in music, Adorno studied composition under Alban Berg in Vienna and wrote extensively on Schoenberg, Stravinsky, Beethoven and Wagner, among other composers.) How might music be said to 'reflect' contemporary society? Such a question could only be answered on the basis of its form. Adorno's argument in *Philosophy of Modern Music* (first published 1949) was that music had been one of the principal art forms of the bourgeoisie since the baroque period. However by the early twentieth century, radical modern music of the kind composed by Schoenberg and his associated composers, Berg and Webern, provoked a disjuncture between classical music and its middle-class audience. Their music was radically opposed to the everyday world of listeners, and indeed, in its extreme virtuosity, to many performers, but this entailed that its extreme alienation from society registered the meaninglessness of contemporary society: 'The shocks of incomprehension, emitted by artistic technique, undergo a sudden change. They illuminate the meaningless world' (Adorno 1973a, 131). A literary equivalent of this music might be found in a modernist writer like Samuel Beckett, celebrated also in Adorno's theories. (Indeed, among the notes for Adorno's *Aesthetic Theory*, published posthumously, was the intention to dedicate that work to Beckett.) Lukács's 'reflectionist' theories of literature could only dismiss a writer like Beckett as 'decadent'. (Lukács wrote that Beckett's *Molloy* 'presents us with an image of the utmost human degradation – an idiot's vegetative existence'; in Eagleton and Milne 1996, 152.) Adorno, in contrast, celebrated *Endgame* in terms which are similar to his analysis of contemporary music: 'The interpretation of *Endgame* cannot pretend to proclaim the play's meaning with the aid of philosophical mediation. Understanding it can involve nothing else than understanding its incomprehensibility, or reconstructing its meaning-structure – to the effect, that it has none' (Adorno 1982, 120–1).

Adorno's discussions of literature were thus not primarily considerations of 'content' or 'subject matter' but of such elements as form, style and technique which distinguished art as a form of knowledge from science. It was artistic form which determined how the artist 'portrayed' the objective world, and thus formal laws could not be reduced to Lukács's consideration of form as arbitrary, an addition made by the 'over-inflated subjectivism' of the author. The modernist 'portrayal' can never be real in the same sense as social reality, since the relationship between the object (social reality) and the subject (the artist) is mediated by the creative process itself, the formal laws of art. Thus art is not a reproduction of the real but an aesthetic representation, or image of it. This distance between the artwork and reality then permits art to contradict and even critique the real. Thus, in Adorno's famous phrase, 'art is the negative knowledge of the actual world' (Adorno et al. 1980, 160). It is in the distance between reality and its artistic representation that the work of art is both aesthetic and a valid mode of knowing reality:

Art does not provide knowledge of reality by reflecting it photograph-
ically or 'from a particular perspective' but by revealing whatever is
veiled by the empirical form assumed by reality, and this is possible
only by virtue of art's own autonomous status. (Adorno et al.
1980, 162)

In *Negative Dialectics* Adorno argues that realism 'equips a fallible
language with the attributes of a revealed one' (1973b, 111), exactly
the kind of mistake Adorno also attributes to Lukács. Thus while
Lukács criticises such writers as Joyce and Proust for over-subjectify-
ing, Adorno's response is that he has mistakenly conflated subject and
object, and failed to recognise that their novels preserve a critical
distance from the reality which they portray. While Lukács argues that
the pervasive use of interior monologue entails that the characters of
their novels are cut off from society, Adorno argues that this style
reveals the ways in which individuals are isolated in capitalist society.
This alienation is still a relation to the 'social', the individual is still
positioned within the social totality, albeit one in which she is over-
shadowed or dominated by it. David Forgacs highlights this: ' ...
Adorno adopts the view that the work must be read attentively in
order to bring out what we could call the "double-reality" it contains.
... [I]t is not sufficient to see how Proust and Joyce reproduce an alienated condition, ... one must also see how their work transcends this
condition by placing the individual subject within a social totality that
takes "precedence" over him' (Forgacs 1986, 190). These 'modernist'
novels are thus no less 'realist' than the nineteenth-century novels
which Lukács celebrates. (Indeed Adorno argues that Lukács over-
looks the 'unrealistic' aspects of these texts. See Adorno et al. 1980,
163.)

Despite their obvious differences, Lukács and Adorno shared the
belief that modern society is thoroughly ideological, that our perceptions of reality are alienated, reified, so that dialectical thinking is
necessary to discover the essences which lie hidden. In *History and
Class Consciousness* (1922), Lukács describes bourgeois thought as
characterised by unmediated antinomies: subject and object,
freedom and necessity, the individual and society, form and content.
Because of the intrinsic duality (as opposed to dialectics) of bourgeois
thought, reality 'disintegrates into a multitude of irrational facts and
over these a network of purely formal "laws" emptied of content is
then cast' (Lukács 1971, 155). Bourgeois thought is unable to see the

ways in which these elements are mediated within a complex system, unable to see their interrelatedness. Thus a concept of totality is necessary if we are to consider the relation between parts and the whole, and the interrelatedness of parts. Here the influence upon Adorno is strong, for Adorno's own theories of 'totality' are responses to and continuations of *History and Class Consciousness*. In Adorno's writings, modern society appears as an administered world, completely controlled by bureaucracy, administration and technocracy. Capitalism is categorised by monopolies rather than the market forces of the nineteenth century. Within this totality, the freedom of the individual is wholly illusory, personal freedom having been destroyed in an age of concentrated capital, planning and mass culture.[14] Society and consciousness then become totally reified, appearing to be immutable, unchanging forms, solidified as objects. The capacity for critical thinking appears an impossibility. But the apparent impasse could be broken by means of art, and more precisely, the specific forms of art. And this is true of both theorists. In Lukács's writing there is the utopian gesture of the realist form, that which could integrate subject and object, an integration which is unrealised in contemporary society. The contradictions of society are reflected in the content of the work but reconciled in its form.[15] In Adorno's theory, the modernist form itself displays the contradiction. When subjectivity is reduced to a 'mere object' by exchange value, avant-garde movements resist reappropriation by the market system.[16] The practices of surrealism, for example, have been interpreted by Jameson as 'a convulsive effort to split open the commodity forms of the objective universe by striking them against each other with immense force' (1974, 96). Thus both Lukács and Adorno view art as a means to a true(r) knowledge of society, differing 'only' as to the form which this art-as-knowledge should take.

For Adorno however, critical thought itself might also achieve a freedom outside of the system, and such thinking would itself take the form of the modernist art work. Through the use of 'provocative formulation', 'startling exaggeration' and 'dramatic emphasis' in his writings (Held in Bottomore 1991, 5), Adorno hoped to undermine ideologies and to create conditions through which the social world could once more become visible. The opposition to closed systems of thought (such as Hegelian idealism, or orthodox marxism) can be seen in his own style, particularly in the extensive use of essay, aphorism, deliberate discontinuity (as in *Dialectic of Enlightenment*) and fragments (*Minima Moralia*). These styles demand that the reader engage creatively with Adorno's own unsystematic thought since the reader needs to make a critical effort to construct the logic of the argument. Style must negotiate between the immediacy of the object (here the work of art) and the abstraction of thought, the concepts by which the object will be perceived (aesthetic theory or criticism). This negotiation is thus a dialectic, between non-identity (the difference of all works to themselves and each other) and identity (we can think in concepts only in terms of the possibility of similarity). Many commentators have remarked on how each sentence of Adorno's itself strives to be dialectical. Jameson, for example, writes that: 'As with aesthetic modernism itself ... what you are able to construct in language has a certain truth by virtue of that very wresting of language, not merely from silence as such, but from the baleful properties of the proposition form, the perils of thematization and reification, and the inevitable (and metaphysical) illusions and distortions of the requirement to begin and end at certain points, and to appeal to this or that conventional standard of argument and of evidence' (1996, 11).[17]

Adorno's hostility to systemisation is also evident in his attacks on 'political art' as programmatic. This hostility underlies his opposition to socialist realism (rather unfairly identified with Lukács), Sartrean engagement and Brechtian theatre. Adorno criticised Sartre's idea of a committed art because his theories of commitment rely on the notion of content as the embodiment of the 'meaning' of the text and on an excessive subjectivism, as if authors have only to make their 'free' choice, a mark of their – and their readers' – 'authentic' existence. Implicit in the first of these is an objection to denotative language as, however politically 'radical' its content might appear, it is bound to remain utterly conformist because of its form. Thus this critique continues Adorno's privileging of non-realist forms.[18] The second objection – that of the 'objectivity' of the form of art – argues that theories, like that of Sartre, which fetishise the author's intentionality, forget that the text is objective in its intrinsic sociality, while they also overestimate the possibilities of 'freedom', 'choice' and 'authenticity' in an administered society.[19] This argument can be seen in the following excerpt from Adorno's *Negative Dialectics*:

> For the theory of committed art, as it is current today, presupposes a superiority and an invulnerability to the basic reigning fact of life of

exchange society – namely, alienation between human beings and also between objective spirit and the society that it expresses and judges all at once. The theory of commitment demands that art speak directly to people, as though the immediate could realize itself immediately in a world of universal mediation. (Adorno 1973, 120)

Political art compromises the autonomy which is the mark of 'authentic' art to Adorno so that writers such as Kafka and Beckett, it is argued, 'compel' the change of attitude which committed works 'merely demand' (Adorno 1980, 191). But the confidence in the 'compelling' nature of such modernist writers illustrates Adorno's own fetishising of a particular *type* of literature and thus reveals the deeper complicity of his theory with that of Lukács. Both espoused a specific form of art and elaborated its intrinsic suitability for a marxist aesthetic. And as a consequence both overlooked the ways in which their ostensibly competing theories intermeshed and the ways in which their definitions of the opposing form were imbalanced (and undialectical). In their commentary on these debates, Livingstone, Anderson and Mulhern argue: 'Lukács inveighed against the irrationalist element in modernism, but was wholly insensitive to its positive disruptive moment: Adorno was justly contemptuous of the "optimism" prescribed by Soviet orthodoxy, but was unable or unwilling to acknowledge the equally reactionary "pessimism" of Western liberal orthodoxy' (in Adorno et al. 1980, 149). They contrast these theoretical closures with Brecht's undogmatic definition of realism as a 'political and ideological *end* whose formal *means* were variable' (149). This was evident in the discussion of the Berliner Ensemble above in which the company performed both experimental 'epic' works and the 'realistic' plays of the classical tradition.

While many commentators have criticised Lukács and Adorno in similar terms to those of Livingstone et al., their exchanges may be marked by the polemical nature of the exchange itself.[20] This is certainly true of Adorno, whose theories do not always privilege modernist form so much as the formal laws of all works of art:

> ... every aesthetic work is an individual product and so always an exception in terms of its in-dwelling principle and its general implications, whereas anything which fits in with general regulations disqualifies itself from a place in the world of art. (Adorno et al. 1980, 172)

Adorno's distinction here is not between realism and modernism but an implicit distinction between the 'aesthetic work' and the popular art of mass culture, a significant focus of his writing elsewhere (see Adorno 1991). Adorno's writings on the culture industry are not, as Jameson has argued (1990, 144), theories of 'culture', but of an industry, of the ways in which culture is produced from reproduction and mass consumption by a system which simultaneously organises 'free' or leisure time, that last domain of 'freedom' under capitalism, into a system of production too. The culture industry continues the encroachment of capitalism into our every moment, while it presents itself as the gratification of desire and freedom. The culture industry is thus thoroughly ideological, nowhere more so than when we refuse to recognise it as dominant. While we will happily pay for the pleasures of the new *Star Wars* trilogy, Lucasfilm backs such a project and indulges our desires primarily so as to maximise company profits. *Titanic* (1997) included a critique of class division, in its portrayal of romance between the genteel Rose and the unemployed artist, Jack, and in its sympathetic identification with the poor on board who were prevented from escaping. Many commentators and reviewers interpreted the film as a satire on the hubris of capitalism, represented by the ship itself. But we need to remember that, whatever its ideological 'message', it is also a film which cost over $200 million to make and which, within six months of its initial distribution, had taken $1.7 billion worldwide, even before television and video rights had been sold.

Adorno's argument was also that our happy leisure hours only inoculate us against effecting political change, so that the entertainment industry becomes a means of political quietism. His argument suggests that there is a thin line between the workings of fascism and the Hollywood industry of 1950s America. This is an interesting correlation, but, as the following chapter's discussion of cultural studies will show, it is also an exceedingly problematic one. Adorno's own stridency is evident in his attack on jazz music as degenerate (though, in publishing this essay under the pseudonym of 'Hektor Rottweiler', Adorno seems to have been aware of the ferocity long before his critics used this essay to dismiss his work). In contrast to mass entertainment, the aesthetic work which is formally difficult remains relatively 'autonomous' from capitalism. Characterised by contradiction, it refuses conventional codes of meaning, and thus prevents itself from the dominative effects of instrumental meaning. Such a work achieves a distance from the otherwise all-pervasive 'culture industry'. The issue of 'high' versus 'low' art is deeply implicated in the debates concerning realism and modernism since 'realist' forms often appear to be less formally innovative, and consequently, more accessible. The arguments of accessibility and popularity have continued to be influential, for if art is to be a potentially political, emancipatory force, it will have to reach more than intellectual elites. This is certainly the argument of Lukács, Brecht, and even Bloch when he defends the incipient 'populism' of expressionism by its inclusion of folk art.

It would be unfair to allow the impression that Adorno privileges modernist art to stand. In his writings, aesthetic works of 'high' art are not innocent of ideology, and are in their own way moulded by the workings of capitalism. Such works are 'autonomous' only because they have excluded the working classes throughout their tradition because the market of 'high art' is 'free' insofar as it is unconstrained by need. Kant's definition of the work of art as 'purpose without purposefulness' is thus revealed as 'uselessness' which frustrates and thus (apparently) escapes the domination of the market, but which is itself a product of that market. In *Prisms* (1967), Adorno writes: 'all culture shares the guilt of society. It ekes out its existence only by virtue of injustice already perpetrated in the sphere of production' (19). Furthermore, Jameson argues that Adorno's distinction between the mass work of art and the aesthetic work is to be found in their representations and (non)/fulfilment of happiness. Adorno's is consistently a pessimistic, gloomy view of contemporary society. In *Negative Dialectics* he wrote: 'No universal history leads from savagery to humanitarianism, but there is one leading from the slingshot to the megaton bomb' (1973b, 320). Adorno certainly opposes the classical marxist belief that capitalist forces of production would generate a free society; for him, twentieth-century capitalism is moving not toward greater freedom but toward further domination and integration, an 'administered' totalised society. Thus happiness is that which does not and cannot yet exist, it is only what is not yet possible or achievable, the promise of its occurrence. As Jameson argues: '[w]hat is inauthentic in the offerings of the Culture Industry then, is not the remnants of experience within them, but rather the ideology of happiness they simultaneously embody: the notion that pleasure or happiness ... already exists, and is available for consumption. ... [Both] "genuine art" and that offered by the Culture Industry raise the issue and possibility of happiness ... and neither provides it; but where the one keeps faith with it by negation and suffering, through the enactment of its impossibility, the other assures us it is taking place' (1990, 147).

We must remember that all these writers lived through fascist oppression. After the Nazi seizure of power in Germany in 1933, Bloch was branded a political enemy and escaped to Switzerland, Benjamin went into exile in Paris, Lukács to Moscow and Brecht escaped to Denmark while his books were burned publicly by the Nazis. By 1938 Adorno had left Germany, joining his colleague Max Horkheimer in New York, where the Institute of Social Research was now based after its own removal from Frankfurt. When we read Adorno's writings on the culture industry, we might remember his most notorious injunction: 'No art after Auschwitz' and his discussion of this in his essay on 'Commitment'. In the latter essay, Adorno balances art's impossibility after Auschwitz with its necessity. The knowledge of suffering simultaneously demands and prohibits the continued existence of art:

> [I]t is now virtually in art alone that suffering can still find its own voice, consolation, without immediately being betrayed by it. The most important artists of the age have realized this. The uncompromising radicalism of their works, the very features defamed as formalism, give them a terrifying power, absent from helpless poems to the victims of our time. But even Schoenberg's *Survivor of Warsaw* remains trapped in the aporia ... There is something embarrassing in Schoenberg's composition – not what arouses anger in Germany, the fact that it prevents people from repressing from memory what they at all costs want to repress – but the way in which, by turning suffering into images, harsh and uncompromising though they are, it wounds the shame we feel in the presence of the victims. For these victims are used to create something, works of art, that are thrown to the consumption of the world which destroyed them. (Adorno et al. 1980, 189–90)

Adorno wrote passionately and mournfully on contemporary inhumanity and domination. The last of his theoretical sparring partners – Walter Benjamin – cannot, like Lukács, Bloch, Brecht and Adorno himself, be said to have 'lived through' fascism: he committed suicide in September 1940 while attempting to escape from Occupied France to Spain.

Although Benjamin and Adorno both wrote celebrations of modernist art, their disagreements reveal that the debates of this chapter cannot be straightforwardly reduced to a contest between realism and modernism.[21] Benjamin's own aversion to a 'realist' model of reflection is evident in his rewriting of the base-superstructure problematic:

> Concerning the doctrine of the ideological superstructure. At first it seems as if Marx here wanted only to establish a causal relation between superstructure and base. But the observation that the ideologies of the superstructure reflect the relations in a false and distorted manner already goes beyond this. The question is, namely: if the base somehow determines the superstructure in the material of thought and experience, but this determination is not one of simple *reflection*, how is it then to be characterized, leaving aside the question of the cause for its emergence? As its *expression*. The superstructure is the expression of the base. (Quoted in Cohen 1995, 28; emphasis added)

Benjamin attempts to counter the mechanistic reading of base-superstructure relations by allying marxism with a variety of non-marxist discourses, the most important of which is psychoanalysis. For while Benjamin reads from Marx that the superstructure is the expression rather than reflection of the base, his rewriting of this relationship as one of 'expression' is inspired by Freudian researches as to how repressed forces are expressed in dreams. The passage above continues with the Freudian analogy of the dream: 'The economic conditions of a society's existence come to expression in the superstructure, just as the overfilled stomach of someone who is sleeping, although it may causally determine the dream content, finds there not its reflection but its expression'. Benjamin's break here with the orthodox marxist preoccupation with Enlightenment concepts of representation and causality is one of the reasons why he is a marxist theorist of particular interest to 'post-marxism'. We might compare, as Margaret Cohen suggestively does, the revisioning of the base-superstructure problematic by Benjamin and Althusser. Althusser too problematises orthodox marxist reflectionism when he writes: '[t]he economic is *never clearly visible*' (1979, 179).[22]

Benjamin's use of psychoanalytic ideas is one of Adorno's (many) objections. For Adorno, psychoanalysis is implicated in bourgeois ideology and thus cannot be used as a type of science by which we might understand ideology. Benjamin adapts Jungian theories of a collective unconscious to suggest that images of pre-capitalist relations remain residual, awaiting a theory by which the cultural critic might transform collective dreams into 'dialectical images' which will have the potential to 'awaken the world from the dream of itself' (Benjamin quotes here from Marx; see Cohen 1995, 21–2). But this apparently 'social' use of psychoanalysis merely compounds the problem of excessive subjectivism for Adorno. Here, he argues, Benjamin is merely transferring analyses of individuals to society, and thus the centrality of the bourgeois individual subject is retained and even strengthened. Adorno's foundational dialectic between alienated subjects and alienating objective conditions is swept aside by the introduction of a collective, prematurely classless unconscious.[23]

The disagreement over the role of collectivity in thinking is linked also to that of mass, or popular culture. Susan Buck-Morss argues that their differences over the Baudelaire drafts were influenced by their 'evaluation of the collective's utopian desire (and hence the degree to which mass culture could be redeemed). Benjamin affirmed this desire as a transitory moment in a process of cultural transition. Adorno dismissed it as irredeemably ideological' (Buck-Morss 1989, 121). This difference between the two friends is paralleled by their disagreement over the potential of new technologies. For Benjamin, new practices, such as contemporary film, encouraged a new mode of reception: in place of the 'aura' or the unapproachability of the traditional art work, comes the immediate 'shock' of the audience confronted with something new. And as a consequence of this shock, the mass audiences of mechanically reproduced art would not merely consume the work but would adopt a critical stance, not only to the art work but to the capitalist society which produced it. Adorno was opposed to what he saw as Benjamin's prematurely optimistic separation of technology from the bourgeois social relations of its use (see, for example, Adorno 1991, 157–8). However, if we think of alienation not in terms of the reification of social relations, but as the effacement of production, then modern technology becomes the means through which we can perceive commodification. Thus Benjamin is able to identify even in the commodity a revolutionary potential. In his analysis of nineteenth-century Paris, Benjamin argues that the development of the shopping arcades created not just a new style of consumption, but also a new kind of looking and a new consumer subject who looked. Rachel Bowlby uses this analysis in her readings of Zola, Gissing and Dreiser, writers who, she argues, were responding to the sudden expansion of consumer culture and whose naturalistic styles are appropriate modes for such a culture. Selling itself is transformed by and into display in the arcades, which 'appear as places of culture, fantasy, divertissement, which the customer visits more for pleasure than necessity' (1985, 6). Bowlby's readings reflect the ways in which popular culture has been defended by cultural studies approaches, as we will see in the next chapter, and counter Lukács's critiques of naturalism as fetishising surface.

Benjamin's confidence in the possibility of modern communications and mass art was explicitly influenced by Brecht's maxim: 'Don't start from the good old things but the bad new ones' (Adorno et al. 1980, 99), an inflection of Marx's argument that history progresses by its bad side. Film is the paradigmatic cultural form of modernity, but Benjamin traces the origins of modernism to the emergence of the city's technologies in the Paris of the Second Empire. Baudelaire is celebrated as the first modernist, a modernism traced through the simultaneity of his writing with the appearance of the daguerreotype, the panorama, advertising, the arcades (commercial passageways), the great expositions, and the use of cast iron, all of which altered the experience of city life. Social experience in the capital is now characterised by the 'shock' which will later become the formal principle of cinematic perception. It is the experience of 'shock' which links the factory worker with the stroller, or *flâneur*, pushed along or jostled by the Parisien crowd on the crowded pavements ('The shock experience which the passer-by has in the crowd corresponds to what the worker "experiences" at his machine'; Benjamin, 1997, 134); with the film-gazer ('[t]hat which determines the rhythm of production on a conveyor belt is the basis of the rhythm of reception in film'; 132), and with the gambler ('[t]he jolt in the movement of a machine is like the so-called *coup* in a game of chance'; 134). The prevalence of shock effects means that urban experience is one of immediacy, or 'living through' (*Erlebnis*) rather than the auratic or Proustian experience of richly recollected inwardness (*Erfahrung*): 'The greater the share of the shock factor in particular impressions, the more constantly consciousness has to be alert as a screen against stimuli; the more efficiently it is so, the less do these impressions enter experience (*Erfahrung*), tending to remain in the sphere of a certain hour in one's life (*Erlebnis*)' (Benjamin 1997, 117). Benjamin's theory here appropriates Freud's theory of trauma, of the way in which consciousness functions so as to prevent shock-effects, in *Beyond the Pleasure Principle*. Benjamin does not denounce the experience of shock as a depressing expression of modern capitalism, submitting the self to alienation, to fragmentation. Rather the effects of shock are registered as moments of revolutionary potential, moments which might disrupt imaginary unities. *Les Fleurs du Mal*, despite the apparent conventionality of its lyric forms, contains a modernist aesthetic, not in a representation of material conditions, but in its inscription of reactions to material conditions. Not the city but the experiences of the neurasthenic, of the big city-dweller, of the customer.[24] Despite the apparent differences in style, Baudelaire's poetry thus shares with the juxtapositions of surrealism and cubism and the montage-effects of Eisenstein's expressionist cinema an inscription of the shock effects of modernity.[25] A more contemporary example might be Abel Ferrara's film *Bad Lieutenant* (1992). Depicting the spiritual degradation of a cop in contemporary New York City, this low-budget film uses hand-held cameras, improvisatory acting styles and long-editing takes to create a documentary style of visual narrative. At the centre of the film, however, and the turning-point for the 'bad lieutenant' (Harvey Keitel) himself, is the rape of a nun. This scene is shot in a studiedly different style, with surreal montage effects of shots of religious iconography interspersed with intimations of the violence of the rape itself. Thus this scene jars against the 'mainstream' viewing of film, with its search for coherence.

Benjamin and Adorno also differed on the question of surrealism and this, as Margaret Cohen has illustrated, is related to their quarrels over the drafts of the Baudelaire project or *Passagenarbeit*. Benjamin himself claimed the connections between his project and surrealism consistently during the twelve years he spent on it.[26] Adorno criticised the second draft of the *Passagenarbeit* because, he argued, Benjamin's dialectic lacked mediation, instead offering an excessive 'concreteness' in the tendency to relate elements of Baudelaire's poems directly to 'adjacent features' in the social context of Paris. Baudelaire's wine poems, for example, are juxtaposed with wine tax duty and the prohibition on taverns outside city limits of the time. The mediation Adorno demands is that cultural traits should be mediated through the total social process, rather than related to corresponding features in the economic base. Benjamin links Baudelaire's poems on wine with taxation but omits the social and economic

tendency within which both operate and thus attributes to phenomena 'precisely that kind of spontaneity, palpability and density which
they have lost in capitalism' (Adorno et al. 1980, 129). Benjamin has
lost the theoretical perspective which would prevent this falsification
in succumbing to his own form of 'positivism'.[27] In his reply,
Benjamin argues that this draft is only a section of a much larger
sequence, in which he would frame this discussion within a theoretical discussion of the poet and the city.[28] More suggestive, however, is
the ways in which Benjamin's own writing paralleled that of the surrealists, whom Adorno also attacked for their fetishism of immediacy
and subjectivity, the violent yoking of arbitrary elements (see
Adorno's essay on surrealists in *Notes on Literature I*). Benjamin
differs from the surrealists however in the ultimate pessimism of their
message in which potentiality is never achieved (see Cohen 1995,
199). Benjamin, as Eagleton has argued, 'is in search of a surrealist
history and politics, one which clings tenaciously to the fragment, the
miniature, the stray citation, but which impacts these fragments one
upon the other to politically explosive effect' (1990, 338).

Realism/modernism/postmodernism

This chapter has thus far retraced the marxist literary and cultural
debates of the 1930s to the 1960s (although it has had to exclude many
voices, including those of Marcuse and Sartre). But this focus is of
more than historical interest to contemporary marxist cultural theories. For one thing, there has been a contemporary rejuvenation of
interest in these thinkers.[29] And these debates have been revisited in
attempts to map our contemporary situation, the postmodern. If the
'post'modern is defined in terms of its difference from or even its
erasure of the 'modern', then modernism is itself evaluated differently.
And in such a climate, the earlier realism/modernism debates have
been re-viewed.[30] The most significant marxist theorist of the postmodern is the American critic Fredric Jameson, whose own approach
is thoroughly imbued in the 'Hegelian' tradition of marxist theory
which many identify with Lukács. Jameson's work is often influenced
by antithetical marxisms. *The Political Unconscious*, for example,
draws upon both structural marxisms (associated with Althusser and
Macherey) and Hegelian marxisms (associated with Sartre and
Lukács). But his synthesis of competing marxisms and his emphasis

upon social *totality* as a standard of judgement for the literary text are both 'Hegelian' manoeuvres.[31] Thus Jameson's work has continued to keep older forms of marxism alive, and allowed the 'Hegelian' work of Lukács to survive the attack upon it by structuralist marxisms.

Jameson has certainly been one of the most persuasive defenders of Lukács's theories of realism.[32] Jameson's argument is that postmodernism needs to be analysed in a dialectical relationship with modernism, but in order to prevent this analysis becoming a binary opposition, it requires a third term, the (in itself complex) mode of realism. He identifies realism, modernism and postmodernism as the dominant (but not exclusive or determinant) cultural modes of respectively market capitalism, monopoly capitalism and multinational capitalism. Indeed, Jameson uses these three terms not to designate purely aesthetic or stylistic descriptions, but to pose the problem from the outset of the mediation between formal or aesthetic concepts and periodising or historical ones.[33] His argument relies on the sense that contemporary, or post-war society, is marked by a constitutively different kind of society, variously termed multinational or media capitalism, or in Guy Debord's terms, spectacle or image society. Multinational capitalism is distinguished from earlier twentieth-century forms ('monopoly' or 'imperial' capitalism) by the emergence of new forms of business organisation (multinational or transnational corporations such as McDonald's, ICI, Dupont, Microsoft, Coca-Cola) and concomitantly a new vision of a world capitalist system which includes the international division of labour and a crisis in traditional labour (the cheapest First World products are manufactured in Third World sweatshops), a 'vertiginous new dynamic' in international banking (millions lost in seconds on the stock exchange, and Second and Third World debt), new forms of media interrelationship, computers and automation, money as status evident in the emergence of 'yuppies' and rural and urban gentrification (Jameson 1992a, xviii–xix). Whereas modernism might be defined as a consequence of incomplete modernisation, postmodernism represents the triumph of modernisation, since it emerges at a time when even the term 'modernisation' no longer has any application (everything now already being 'modern'), a time when the archaic traces of the pre-modern past have been eradicated (see 1992a, 366). Thus the base-superstructure problematic is no longer appropriate for a postmodern society in which culture has become thoroughly commodified. 'Culture' is itself now fully infrastructural, so absorbed in the economic that it cannot be disentangled from it, so that today one cannot talk about culture without simultaneously discussing economics and vice versa. '[E]very position on postmodernism in culture – whether apologia or stigmatization – is also at one and the same time, and *necessarily*, an implicitly or explicitly political stance on the nature of multinational capitalism today' (Jameson 1992a, 3).

Jameson's understanding of dialectics as the possibility of grasping capitalism as both liberating and exploitative, progressive and regressive, means that he himself studiously refuses either to castigate or celebrate realism, modernist or postmodern culture. In his reading of Conrad's *Lord Jim*, for example, he contrasts the impressionist style of Conrad's ('high') modernist aesthetics and the romance conventions of mass culture. Such oppositions reveal, in a Machereyan reading, the novel's symptomatic splits. Impressionism and romance are recourses against the rationalisation and reification of nineteenth-century capitalist society. In the transitional period in which capitalism first transforms society it overlays older, traditional and pre-capitalist forms of society with the characteristic logic of capitalism as a system: a means/ends instrumentality which values efficiency, calculation and profit. This is the moment of rationalisation (or in Lukács's term 'reification') which Conrad's novels address in situating their plots in the margins of imperialism, in Patusan (*Lord Jim*) and in Costaguana (*Nostromo*). But reification also produces side-effects which then develop semi-autonomously. In Jameson's example, the privileging of rationality under capitalism leads to a split whereby sense perception is divorced from an increasingly abstract rationalism. Conrad's aestheticising style can be understood as both a consequence of this transition and a strategy by which his novels resist it. In the style's foregrounding of the senses, reality is turned into image. This is an embodiment of reification, but it also projects beyond it, so that the literary text in its potential to resolve real contradictions on the level of symbol is both a figure of ideology in Althusser's sense and also an emancipatory ideal. Literature transcends the real, even if only symbolically. Conrad's style and the experience of industrial capitalism during the heyday of imperialism belong to separate realms and as such are relatively autonomous of each other. But in thinking through the text at the level of mediatory codes (through which both text and context can be discussed), Jameson resynthesises the elements of life which capitalism had torn apart and thus, he argues, realises the utopian potential of the text.

Jameson's readings also attempt to reopen discussion of the realism/modernism debate, in such a way that its conclusions would not be decided in advance. (Modernism is usually judged to have 'won' in terms of twentieth-century marxist theories.[34]) Thus Jameson defines the terms realism and modernism more broadly than is usually the case. For example, Jameson resists the absolute linear, chronological or even evolutionary sequence which this transition implies. In 'The Existence of Italy' he discusses film in terms of realism, modernism, postmodernism, despite its being an exclusively twentieth-century form (1992b, 155–229) and 'realism' is identified less with the (Victorian) 'period' of market capitalism as with the 'conquest of a kind of cultural, ideological, and narrative literacy by a new class or group' (156). This allows realism to be situated in, for example, early eighteenth-century England (when the novel's emergence can be traced against the rise of the middle classes) and in the mid-twentieth century (when cinematic realism – such as the Italian 'neo-realism' of Rossellini and De Sica, or the British social realism of Lindsay Anderson and Tony Richardson – is associated with the confidence of the industrial working classes, in which they become filmic subjects in their own right). This argument is implicitly linked with Lukács's theory of realism, which was not defined by reflectionism or theories of representation. Critical realism was never a matter of photographic accuracy (which would be truer of naturalism), but a mode of narrative (rather than description) which permitted an articulation of historical and social forces which ideology attempted to efface. Such counter-cinematic forms as Italian neo-realism, or the social realism of the contemporary British film-maker Ken Loach, for example, are marked by a rejection of the ideological stereotypes of mainstream Hollywood cinema for a documentary style (common production modes of realist counter-cinema include non-professional actors or, at least, non-'stars'; visual authenticity of real locations; hand-held cameras; naturalistic dialogue). In *Ladybird, Ladybird* (1994) Loach allowed the story of a mother's fight to prevent her children being taken away from her to be told from her perspective. We see how the social workers judge her on her past: a series of abusive partners and, as a single mother, her mistake in locking her children in a hostel room while she went to work. Now that Maggie (Crissy Rock) is in a loving relationship, those in social welfare continue to judge her according to their preconceptions of her life. Scenes in which Maggie and Jorge find successive new-born babies taken from them by welfare, just after delivery, emphasise their sense of powerlessness. Loach's realism allows him to portray the tragedy of poverty in which people have few real choices and find themselves in situations they can do little to alter. The film reminds us that definitions of 'realism' which rely upon plausibility or 'verisimilitude' may be too narrow for the harrowing events which are 'real' for many people. It is a reality which is rarely enough represented.

Jameson also argues that realism in the late twentieth century has assumed forms which Lukács would have been unlikely to recognise, such as 'magic realism', contemporary postcolonial writing, and even advertising. Such 'postmodern' realisms are permissible because modernism itself has altered the ways in which we decide what is 'realistic'. As modernist art has become institutionalised, canonised and commodified (Picasso postcards are bestsellers and Beckett's plays are accepted as ways of *representing* the modern condition), what at first seemed anti-realistic can be re-viewed. But postmodern realisms are also necessarily different from their nineteenth-century forms: Lukács's celebration of realism was as a mode which narrated the relation between the individual and society, the particular and the totality. But Jameson's conception of a social 'totality' in the postmodern period is of one which cannot be represented (though this does not mean that it cannot be known).[35]

Equally, however, modernism's implicit attack on realism has also permitted a recognition of the ideology of realism. Where realism was once celebrated as a mode of exposing ideology (Lukács), realism itself, like all modes, might itself be seen as ideological. This chapter began with a discussion of the ways in which realism is cognitive as well as aesthetic and as such was valorised by the official Communist Party. Poststructuralist attacks on realism as an aesthetic mode have, however, censured it as an essentially 'bourgeois' form. Realism promotes a pretence of transparency or illusionism (in disguising its mode of production, the fact that it is a production); naturalises its perspective (in presenting itself as commonsensical); fixes a narrative closure (in aspiring to determine the interpretation of its reader or viewer); and either empties the reality which it represents of its contradictions or organises these hierarchically, thus reconciling them, rather than permitting them to interrogate and contradict each other. Such critiques of realism are associated with Barthes (who wrote of the 'reality effect'), the writers associated with *Screen* (principally Stephen Heath and Colin MacCabe) and Catherine Belsey. For

Stephen Heath, in a reading which blends Lacanian, Brechtian and Barthesian influences, representation confirms the subject in an imaginary self-coherence, gliding over the subject's setting in position, the very process and structure in which she is constructed. Heath finds among the 'lessons from Brecht' that of distanciation through estrangement, so that this moment of illusory fullness is broken, as the subject is reminded of the mode of representation.[36] For MacCabe, the classic realist text is grounded in a dominant narrative voice which presents itself as the voice of knowledge. George Eliot's narrator in *Middlemarch*, for example, is the guarantor of meaning, the voice which exposes the limitations of her characters whose speeches are separated from this more 'truthful' voice by the inverted commas which enclose them. In the following passage the reader is encouraged to view Mr Brooke from the same position of omniscience as that of the author/narrator. Mr Brooke is surprised by the response to him from the drunken, violent Dagley when he visits his farm, but the narrator makes us recognise this surprise as self-delusion: 'He [Mr Brooke] had never been insulted on his own land before, and had been inclined to regard himself as a general favourite (we are all apt to do so, when we think of our own amiability more than of what other people are likely to want of us)'. (See MacCabe 1979, 13–38.) It is this ultimate narrative voice which controls the narrative: 'The unquestioned nature of the narrative discourse entails that the only problem that reality poses is to go and look and see what *Things* there *are*. ... The real is not articulated – it is' (Rice and Waugh 1992, 138). Thus realism consists not in the work's content, its 'realistic' subject-matter, but in its mode of presentation.[37]

In these readings, the language of realism is interrogated by deconstructive scepticism. In MacCabe's account of classic realism, for example, the voice which represents itself as 'truth-speaking' is vulnerable to the same slippages and deferrals of meaning which haunt all language. But there is a political dimension to these epistemological discussions which MacCabe does not pursue (though Belsey, in placing classic realism as a product of, and simultaneous with, industrial capitalism does so obliquely). For the 'truth-speaking voice' is also an adoption of authority in a discourse which is then strictly hierarchical. Simon Dentith has written of the parallels between MacCabe's critique of classic realism and Bakhtin's criticisms of monologism, but he notes also this divergence: where MacCabe's focus is epistemological, Bakhtin's is ethical and social, in which 'the objection to the monologic "discursive hierarchy" is that it represents a politically unacceptable arrogation of authority' and the celebration of polyphony is not simply 'a celebration of the other's word but a responsible engagement with it – though of course with no attempt to arrogate the final word' (Dentith 1995, 94). Maria Edgeworth's *Castle Rackrent* (1800) explores just these issues. This novel consists of (at least) two voices, that of the illiterate Irish peasant Thady and that of the English (or Anglo-Irish) editor, who transcribes Thady's tale and 'translates' his vernacular so that the novel's English readers can understand his account of the Rackrent family. The editor is the ostensibly 'neutral' scholar, adding the textual apparatus of footnotes and glossary. But the novel permits us to see that the authority of his status might also be a form of domination. Before Thady's account even begins, the editor is already telling his readers the significance of the 'Monday' on which Thady begins his account, for the work-shy Irish are forever postponing things until a Monday. Edgeworth's experimental realism in *Castle Rackrent* permits her two voices to comment upon one another, but the editor, as the educated man, always has the last word. Thady cannot comment directly upon the editor's notes, and thus these are ironised only if we read them, and the supporting voices they invoke (such as the English colonial writers Gerald of Wales and Edmund Spenser) from the perspective of Thady's Irishness. Edgeworth's novel is then hierarchically dialogic.

MacCabe's analysis also risks an exaggerated formalism in celebrating anti-realism as an absolute good. His opposition to Lukács's celebration of classic realism becomes a mirror image of it, in which the argument becomes a question of the intrinsically 'progressive' or 'regressive' effects of that realism.[38] But if we situate the practices of 'realism' or 'modernism' within specific contexts, the effects of their practices cannot be so (pre-)determined. This is largely Jameson's argument, but it is also Brecht's. As Eagleton has argued (1980), Brecht was not opposed to representation in itself; he was opposed to *non-contradictory* representation. (And, Eagleton argues, the influential 1974 volume of *Screen* edited out Brecht's contradictions 'in the interests of presenting him as an *avant-gardist*'; 1980, 163.) For Brecht, representational modes do not always have realist effects: realist writing and film-making may be more radical, in reaching a wide audience, for example, than modernist experimentalisms, enjoyed only by educated elites. Thus collapsing formalist radicalism into socialist radicalism may be all too premature.

Notes

1. This letter is reprinted in Craig (1975, 269–71).

2. The Congress's most infamous comment on modernism is Karl Radek's denunciation of Joyce's *Ulysses* as a 'heap of dung, crawling with worms, photographed by a cinema apparatus through a microscope' (Milner 1993, 27). Such an attack is an important, if implicit, context for Adorno's defences of modernism.

3. 'Symbolism' is most associated with French poets of the later nineteenth and early twentieth centuries (Baudelaire, Rimbaud, Verlaine, Mallarmé and Valéry) whose intense mixing and blurring of the senses and poetic images was an attempt to portray the 'reality' of consciousness through suggestion and evocation rather than through direct description. In 'expressionist' works of the early twentieth century, reality is shown to be distorted by emotional or irrational perspectives (Van Gogh, Strindberg and Wiene's *The Cabinet of Dr Caligari* are examples in painting, theatre and film). 'Imagism' is associated primarily with the poetry of Ezra Pound (and flourished from 1910–17), in which short, impersonal lyric poems attempt to treat the object with precision rather than with overt symbolic intent. 'Vorticism', associated with Wyndham Lewis and Ezra Pound (flourishing between 1912–15), depicted abstract compositions of bold lines, sharp angles and planes. 'Dada' styles used collage to arrange objects and words into meaningless and illogical patterns whose import was frequently nihilistic. In 'cubist' art objects are represented as geometrical forms. 'Futurism' espoused speed, war and Fascism, rejected all grammatical and artistic conventions, and was given expression in Marinetti's Manifesto of 1909. Russian 'constructivists' in the 1920s attempted to adopt a technological approach to writing. 'Surrealism', drawing upon Freudianism, patterned itself upon dreams, hallucination and other forms of the unconscious mind to free art from logic and convention. André Breton published a manifesto of surrealism in 1924.

4. All quotations are taken from Milner's discussion of 'communist materialism' (Milner 1993, 23–32). See also Sim (1994, 83–5 and 125–6).

5. John Frow argues that Lukács's writings became communist orthodoxy and are of a piece with his ambiguous defences of Stalinisation, despite later professions that his attacks on modernism were directed against socialist realism (Frow 1988, 16). Jameson notes that Stalin belatedly authorised a version of the policy advocated by Lukács in the Blum Theses (in Adorno et al. 1980, 203). In a late interview, Lukács remarked that one of the things which attracted him to Stalin in the late

1920s/early 1930s was his criticism of Plekhanov's aesthetic theory of realism (see Sim 1994, 125).

6. 'Zola's theatre director continually repeats: "Don't say theatre, say bordello." Balzac, however, [in *Lost Illusions*] depicts *how* the theatre becomes prostituted under capitalism. The drama of his protagonists is simultaneously the drama of the institution in which they work, of the things with which they live, of the setting in which they fight their battles, of the objects through which they express themselves and through which their interrelationships are determined.' (Lukács 1970, 114). Other arguments in this essay include that 'Narration establishes proportions, description merely levels' (127) and that description contemporises everything while narration recounts the past (130).

7. 'The "centre" figure need not represent an "average man" but is rather the product of a particular social and personal environment. The problem is to find a central figure in whose life all the important extremes in the world of the novel converge and around whom a complete world with all its vital contradictions can be organized' (Lukács 1970, 142).

8. All of these are reprinted in Adorno et al. *Aesthetics and Politics* (1980).

9. 'Experience' itself seems to have taught Lukács something of the accuracy of Bloch's arguments. See the anecdote related by Eagleton: 'Arrested by the Communist Party in 1956, deported, locked up in a castle and held without trial in Rumania, Lukács is reputed to have said that Kafka was a realist after all' (Eagleton 1996, 141).

10. See Adorno et al. (1980, 14) for a discussion of the Bloch-Lukács exchange and of how both writers do not discuss how social unity is contradictory (an implict context for Bloch's discussion of montage).

11. I have translated *verfremdung* as 'estrangement' rather than the more common 'alienation' because Brecht's 'alienation' is used contrarily from Marx's definition of alienation under capitalism. It also reveals a link with the Russian Formalist argument that literature 'estranges', 'de-familiarises' or 'makes strange'. Formalism was antithetical to marxist literary theories in that it studied literature in separation from its historical and social context. However this common definition of 'formalism' is itself misleading in its omission of second-wave revisionary formalists – Vološinov, Bakhtin, Medvedev – who incorporated primary formalist theories within marxist theories of context. The formalist theory that all art 'estranges' is later echoed in Althusser's 'Letter on art' in which literature is endowed with the potential to expose ideology (see Chapter 2). Althusser, who rarely discusses literature, devotes one chapter to the theatre of Bertolazzi and Brecht in *For Marx* (1990, 129–52).

12. Amendments to the text are not prohibited, but the Ensemble begin with the premise that they will prove the usefulness of their analytical method even without adding new text (259). One suggestion is ruled out by Brecht as a 'major intervention', one which would raise expectations which it would be difficult to fulfil in later scenes (259). Willett's notes to this section detail how the scene was eventually performed (see 265).

13. Quoted in Desmond Shawe-Taylor (1997, 11).

14. Given this theory of society, Jameson argues that Adorno's writings envisage a place for the possible emergence of postmodernism (1996, 247). As an analyst of 'total system' and late capitalism, Adorno is an analyst of the 1980s onwards (8). See below on postmodernism.

15. For this argument, see, for example, Eagleton (1990, 324): 'The work of art ... comes to the rescue of a commodified existence, equipped with everything in which the commodity is so lamentably lacking – a form no longer indifferent to its content but indissociable from it; an objectifying of the subjective which entails enrichment rather than estrangement; a deconstruction of the antithesis between freedom and necessity, as each element of the artefact appears at once miraculously autonomous yet cunningly subordinated to the law of the whole. In the absence of socialism, then, it will prove necessary to make do with art.' Eagleton reads modernity in the light of Williams's argument that modernism is marked by the divergences between metropolitan and colonial identities, and applying this obliquely to the Adorno-Lukács debate sees critical realism as impossible for colonised writers such as Joyce, Flann O'Brien and Beckett. (See 1990, 320ff. and also 1995, 'Form and Ideology in the Anglo-Irish Novel'.) See also Jameson in Eagleton et al. (1992).

16. Peter Bürger distinguishes between modernism's attack on traditional writing techniques and the avant-garde attack on and attempt to alter the institutionalised commercialisation of art. See 1984, *passim*.

17. See also Eagleton (1990, 342): 'a style of philosophizing which frames the object conceptually but manages by some cerebral acrobatics to glance sideways at what gives such generalized identity the slip'. Adorno's style however is criticised by some – here by Rodney Livingstone, Perry Anderson and Francis Mulhern: 'Dialectical tropes and epigrams that do not so much explain modernist art as re-create its moods and tempers served here for the kind of conceptual clarity that Lukács, for all his errors and evasions, rightly took to be the task of theoretical exposition' (Adorno et al. 1980, 146). This parallels the question of accessibility in relation to realist and modernist art-forms. See below.

18. For example, Adorno writes: 'Eulogists of "relevance" are more likely to find Sartre's *Huis Clos* profound, than to listen patiently to a text whose language challenges signification and by its very distance from meaning revolts in advance against positivist subordination of meaning' and 'This hostility to anything alien or alienating can accommodate itself much more easily to literary realism of any provenance, even if it proclaims itself critical or socialist, than to works which swear allegiance to no political slogans, but whose mere guise is enough to disrupt the whole system of rigid co-ordinates that governs authoritarian personalities' (Adorno et al. 1980, 179).

19. In this regard Adorno's argument can be seen to anticipate Pierre Macherey's theory of art as 'production' in the determination by genre, language, narrative conventions and so on. See Chapter 2. Adorno accuses Sartre of fetishising 'spontaneity' and thus, ironically, causing it to reify: ' ... since the pure immediacy and spontaneity which he hopes to save encounter no resistance in his work by which they could define themselves, they undergo a second reification' (Adorno et al. 1980, 181).

20. For other critiques of the Adorno-Lukács debates, see Bennett (1979, 136) and Peter Bürger on the inconsistency between Lukács's normative aesthetic theory and his marxist philosophy of history; and his failure to distinguish between modernism and the avant-garde (in Corredor 1997, 49 and 51). Stuart Sim however discusses Lukács's writings on Solzhenitsyn as an example of how Lukács was willing to depart from standard forms of realism (1994).

21. The debate has also to a large extent dictated whether Benjamin is interpreted as sufficiently 'marxist'. See Cohen (1995, 28ff.): e.g. Habermas's agreements with Adorno, Buck-Morss's defence of Benjamin (see below).

22. There are significant similarities between Benjamin and Althusser in relation to the base-superstructure model. See the discussion of Althusser in the section on 'base and superstructure', Chapter 1 and Cohen's excellent discussion of both the similarities and divergences between the two (1995, 30–6).

23. Buck-Morss defends Benjamin's analysis from the attack of 'classlessness', for example, in reading the analogy of the 'overly full stomach' as obviously symbolising the bourgeoisie, and thus the so-called 'collective' unconscious as the dream of the dominant class. See Cohen's summary of these arguments (1995, 29) and Buck-Morss (1989, 281–2).

24. See Williams's implicit disagreement: ' ... it is not the general themes of response to the city and its modernity which compose anything that can be properly called Modernism. It is rather the new and specific location of the artists and intellectuals of this movement within the

changing cultural milieu of the metropolis' (Williams 1996, 44). See also n.15, above.

25. Cohen argues that Benjamin's theory of 'shock' is more applicable to the surrealist practices of Breton than Baudelaire's latent romanticism. (See Cohen 1995, 208–15.)

26. See Cohen (1995, 8 and187). Cohen defends Benjamin's 'psychoanalytical' or 'Gothic' marxism against the critiques of the Frankfurt School and other marxisms (see 18ff.).

27. 'Positivism' or 'Positive philosophy', as originated by Auguste Comte (1798–1857), is defined by the doctrine that man can have no knowledge of anything but phenomena, a knowledge which is relative, not absolute. Jameson discusses its specific usage in Adorno's writings (1990, 89–90): ' ... in general to be taken to mean a commitment to empirical facts and worldly phenomena in which the abstract ... is increasingly constricted, when not systematically pursued and extirpated as a relic and a survival of older traditional "metaphysical", or simply old-fashioned and antiquated thoughts and categories' (89).

28. Benjamin submitted a third draft to Adorno: 'On Some Motifs in Baudelaire' to which Adorno responded with enthusiasm. Livingstone et al., however, note that this draft loses the strength of the second draft – its 'intense absorption and mastery of cross-connected historical materials' – without compensating gains in theoretical perception (Adorno et al. 1980, 105).

29. For example, Eagleton's celebration of Benjamin (1981); Jameson's celebration of Adorno (1990; reprinted 1996); recent reappraisals of Lukács (Corredor 1997); of Adorno (Hohendahl 1996; Nicholsen 1997; Jarvis 1998; Armstrong 1998) and of Bloch (Daniel and Moylan 1997). Adorno's *Aesthetic Theory* was first translated into English in 1984. Since then, Beech and Roberts (1996) argue, there has been a return to aesthetics on the Left, after the considerations of aesthetics as ideological which were pervasive in marxist debates of the 70s and early 80s.

30. Eagleton has suggested that criticisms of Lukács's anti-modernism as being 'reductive' need to be re-examined in the light of 'analogous and even more reductive antipathies to modernism [which] have become hegemonic via debates associated with postmodernism' (Eagleton 1996, 141) whereas Robert Young has argued that attacks on poststructuralism for denying history repeat Lukács's attacks on modernism, and that both are myopic in looking only for the 'History' which they wish to see there (1990, 23).

31. In subsuming all other approaches within marxism, Jameson's theory parallels Hegel's view of history as the unfolding of progressive stages in which new ideas and cultural forms develop by 'sublating' older ones,

that is by simultaneously adopting and transcending them, reconciling and preserving them. So too in Jameson's writings, no theory, however 'partial', cannot be usefully assimilated. In Bhaskar's discussion of dialectics, we can see obvious parallels between Hegel and Jameson's approach: 'For Hegel truth is the whole and error lies in one-sidedness, incompleteness and abstraction; it can be recognized by the contradictions it generates and remedied through their incorporation in fuller, richer, more concrete conceptual forms' (in Bottomore 1991, 144). Yet the suspicion remains, as Eagleton has argued, that Jameson is able to assimilate competing theories only because his analysis remains on the level of pure theory, suggesting, to put it in its crudest terms, that we need only see the 'whole' in order to put the world to rights. That the more structuralist marxisms associated with Eagleton and Hall in Britain have been less popular among American marxist theorists reveals the absence of a grass-roots marxism in America since the McCarthy era.

32. See in particular Jameson (1974, 160–205). In *The Political Unconscious* (1983), however, Jameson's own reading of Balzac's realism involved important critiques of Lukács's readings (151–84).

33. See Jameson (1992a, 95–6) for a brief discussion of these transitions in terms also of signification. Associated technologies might be steam (market capitalism), electricity and cars (monopoly), computers and nuclear power (multinational). Alex Callinicos argues that modernism and postmodernism as aesthetic movements and monopoly and multinational capitalism cannot be differentiated in the schematic way Jameson suggests (see 1989, passim).

34. Franco Moretti argued that contemporary marxist criticism tends to be 'little more than a left-wing "Apology for Modernism"' (in Grossberg and Nelson eds. 1988, 339). Such 'modernist marxists' include Kristeva's celebration of the texts of Lautréamont, Joyce and Rimbaud for the ways in which they deconstruct ideological closures. That modernism 'won' over realism needs to be considered in the context of socialist realism and its influence in terms of inspiring strenuous resistance not only to such doctrinaire judgements, but also to realism itself.

35. Jameson himself distinguishes between 'totality' and 'totalisation'. See Jameson (1992a, 332–3).

36. Heath's essay, 'Lessons from Brecht', *Screen* 15 (1974), 103–28 is reprinted in Mulhern (1992). See also Easthope (1991, 69): 'The text, whether literary or not, provides a position in which the reader identifies himself or herself: the realist text, by containing its own textuality, aims to secure for the reader a position of dominant specularity, seemingly autonomous, "outside looking on"; the modernist text in contrast,

by foregrounding its own textuality, puts the reader's security in question.'

37. MacCabe's essay 'Realism and the Cinema; Notes on some Brechtian Theses', *Screen* 15: 2 (1974) is excerpted in Rice and Waugh (1992). See also MacCabe (1979, especially Chapter 2, 'The end of a meta-language: from George Eliot to *Dubliners*') and Coward and Ellis (1977a). Such positions are also close to structuralist forms of marxism in the resistance to claims of 'experience' as legitimising, as for example, in the following: 'Belief in simple referentiality is not only unpoetic but also ultimately politically conservative, because it cannot recognize that the reality to which it appeals is a traditional ideological construction, whether one terms it phallomorphic, or metaphysical, or bourgeois, or something else. The politics of experience is inevitably a conservative politics for it cannot help but conserve traditional ideological constructs which are not recognised as such but are taken for "the real"' (Jane Gallop, quoted in Docherty 1993, 440).

38. The most interesting writings on the realism-modernism debates are thus those which interrogate and frustrate these terms as labels, as badges of position. For example Docherty's unexpected invocation of Lukács in his discussion of postmodernism: genuine avant-garde work for Lukács was prophetic, and thus 'realist', though it could only be so judged retrospectively (Docherty 1993, 17). Docherty quotes the following from Lukács – 'Whether a writer really belongs to the ranks of the avant-garde is something that only history can reveal, for only after the passage of time will it become apparent whether he has perceived significant qualities, trends, and the social functions of individual types, and has given them effective and lasting form ... only the major realists are capable of forming a genuine avant-garde' – and thus compares Lukács with Lyotard's theory of the future anteriority of the postmodern. Lukács admits the schematic degree of his own theory in 'Narrate or describe?': 'There are no writers who renounce description absolutely. Nor, on the other hand, can one claim that the outstanding representatives of realism after 1848, Flaubert and Zola, renounced narration absolutely. What is important here are philosophies of composition, not any illusory "pure" phenomenon of narration or description.' (Lukács 1970, 116.) A further example would be Williams's emphasis on the diversity within both 'modernism' and 'realism'. See, for example, 'Metropolitan Perceptions and the Emergence of Modernism' (Williams 1989) and 'Forms of English fiction in 1848' (Barker et al. 1986). For an excellent essay on Williams's relationship to the debates of this chapter, see Tony Pinkney's introduction to Williams (1989).

4   Cultural Studies

'[culture] ... the number of times I've wished that I had never heard of
the damned word. I have become more aware of its difficulties, not
less, as I have gone on.'
(Williams 1981, 154)

'There was never a prior moment when cultural studies and Marxism
represented a perfect theoretical fit. From the beginning ... there was
always-already the question of the great inadequacies, theoretically
and politically, the resounding silences, the great evasions of
Marxism – the things that Marx did not talk about or seem to understand which were our privileged object of study: culture, ideology,
language, the symbolic. These were always-already, instead, the
things which had imprisoned marxism as a mode of thought, as an
activity of critical practice – its orthodoxy, its doctrinal character, its
determinism, its reductionism, its immutable law of history, its status
as a metanarrative. That is to say, the encounter between British
cultural studies and Marxism has first to be understood as the
engagement with a problem – not a theory, not even a problematic.'
(Hall in Morley and Chen 1996, 265)

With the explosion of literary theory and cultural studies, marxist
theories need to be more vigilantly self-reflexive than before. Theory
has become commodified: it sells books, conferences, even university
programmes (when university funding is linked with student
numbers, universities compete for 'trade' like any other business).
Such intense and inescapable commodification is part of the 'late
capitalism' which Jameson designates as typical of western capitalism
since the 1950s. Indeed much of the current malaise affecting
marxism might be explained by the feeling that even its own theoretical endeavours can so easily become products of global capitalism. Of
the various forms of marxism, cultural studies has been affected by
this more than any other. This is largely because of the very modernity
of cultural studies as a discipline, and its formation within the

academy. An academic field which is traditionally traced to the 1950s and which, as the twenty-first century begins, continues its 'indisputable boom' (see Morley and Chen 1996, 361), cultural studies has always been constructed within and out of the contemporary. Many of its traditional objects of study – youth subcultures, popular fiction, film, magazines, newspapers and other contemporary media, and the cultural constructions of race and gender – are features of the 'postmodern' society of contemporary capitalism. Unlike other marxist approaches, cultural studies has no accompanying political form, and its international interests, its curiosity about all cultures, have ironically made it a product which can be sold on a global scale. Popular culture is produced by the mass culture industries, those associated with Twentieth Century Fox and Rupert Murdoch, with Bill Gates and EMI, for example. But popular culture is now also a 'product' of academic institutions and their own industry, pun intended, for popular culture sells academic books and degree courses.

From a 'marxist' position then, cultural studies is suspiciously complicit with contemporary advanced capitalism. But cultural studies is also a critique of marxism, and originated in the mid-twentieth century as a response to those aspects of post-war society which traditional marxist accounts could not understand: the enormous influence of the new media of radio, film, television; working-class affluence; and consumer capitalism. The origin of cultural studies is most usually located in the work of historians and literary critics associated with the British New Left of the 1950s and as such it was opposed to marxism, or at least the orthodox or economistic marxism then dominant. The New Left of the 1950s broke from traditional communism. Stuart Hall writes that he 'came into Marxism backwards: against the Soviet tanks in Budapest, as it were' (Morley and Chen 1996, 264) while for Williams, the decisive break was not after the Hungarian Revolt of 1956, but the intervention of the Russian army in the East German rising of June 1953 (Williams 1981, 88). But the New Left of the 1950s was formed not only out of disillusionment with Soviet communism, evident in the events of 1953 and 1956 and in the trials against Stalin after his death in 1954. The widespread conservatism of 1950s Britain also undermined the traditional view that the working classes would inevitably work to create a socialist society. (The Conservative electoral successes – elected in 1951, the Conservatives enjoyed uninterrupted power until 1964 – are often traced to the erosion of traditional working-class support for Labour.)

So the relationship between cultural studies and marxism was one, in Hall's words, of 'working within shouting distance of marxism, working on marxism, working against marxism, working with it, working to try to develop marxism' (Morley and Chen 1996, 265).

The close affinity between marxism and cultural studies, and the simultaneous antagonisms between them, are also evident in their respective approaches to cultural texts. In the serialisation of Dickens's novels, for example, marxist readers such as Norman Feltes (1986) have seen the increasing commodification of the book trade. For Feltes, book production until the Victorian period was characterised by petty-commodity production: books were sold on the market, but the characteristically exploitative nature of capitalism (by which surplus value is extracted through control over the labour process) was absent. It is only with the attempts to cultivate a mass market in the Victorian period that book production becomes a form of mature capitalism. For Feltes this is exemplified in serial publication. Dickens's *Pickwick Papers* (1836–7) was the first fiction to be sold in monthly parts and as such it both reached and produced a mass audience. Not only did the series permit the identity of a mass bourgeois audience to be created (or interpellated), but it also drew ever greater surplus value from the author as producer. The publishers Chapman and Hall bought Dickens's intellectual labour for nineteen months and required each month a discrete text of determinate length, which would form part of the series overall. That *Pickwick*'s style has been described as a 'constant, rapid, and virtually limitless multiplication of its own effects and forms in new inventions and combinations and configurations' is as much a product of the serial publication as it is of any conscious or creative decision on the author's part to write about the members of the 'Pickwick Club'. A cultural studies approach, in contrast, might typically discuss Dickens only in the context of contemporary non-canonical writing, such as Victorian street ballads and 'penny' fiction. Or in the context of our equivalents to Dickens's serial fictions: television programmes like *Homicide: Life on the Street* or *The X Files*, which maintain narrative lines over many years and use similar 'cliff-hanger' narrative suspensions at the end of each episode. Because cultural studies are more interested in the issue of 'consumption' (or reception) than of 'production', their objects of study are usually those 'mass cultural' texts which were and are read by the greatest number, rather than the canonical authors who have often been read by comparatively few.

(Since *Pickwick Papers* sold forty thousand copies each month in 1836–7, Dickens is not typical in this regard.) However the distinction between a focus on consumption and on production is a rather heavy-handed one, since in marxist analysis, the two are not separate in this way. ('Consumption' can only be thought of in opposition to production if we reduce production to 'factories making goods, capitalists making profits' instead of seeing it as a complex process of which consumption is one phase.[1]) And the shift in focus between 'canonical' and 'popular' culture has been so revolutionary that contemporary marxist literary theories seldom ignore the popular and thus might be seen as themselves a form of cultural studies. Cultural critics today refuse the classifications by which certain objects of study are separated and are approached from distinct disciplinary approaches (such as anthropology, economics, history, literary studies). Luke Gibbons, in *Transformations in Irish Culture* (1996), for example, eclectically discusses installation art and television soap operas (*The Riordans, Glenroe*), the writings of James Joyce and the popular postcards of John Hinde. And in doing so, Gibbons writes as if the division between high and low art is a thing of the past. Gibbons's book is an excellent study of Irish culture, but it also, if only implicitly, suggests why the inclusion of popular culture is so necessary. The power and influence of a television soap opera is incomparably greater than the art of Willie Doherty, so that while Doherty's art continues to comment powerfully on contemporary Northern Ireland, it does not have the same effectivity as popular culture. And it is this effectivity which makes popular culture a necessary subject for marxist analysis.

The question of how 'marxist' cultural studies might be will be considered later in the chapter. First I will sketch a brief history of cultural studies as a kind of intellectual map which will suggest something of the history of cultural marxism in Britain in the late twentieth century, a map which will situate both theories and theorists already discussed in this book.[2] This is a convenient narrative, and one which many cultural studies theorists would resist. Indeed, cultural studies frequently denies that it is a discipline at all, since it was conceived as a project which would be inter-disciplinary (using and linking disciplines usually segregated: sociology, literature, history, anthropology, to name those most important in the earliest years of cultural studies) and even anti-disciplinary (since its inter-disciplinary nature was a rebuke and a challenge to those who set limits to their own mode and objects of enquiry). Thus there have been almost as many refusals of the traditional 'history' of cultural studies as there have been books to explain this formation.[3] Williams himself, in a lecture in 1986, argued that the origin of cultural studies was not to be found in texts, such as his own *Culture and Society* (1957), but in the adult education classes of the 30s to late 40s.[4] Williams's correction is appropriate for a cultural critic who always emphasised social practices rather than texts. But it is also a history which only those involved in such teaching could sketch. It is a history, then, which privileges the experiential over the textual, and as such is inaccessible to any except participants in the formation of cultural studies. This question too (of the experiential as opposed to the theoretical) is part of the debates about and within cultural studies. Thus the type of historicising of the cultural studies project evident in such a survey is merely one history among many, but I have retained it here because it is a history which conveniently mirrors the kinds of trajectories and transitions which marxist aesthetic theories were undergoing in post-war Britain.

A (traditional) history of cultural studies

In the work of Hoggart and Williams, cultural studies 'began' in a curious mixture of marxism and Leavisite reading practices.[5] Both Hoggart and Williams had been trained in Leavisite literary criticism but turned this methodology of sensitive, moral reading to the culture of the working class with which they had grown up as children and which Leavis himself had so disdained. F.R. Leavis feared 'mass' culture and its incipient threat to the 'great tradition' of literature which he had celebrated throughout his career. For him, culture was embodied in 'great' art and literature which was beyond commercial pressures and which, in being so, would promote an 'awareness of the possibilities of life' (Leavis 1962, 10). Thus Leavis's legacy was both an opportunity and an obstacle for Hoggart and Williams: here was a break with the New Critical practice of divorcing literature from any context other than an immediate reading of the words on the page, but the turn towards society was problematic too since it was based on vague goals in which the 'possibilities of life' and the 'great tradition' seemed to be whatever Leavis himself argued them to be. And, since Leavis was a critic in the mould of nineteenth-century liberalism, the 'possibilities of life' often sounded like the embourgeoisment of the working class, or the gentrification of the middle classes. Leavis, like Matthew Arnold before him, celebrated culture as the means of 'educating' the masses, in which such 'education' was often nothing but a thinly disguised aim of taming them. Such liberalism is exemplified in the figure of Sir Robert Peel, founder of the Metropolitan Police Force and future Tory Prime Minister who, after the 1832 agitation for parliamentary reform, supported the campaign to situate the National Gallery in Trafalgar Square since, he argued: 'In the present time of political excitement, the exacerbation of angry and unsocial feelings might be much softened by the effect which the fine arts have ever produced on the minds of men' (quoted in Minihan 1977, 56). Similarly, Arnold's essay 'Culture and Anarchy' (1869) was written in response to the Hyde Park Riot following the failure of the 1867 Reform Bill (see Williams, 1980).

In *The Uses of Literacy* (1957), Hoggart described working-class culture as characterised by ties of solidarity, a commitment to community, home and neighbourhood and a sense of its own collective identity. While this was certainly not Leavis's definition of culture, it paralleled Leavis's work in its attempt to read culture as part of society and in its fears of a capitalist 'mass culture' which would threaten traditional, 'authentic', working-class culture. Above all, Hoggart feared the 'Invitations to a Candy-floss world' and the 'Sex in Shiny packets' which were, for him, the terms of 'the newer mass art'. Hoggart's largely autobiographical account of working-class experience has been criticised as nostalgic by many subsequent commentators. Reyner Banham, for example, an architectural critic and, like Hoggart a Left-wing intellectual from a working-class background, fondly remembers a childhood imbued with American popular culture: *Mechanix Illustrated*, Betty Boop, the films of Chaplin and Keaton. 'Thinking back, the cultural background against which I grew up was a very curious one indeed, if one is to believe the sort of things in Hoggart' (quoted in Dworkin 1997, 85). The parallel between Hoggart and Williams and Leavis is thus a striking image of the way in which early cultural studies was created out of traditional English studies. Later, cultural studies would divorce its work from that of traditional literature departments, with their evaluative traditions of 'great' and 'popular' art, high-, middle- and low-brow cultures. But with the first emergence of a 'postmodern' consumer society, popular or 'Americanised' culture was seen as a threat to the authenticity of working-class experience, as it had been to the elite culture which

Leavis defended. (There is an obvious parallel here too with the work of the Frankfurt School, particularly Adorno's critiques of the 'culture industry', discussed in Chapter 3.) A young Stuart Hall, in an article in the *Universities and Left Review* (winter 1958), defined socialist humanism by quoting Leavis's description of the nineteenth-century novel as displaying 'a vital capacity for experience, a kind of reverent openness before life, and a marked moral intensity'.[6]

We can see something of the affinities and differences between Leavis and Williams and Hoggart in the ways in which all three referred to D.H. Lawrence. Leavis included Lawrence among his list of great writers and preferred him to Joyce because of his self-professed religiosity, quoting with applause Lawrence's argument that his novels were written out of the depth of his religious experience, rather than out of the 'vulgarity and disagreeableness of the common people' (Leavis 1972, 36–7). For Leavis, evidently, Lawrence could only be appreciated insofar as he transcended his class origins. For Hoggart and Williams, Lawrence is an attractive writer, combining as he does the 'high' cultural tradition of the canonical Victorian novel with working-class concerns. Indeed Hoggart argues that *Sons and Lovers* brings us closer to working-class life than 'more popular or more consciously proletarian fiction' (1958, 16). Neither Hoggart nor Williams are interested in such phenomenally popular novels as those published by Horner in late Victorian London: Dr Rossvally's *Charlie Coulson*, for example, which sold four hundred and fifty thousand copies (see Neuburg 1977, 228–30). There is little serious interest in what working-class people actually read in their early work. Williams's *The English Novel from Dickens to Lawrence* is so consciously tied up in a dialogue with Leavis's *The Great Tradition* that it inevitably seems as complicit with Leavis's work as it does with forging its own. Williams's selections in his book almost entirely invert those of Leavis. Leavis excludes Dickens from his tradition; Williams includes a full chapter on Dickens. Leavis emphasises the later work of George Eliot; Williams the early Eliot. Leavis omits Hardy and includes James; Williams omits James and includes Hardy. Leavis praises *Women in Love* above all other Lawrence novels; Williams prefers *Sons and Lovers* and *Lady Chatterley's Lover*. Such inversions demonstrate Williams's familiarity with Leavis, as much as his disagreement with him, a familiarity evident too in the methods of analysis of *The English Novel*, in which the focus of discussion is on passages excerpted from the novels for close inspection. Williams, as he later acknowledged, 'knew *The Great Tradition* by heart' (1981, 245).

However, the significant differences between the work of Leavis and the early work of Hoggart, Williams and Hall also need to be acknowledged. The most profound of these changes was in the very definition of culture itself. In *Culture and Society* (1958), Williams began by examining the historicity of the concept, the way in which the idea of culture was forged as a response to problems in new forms of industry, democracy and class in the late eighteenth and early nineteenth centuries. As a deepening capitalism made lives mechanised, depersonalised and isolated, culture became the bulwark which would protect the moral and intellectual activities of individual people, their private and personal lives, and thus provide them with an alternative order to that of capitalist production and the market. Culture became the domain in which alternative values could be fostered, values which could criticise and even transform nineteenth-century society. Thus throughout the nineteenth century culture came to stand for a whole way of life, articulated by such writers as the Romantic poets, Carlyle, the 'social problem' novelists – Gaskell, Dickens, Disraeli, Kingsley and Eliot – Matthew Arnold and William Morris. Williams's cultural mapping here duplicates Leavis's celebration of the 'great' English writers as the guardians of English culture. But Williams's account was simultaneously a critique of Leavis, of the way in which he had narrowed the definition of culture so that it excluded other forms of culture in its exaggeration of the English literary canon. Leavis's culture included only the 'high' cultural products of individual, independent, 'great' writers and artists, and, in the work of his more conservative followers, such a culture was then able to be reappropriated as an opposition to democracy, socialism, the working class or popular education. (In Leavis's terms, culture is distinct from society, although paradoxically, it is also that which will make society whole again.) Quite independently of Hoggart's work, Williams also believed that culture included customs, manners, family memories, institutions, forms of knowledge, in short 'ways of living'. Culture was the way in which people within communities and communities within societies defined and lived out their identities. When Williams and Hoggart shifted the emphasis away from culture as text to culture as experience, they were able to restore a dignity to those working-class communities which Leavis viewed as bereft of culture, as 'uncultured'. Instead of seeing 'high' culture as a tool which might uplift the moral and spiritual being of the working class (although this was still part of how they saw culture), their definitions incorporated anything which those people chose to read or do, their beliefs and values, their ways of working and interacting with each other. In the following extract from *Culture and Society* (1957), Williams defines working-class culture in this way:

> It is not proletarian art, or council houses, or a particular use of language; it is, rather, the basic collective idea, and the institutions, manners, habits of thought, and intentions which proceed from this. Bourgeois culture, similarly, is the basic individualist idea and the institutions, manners, habits of thought, and intentions which proceed from that. ... The working class, because of its position, has not, since the Industrial Revolution, produced a culture in the narrower sense. The culture which it has produced, and which it is important to recognize, is the collective democratic institution, whether in the trade unions, the cooperative movement, or a political party. (Williams 1963, 313)

Both Hoggart and Williams redefined culture as a social practice, so that to separate the study of individual cultural forms from the 'whole way of life' in which they were embedded and which they constituted, would be to misrepresent culture itself. We might see Williams's definition as an attempt to resist the suggestion of separation implied in an interest in 'culture *and* society'. But this definition itself also meant that 'culture' would always be a complex concept, in Stuart Hall's words 'a site of convergent interests, rather than a logically or conceptually clarified idea' (in Bennett et al. 1981, 21).[7]

It is tempting, and common, to interpret the ambivalences which Hoggart and Williams display towards the Leavisite tradition as products of their own histories: both were from working-class communities (Hoggart from industrial Leeds, Williams from Pandy, a mining village in South Wales), but were somewhat distanced from these upbringings by their scholarship training at university (Hoggart at Leeds, Williams at Cambridge). So in their writings, the celebration of traditional working-class rhythms and customs of life was held in tension with the desire to 'save' the working class from the kinds of 'mass' literature it enjoyed but which their university education had taught them to disdain. Williams wanted to defend communities like that of Pandy from the charge that they were 'uncultured' and yet the incipient Americanisation of pulp fiction and best sellers which they enjoyed was measured against the texts he now read and taught in adult education classes in Cambridge. However, in seeking to understand why the working classes enjoyed a culture which traditional literary criticism disdained, Williams shifted the study of 'culture' from exclusively textual analysis (which left only bewilderment in the face of comic books and popular dime novels) to the analysis of the experiences themselves. And it was this transition which enabled the later work of Hall and the Centre for Contemporary Cultural Studies in their explorations of the ways in which popular culture might be potentially subversive, rather than demeaning.

At first the Centre at Birmingham continued to reflect the same kind of ambivalences towards popular culture which had deformed the 1950s work of Hoggart and Williams. The Centre was first formed as an annex to the English department at Birmingham University and its original goal, outlined and defended by Hoggart in his inaugural address in 1964, was to apply the traditional methods of literary criticism to the new domains of popular and mass culture. (See Hoggart 1970.) Admittedly, this also entailed a recognition that new criteria would have to be found for the evaluation of specific texts, but their early judgements tended to parallel normative standards, those standards which were always already set by high culture. For example, Stuart Hall and Paddy Whannel's book *The Popular Arts* (1964) usefully distinguished between 'popular' and 'mass' culture, but ultimately its judgements were based on unquestioned assumptions: jazz was preferable to rock 'n' roll because it was as creative as classical music, just as film was celebrated over television. Hall and Whannel may have bestowed a respectability on jazz, which, for example, Adorno's censures had denied it, but their distinctions merely replicated earlier judgements. These distinctions were made because the mode of analysis was fundamentally intrinsic. Jazz was 'superior' to rock 'n' roll, judged by such criteria as rhythmic variety, musical diversity, personal expression and imagination, all of which could be decided by reading musical scores or listening to recordings. But this exploration failed to explore the implication of these particular forms within Williams's 'whole way of life'. It never considered the function of pop music in the communities which listened to it, their responses to it or the relation between popular culture and social struggle. Thus only Hall and Whannel's object of study, not their methodology, differed from that of traditional Leavisite readings. And what had

been lost from Hoggart and Williams's 1950s work was any commitment to political engagement. As Simon During has argued: 'Most
individuals aspire and struggle the greater part of their lives and it is
easier to forget this if one is just interpreting texts rather than thinking
about reading as a life-practice' (During 1993, 2).

After the publication of E.P. Thompson's major work, *The Making
of the English Working Class* (1964) however, there was a greater
impulse to connect culture with social struggle. Thompson's book
eradicated the distinction between 'high' and 'mass' art by perceiving
popular culture as a form of resistance, and simultaneously redefined
Williams's definition of culture (as a 'whole way of life') as a 'whole
way of struggle'. In a move analogous to Macherey and Balibar's
questioning of 'Literature' as an institutionalised practice in the
1970s, the work of the Birmingham Centre supplemented the critical
interpretation of texts with an examination of their effects on audiences, and an analysis of their social contexts and cultural signifi-
cances. Thus literary criticism moved out towards social theory. Four
texts from the late 1970s might be cited as representative of this development: the collectively written *Resistance through Rituals: Youth
Subcultures in Post-War Britain* (1976), edited by Stuart Hall and Tim
Jefferson; Paul Willis's *Learning to Labour: How Working-Class Kids
Get Working-Class Jobs* (1977); Dick Hebdige's *Subculture: the
Meaning of Style* (1979); and David Morley's *The 'Nationwide'
Audience* (1980). With their focus on youth groups and television,
these texts appeared to constitute a break with the traditions of
Western marxism: generational conflict was as important to these
analyses as class conflict and the serious treatment of such popular
cultural forms as television challenged marxism's traditional fascination with so-called 'high' art, epitomised by Adorno's pessimism in
the face of a burgeoning culture industry. Indeed, many have recognised in the cultural studies of the 70s the origins of a 'post-marxism'.
If so, this turn was itself partly due to the influence of continental
marxisms which were translated, often belatedly, into English from
the mid-60s onwards and disseminated by the buoyancy of such jour-
nals as the *New Left Review* (founded 1959).[8]

The most influential theorists for cultural studies at this time were
Gramsci and, to a lesser extent, Althusser.[9] Althusser was the first of
the two theorists to influence British cultural studies, although his
influence was most pronounced in film theory, as embodied in the
journal *Screen*. Althusser's work challenged the 'culturalism' or

'humanism' of the work of Thompson, Hoggart and early Williams. Their work might be distinguished from Althusserian structuralism by their focus on 'culture' rather than on 'ideology', a focus, moreover, which was sympathetic to empirical modes of thought, so that, they believed, the experiences and history of the past could be reconstructed and celebrated. And not the least of these differences was the distrust of abstraction, the commitment to the historically specific, a wariness of theory itself. In stark opposition to this, Althusser's theory of ideology argued that 'experience' could not be accepted as a given, something which might ground accounts of culture because experience itself was determined by culture. Experience was an 'effect' of social practices, not the unique initiator of them. It was not a reflection of the real, but an 'imaginary relation' through which people lived the real conditions of existence. This was a fundamental challenge to the culturalism associated with Hoggart, Williams and Thompson, which viewed culture as an expression or product of human consciousness. Culture, in the terms of 'humanist' marxism, always contained the possibility of emancipation, of potential amelioration or of subversion. This was culture as a form of praxis. In the terms of structuralist marxism, culture was 'always-already' determined by structures, so that culture became almost entirely synonymous with ideology, with domination. This argument was especially useful to the contributors to *Screen*, who used Althusserian and Lacanian analyses to articulate how the perspective produced by film-gazing was fixed in advance. Laura Mulvey (1975) argued, for example, that women at the cinema are coded as 'masculine', drawn into masculine positions of spectatorship and identification. The camera constructs the female star as the locus of erotic desire, a spectacle to be looked at by the male characters, and through their point-of-view shots, by the spectators of both sexes. Sternberg's films of Marlene Dietrich, such as *The Scarlet Empress*, are cited as exemplary of this by Mulvey, since Sternberg's remark that he could have projected his films upside-down illustrates that spectacle took priority over narrative.[10] So too, in the lavish beauty of the Regency settings of recent Jane Austen adaptations, the viewer is coded as the bourgeois, envious, aspirant voyeur. But the turn towards sociological study at the Birmingham Centre meant that Althusser's brand of Lacanianism was resisted as much as it was accepted by cultural studies. Althusser's refusal of human agency was too absolute for those who studied the ways in which youth groups, drug users or television

viewers constructed meanings, meanings which sometimes negotiated or even opposed those predetermined by the productive mode,
structure or system. Thus Althusserianism was rejected as a doctrine,
even though its positioning of culture within a relatively autonomous
sphere enabled cultural studies to turn to the question of 'style', as a
dimension relatively untouched by material determination.

Attempts to fuse structuralism and humanism were characteristic of
the work of the Centre throughout the 1970s. Stuart Hall summarises
the respective strengths of what he calls the 'two paradigms' of structuralism and culturalism in his essay of that name (see Bennett et al.
1981, 30–6). Both movements are necessary if cultural studies is to
achieve the balance of Marx's statement that 'men make their own
history ... on the basis of conditions which are not of their making'.
While culturalism reminds us of the possibilities of political organisation, that men and women can so organise themselves as to resist and
even defeat the forces which exploit them, it would be naive to think
that men and women need only decide to change conditions in order
for change to come about. We are always positioned as agents by
structures which are beyond our individual, and often collective,
control. In combining recognitions of human potential and constraint,
Hall urges us to keep faith with Gramsci's motto: 'pessimism of the
intellect, optimism of the will'. Hall also sees the attempt to reconcile
structuralism and culturalism as a balancing of the claims of abstraction and particularity, theory and empiricism. Indeed, it is too simplistic to characterise the debate in terms of theoreticism versus
empiricism, since all thinking requires a theoretical level. Even empirical knowledge requires interpretation, and interpretation in turn
requires a theoretical positioning. The 'facts' never do 'speak for themselves'. Thus culturalism will continue to be – theoretically, method-
ologically, inevitably – naive if it does not heed the lesson of
structuralism: that thought does not reflect reality, but is articulated
on and appropriates it. And the debate needs to be articulated as a
debate between levels of abstraction, rather than that between
abstraction and some form of immediacy.[11] Hall also celebrates
Althusser's theories of 'overdetermination' and 'relative autonomy'
(see Chapter 1), because these concepts permit us to understand a
totality which is constituted by specific practices which are unified by
their difference as much as by their identity. Culturalism's view of the
totality is constrained again by reflectionism, so that the contradictions of, for example, human activity are judged as expressive of the

contradiction of the economic base (the contradiction between the forces and the relations of production). In this way, the totality is always thought of in terms of parallels or homologies, which courts the danger of returning theoretically to a simplistic base-superstructure paradigm. Culturalism tends to perceive society in terms of a holistic 'wholeness' rather than the fluid, heterogeneous, fragmentary and even sometimes isolated or atomised character of social formations.

Despite these major reservations about culturalism as it was practised in the early years of cultural studies, Hall is also open to the ways in which culturalist emphases are crucial. While structuralist approaches have introduced the issue of ideology as central to cultural studies, culturalism reminds us that ideology is not simply imposed from above, but is constantly fought over, negotiated and subject to challenge. 'Experience' is not always merely an effect of the system as 'structure', as Althusser's theories often imply. Thus cultural studies is an attempt to sustain the possibility of intervention, not least in its own work. And the attempted fusion of structuralism and culturalism might be seen as one such intervention. It highlights the way in which these positions have become more entrenched as a consequence of the debate itself: Williams's defence of 'experience' was motivated in part in reaction against the Althusserian elision of the subject. And this polemical positioning tends to hide how Williams's form of empiricism was itself distinguished from what we might call 'vulgar empiricism' and its complacent belief in the unmediated access to reality. Williams's is a radical empiricism which sees in language not a transparent medium through which consciousness might be delivered, but a resistance of its own (see Williams in Gable 1989, 92–3). Williams was to turn increasingly to the work of Medvedev, Vološinov, and Bakhtin (see, for example, 'The Uses of Cultural Theory' in 1996; a lecture first delivered in 1986).

However, such nuances are frequently lost in accounts of the debate between structuralism and culturalism. The pressure of the argument between the 'two paradigms' undoubtedly skewed positions. Richard Johnson, for example, argued that Thompson's attack on Althusserianism in 'The Poverty of Theory' (1978) exemplified a more general tendency of the Left to hold its debate in crippling, absolutist terms. This is certainly evident in Dennis Dworkin's account of the debate between Thompson, Hall and Richard Johnson in 1979 (Dworkin 1997, 235ff.), in which arguments became embroiled over the nature of debate itself and many present recognised that such polemical stances were part of the problem rather than the solution to their differences.[12] The attempted fusion of culturalism and structuralism by the Centre in the 70s might be interpreted as an attempt to move beyond such gladiatorial styles of argumentation, influenced by feminism's questioning of aggressive forms of debate. But the celebrated 'fusion' of the two paradigms might also be seen as a papering over of the cracks between competing marxisms. Rosalind Coward, in a review of *Resistance through Rituals* (1977b), argued that the attempted 'fusion' failed to recognise the ways in which the two paradigms could not be reconciled. Culturalism celebrated subcultures as expressions of a working-class, marginalised consciousness distinct from, and sometimes oppositional to, the culture of the dominant class. Thus social practices were directly linked to and determined by class position (an 'old-fashioned', base-superstructure type argument which Coward thought reductive) at the same time as being free from the structures of capitalism.[13]

Because Althusserianism was positioned overtly as a challenge to the central theoretical premises which had founded and continued to influence cultural studies, the Centre turned towards other marxist theorists, particularly Gramsci. Gramsci's *Selections from the Prison Notebooks* was translated into English in 1971 and was quickly embraced as a potential reconciliation of the competing claims of structuralism and culturalism. Gramsci's theory of hegemony allowed cultural studies to analyse social practices as being determined by constraints (as Althusserianism stressed) but without abandoning the argument that they are themselves also potentially determining (as culturalism demanded). Thus Gramsci appeared to offer cultural studies practitioners a resolution of the impossible: that social practices were shaped by both historical boundedness and active agency, both making and being made by history. Vološinov's theory of the multiaccentuality of the sign also permitted meanings to be sites of struggle, in which variant and oppositional interpretations would be possible. These arguments are articulated in the studies named above. In *Learning to Labour*, for example, Paul Willis stressed that the disaffection of working-class boys was both a product of their gloomy prospects within the system and a culture which they constructed out of their own awareness of the system. Their apathy was thus not a reflection of laziness or ignorance, but of their very understanding that the kind of dead-end jobs they would fill after school, their exploitation by the system, were necessary to capitalist production. David

Morley studied the responses of a variety of groups to the daily BBC current affairs magazine programme *Nationwide* and found that even though the programme attempted to predetermine a response (that its viewers would share with the presenters their 'common sense' view of the issues), not all groups passively consumed this message. Some recognised the ideological bias of the programme but suspended their cynicism while watching (a form of 'negotiation'); others rejected the message completely.[14] The *Resistance through Rituals* anthology included studies of drug users, skinheads, teddy boys, the West Indian immigrant subculture of Rastafarianism and reggae music, groups more usually labelled as 'deviant' and hitherto deemed unworthy of serious academic study. Dick Hebdige (1979) celebrated the radical potential of such subcultures as punk, reggae and mods as refusals of bourgeois institutions and values. The Sex Pistols' punk-anthem, *Anarchy in the UK*, for example, is equated with the bohemian avant-gardes of Paris in its conscious rebellion against everything middle class. Jean Genet in his autobiography, *Thief's Journal* (1948), had argued that style could be a form of refusal, and Hebdige picks up on this legacy, and on Camus's and Sartre's assertions that rebellion is a mode of freedom, in order to treat his 'subjects' with a seriousness and dignity they would have rejected: 'I would like to think that [Genet's form of] Refusal is worth making, that these gestures have a meaning, that the smiles and the sneers have some subversive value, even if, in the final analysis, they are, like Genet's gangster pin-ups, just the darker side of sets of regulations, just so much graffiti on a prison-wall' (1979, 3). The writers within the Centre, then, celebrated the cultures of these groups as challenges to the dominant culture, white, middle class, aspirant. They interpreted these subcultures as ways of expressing and realising their own subordinate position in relation to the dominant culture, but they were also challenges to that culture, whose dominance was expressed in the attempt to contain all others within its own range, to become the most 'natural' or seemingly 'universal' culture (see CCCS 1976, 12).[15] This anthology, and the work of the Birmingham Centre which it represented, must have seemed revolutionary in the context of the 1970s, when a department which had originally been an 'annex' of the university's English literature department began to apply techniques of reading literary texts to social subgroups, including the most marginalised groups in society. (Indeed the work of many cultural studies departments is still condescended to by much of the conservative press.)

However, like *The Popular Arts*, these texts were more revolutionary in the objects of their studies than in their methodologies. Despite the obvious debt to Gramsci's theories of hegemony and ideological struggle, they remained overwhelmingly and unreflexively empirical. (In *The 'Nationwide' Audience*, for example, Morley used the responses given in interviews as evidence of the viewers' experience of watching the programme, and thus failed to address both the question of his own involvement, and the ways in which viewers would articulate their own experiences in the interview.) In the particular way in which cultural studies read Gramsci, Gramscianism often became a theoretical ally of culturalism rather than a potential mediator between the competing claims of the two paradigms. Gramscian work in cultural studies tended to overestimate the political power of articulation. While these commentators might celebrate the potential radicalism of mods, punks and skinheads, they failed to address the way in which these youths were nevertheless trapped within a cycle of economic poverty and a lack of opportunity. Rebellious styles did not alter policing modes or employers' practices; if anything, they exacerbated them. Meanwhile these styles were themselves liable to be incorporated within a system which privileged novelty and even, if only superficially, rebellion: all such articulations were in turn to become fashionable, commodified. In later reworkings of his study of subcultures, Hebdige (1989) was to concede that he had underestimated the power of commercial culture to appropriate, and even produce, the very styles he had analysed as instances of 'refusal'. Punk's complicity with the media – its use of the press, advertising, television and radio – had previously been read as ironic. Now it seemed as much like marketing savvy. But relatively few of the studies which were inspired by Clarke, Hebdige and others attempted to balance subculture as resistance with commercial culture as hegemony in this way. Later studies were to find resistance everywhere, even in the commodity itself. At this point, the marxist mode of cultural studies can be said to have been thoroughly abandoned.

Of course, it is easy to see the claims made for 1970s youth as absurd now, from the perspective of millenial Britain. We cannot but remember these youth rebellions simultaneously with the history of their lack of success: after the revolutionary carnivals of 1968, the police occupation of the London School of Economics in 1969; the increasingly expert surveillance and policing of demonstrations and protests in the 70s and 80s; the brutal policing of the 1984 miners' strike; the Criminal Justice Acts of the 1990s. But even at the time of their first publication, all four texts shared an avoidance of issues which were becoming increasingly glaring. All failed to account for the ways in which gender and race were implicated in their research. *Resistance through Rituals* included just one essay on the relationship between male youth subcultures and their female peers. Willis defended the culture of the 'lads' from academic condescension, but he failed to discuss the ways in which this same culture was defined partly through its ill treatment of girls and non-white peers. Similarly John Clarke's study of skinheads in *Resistance through Rituals* failed to address their practice of 'Paki' and 'queer' bashing. And only later, as a consequence of feminist debates, would Morley revise his *Nationwide* survey so as to include the domestic context of television viewing, the influence of the family group on the perceptions of the individual viewer. In this way, the three texts were not fully representative of the 'new' New Left after 1968 (as opposed to the 'old' New Left of the 1950s). This 'new' New Left was an umbrella term for a diversity of interests which were only loosely connected: anarchist, independent marxist, black power, situationist, student, dissident Trotskyist, Maoist, socialist-feminist, communist. These groups shared less of a link with British labour traditions, a distinction which was evident in their formations and style. In place of the 'old' Left's 'managerial' style was a preference for local, grassroots action and spontaneous, *ad hoc* formations. And this political climate had implications for the way in which culture might be defined. The early work of Hoggart, Williams and Thompson had tended to emphasise culture as the expression of a group's consciousness. Now, parallel with the 'theoreticist' challenge to the reflectionism implicit in this theory, was the sense of multiple and often conflicting identities in which a straightforward, univocal 'consciousness' was increasingly impossible. Culture thus became recognised as a field of signification rather than an expression of a group's consciousness.

In charting the rise and challenge of gender and race as key issues, Patrick Brantlinger argues that 'ideology' should be replaced as the key concept by 'representation'. 'Ideology' has become so identified with the narrow sense of 'false consciousness' that it is difficult to use the term to distinguish between degrees of truth and falsity or indeed to avoid a complacent assumption of the identity of 'truth' or 'falsity'. 'Representation', however, allows culture to be identified as a 'field of struggle in which the stakes are accurate, just, and direct representation by groups and individuals instead of misrepresentations by others' (Brantlinger 1990, 104). This replacement settles both challenges, that of structuralist or anti-reflectionist theories, and that of simultaneous claims (by women, gay and black movements). Debates over representation encompass a spectrum of cultural politics in which marginalised groups might articulate their misrepresentation by the ideological power of others, whether in the artistic or literary canons so powerfully maintained in school and university courses, by accepted 'standards' of language practice, or by the institutions of the government, the legal system and the economy. It also necessitates that cultural studies includes within its parameters its own institutionalisation as an academic discipline.

The issues of class, race and gender might have been articulated together. Black and Asian, female and working class are all defined as 'minority' groupings despite their constituting 'major' sections of the population. And all share a marginalisation by the dominant culture of the aspirant, white, male, predominantly middle class. But throughout the late 70s and 80s in Britain, the issue of class receded as those of gender and race predominated. To an extent this was merely a correction of a previous imbalance in cultural studies work and the resurgence of long-suppressed issues. Key texts of the late 70s and 80s included studies of racism in Britain – the Birmingham collective's *Policing the Crisis* (1979) and *The Empire Strikes Back: Race and Racism in 70s Britain* (1982), Paul Gilroy's *There Ain't No Black in the Union Jack* (1987) – and feminist work such as the Women's Studies Group (started in October 1974), their journal *Women Take Issue* (1978), and Dorothy Hobson's *Crossroads: The Drama of a Soap Opera* (1982). While Hebdige's work on subculture had emphasised the importance of black music and culture to the punk movement, and had reminded his academic audiences of the important allegiances between black and punk movements (as in the 'Rock against Racism' concerts to protest against the National Front), there had been little sustained interest until the Birmingham collective's response to the widespread fear of attack by black youths in the early 1970s. As a consequence of the way in which they reported the 'Handsworth Case', in which a young black man was given a sentence of twenty years for involvement in a mugging, the media had helped to legitimate heavy policing of the black population by fostering panic. Althusserian theories permitted black working-class culture to be considered even through its discontinuities and non-correspondences with contemporary economic, political and ideological levels. The challenge to the earlier work of cultural studies from feminism also developed in the late 70s. The first ten issues of the Birmingham Centre's *Working Papers* had contained only four articles on issues concerning gender. In 1978, the Women's Studies Group took sole responsibility for the volume, which they entitled, *Women Take Issue*, a 'taking issue' not only with sexism in society and in the Centre, but also taking over the issue of the volume itself. Many of the articles were direct responses to earlier papers: Angela McRobbie's essay 'Working Class Girls and the Culture of Femininity' took the work of Willis and Hebdige to task for failing to address adolescent girls in their studies of youth cultures. Girls, she argued, demonstrated the same oppositionality to school as Willis's lads in *Learning to Labour*, but their resistance to the culture of school merely confirmed their subordination: 'Marriage, family life, fashion and beauty all contribute massively to this feminine anti-school culture and, in doing so, nicely illustrate the contradictions inherent in so-called oppositional activities' (CCCS 1978, 104).[16] One of the earliest projects by the Women's Studies Group, *Images of Women in the Media*, analysed the representations of women in the media: as housewives, mothers, sex objects, career women. But later work would move away from the exclusive interest in media produced by and aimed at men, to the women's magazines, popular romances, television and film melodramas and soap operas aimed specifically at women. Hobson's study of responses to the popular soap opera, *Crossroads*, which focused on life in a motel in the Midlands, developed from Morley's work on the *Nationwide* audience, by placing herself in the living room with the women she was studying and by sympathetically 'chatting' to rather than conducting surveys with them. The domestic context of watching was something which Morley had never consid-ered: 'To watch a programme at meal time with the mother of young children is an entirely different experience from watching with a seventy-two-year-old widow whose day is largely structured around television programmes' (1982, 111).

The decrease in work on class might also be seen as, on one level, a collusion of cultural studies with the prevailing New Right, or Thatcherism. Thatcherism's long years of power (1979–97) were achieved through the capture of the working-class vote by the Conservatives. In a direction which seemed to mirror Labour disap-pointments and the 'new affluence' of the 1950s, working-class voters increasingly evaluated the world in economic, rather than class terms. And, additionally, Thatcherism addressed this constituency in its appeals to non-economic values which they might share with all other classes: the virtue of hard work, the respectability of owning your own home, so-called 'family values' and pride in Britain's status as a world player (as, for example, the Falklands War apparently demonstrated). Thatcherism's trans-class appeals fostered an ideal image of hard-working family life, an image which necessitated traditional gender roles of husband and wife, father and mother. Its appeals also overrode differences between classes in a new English patriotism which defined social cohesion chauvinistically, to the exclusion of foreigners, including those 'within'. Thus women and ethnic minorities became the 'others' of Thatcherism's discourse.

In his introduction to *The Cultural Studies Reader* (1993), Simon During claims that cultural studies was formed by, as much as it attempted to comment upon, Thatcherism. This simultaneity is explained both in terms of the nature of Thatcherism, as in the account above, and in what During terms the relatively 'de-politicised' analyses of cultural studies under the influence of the French theorists Pierre Bourdieu, Michel de Certeau and Michel Foucault. The so-called 'French model' analysed the specificity of social practices within such disparate institutions as school, family, church, peer groups, political parties, work and so on. Each institution, or, in Bourdieu's term, 'field', 'both defines itself against and is suffused by others: for instance, relations in the workplace may be modelled on the family ("paternalism"), though the family is simultaneously a "haven" from work. However, highly rationalized fields (like schools and factories) interact least directly with other fields – they form their own "world"' (During 1993, 11–12). Any one individual will habit a multiplicity of such spheres. In addition, each field contains its own distinctions – cinema-goers, for example, might be casual attenders or film buffs – which are largely self-determined practices, although some fields (such as schools and businesses) will be more deterministic than others. There are more limited forms of behaviour at school, for example, than in the pub. These choices might be ways of accepting routine or social positioning (Bourdieu, for example, showed how members of the working class who were unable to afford certain goods made a virtue of necessity by saying they didn't like them anyway) or of resisting, transforming, even undermining the *status quo*. As representative studies of transgressive practices, During cites

Dyer (1977), Stallybrass and White (1986) and Michel de Certeau (1984). Richard Dyer celebrated the ways in which Hollywood musicals offered possibilities of countering capitalism through their very escapism. Peter Stallybrass and Allon White charted a history of the 'carnivalesque', that moment of bodily pleasure which exceeded all attempts to structure and control it. And Michel de Certeau wrote of how walking in the city was one way in which the controls and rigidities of urban planning were dynamically rewritten. All works of this type explore social and cultural responses and effects such as pleasure, identification, corporeality, fantasy, desire, critique, transgression. This 'French model', like the British-inspired use of Gramscian hegemony, balances the specificity of individual choices with the determination by social structures. But, unlike earlier British cultural studies projects, its implications are that social practices are so heterogeneous and fragmented that no political organisation, which might actively transform the structures themselves, is possible:

> Because it conceives of social fields as 'partially autonomous', the French model cannot affirm a central agency that might direct a number of fields to provide a more equitable distribution of resources. In this, it is remote from traditional social democratic politics. Instead there is a drift to affirm both culture's Utopian force and those forms of resistance ... only possible in the cracks and gaps of the larger, apparently impregnable, system. (During 1993, 12–13)

During's criticisms of what he calls the 'French' model of cultural studies have been taken up by a number of marxist commentators on the cultural studies project as a whole.[17] Cultural studies in the 1990s has continued to flourish – now on a global scale. What has been lost, however, is its political edge. Cultural studies in the 1990s has found resistance and subversion in fantasising, children's toys, playing video games, Madonna fandom, even shopping. Robin Potter, researching Madonna in 1993, found over ten thousand books and researched articles written in English (cited in Davies 1995, 138). John Fiske, for example, has written of how Madonna offered empowerment to young girls with her bravado and unabashed exhibitionism, a powerful female in control of her own sexuality. And by taking the trappings of the brothel (underwear worn as outerwear, lacy gloves, garter belt and stockings) and of the church (the crucifix-necklace, her name) into her public world, Fiske argues, the act of freeing these products from their original context 'signifies the power ... of the subordinate to exert some control over the process of making meanings' (1996, 137). I should have thought, given Madonna's power and success, that 'subordinate', while it might have been true of her temporarily empowered teenage fans, was hardly appropriate for Madonna herself. A similarly premature celebration of popular culture is also evident in Jane Root's study of television viewing, *Open the Box* (1986). In her analysis of the popular 80s game-show, *The Price is Right*, Root talked of the 'spontaneous' and 'natural' pleasure of the studio audience, but her description of the programme seems inconsistent: '*The Price is Right*'s key to producing natural performances is its elaborate physical environment. Bright lights, expensive glittering backdrops, excited warm-up routines and loud music help to nurture a rowdy, uninhibited party atmosphere. Ideally, the participants then forget that they are in the studio' (198–9). That the audience was also being carefully manipulated is presumably too 'marxist' (or 'Frankfurt School-ish') for her study. But these kinds of studies are warped by their continuing resistance to a kind of marxism which seems to exist only as an imaginary opponent, whether that is presumed to be 'vulgar' feminism or the Frankfurt School. And this degree of over-compensation is beginning to seem absurd.[18]

Cultural studies approaches to popular culture have usefully countered many aspects of vulgar marxist approaches to culture. Cultural studies has rescued consumers from the condescension of marxist approaches, by seeing their pleasures as real, rather than as a form of duping by the market and by being alert to the ways in which they approach mass culture critically, rather than passively. They have taught us that reading practices cannot be read off from the conditions of textual production. *Dallas*, for example, was an American television soap opera, designed and marketed as an exclusively financial gesture, and glossily displaying the kinds of lifestyle only available to the wealthiest, and often most ruthless, businessmen (in this case, oil tycoons). But, as Ien Ang's studies discovered (1985) a Dutch marxist and feminist could both enjoy the programme because they read its extreme sexism and advocacy of capitalism as ironic critiques of the very systems it appeared to endorse. And cultural studies has shown how consumerism is more than a merely economic activity, but also involves our desires, aspirations, identities, or our need for consolation or communication. While these have been enabling theories, there has also been a tendency to understand almost all cultural activity as a form of resistance to inequalities of power and possession. Cultural studies all too frequently mimics the consumer capitalism which it claims to analyse and even, surely more wide of the mark, to challenge. The celebration of the subversive pleasures of shopping, for example, certainly excludes those women for whom spending the always-limited housekeeping money is a trial, not an event, and for whom consumer choice just does not exist.[19]

The accusation of theoretical complicity with capitalism was also made of the analyses of Thatcherism by Stuart Hall and his co-editor on *Marxism Today* (1977–91), Martin Jacques, and of the anthology which they co-edited, entitled *New Times: The Changing Face of Politics in the 1990s* (1989).[20] The work of Hall and Jacques, however, remained within marxist paradigms, if only within so-called 'post-marxist' ones, in a way which the vast majority of their contemporary cultural theorists did not. Jessop et al. attacked Hall's Gramscian analysis of Thatcherism, in which Conservative political power was maintained by a revolution in cultural as much as in economic terms, as a form of 'idealism'. Hall's analysis, they argued, had ignored the economic changes brought about by the Thatcher administration, the turn, for example, from manufacturing industry to finance capital. While this was an important corrective to the exclusively cultural focus of Hall's work in the 80s, it was less true of the *New Times* project, in which several of the essays addressed the question of capitalist formations. The vehemence of the attacks suggested that conventional pieties – such as the dominance of economic modes of production and the more trivial concerns of culture – were being destroyed. (Michèle Barrett noted that for classical marxists any serious consideration of ideology is too serious.) But the *New Times* project was at the very least a worthy attempt to address the questions which contemporary society needs marxism to confront. And the complexity of contemporary capitalism entails that few answers can be dogmatic. Paul Gilroy, for example, in his essay in the anthology, refused to label consumerism as a form of exploitation or reified subjectivity. Of course it is both these things, but it also offers potential recuperation. Discussing records and record sleeves, Gilroy writes:

> 'Consumption' is a vague word that trips far too easily off the dismissive tongue. People *use* these images and the music that they enclose for a variety of reasons. For the black user of these images and products, multivariant processes of 'consumption' may express the need

> to belong, the desire to make the beauty of blackness intelligible and
> somehow to fix that beauty and the pleasures it creates so that they
> achieve ... at least a longevity that retrieves them from the world of ...
> racial dispossession. However trivial the black music record sleeve
> may seem to the outsider, it points to a fund of aesthetic and philo-
> sophical folk knowledge which the record as a commodity has been
> made to contain *in addition* to its reified pleasures. (Gilroy 1993, 256)

By the time *New Times* was published, even Jessop and his colleagues
were beginning to admit that ideology was important, as Thatcherism
continued its hegemonic control over Britain. However it is difficult to
see how the poor, the unemployed and the homeless might find such
self-affirmation in consumer culture. Sivanandan, in a chapter entitled 'Thatcherism in drag' (1990), mocked the logic of the consumption theorists in remarking: now we know why the poor in London
sleep in cardboard boxes – because cardboard boxes are a wonderful
way to signify poverty! Cultural self-expression is not only difficult or
impossible for the poor but also largely irrelevant to their real needs.
As Diana Coole has argued: 'Their major preoccupations must lie in
survival; and, beyond this, what they share – and what identifies them
as members of a class – is only the economic plight that statistics and
everyday life monotonously reproduce' (Coole 1996, 21). The poor
can take little pride in so-called 'group identity'.

In the 1990s, cultural studies began attempts to repoliticise its
project. The increased interest in cultural policy studies entailed a
turning towards institutional conditions, and away from the more or
less exclusive concern with textual signification and interpretation
which characterised so much work in the 70s and 80s. Bennett (1992)
and McGuigan (1996), for example, have both examined the museum.
This turn was also generated by a new self-consciousness about the
ways in which cultural studies, in becoming a 'fashionable' discipline,
was in danger of itself becoming reified, commodified. David Morley
(1992), for example, advised that the internationalisation of cultural
studies had led to an emphasis on 'higher levels of abstraction' and
the development of a market for 'theory' which 'travels' well (4). And
John Frow has cautioned against a theoretical blindness which has
made cultural studies unaware of how it has itself contributed to what
it ostensibly only studies: '"Style" becomes a figure of the organic
relation to a community (or an anti-community), rather than of the
simulacral production of authenticity within a highly industrialized

fashion system *to which cultural theory has itself significantly contributed'* (1995, 12; original emphasis). Yet the analysis of structured class inequality remains missing from most cultural studies work. This is a serious failing at a time when the 'Blair' revolution seems to follow the Thatcherite occlusion of social justice and its imperative of the redistribution of wealth. Undoubtedly, something of the theoretical and moral resistance to capitalism which characterised the work of the first cultural studies has been lost.[21] Such nostalgia admittedly must appear rather paradoxical for a chapter which opened with marxist criticisms of the 'new' Left of the 50s and early 60s, but, like Francis Mulhern, we can only turn towards alternative traditions to trace what is missing from the present: '[The] rising tendency in cultural studies gives itself to a certain *anarchoreformism*, permanently giddy in the conviction that micro-subversion is everywhere, in a totality which, at the same time, it is theoretically *passé* to name, let alone seek to dismantle' (Mulhern 1996, 36).

The question of popular culture

'Beating popular fiction over the head with the three volumes of *Capital* is, politically, beside the point; what is needed are terms of theorization which will enable writers and critics to intervene, in a strategically calculated way, *within* the processes of popular reading and writing.' (Bennett, in Mulhern 1992, 206)

'In place of a theory of value, ... Marxism's concern should be with the analysis of "the ideological conditions of the social *contestation* of value". So far as the *making* of evaluations is concerned, this is a matter for strategic calculation – a question of politics and not of aesthetics.' (Bennett in Mulhern 1992, 200)

In the introduction to *The Politics and Poetics of Transgression*, Stallybrass and White discuss how the idea of the 'classic author' was derived from ancient taxation categories. When Aulus Gellius (c.123–c.165) divided citizens according to their property qualifications, those of the first taxation category came to be known as *classici*, as distinguished from the commonality (*proletarius*). That such an explicitly economic status should inform later ideas of writing, by which the most esteemed authors become known as 'classic', is not a surprising one for cultural studies. For cultural studies, more than any other approach, has called the ways in which we define the 'literary' into question and revealed the kinds of ideological power which are exercised when we discriminate between the 'great traditions' of literature and the literature which is produced for a mass market: bestselling genres such as romance fiction, spy thrillers, comics. Feminist approaches to literature have also called our definitions of 'Literature' into question, since so many of these definitions included few, if any, women writers, with the possible exception of Jane Austen, George Eliot and Virginia Woolf, who then figure as exceptional figures rather than, as cultural history reveals, commonplace. But it is cultural studies which has made the study of popular formations an established academic discipline and has transformed the ways in which we study and teach literature. The growing popularity of such genres as the gothic, science-fiction and detective fiction in university syllabi is an indication of this. (Marie Corelli's novel, *The Sorrows of Satan*, 1895, which sold seventy thousand copies in its first two months of publication and went to thirty-seven editions in its first three years, has been reissued by Oxford World's Classics, for example.)

Cultural studies' recuperation of the popular began as a quarrel, not only with the Leavisite or Arnoldian canons, but also with those tendencies within marxist literary theories to collude with such canon formation. Tony Bennett, for example, has argued that marxist approaches often saw 'Literature', however variously the best literature might be defined within the parameters of 'high' culture, as escaping ideological deformation while popular literature was viewed as ideological. But in doing so, marxists abandoned popular culture as a possible field of struggle. Bennett's target here was largely the Frankfurt School, and especially the chapter on the 'culture industry' in Adorno and Horkheimer's *The Dialectic of Enlightenment*. Many in the Frankfurt School argued that, although high culture is both elitist and delusory as a would-be transcendental domain, at least its transcendence promises a non-alienated alternative to commodification.[22] In contrast to this position we might cite the increasing affirmation of popular culture by postmodern theories, in which the power of the culture industries is not seen as equal to their influence, and the ideological messages of mass culture are resisted as much as consented to. If, as Jurij Lotman and Umberto Eco have argued, the distinction between popular/mass art and modernist/high art is that of seriality as opposed to innovation, then postmodern culture with its own celebration of iteration and repetition is in a position to valorise and enjoy popular/mass art (see Frow 1995, 21–2). The erosion between 'high' and 'low' culture can be dated long before postmodernism however: Anthony Trollope, for example, thought of his novel-writing as a trade, the eighteenth-century theatre offered productions of operas by Handel and rope-dancing feats, versions of classical tragedy and pantomime farces, often on the same evening.

The ostensible polarity between the 'high modernism' of the Frankfurt School and the 'populism' of postmodernism has also obscured the differences within these camps and their very different contexts. The Frankfurt School's experience of exile in America during the Second World War, or the ways in which the chapter on the culture industry from *The Dialectic* has been read in isolation, for example, might explain why the polarity between modernists and postmodernists has been rather caricatured. Recent studies, and Adorno's own later work, suggest that Adorno's position as a European elitist has been exaggerated.[23] Adorno's criticisms of Wagner, for example, suggest that even before going to America, he did not associate 'bad' mass culture exclusively with American popular culture. Adorno's argument was rather that in an age of industrial capitalism high culture and mass culture are entwined and ultimately inseparable because they are rooted in the same social conditions. This undoes the binary opposition between 'high' and 'low' culture. Indeed, in the late twentieth century, works of 'high' culture are produced in exactly the same serial forms as 'low' culture (the paperback, television, compact disc, film). And the 'high' arts – opera, ballet and art exhibitions – are increasingly sponsored by corporate business in a way which openly undermines the 'autonomy' of culture. In 1996, for example, the Museum of Modern Art in Oxford held an exhibition of contemporary British painting with the title: 'Ab*so*lut Vision', playing on the words 'About', 'Absolute' and 'Absolut' (a brand of vodka). One painting in the exhibition was specially commissioned by Absolut vodka – Chris Ofili's painting 'Imported' included an image of their brand of vodka bottle. 'Sponsorship' is evidently equivalent to advertising. (See Wu 1998.) Jameson's argument that Adorno's cultural pessimism was anticipatory seems correct in such a context.

Adorno's argument, however, does refuse popular culture as a possible site of freedom. In contrast to Adorno, Bloch found emancipatory aspects in mass culture (shop windows, best-selling novels, fashion, magazines, film), and Lefebvre in 1950s Paris argued that everyday life is a proper site of critical interrogation. These marxist traditions are picked up by Jameson. For example, in his essay 'Reification and Utopia in Mass Culture', Jameson reads such popular Hollywood films as *Jaws* and *The Godfather* as both ideological and emancipatory. The fascination with the Mafia, for example, mystifies the ways in which the deterioration of contemporary life is an economic, not a moral issue, suggesting that it is the dishonesty of gangsters rather than the profit motive of corporate business which has led to American unhappiness. But in the image of the (albeit Mafia) family itself, of communal solidarity, the film presents a utopian image of collectivity. Similarly *Jaws* is seen ultimately to contain the potentially transgressive fears and desires of the audience (the shark, for example, might embody nature confronting the advanced, artificial culture of America; or disruptive sexuality threatening family values; or corporate businesses threatening communities). But the film also permits utopian images of family and of communal solidarity. Jameson's recuperation of these Hollywood films is then a deliberately partial one: 'works of mass culture cannot be ideological without at one and the same time being implicitly or explicitly Utopian as well: they cannot manipulate unless they offer some genuine shred of content as a fantasy bribe to the public about to be so manipulated' (1979, 144). This argument continues the Frankfurt School position of seeing mass audiences as cultural dupes, while, by rhetorical sleight of hand, turning this to advantage. And undoubtedly, something of the films is being lost in such readings: the ways in which the Mafia in the first two *Godfather* films is shown to be formed out of racial and class discriminations against the Italian-American community, for example.

Jameson's characterisation of 'mass culture' as the dialectical opposite of 'modernism' also attempts to refuse the problem of valuation, replacing subjective judgement with the polarisation of mass and modernist art as 'an objective contradiction which has its own social grounding' (1979, 14). But it also holds modernism and contemporary mass culture in place, as separate, homogeneous blocks. The study of popular culture is always more than an expansion of the 'canon', in which silenced voices from the past, or contemporary popular experiences are incorporated into syllabi as necessary additions. The recuperation of popular culture is not only a celebration of those genres previously derided, but a transformation in the ways in which we approach 'high' culture itself. Popular culture is not intrinsically radical, but its study has a radicalising effect insofar as it can reveal constructions of 'high' literature as a form of cultural power and exclusion.[24] Cultural studies has also revealed the ironies in such canon formation, as 'high' literature has constantly drawn upon popular narratives such as the adventure story, the melodrama and the romance to restore vitality. The 'division' between high and low cultures is permeable, ambiguous and often transgressed, the line between the 'refined' and the 'popular' often blurred. The novels which we now study as among the first of their kind, such as Defoe's *Robinson Crusoe* and *Moll Flanders*, developed out of a flourishing popular culture of travel narratives and prison memoirs. The classical composer Haydn drew upon popular song in his arrangement of Scottish folk songs, while eighteenth-century chapbooks, those cheap, unbound editions, published not only popular tales but also polite novels and classical stories. The Victorian three-decker novel or the Victorian novel serialised in magazine form shares the same kind of plot-twists and narrative suspensions as the *X Files* television programme. As Stallybrass and White have argued, 'high' and 'low' are interrelating and dependent categories. Because 'low' culture is both reviled and desired, it becomes part of 'high culture', its fanta-sised 'other'. (Stallybrass and White conclude their study with a discussion of the way in which popular culture as an object of study – including their own book – reveals the desires and guilt of bourgeois academics and students.)

Thus the study of popular culture calls into question the ways in which we define and isolate 'high' culture, striking at the heart of arguments concerning literary 'value'. Chapter 2 has already suggested that the criteria by which we decide aesthetic 'value' are inevitably ideological. We need to remember that such criteria not only change continually, but are frequently motivated by extra-aesthetic concerns. Milton's poetry, for example, is inescapably the work of a committed republican who lived through one of the most turbulent periods of English history, through the experience of England's only regicide and republican government. But in the first decades of this century, Milton's poetry was derided, as the meta-physical poetry of Donne – complex, highly figurative, ostensibly a-political – was fêted, most famously by T.S. Eliot. While Eliot sometimes made the source of his 'aesthetic' judgements clear (he admitted, for example, that he found the ideas of Shelley 'repellent'), political disagreements were frequently passed off as purely 'aesthetic' concerns. We should remember that ideas of 'literary taste' were first developed in the eighteenth century in which the marginalisation of such popular cultural forms as ballads, folktales, woodcuts and seasonal festivals developed simultaneously with the development of a less courtly, more commercial culture in which the theatre, music, literature and painting were given a special collective identity and judged according to the prescriptions of 'good taste'. Countless pamphlets, essays and books attempted to decide the nature of 'taste' and the inconsistencies among them reveal something of the ambivalences within which we still work. If taste was a matter of feeling, then it was potentially available to everyone. Francis Hutcheson, in *Inquiry into the Original of our Ideas of Beauty and Virtue* (1725), argued that an appreciation of beauty did not require a specialised knowledge. But while the 'sociable man' of Addison and Steele's *Spectator*, for example, suggested that taste was determined by personal qualities rather than rank, the language used simultaneously suggested that it was not a quality found among rural peasants or the urban poor, most of whom lacked the wealth, leisure and literacy to enjoy aesthetic pleasures. A refined appreciation of art was also a disinterested one, but, as Addison made clear, disinterest was the product only of leisure and wealth: 'A Man of Polite Imagination is let into a great many Pleasures that the Vulgar are not capable of receiving. He can converse with a picture, and find an agreeable companion in a Statue' (*The Spectator*, 21 June 1712). While financial independence was not itself a guarantee of good taste, it certainly made good taste possible in the first place.

Robert Young (1996) has argued that Stallybrass and White shift between the categories of social division (bourgeois v. lower classes, for example) and the categories of cultural division (the refined v. the philistine, polite v. vulgar, civilised v. savage). But the history of the formation of 'taste' in the eighteenth century indicates that class and cultural divisions were often synonymous. Whether they remain so has been the subject of recent debates. John Frow has argued that high culture is now tied to an educational elite, or 'knowledge class' which possesses cultural capital, and to which intellectuals (including cultural studies researchers) inevitably belong. He calls for a recognition of the ways in which we – researchers and students – are endowed with specific class interests which are ultimately institutional. This does not mean that we should disparage the cultural capital we possess, but that we should recognise it as both an 'instrument of knowing (and in that sense *potentially* universal), and an instrument of class distinction' (1995, 168). In an ongoing debate in *The New Left Review*, Beech and Roberts have argued that contemporary marxist theory is marked by a blindness to cultural division. While the aesthetic is celebrated as a semi-autonomous sphere in which social division can be critiqued, in what Beech and Roberts argue is a misreading of Adorno, the cultural division within which the critic herself is implicated is ignored. Thus the most pressing question for them is: 'can the promises of aesthetics be made good in a divided culture?' (1996, 117).[25] Their theory of the 'philistine' and their valorisation of 'modes of philistine attention' are attempts to escape the impasse of current debates between marxist critical and cultural theories, in which the consumers of mass culture are seen as either dupes or radicals. This, according to Robert Young, is the 'double bind' for a leftist critic:

> On the one hand, a high cultural aesthetic or formalism eschews the vulgarity of the outside, a means of establishing bourgeois identity and of identifying the institution with its values in opposition to the vulgar world outside. On the other hand, those on the left who challenge this, and regard the outside with fascination and nostalgia and seek to turn it into their object of study are, according to Stallybrass and White, merely indulging in a fetishization of the excluded other – a form of hysterical eroticization. (1996, 13–14)[26]

Neither Beech and Roberts, Robert Young, nor John Frow claim to be able to resolve this contradiction, but their work is part of the ongoing immanent critiques within marxist approaches to culture. Ultimately, value-judgements are inevitable and they will continue to be implicated within power relations and inequalities which are often constituted elsewhere. However we can situate our value-judgements within an awareness of the debates of valorisation and counter-valorisation and the arguments concerning their motivations. Tony Bennett, in an article written in advance of many of these debates, argues for this qualified solution ('Marxism and Popular Fiction', 1981; reprinted in Mulhern 1992). To claim that Joyce's prose fiction opened up new possibilities for language in a way that the novels of Conan Doyle did not, to privilege one over the other for this reason is, he argues, to situate them within a scale of values which the critic, not the texts, brings to bear on that judgement. Value is not a property of the text alone: 'Texts do not *have* value; they can only *be valued*' (in Mulhern 1992, 295). The question we need to pose is not which is the more valuable, but 'valuable *to whom* and *in what conditions*?'. And these questions are invariably extra-textual, often residing in formulations of 'taste', or of the cultural capital which marks its possessors as those-who-might-posit value. Marxist approaches to literature and culture have not always been nearly as self-reflexive on this point as they ought to have been. But the debates between marxist critical and cultural theory, and the debates within cultural studies, suggest that marxist approaches are continuing, but also adapting. And while relatively few critics today identify their work as marxist, so long as the practice of cultural studies includes a consideration of the deleterious, as well as the potentially enabling aspects of culture as an industry, the link with marxism remains as an informing tradition.

The simultaneous distance from and incorporation within marxism makes cultural studies appear as a form of 'post-marxism' before the adoption of this term by Laclau and Mouffe in 1978. The history of cultural studies as a discipline not only reflects movements in marxist aesthetic theories in Britain since 1950, but the project of cultural studies itself has also shaped these movements. The relationship between cultural studies and marxism has thus always been a somewhat ambivalent one. Today, the greatest part of cultural studies has lost any marxist dynamics it might once have had, particularly as the currently popular studies of everyday life, of the subjectivities of race, gender and sexuality, and of popular culture, begin to omit considerations of class inequality or any critique of capitalist consumerism. But despite and even because of such occlusions, cultural studies remains of especial interest for contemporary marxist theories, for it is in cultural studies that the attempted hybrids of marxism have been forged, crossing marxism with psychoanalysis, feminism, postcolonialism, semiotics, poststructuralism and postmodernism. Last and not least of these reasons is the now global spread of cultural studies as an academic discipline, a growth which has kept marxist concerns as part of current debates and has introduced marxist theories to a new generation of cultural studies, 'communications' or media students at a time when the easiest, and intellectually laziest option is to write off marxism after the demise of Soviet communism in 1989.

Notes

1. See, for example, Lovell's definition of the 'use-value' of a commodity as 'the ability of the commodity to satisfy some human want' which, according to Marx, 'may spring from the stomach or from the fancy'. 'The use-value of a commodity is realised only when it is consumed, or used' (1980, 57).

2. For histories of cultural studies see Turner (1990); During (1993, introduction); Brantlinger (1990); Dworkin (1997); Steele (1997). Of these, only Steele diverges from the traditional account which I summarise below. See also notes 3 and 4 below.

3. Bill Schwarz, writing in 1994, professes himself to be 'astonished by the volume of surveys flowing from the presses' (1994, 390) and suggests that this proliferation represents an attempt to establish 'a myth of origins which eases the journey of cultural studies into the academy' (381). Paul Jones mocks the ways in which these histories have created a canon of cultural studies texts in which the founding fathers are Raymond Williams and Richard Hoggart in an essay entitled 'The myth of "Raymond Hoggart"' (1994).

4. See Williams (1996, 154–5). Christine Geraghty (1996, 352 n.3) also suggests earlier antecedents, such as Humphrey Jenning's documentary *Spare Time* (1939) in which working-class communities are observed through the integration of industry and culture, and other formations, such as the growth of paperback printing in Britain, which allowed *The Uses of Literacy* to become a best seller to 'those middle classes whose contradictions it addressed'. Jon Stratton and Ien Ang question conventional histories of cultural studies: see Morley and Chen (1996, 361–91). Like Williams, Hall has refused the authority of 'founding father' which many commentators have bequeathed to him (see Morley and Chen 1996, 263) and argued that the experience of immigration in post-war Britain was as formative as the anti-Statism of the New Left. An alternative history of cultural studies could be sketched through the work of Lefebvre, particularly his *Critique of Everyday Life* (1947; 1958).

5. Dworkin argues that T.S. Eliot and Leavis were both influences on early cultural studies: Eliot, ironically, could be said to have anticipated the study of popular culture in his expansive definition of culture beyond the literary and the artistic. However Eliot's definition was of a culture defined and disseminated by an elite, a culture 'from above'. Dworkin also argues that for Leavis, the marxists were not radical enough: 'For Leavis and *Scrutiny*, the roots of the contemporary social crisis were not material but spiritual and cultural' (81). There appears to be a notice-

able defence of Leavis gathering ground: see also David Simpson's view that 'Leavisism ... was not so much an incarnation as an expiring simplification of Leavis's own critique, soon domesticated from its angry beginnings into a lazier form of assumed common sense' (in Prendergast 1995, 32).

6. Stuart Hall, 'In the No Man's Land' in *Universities and Left Review* 3 (Winter, 1958): 87. Quoted in Dworkin (1997, 60).

7. Hall discusses Thompson's *The Making of the English Working Class* as a third 'founding' text for cultural studies. I have not discussed Thompson in this way due to the brevity of this account, and also so as to stress the formation of cultural studies out of literary criticism, both an enabling and disabling formation.

8. Adorno, Goldmann, Lukács and Galvano Della Volpe were all concerned with the relations between culture and society, while Sebastiano Timpanaro, Lucio Colletti and Karl Korsch also contributed to the debates on marxism.

9. Hall argues that the (structuralist) work of Lévi-Strauss has been under-estimated in most accounts. I have omitted Lévi-Strauss because, despite his claim that he is working within marxist paradigms, he is not conventionally recognised as belonging to the marxist tradition which I outline in this book. This, of course, is a deeply unsatisfactory rationale, but one dictated by the parameters of this study.

10. More recently Mulvey has revised this essay, in arguing that the woman screen-watcher oscillates between masculine and feminine positions of spectatorship and identification, restless in her 'transvestite clothes' (1990, 35).

11. See also Hall's essay in Eagleton (1990): 'The indissolubility of practices in the ways in which they are experienced and "lived", in any real historical situation, does not in any way pre-empt the *analytic* separa-tion of them, when one is attempting to theorize their different effects. The ways in which everything appears to interconnect in "experience" can only be a starting point for analysis. One has to "produce the concrete in thought" – that is, show, by a series of analytic approxima-tions through abstraction, the concrete historical experience as the "product of many determinations"' (62).

12. Compare, however, Steedman's celebration of Thompson's angry attack on Althusser in *The Poverty of Theory*: 'not only an attack ... but also a staging of the writer's exasperation, by means of hyperbolic self-dramatisation. Moreover – perhaps – Thompson knowingly puts you in the position of delicious uncertainty, of never being able to make up your mind between his honest anger and his baroque performance of it' (Steedman 1997, 26).

13. For the Centre's reply see Chambers et al. (1977–8).

14. Morley's study was inspired by Hall's essay 'Encoding/Decoding' (reprinted in During 1993) in which the production of meaning ('encoding') is theorised as the interpretation which is 'structured in dominance', but which does not prevent the reception of the meaning ('decoding') from escaping this attempted control, and even from being multiple or polysemic, even though its limits are set by the dominant definition, or 'encoding' process. This essay was influenced by Vološinov's argument that the linguistic sign was a site of struggle, of negotiation (see Chapter 1) and by Gramsci's theory of hegemony as ideological struggle (see Chapter 2).

15. Brantlinger links this work with Barthes's project in *Mythologies* of exposing the class basis of the seemingly 'universal' bourgeois ideology of capitalism. Barthes's influence on cultural studies – like that of Lévi-Strauss – has been omitted from this chapter, even though both identified themselves as working within marxist paradigms.

16. For a later critique of Willis, Hebdige et al., see McRobbie (1980).

17. See, for example, Frow's criticisms of Bourdieu and Certeau (1995, 16–59): 'Both tend to fix an essential domain of the popular, without ever specifying its institutional characteristics; both work with a top-down model of social domination; and both tend to slight the complexities of the relations of the class (or class fraction) of intellectuals to "high" culture and to "popular" culture' (60).

18. See Morris (1996) for the argument that cultural studies has caricatured marxism to justify its own practices.

19. Meaghan Morris's discussion of shopping is an exception to this because it asks such questions (1993). For critiques of what During calls 'cultural populism' in cultural studies, see David Harris (1992), who argues that cultural studies has transformed itself from a theory of the politics of ideology to the politics of pleasure (which he explains as being a consequence of a partial reading of Gramsci, one which denies his attempt to radicalise the working class); Steven Connor has countered the tendency in cultural studies to read rock music as necessarily liberalising (1989, 189–90); and Meaghan Morris has rebuked the 'voxpop style of cultural studies ... offering us the sanitized world of a deodorant commercial where there's always a way to redemption' (1996, 161). See also the section on 'The Politics of the Popular' in Storey (1994), especially Schudson, Webster and McGuigan.

20. For attacks on Hall's earlier work on Thatcherism see Jessop et al. and on the *New Times* anthology, Frith and Savage – all published in the *New Left Review*. And compare Leys's defence of Hall's emphasis on culture rather than political economy (1990).

21. Colin Sparks (in Morley and Chen 1996) argues that direct engagement between cultural studies and marxism lasted only around twenty years. His article discusses the ways in which the work of Williams and Thompson continued an engagement with the concerns of marxist socialism, but his designation of early cultural studies as 'Before Marxism', and of Hall's engagement with Laclau as 'the road from Marx', threatens to collapse 'marxism' into one, in this case, Althusserian strand. Sparks offers many criticisms of Althusserianism and pays homage to a receptivity to strands of marxism – 'The category of "marxism" is an extremely broad one, and there is little point or profit in trying to decide whether someone can legitimately claim to be "marxist" or not' (95) – but the impulse of his essay implies such a narrow definition that cultural studies is doomed to be excluded from it.
22. See, for example, Herbert Marcuse, 'The Affirmative Character of Culture' (1937; 1968).
23. See Adorno (1975) and, countering the argument that Adorno was resistant to new forms of technology, Levin (1990).
24. However, this is increasingly less true of contemporary art. See Schwarz (1989, 254–5) and Frow (1995, 25): 'for consumers of "low" culture the sense of illegitimacy or of cultural inferiority that characterized previous regimes of value has now largely dissipated' (25).
25. For continuations of this debate, see Bull (1996), Bowie (1997), Bernstein (1997), and Beech and Roberts (1998).
26. See also Gary Hall (1996) for an extended discussion of the position of the academic critic regarding popular culture.

Part II

Applications and Readings

Marxist Readings

While marxist theoretical debates continue to flourish today, especially with the identification of a new tradition of 'post-marxism', marxist readings of literature and culture are becoming less common. Partly this is because many contemporary marxist readings are transversed by the issues of gender and race (as, for example, in the work of Laura Brown or Patrick Brantlinger, and in Eagleton's increasing turn towards Irish writing), so that they might just as easily be defined as 'feminist' or 'postcolonial'. Additionally, marxism as the theoretical inspiration for readings often remains implicit (one example would be Regenia Gagnier's work on Oscar Wilde). While I regret this absence of marxist readings, since I believe that such issues as social class are still central to our work, I would also argue that it is an indication of marxism's surprising flexibility – 'surprising' because marxism as a practice is so usually associated with deterministic, pre-programmed readings and responses.

Marxism in itself is not a method of reading, however, but a body of economic and political theories. Eve Tavor Bannet has argued that culture will always be overdetermined by other issues and assumptions in marxist cultural studies, that '[i]n the marxist paradigm, discourse on literature is grafted *post festum* onto a dense and well developed body of theories about knowledge, culture, society, politics, history, language and "man"' (1993, 4). But this need not be a failing in marxist approaches to literature and culture, if culture's own specificity, its own mode of working and even its own partial autonomy from these contexts are simultaneously acknowledged. This combination – of political commitment (and the firmly held beliefs about society which are part of that commitment) and respect for the text's own identity – would create an ideal marxist reading. And most marxist readings, my own included, do not always succeed in this ambitious, but ideal, combination. However, marxist literary and cultural theories at least do not entail set assumptions about ways of reading, or even about the answers which such readings might provide. The extraordinary diversity of marxist arguments about literature and culture is an indication of this. Marxism does present assumptions about what texts are studied: my choice of the lower-class poet Mary Leapor is already an obviously marxist one, for example. Marxism does dictate the ethical priorities in coming to a text: there is an automatic loyalty to the labouring-class poets rather than to their patrons. And marxism does predetermine the kinds of questions we might ask of a cultural or literary text: what is the relationship between Wilde's aestheticist novel *The Picture of Dorian Gray* or Jane Austen's fiction, and their contexts? But other marxist approaches could read these texts differently, and even suggest different answers to marxism's questions.

This is partly because cultural texts themselves can highlight problems with 'theory'. It is not the case that we might sufficiently refine the 'theory' until applying it was a simple matter of using it to produce an answer. Applications often raise as many questions as they seek to answer. Those theoretical approaches which find in the text what they were looking for are merely self-validating. In his book in this series, John Brannigan (1998) has argued that this is true of most new historicist readings, but it is also true of 'vulgar' uses of all theories (using poststructuralist readings merely to confirm indeterminacy, for example) since literary texts are not reducible to the kinds of questions we pose of them. Many marxist readings are more 'vulgar' than the theories which inspire them, because of an inherent difficulty in taking the subtlety and complexity of the best theory into reading practices. Marxist readings are always concerned with the connections between, for example, literature and the non-literary. While marxist theories of society and history ideally gesture towards ever greater complexity, marxist readings probe literary texts which are both part of and apart from society. Literary texts are discrete from society, in that they have their own, 'aesthetic' modes of being, but they are also necessarily implicated within society. The difficulty in marxist readings of literary texts is one of the relationship between the part (the text) and the whole (society), for to read the text as a microcosm of society is to 'reduce' the text to society, but to read the text interpretatively, 'on its own terms', is to reduce society to the text.

Many marxists have addressed just this question in both their readings and their theories. John Barrell, in his readings of Shakespeare, Milton, Clare and other poets (1988), successfully unites the kinds of close reading we associate with formalism and practical criticism with the materialist and political concerns of marxism and feminism. In *The Ideology of the Aesthetic*, Eagleton discusses Benjamin's 'constellatory epistemology' as an attempt to grasp the concrete in all its particularity and abstractness, to combine the empirical and the conceptual (see 1990, 328–39).[1] Adorno's writings argued that aesthetic form is immanently social, but that social factors do not explain away aesthetic form. And in his reading of Conrad, Jameson attempts to combine heuristic with deductive procedures (1983, 206–80). He refutes the idea that historical subtext is 'extrinsic' to the text, something which he, not the text, brings to bear upon it. Instead his 'formal' analysis is defined as 'contextual', a definition we think of as paradoxical only because such theoretical strategies have tended to be situated as oppositional to one another. Formal patterns in the work are read as symbolic enactments of the social within the formal (77). His initial approach to the work is an immanent, heuristic description of its formal and structural properties. He begins, for example, with the impressionistic style of *Lord Jim* and *Nostromo*, the ways in which it foregrounds sensory perceptions:

> Everywhere there were long shadows lying on the hills, on the roads, on the unclosed fields of olive trees; the shadows of poplars, of wide chestnuts, of farm buildings, of stone walls; and in mid-air the sound of a bell, thin and alert, was like the throbbing pulse of the sunset glow. (Conrad 1963, 63)

But his reading is also deductive insofar as its hunt for formal contradictions is motivated by its aim of transcending the purely formalistic, its ultimate intention to relate these contradictions to history as the subtext of the work. For Jameson, capitalism's privileging of rationality entailed that sense perception was divorced from an increasingly abstract rationalism. Conrad's impressionism is then understood as both a consequence of this reification and a strategy by which his novels resist it.

Jameson's argument is also that a marxist reading is not merely contemplative, but makes a difference to the object of study. My own claims for the readings which follow are certainly more modest. While cultural study certainly has implications for political change, and might even be said to intervene, to have some effect on the world beyond the academy, it is also limited in what it might achieve. The retrieval of working-class voices from the past – as in the first of the readings here – undoubtedly helps us to understand the periods in which they lived and wrote. But it is of little use to today's exploited. But to stop such marxist endeavours as the recuperation of popular culture would be to enable dominant, hegemonic constructions of both culture and history to remain uncontested. And to stop marxist readings of such canonical authors as Austen and Wilde would be to concede to other, often more conservative modes of interpretation. Ultimately these chapters might also fail to balance contextual imperative with textual and interpretative specificity. It is for the readers of *this* book to decide whether these readings are too 'deterministic' in their use of context or excessively formalistic. I have attempted to be self-reflexive in the conclusions of each chapter, where potential problems with the readings adopted are suggested. Often these concern the questions of gender or sexuality and the ways in which a narrowly marxist approach might fail to address such issues, although a properly marxist approach should call the separation of 'marxism', 'feminism', 'postcolonialism' and so on into question.

These readings do not aim to provide a model ('here's-how-to-do-it'), because there is no such thing as a 'properly' marxist analysis of culture. What these readings do show, however, is an interaction between marxist concerns and cultural texts, and how this interaction ought to preserve the integrity of both theory and text, without making the text subservient to the theory or vice versa. Complex literary texts will always appear excessive, as no reading can ever exhaust the text's possibilities. Ultimately the literary text is not reducible to the kinds of questions we ask of it. But a recognition of this, as Martin Ryle has suggested, 'reminds us of the relativity of our definition of what matters' (1988, 25). And marxism is, at the very least, a situated knowledge which is more ready to acknowledge its own positioning than other theoretical approaches.

Notes

1.   See also Marx's discussion of the concrete and the abstract in the introduction to *Grundrisse* (Marx 1973, 100ff.).

5 A Labouring Woman Poet in the Age of Pope: Mary Leapor's 'Crumble-Hall' (1751)

'No one is more susceptible to the charms of the gentry's life than the
historian of the eighteenth century. His major sources are in the
archives of the gentry or aristocracy. Perhaps he may even find some
of his sources still in the muniments room at an ancient landed seat.
The historian can easily identify with his sources: he sees himself
riding to hounds, or attending Quarter Sessions, or (if he is less ambitious) he sees himself as at least seated at Parson Woodforde's groan-
ing table. The "labouring poor" did not leave their workhouses
stashed with documents for historians to work over nor do they invite
identification with their back-breaking toil.'
(Thompson 1993, 17–18)

In her study of popular culture, Morag Shiach traces the emergence of
this concept to the 1730s and the appearance then of distinctive ways
of talking about the cultural role and significance of the people. In
1730, the eighteenth-century tradition of lower-class writing can be
said to begin with the publication of *The Thresher's Labour* by
Stephen Duck, a Wiltshire farm worker. This first volume of poetry ran
to ten editions in 1730 and was read by Queen Caroline, who quickly
transformed the 'thresher' into the keeper of her library at Richmond.
Queen Caroline could hardly be considered an advocate for the arts:
German by birth, she spoke French with her family and never had
more than a limited command of English. But, as E.P. Thompson
remarks in his introduction to a modern edition of Duck, 'she was a
good judge of the gestures of patronage, at a time when ostentatious
liberality was part of the necessary public image of the great' (1989,
vi). The list of subscribers at the front of the 1736 edition of Duck's

collection, *Poems on Several Occasions,* was headed by His Royal Highness, the Prince of Wales, and included four princesses, 17 dukes and duchesses, 43 countesses, earls, marquises and viscounts, the archbishops of Canterbury and York, and eight other bishops, three Lord Chief Justices, the Master of the Rolls, Sir Robert Walpole, the Speaker of the House of Commons, the Recorder of the City of London, 39 Ladies, 37 Lords, a multitude of baronets, gentry and clergy, and even a few humble mortals, including Alexander Pope and Jonathan Swift. But, as even this introduction to Duck suggests, the discourse of popular culture is a product of talking *about* popular culture, rather than of speaking from within it. For, as Shiach notes, the discourse of popular culture reveals as much, if not more, about the state of the dominant culture than it does about its ostensible object.

Patronising plebeian poets

One of the most striking aspects of eighteenth-century society is the apparent gulf between plebeian culture and the classical culture required of educated men. In E.P. Thompson's analysis this is largely a consequence of the 'gravitational pull' of the extremes of wealth and poverty, as the middling classes were absorbed into the upper by relations of clientage and dependency, in short by their 'aspirant' status (1993, 56).[1] But in our literary histories the apparent gulf between 'high' and 'popular' culture may also be a result of the peculiarly 'Romanticist' nature of our studies of eighteenth-century culture, the way in which we read eighteenth-century literature through the prism of Romanticism.[2] And this might explain why we have forgotten the tradition of eighteenth-century lower-class writing. Traditionally it is with Rousseau, and the increasing dominance of 'Romantic' modes of feeling, that we associate the increasing interest in nature, the valorisation of untrained spontaneity, and the fascination with the 'primitive', the uncivilised, 'natural' man, in which the peasant and 'his' special relationship with the land is celebrated. And all of these we identify with Wordsworth's poetic manifesto, the 'Preface' to *Lyrical Ballads,* in which he outlines his advocacy of the 'language of low and rustic life'.[3] Yet the eighteenth century also witnessed the fêting of numerous lower-class poets, of whom Duck is only the first. Between 1730 and 1820 the following poets published work: Stephen Duck (farm worker), Robert Dodsley (weaver), Robert Tatersal (bricklayer), Mary Masters (uneducated), Mary Collier (a laundress and occasional field hand), Mary Leapor (daughter of a gardener, she worked for a time in the kitchen of an estate), William Falconer (sailor), Phillis Wheatley (black slave), Susannah Harrison (domestic servant), Robert Burns (son of a peasant or 'cottar', he worked for a time as a farmer), John Bryant (tobacco-pipe maker), Ann Yearsley (milkmaid, described by Hannah More as 'a Milker of Cows, and a feeder of Hogs, who has never even *seen* a Dictionary'), James Woodhouse (the 'shoe-maker poet'), Robert Bloomfield (farm labourer), Ann More Candler ('Suffolk cottager'), Elizabeth Bentley (daughter of a journeyman cordwainer), Elizabeth Hands (domestic servant, later wife of a black-smith), Janet Little ('the Scotch milkmaid') and John Clare (peasant). And this list includes only those poets increasingly familiar in eighteenth-century studies.[4]

Listing such poets is a reminder that the cult of the primitive did not originate with Rousseau and that the supposedly 'Romantic' qualities of spontaneity and artlessness were celebrated as early as the 1730s and 1740s.[5] Not only did all of these poets publish their work, but their publications advertised their lower-class origins. John Bancks's volume of poetry was entitled *The Weaver's Miscellany* (1730) and Robert Tatersal's *The Bricklayer's Miscellany* (1734), for example. While the celebration of the 'natural', untaught genius enabled many of these poets to publish, ensuring as it did subscribers for prospective volumes, this fêting was undoubtedly double-edged: lower-class writers achieved a popularity unprecedented until this time, but at the risk of fetishising their relative poverty. These poets were 'patronised' – supported and humiliated – simultaneously.[6] To find signs of intelligence in working people anything other than ordinary is an insult, and one obviously felt by James Woodhouse:

> As tutor'd Bears are led from place, to place,
> Displaying biped gait, and burlesque grace;
> Their action clumsey, and their shape uncouth,
> While grunting bagpipe greets the gaping youth ...
> So was he sent the twofold City through,
> For Cits, like Swains, are pleas'd with something new,
> That each Subscriber's eyes might freely range,
> O'er Clown, so clever! Spectacle, so strange! (See Greene 1993, 161)

Woodhouse's poem demonstrates how 'peasant' poets had to perform and how humiliating and deceptive that role was.[7] They had to maintain a delicate position somewhere between illiteracy and learning, indigence and wealth, for to be raised to a status seemingly above themselves would be to destroy their status as 'labouring poets', often the very reason why they were so fêted. Thus the capitalist aspects of print culture invoked the dilemma of the lower-class poet. She needed patronage in order to publish, but she needed to benefit from print just enough to maintain her current status. This dilemma was most clearly exemplified in the acrimonious relationship between Ann Yearsley and her principal patron, Hannah More. In a prefatory letter to Yearsley's *Poems* More wrote:

> It is not intended to place her in such a state of independence as might reduce her to devote her time to the idleness of Poetry. I hope that she is convinced that the making of verses is not the great business of human life; and that, as a wife and a mother, she has duties to fill, the smallest of which is of more value than the finest verses she can write: but as it has pleased God to give her these talents, may they not be made an instrument to mend her situation, if we publish a small volume of her Poems by subscription? . . . it is not fame, but bread, which I am anxious to secure for her. (Quoted in Turner 1994, 108)

Turner adds that the cautious tone of this passage mirrors More's ambivalences, for although she supported education for the poor, she retained a conservative interpretation of how this education should affect their lives. Later, her works on education advocated only such instruction for the poor as might enable them to be better servants. Thus More's support of Yearsley ran up against fundamental ideological problems and impasses. She desired Yearsley to remain 'in her place' and yet she also wanted to improve her 'tone', to make her a writer who would be acceptable to the sensibilities of middle-class readers and, of course, for her as a patron. When Yearsley claimed that she had encountered classical allusions through prints hanging in shop windows, she managed on this occasion to resolve these contradictions: to be lower-class and learned.[8]

More was extremely successful in collecting subscribers for Yearsley: over 1000 in total, including Reynolds, Blake, Walpole, at least 115 members of the aristocracy, the Lord Primate of Ireland, and the Bluestockings. But Yearsley was unhappy at the way in which More and Montagu commandeered the subscription funds: they invested the £350 raised through subscriptions so that it would allow a yearly stipend of £18. This would appear to confirm that More was mainly interested in making Yearsley comfortable without removing her from her 'natural' station. But £350 – and with subsequent editions, it came to more than £600 – seemed to Yearsley to promise a more radical mending of her family's circumstances than could be brought about by More's careful doling out of small sums here and there. Yearsley's demands were to have more control over what she perceived to be her money, rather than have it regulated by her literary patron. Donna Landry argues that Yearsley's aspirations to gentility were, to her, synonymous with her aspirations to poetic composition – poetry was that signifier of middle-class 'good taste', and that these aspirations were hypocritically severed by her middle-class patron (a woman who might herself be seen to have made her fortune through print).[9]

Certainly, as Shiach has argued, polite interest in these lower-class writers lay in the extent to which their writings 'could support particular theories about the relations between nature and poetic writing, rather than in any desire to re-evaluate the cultural and social role of the peasantry' (Shiach 1989, 6).

Rural authenticity?

Explanations of the popularity of the labouring poets lie, however, not only in their peasant status, but in the tradition of writing about the countryside. As the list above suggests, most, and certainly the most renowned, worked the land. Indeed, Shiach argues that Tatersal's poetry fails to resonate insofar as, unable to appeal to nature as a moral force, he 'lacks a poetic tradition which would render his landscape meaningful' (1989, 54). Thus one explanation for the popularity of labouring-class poetry in this period might be traced to the history of literary genres, especially the increasing popularity of the georgic and its dominance over the pastoral in the eighteenth century. Pastoral and georgic are both genres which were developed in classical Greece and Rome: pastoral in the *Idylls* of Theocritus and Moschus (3rd century BC) and Virgil's *Eclogues* (42–37 BC), georgic in Hesiod's *Works and Days* (8th century BC) and Virgil's

Georgics (37–30 BC). Although early Greek pastoral reflected upon the working year and seasonal conditions of country life, in its later development it became identified only with an idyllic vision of the countryside. In Renaissance pastorals, shepherds and shepherdesses commonly live without care in an ideal climate and sing only of love and death. In this development, pastoral became identified with an idyllic past, against which the contemporary corruptions of court and city could be contrasted. It thus became an idealising genre which nevertheless gave expression to very 'real' desires and dissatisfactions. The georgic mode, in contrast, retained its earliest characteristic as a record of agricultural techniques, and thus became identified with descriptions of rural labour as such descriptions became increasingly impermissible for the idylls of pastoral verse. Something of a debate between these two genres was raised in the early eighteenth century, when Pope defended the idealisms of pastoral against attempts to make pastoral more realistically 'English'. Pope's essay on pastoral in *The Guardian* (Rogers 1993, 559ff.) was a response to a series of essays on pastoral poetry in the same journal (1713), probably written by Thomas Tickell. Tickell, in praising the pastorals of Ambrose Philips (1708), argued for greater realism, calling upon English authors to alter the classical models of pastoral in the interests of probability, so that English fairies would replace classical gods; that hyacinths and 'Paestan' roses would be replaced by king-cups, endives and daisies; and Hobbinol, Cuddy and Colin Clout would replace Daphnis, Alexis and Thyrsis as names of shepherds. The shepherd of Tickell's pastoral should speak as English peasants do, should sing of English peasant sports and customs and, instead of an idyllic carefree existence, should be troubled by such anxieties as a thorn in the foot or a stolen lamb. In the following year, Gay published the satirical *The Shepherd's Week* (1714) in which Tickell's argument was also lampooned with shepherds entitled Bumkinet, Cuddy and Cloddipole.[10] But the growing popularity of the georgic might be read as a response to this debate too: John Philips's *Cyder*, with its detailed advice on orchard-management, had already been published (1708; and Gay had published a comic burlesque, *Wine*, within the same year), and this was followed by James Thomson's *The Seasons* (1726–30; revised editions 1744, 1746), describing the annual round of agricultural life and labour and later by Christopher Smart's *The Hop-Garden* (1752), John Dyer's *The Fleece* (1757), a poem on the woollen trade and all aspects of sheep farming, and James Grainger's

The Sugar Cane (1764), one of several georgic poems on Caribbean agriculture.[11]

However, we should beware of reading the debate between Tickell and Pope as one of 'realism' versus 'idealism', with georgic as the mode which conveniently resolves the issue. Tickell's pastoral was itself a way of, selectively, seeing:

> It is indeed commonly affirmed, that truth well painted will certainly please the imagination; but it is sometimes convenient not to discover the whole truth, but that part which only is delightful. We must sometimes show only half an image to the fancy; which if we display in a lively manner, the mind is so dexterously deluded, that it doth not readily perceive that the other half is concealed. Thus in writing Pastorals, let the tranquillity of that life appear full and plain, but hide the meanness of it; represent its simplicity as clear as you please, but cover its misery. (Quoted in Barrell 1983, 1)

Tickell's examples of the thorn in the foot or a stolen lamb were, after all, only relatively 'idyllic' cares and his reformulation of pastoral only a partial one. Realistic touches – such as a vernacular English idiom and contemporary, quotidian details – were to be included only so that readers of pastoral might believe in what was still, indubitably, a fiction (see Barrell 1983, 14–15). Thus even Tickell's pastoral remains a courtly, aristocratic way of seeing the countryside. In Duck's poem, 'Gratitude, A Pastoral' (1736), he recognises that to be a 'meanly born' shepherd is a contradiction in terms – within the terms of courtly pastoral and its allegories of aristocratic virtue in the guise of shepherd life. As Barrell notes: 'In writing formal pastorals, he is aiming above, not below his station, and his attempts to assume the "shepherd's weeds" cannot disguise his origins, but only make them more conspicuous' (Barrell 1983, 11).

Yet it was primarily the aristocracy who supported the cult of the peasant poet. Only later in the century did middle-class readers, such as Hannah More or the contributors to Arthur Young's periodical *Annals of Agriculture* (1784), express any enthusiasm for the poetry of rural life.[12] Perhaps this was because, as economic power shifted from agriculture to commerce and industry, the aristocracy became more interested in their country seats as working, productive estates. If wealth and political power were to be maintained, the landed gentry would need to busy themselves with estate-management and intensive farming methods, and ensure strict entailment of their estates. But simultaneously they desired to appear above such needs. For Barrell, this paradox might be read in the poetry and painting of rural life, and particularly in the compromises which the georgic permitted.

While the georgic might seem the more capacious genre, permitting those representations of labour and production which the pastoral (whether that of Tickell or Pope) omitted, georgic poems of the eighteenth century served not labouring-class, but capitalist and upper-class interests. For England's first form of capitalism was agrarian rather than urban, and its first beneficiaries were aristocratic rather than middle class. As Williams has argued, the protest poetry of the Romantic poets – the ways in which they celebrate the virtues of a countryside under threat from industrialisation – has tended to obscure that it is capitalism that threatens communities and social ties rather than industrialism.[13] And the class which contributed most to the formation of a bourgeois capitalism in England was not the urban middle class, but the country landowners, for it was their practices which introduced wage labour, the revolution of production by new technologies, and the economic science of increasing yields through intensive farming, rack-renting, engrossing and enclosure.

Here the georgic provided a complementary alternative to the pastoral, rather than an antithetical impulse. Dyer's *The Fleece*, for example, blended pastoral and georgic in moving smoothly from its depiction of shepherds to that of the commercial relations of eighteenth-century England. Many of these georgic poems proclaim wealth as a matter of national pride, as the economy rivals military power in the discourse of patriotism (see Lucas 1991, 38). In Thomson's *The Seasons*, farm labourers are happy toilers and picturesque accompaniments to the larger narrative of Britain's commercial dominance of the world. The description of the ploughmen in 'Spring' (ll.32–77), for example, modulates into a paean to the British export trade:

> Ye generous Britons, venerate the plough;
> And o'er your hills and long withdrawing vales
> Let Autumn spread his treasures to the sun,
> Luxuriant and unbounded. As the sea
> Far through his azure turbulent domain
> Your empire owns, and from a thousand shores
> Wafts all the pomp of life into your ports;

So with superior boon may your rich soil,
Exuberant, Nature's better blessings pour
O'er every land, the naked nations clothe,
And be the exhaustless granary of a world! (ll.67–77; Sambrook 1972, 5)

Georgic ideally combined a classical model with the contemporary Englishness so desired by Tickell; the decorous and ornate language advocated by Pope with the 'humdrum', commercial aspects of agriculture. Its success, as Barrell argues, lay in its perfect blend of delicacy and practicality (Barrell 1983, 12).[14] And there was a classical precedent for even this conjunction of the rural and the patriotic: Virgil's detailed accounts of husbandry and the images of the innocent, pious and happy husbandman were married to a narrative of national power (see Sambrook 1972, xi).[15]

The commercial and imperial boasts of these georgic poems remind us that the depiction of labourers at work was not automatically progressive. In his essay 'Ideas of Nature', Williams urges us to read the absences of rural poetry and painting symptomatically: '... a considerable part of what we call natural landscape ... is the product of human design and human labour, and in admiring it as natural it matters very much whether we suppress that fact of labour or acknowledge it' (Williams 1980, 78). The absence of labour serves to occlude the kind of mundane exploitation which makes the land profitable for those who own it. But depictions of the working poor might equally be prescriptive images of the 'deserving' poor, possible recipients of benevolence, and these depictions in turn occlude those vagrants and beggars who are not sustained through wage labour and who are increasingly seen as a drain on parish funds.[16] Working life seen 'from above' was life in the service of national and upper-class prosperity: 'On every hand/ Thy villas shine. Thy country teems with wealth; / And Property assures it to the swain,/ Pleased, and unwearied, in his guarded toil' (Thomson, 'Summer' ll.1453–6; Sambrook 1972, 77).

These varied arguments help to explain why Duck's *The Thresher's Labour* enjoyed considerable popularity in 1730s England, a poem which exposes the monotony, financial insecurity, exertion and exhaustion of the thresher's work, at the mercy of farmers, a daily or weekly rate of pay and the surveillance of the employer. But while the details of this work make his poem arguably part of the georgic tradition, the controlled anger of the poem's rhyming couplets, and their suggestion of endlessly repetitive labour, give it a subversive force which is counter to the didacticism of other eighteenth-century georgic poems: 'Tis all a dull and melancholy Scene, / Fit only to provoke the Muses Spleen' (in Thompson 1989, 4). This mixture of conformity and subversion is typical of many of the labouring-class poets of this period. While they tended to conform to popular taste, they also often used poetry to express what their patrons must have regarded as quite unpoetic – sometimes rather bitter feelings about their own exclusion from education and culture.[17] And it is the tension between 'the aspiration towards simplicity and transparency, and the actual facts of contradiction and negotiation' (Shiach 1989, 70) which reveals something of the ideological impasses and transgressions of a society in transition.

Upstairs, downstairs in an eighteenth-century country house [18]

> '... the [country-house] poems were customarily presented as records of the country houses, and so of the organic rural society England had once been, and so of the pattern of real civilization, later destroyed by capitalism. But as you moved to criticize that, the same people were always prepared to shift their ground and say: "After all it was only a convention." I decided that this had to be challenged ...' (Williams 1981, 304)

We have already seen how the writing of eighteenth-century labouring-class poets is inevitably 'intertextual', both in its reworking of conventional genres and poetic models and its dialogue with prevailing expectations of 'untutored genius'. This chapter will continue with a reading of Mary Leapor's poem 'Crumble-Hall' (1751), which is reprinted as an appendix to this volume. This poem suggestively plays with the genre of the 'country-house poem', but its class perspective means that the genre is also called into question.

Poems on country estates are chiefly associated with the seventeenth century, with such poems as Lanyer's 'Description of Cookeham' (written 1610); Jonson's 'To Penshurst' (1612) and 'To Sir Robert Wroth'; Herrick's 'A Panegyrick to Sir Lewis Pemberton' and 'The Country Life: To the honoured M. End[ymion] Porter'; Carew's 'To Saxham' and 'To my friend G.N. from Wrest' (1640); Marvell's 'Upon Appleton House' (c.1652).[19] All of these are offered as complimentary tributes to the estates' owners or occupants at a time when the country gentry were fashioned as extensions of monarchic power. Charles I's proclamation of 1632 exhorted the virtue of country retirement to his nobility and attempted to stem the increasing drift of the country gentry to the city and the attractions of court life. When the gentry resided in their country seats, Charles wrote, 'they served the King in several places according to their degree and ranks, in aid of the government, whereby, and by their housekeeping in those parts, the realm was defended and the meaner sort of people were guided, directed and relieved ...' (quoted in Parfitt 1992, 68). Thus country houses were not just places where rich people lived, but, in Mark Girouard's phrase, 'power houses'. If the house was owned by a local squire, that power was local: the squire dominated over the life of the village and presided, with his fellow JPs, over the county at quarter sessions. If the house was owned by a landowner who was also a member of parliament, that power would extend from the local to the national level. As Girouard summarises, 'basically people did not live in country houses unless they either possessed power, or, by setting up in a country house, were making a bid to possess it' (1980, 2).

Inevitably, then, these country-house poems constitute a thoroughly politicised tradition. They celebrate the virtues of paternalism even when paternalism was becoming increasingly anachronistic in an incipiently capitalist world.[20] As the farm worker became a wage labourer rather than a peasant, so his or her relationship with the landlord became a purely economic one. But the country-house poems continued, even into the eighteenth century, in celebrating a different kind of relationship, in which the relationship was social too: here the labourer ate at the great hall's table, lodged in the barn, was given second-hand clothes or other perquisites in lieu of cash payment. And, lest we romanticise this earlier relationship, E.P. Thompson reminds us that paternalism was as much a conspicuous display of largesse as a genuine responsibility: 'the roasted ox, the prizes offered for some race or sport, the liberal donation to charity in time of dearth, the application for mercy, the proclamation against forestallers' (1993, 46). From a marxist perspective, a paternalist system, exemplified in its 'virtue' of benevolence, is more exploitative than magnanimous for, as John Lucas argues, 'however desirable, [benevolence] is the product of economic arrangements for which the benevolent are responsible' (1991, 31). In the anti-pastoral nature of

Duck's *The Thresher's Labour*, we can see benevolence exposed as ideology – in the eighteenth century:

> Our Master joyful at the welcome sight,
> Invites us all to feast with him at Night.
> A Table plentifully spread we find,
> And jugs of humming Beer to cheer the Mind,
> Which he, too generous, pushes on so fast,
> We think no toils to come, nor mind the past.
> But the next Morning soon reveals the Cheat,
> When the same toils we must again repeat,
> To the same Barns again must back return,
> To labour there for room for next year's Corn. (Thompson 1989, 11)[21]

Duck reveals the feast as a form of bribe or sop, to ensure the continued labour of the workers. But its angry polemic is far removed from the deferential pleasantries of the country-house poems, where idyllic images of harmonious social relations, of easy fecundity and sufficiency are more typical. The country-house genre thus extols the moral, political and economic values of the landed estate and exemplifies the way in which ideological distortion can serve ruling-class interests.

The most influential marxist reading of the country-house genre is that of Raymond Williams in *The Country and the City*, in which he argues that these poems serve to mystify social relations and to occlude the exploitation which ensures the smooth functioning of the estate. Lanyer, Jonson and Carew all omit the tenants and rural labourers whose industry makes the landowner and his property prosperous. And the classical trope of these poems is Nature's giving of its bounty to the landlords in veneration of their virtue. This is clearly evident in Carew's 'To Saxham' (reprinted as an appendix to this volume). Little Saxham, near Bury St Edmunds, was the country seat of Sir John Crofts and Thomas Carew was a frequent visitor because of his friendship with the younger John Crofts. 'To Saxham', like other country-house poems of its type, compliments the owners of the house. But this compliment – as Jonson's to the Sidney family in 'To Penshurst' – depends upon a negative not an idyllic portrayal of the rural economy of the early seventeenth century. The poem flatters the hospitality of the Crofts by insinuating that their generosity is exceptional (ll.11–14 and ll.49–52). Their house is a refuge for the poor and the stranger in an otherwise inhospitable landscape and their hospitality organised around the dinner-table. But this is a dinner-table providentially bestowed by Nature herself:

> The Pheasant, Partiridge, and the Larke,
> Flew to thy house, as to the Arke.
> The willing Oxe, of himselfe came
> Home to the slaughter, with the Lambe,
> And every beast did thither bring
> Himselfe, to be an offering. (ll.21–6)

The omission of labour is significant, especially since the country-house poems are more apparently affiliated to the georgic than to pastoral. Pastoral's idyllic portrayal of nature could not admit such cultural artefacts as buildings, gardens or estates, and the georgic had traditionally incorporated such issues as the seasonal cycle; abundance of produce; contentment with a sufficient estate idealised in terms of the Golden Age; renunciation of grandeur; hunting; and moral virtue, all of which are also important aspects of these poems. But the georgic's main subject, agricultural labour, is either omitted altogether or subsumed into a vision of happy harvesting and festivity. (Carole Fabricant, for example, argues that Herrick's 'The Hock-cart', for all its description of the exertions of the harvest, and despite its overt comparison of farm workers with beasts of burden, merely assimilates this labour into a vision of seasonal renewal and fecundity; 1982, 61.) For this reason, and while acknowledging the considerable differences between many of these poems, Williams ultimately concludes that the country-house genre is a trope in which neo-pastoral is used in the service of a developing agrarian capitalism (1973, 22).

In a response to Williams's work, Alistair Fowler presents a series of counter-arguments, some of which are inconsistent. Fowler's 'literary historical' argument is that Williams has misread the classical motif of *sponte sua* (the voluntary, paradisal yielding of nature without labour) in reading it as a magical automation of agriculture (1986, 6). But whether the motif is used by the ancient Roman poet Virgil in the first century BC or by the English poet Carew in the seventeenth century, it remains a motif which occludes labour and idealises agricultural life as pre-lapsarian. While I would agree that many landowners did not farm their estates at all, their tenants certainly did, and these tenant-holdings and the working landscape associated with them are still aspects of the landscape about which these poems are silent. Despite offering these formal and historical explanations for the occlusion of labour in the poems, Fowler also argues that labour *is* present in the poems. While few (including Williams) would disagree with this in relation to Marvell's 'Upon Appleton House', his defence of such poems as 'To Saxham' (which, he argues, 'at least mentions the "Hinde"') and 'To my Friend G.N.' (in which 'it is the lord who is almost extracted') relies upon a kind of literal presence which is rather disingenuous. While the lord and lady of 'To my Friend G.N.' are present only metonymically or obliquely in descriptions of their hospitality, the entire poem, like all these country-house poems, is offered as a paean to their owners' virtues. The landlords can therefore only be said to be 'absent' in the most narrow sense. The absence of tenants and wage labourers from these poems is an absence of perspective as much as scene-painting. It is the particular way of seeing in these poems which remains blind to those most foundational of all: those who work the land and pay the rents which generate the power and influence of the gentry.

Mary Leapor's variant on the country-house poem is particularly significant in this context, though her poem is not discussed by either Fowler or Williams. Her poem is evidently a portrayal of the country house through the eyes of a servant. Though she never explicitly identifies herself as such – indeed the narrator of the poem is identified only as 'Mira', a name suggestively poetic – there are lots of clues to her labouring-class status.[22] 'Crumble-Hall' opens with an attempt to relinquish writing poetry, a 'crime' for a woman or servant, though the many poems Leapor wrote on the scandal of a lower-class poetic voice suggests the second. Moreover this poet suffers not just the kinds of headaches and whims supposedly typical of eighteenth-century ladies, but 'aching Limbs' (l.3), perhaps the result of stretching after cobwebs out of reach of a broom (l.47). For this is grandeur seen in its inaccessibility for domestic servants: the coat of arms in the great hall is shone only once a year (l.48) and each pewter plate must be rubbed, rinsed and polished till it shines (ll.153–5).

The poem also distinguishes between the easy leisure of those who own the house and the industry of those who sustain it. The busy industry of the women in the kitchens forms a counterpoint to the descriptions of the parlours. In the parlour to the left, famous only for its leather chairs, 'the dull Clock beats audible and slow' (63). Here time passes slowly. Similarly in describing the parlour on the right, the distinction between industry and leisure is pointed by the succession of couplets:

> From hence we turn to more familiar Rooms;
> Whose Hangings ne'er were wrought in *Grecian* Looms:
> Yet the soft Stools, and eke the lazy Chair,
> To Sleep invite the Weary, and the Fair. (ll.80–3)

The tapestries made, presumably, on modern rather than mythic looms (such as those of Homer's Penelope or Ovid's Arachne) suggest an image of industry which is then sharply juxtaposed (with the conjunctive forcing together of 'yet') with that of slothfulness. Only Roger, of the servants, is shown to enjoy such ease, the consequence of a full stomach (but implicitly too of the day's labour). But even in moments of rest, these servants are marked by their labour: in his sleep Roger coughs ('His *able* Lungs discharge a rattling Sound'; l.134, my emphasis) and Colinettus dreams of 'his' oxen and awakes sharply in a panic that the hay might be destroyed by rain (ll.121–4).

Among Mira's most ecstatic moments is her glimpse of the surrounding countryside from the rooftops of Crumble-Hall (ll.105–6), but this is interrupted when Mira finds herself involuntarily returned to the 'nether World', associatively figuring here the hell of life in the kitchens. Mira's prospect of the landscape around is thus presented as a snatched possibility, a momentary escape from the sphere to which she more properly belongs.[23] From the poem's account of Crumble-Hall, the kitchens appear to be on the ground floor, but their description as a 'nether World' prefigures the development of country-house styles in the eighteenth century, as the servants' rooms were pushed further from the living quarters of their masters: 'By the end of the eighteenth century [the servants' rooms] were often sunk so far down that light had to be got to them by digging a pit or dry moat round the house' (Girouard 1980, 218). Leapor's loyalty to the lower classes might also be inferred by her focus upon them. Descriptions of the domestic servants 'Sophronia', 'Grusso' and 'Urs'la' and the farm labourers 'Colinettus' and 'Roger', form a major section of the poem and her attention towards them reverses the more conventional structure of the country-house poem. Jonson's and Carew's poems typically move from descriptions of the setting to those of the buildings to praise of the owners. In 'Crumble-Hall' the owners are almost completely absent and the 'menial Train' of servants are consciously addressed before turning to the house's setting. Leapor's poem thus reverses the more usual prioritising of the estate's grounds with the dismissively abrupt phrase: 'Its Groves anon' (l.111).

'Crumble-Hall' does share with earlier country-house poems their praise of hospitality. As in the poems by Jonson and Carew, such hospitality is lamented as a virtue which is now outmoded. But the important distinction here is that, whereas Jonson and Carew celebrate the virtues of Penshurst or Saxham as exceptions to the prevailing meanness of modernity, Leapor's virtuous household is very firmly located in the past (ll.13–28). And this contrast can be seen in the several experiences of the stranger who comes to Crumble-Hall. In its medieval setting, Crumble-Hall welcomed the stranger (l.14). Now, he is shown feeling his way blindly along the house, fearful of the ghosts which pervade this decaying mansion (ll.54–5). That Crumble-Hall is now long past its original splendour is also pointed up by Leapor's pervasive use of archaisms. Its former inhabitants are distanced from the mid-eighteenth century by being described in stock poetic terms as wights, friar and clown, and the artefacts which display the house's antiquity are now either frightening or ludicrous. The giants over the front entrance 'look severe, and horribly adorn' (34); inside the great hall, the decorative faces include '[s]ome mouths that grin, some smile, and some that spew' (l.40), and a tyrant with distorted eye, crying maids and children. These last lines suggest a specifically masculine brutality, which disturbs the poet, even though (or because) these images adorn the central hall. Where the images are less threatening, as in the painting of 'doughty George' on his 'goodly Steed' (l.73), the use of obvious archaism distances this image into a never-never world of Elizabethan heroism or the merely fictional.[24]

Moreover, in direct contrast with all of the country-house poems listed above, the present owners of Crumble-Hall are certainly not praised. Lord Biron uses his library only as a quiet place in which to sleep, and his indifference to the books around him is evident in their clean pages, free from marginal annotations, and in their dusty state. The 'crumbling' hall bears everywhere the signs of carelessness and oversight: mice scuttle through downstairs passages (l.52) and one upstairs room has become a kind of general store-room for unwanted bits and pieces such as old shoes, bits of harness, wheelspokes and a disused plough, stacks of wool which have been left so long they have become a nesting place for sheep ticks and a surfeit of containers for administering medicine to horses ('drenching-horns'; ll.99–101). The narrator's disapproval is evident in her ironic preface to this description: 'These Rooms are furnish'd amiably, and full' (l.98). There is none of the servility and deference evident in many labouring-class poems, or indeed, the country-house genre; instead there is a direct and familiar relationship with the reader ('Shall we proceed? – Yes, if you'll break the Wall' 83) and much flippancy in describing this country seat (the parlour on the left is 'nothing famous' but for its leather chairs; and the narrator seems almost bored with description when she turns to the parlour on the right, dismissing it quickly, and just about cataloguing its dimensions, its china and tapestry; ll.64–71).

This is a poem which everywhere proclaims its independence from earlier kinds of patronage. Indeed, at one point it seems to mock earlier authors of country-house poems and their needy dependence upon the hospitality which they so celebrated: 'Of this rude Palace might a Poet sing / From cold *December* to returning Spring' (ll.29–30). This couplet threatens to expose the ulterior motivation behind the country-house poet's grateful verses of compliment. Leapor's own poetry was published by subscription after her death and the subscribers to her volumes, especially her second volume, were predominantly middle class. (See Landry 1990, 99–100 and Rizzo 1991, 324.) Leapor's particular patron, addressed as 'Artemisia', was Bridget Freemantle, the daughter of a local clergyman. Their relationship appears to have suffered none of the rancour which later characterised the relationship between Ann Yearsley and Hannah More. Dustin Griffin (1996) suggests that this was because Mary Leapor was quietly deferential. Freemantle's prefatory letter to the second of her posthumous collections (the volume which includes 'Crumble-Hall') reassured the reader that Leapor was no presumptuous and ambitious servant girl seeking to climb her way into higher life. But the good nature of the Freemantle-Leapor relationship might also have been because Freemantle did not aspire to literary fame herself, nor even to especially critical taste, or because Mary Leapor died before her work was published, so there were none of the financial wrangles which set Yearsley and More at odds. We ought to suspect then, that this poem's conventional deference towards 'Artemisia' is as light-hearted as it is also, on one level, true: 'We sing once more, obedient to her Call' (l.11).[25]

However, Leapor's poem might also be read as a response to the eighteenth-century variants on the country-house genre, which include John Pomfret's popular poem 'The Choice' (1700; it went to seven editions within the first two years of publication); William Diaper's *Dryades* (1726); but primarily two of Pope's 'moral essays', *The Epistle to Bathurst* (1733) and *Epistle to Burlington* (1731). These continue the 'Horatian' tradition of the country-house poems, in their celebration of contented frugality and retirement from a rich, corrupt and bustling (urban) world. Ostentatious or luxurious building schemes are censured, while moderate spending and generosity towards the poor are advocated. In *The Epistle to Bathurst*, for example, the meanness and spendthrift ways of Old Cotta and his son, and Cutler and Villers, are contrasted with the 'old Man of Ross', whose benevolence to the poor and sick parallels that of the landed gentleman in Jonson and Carew's country-house poems. As in those poems, such virtuous gentlemen as John Kyrlc (the 'old man of Ross'), Lord Bathurst and Lord Oxford are praised as exceptions to the general, modern rule: those who entertain the unworthy (such as flatterers, gamesters and buffoons) and ignore the poor and oppressed. In *The Epistle to Burlington*, Boyle's restrained, refined Palladian aesthetic is contrasted with the baroque excessiveness of Timon's villa. The gaudy showiness and ostentatious artificiality of Timon's villa is merely an image of his own personal derelictions: an inhospitable host, the dinner courses are rushed and niggardly ('In plenty starving, tantaliz'd in state, / And complaisantly helped to all I hate'; ll.163–4). Burlington, in contrast, is described as the benevolent landlord: ' ... cheerful Tenants bless their yearly toil / Yet to their lord owe more than to the soil' (ll.183–4).

But there are also newer, eighteenth-century notes in these variants on the seventeenth-century country-house tradition. In Pomfret's poem, for example, it is to 'Objects of *true* Pitty' that charity will be given, as the distinction between deserving and undeserving poor is increasingly seen as necessary. And both of Pope's *Epistles* on 'the use of riches' juxtapose moral and utilitarian judgements which are incompatible. The poems set up a system of oppositions in which the excessive behaviour of the miser and the spendthrift (Old Cotta and his son, Cutler and Villers in *Epistle to Bathurst*; Timon in *To Burlington*) is contrasted with the altruism and moderation of the virtuous man (the Man of Ross in *To Bathurst*; Burlington himself in *To Burlington*). Such contrasts would not be out of place in the seventeenth-century country-house poems, since they propose an ethic of hospitality, charity and benevolence. But the poems also suggest that the 'vices' of prodigality and avarice do – providentially – work to the greater good. In the 'Argument' to the *Epistle to Burlington*, for example, Pope writes: 'Yet PROVIDENCE is justified in giving wealth to be squandered in this manner, since it is adapted to the poor and laborious part of mankind' (Rogers 1993, 243). Timon's lavish spending is seen as inadvertent charity, since his prodigality entails that his wealth is diffused:

> Yet hence the poor are clothed, the hungry fed;
> Health to himself, and to his infants bread
> The labourer bears: what his hard heart denies,
> His charitable vanity supplies. (ll.169–72)

Indeed, Timon's vice is ultimately more beneficial even than Burlington's virtuous moderation and good taste: in his own note to the above lines, Pope writes, 'A Bad taste employs more hands, and diffuses expense more than a good one' (in Rogers 1993, 249). Similarly, in *Epistle to Bathurst*, young Cotta's excessive spending splashes wealth around and his father's hoarding becomes the precondition for that good:

> Who sees pale Mammon pine amidst his store,
> Sees but a backward steward for the poor.
> This year a reservoir, to keep and spare;
> The next, a fountain, spouting through his heir,
> In lavish streams to quench a country's thirst,
> And men and dogs shall drink him till they burst. (ll.171–6)

Pope's poems come close to espousing a 'trickle-down' theory of the economy, by which the wealth of the very richest is diffused and percolates down through the social system: 'The sense to enjoy riches, with the art / T'enjoy them, and the virtue to impart' (*To Bathurst*, ll.219–20) and 'Wealth in the gross is death, but life diffused' (l.233). This is closer to Bernard Mandeville and Adam Smith – both early advocates for capitalism – than any marxist would like to be.[26]

We can read Leapor's poem intertextually with these poems. Greene notes that Leapor had 'certainly read' Pope's *Epistle to Burlington* (1993, 137) and there are several echoes or at least parallels between 'Crumble-Hall' and both of these epistles. Timon's superficial interest in collecting, rather than reading books is paralleled by Leapor's description of Biron drowsing in his study; the merman fountains which 'spew' water at the guests at Timon's buffet resemble the sculptures of Crumble-Hall's entrance (l.40) and Pope's criticism of the 'wretched taste of carving large periwigs on [funeral] bustos' is mirrored in Leapor's dislike of the 'severe beards' of the giants outside Crumble-Hall's entrance (ll.33–4).[27] Unlike either of Pope's epistles, or indeed the typical country-house poem of the seventeenth century, however, Leapor's poem has no model alternative to offer. Her criticisms of the landlords of Crumble-Hall are not neutralised by prescriptive images of benevolence elsewhere, and it is this absence which makes her 'nostalgic' turn towards the hospitality of Crumble-Hall in earlier times as much ('truly') utopian as ('falsely') idealising.[28]

In the final section of 'Crumble-Hall', that which addresses the building projects at the estate, there is a further parallel with Pope's work which is of especial interest to this chapter and its particular concerns with ideology and early forms of capitalism. In the *Epistle to Bathurst*, the prodigious spending of Old Cotta's son includes 'improvements' to his estate. But the author's comments on these improvements are ambivalent, especially given the kinds of inconsistencies which I traced above:

> 'Tis GEORGE and LIBERTY that crowns the cup,
> And zeal for that great house which eats him up.
> The woods recede around the naked seat,
> The sylvans groan – no matter – for the fleet. (ll.207–10)

Pat Rogers suggests two readings for the second couplet: 'The meaning may be either, "The inhabitants of the forest lament the despoliation of their landscape and livelihood", or else "the trees screech as they are cut down to provide timber for shipbuilding"' (1993, 641, l.210). The second of these readings may be the more persuasive, if we follow Rogers's reading of 'that great house' as the Hanoverian monarchy and recall the imperial-pastoral images of *Windsor Forest*, in which sturdy English oaks function as a synecdoche for the navy. But it is surely also possible to interpret these lines in a conflation of Rogers's two readings. Enclosure of the commons led to greater productivity in the eighteenth century, by means of which the increasing population in the towns and cities were fed, and Britain's expanding imperial trade was supported. But it also meant the loss of livelihood for many of the labouring poor: those who formerly had raised crops on a patch of waste, or grazed livestock on the common, those who had gathered firewood from the local lord's woods, or gleaned from a landowner's fields after harvest. In the eighteenth century, these customary rights were redefined as crime, theft, trespassing, or poaching.

Leapor's poem raises none of these issues at an explicit level. But we might read the final section of 'Crumble-Hall' as a response to such changes. Here the rapturous depiction of the estate's setting (ll.156–64) serves as the idyll, comparable to the old-fashioned hospitality of the house in earlier times (ll.13–28), which is about to be destroyed by the 'whims' of modern fashion.[29] Trees will be cut down, and nightingales and turtle-doves, nymphs and dryads will flee as the owners extend the house. At one level, we might read this section for its similarities to Pope's condemnation of 'false taste' (an early subtitle for the *Epistle to Burlington*), and his aesthetic of 'natural' landscaping. But, unlike Pope, Leapor here resists cultivation of any kind. While Pope is a severe critic of the artificialities of French-style landscaping, such as symmetrical groves and paths or the studied artistry of topiary, the 'natural' garden which he applauds is itself a form of careful cultivation. (We might compare Lady Mary Wortley Montagu's criticism of Bathurst's gardening schemes with Pope's praise: 'Lands are cut, and mountains level made'; Montagu, *Epistle [to Lord Bathurst]*, l.15.) Thus we cannot draw a simple antithesis in Pope's aesthetic between nature and culture, but only between different varieties of culture – vulgar and tasteful. For Leapor, in contrast, any redesigning of this landscape is an intrusion:

> Shall these [oaks] ignobly from their Roots be torn,
> And perish shameful, as the abject Thorn;
> While the slow Car bears off their aged Limbs,
> To clear the Way for Slopes, and modern Whims;
> Where banished Nature leaves a barren Gloom,
> And aukward Art Supplies the vacant Room? (ll.173–8)

This might be a conservative reaction towards change, an idealised clinging to a pastoral vision. But this section also suggests a revolutionary, if subdued, voice: the poet calls upon the nymphs to haunt the house in 'vengeance' for their exile. Indeed, Rogers's suggested reading of Pope's couplet – 'The inhabitants of the forest lament the despoliation of their landscape and livelihood' – seems more fitting for Leapor's 'Crumble-Hall' than it does of *Epistle to Bathurst*. The poem suggests that the removal of this green space will destroy the contentment of the (labouring) 'hapless swain' and that the 'nymphs', 'dryads' and 'fairy-elves' who will continue to haunt the estate are perceived only by this labouring-class poet (l.168) and by the kitchen-maid Ursula (l.182). We might then return to the ghosts which greet the modern stranger to Crumble-Hall (ll.54–5) and read these spectres as emanations of the house's guilt. In several eighteenth-century vari-ants of country-house poems, the fear of ghosts is associated with vice and guilt, as in the following excerpt from Matthew Green's 'The Grotto' (1732):

> Nor in impress'd remembrance keep
> Grim tapestry figures wrought in sleep;
> The moonlight monsters on the wall,
> And shadowy spectres darkly pass
> Trailing their sables o'er the grass.
> Let vice and guilt act how they please
> In souls, their conquered provinces;
> By Heaven's just charter it appears,
> Virtue's exempt from quartering fears. (ll.131–40; Fausset 1930, 239)[30]

Resistance towards enclosure took much more strenuous forms than a poem like 'Crumble-Hall', of course, though the ways in which 'theft' or 'trespassing' might have been part of the labouring classes' protests are only beginning to be recorded. (See Valenze 1995, 40; Thompson 1991, 66 and *passim*.) And, unlike the popular balladry, chap-books and folktales of the eighteenth century, Leapor's poetry (as indeed other poems by labouring-class authors) was as much constrained as enabled by the conventions of publishing and the fashionable literary genres within which she wrote. We might compare, for example, a poem published anonymously in 1754 – 'Snaith Marsh. A Yorkshire Pastoral' – which opposes enclosure much more directly:

> But far more waeful still that luckless day,
> Which with the commons gave *Snaith Marsh* away,

Snaith Marsh our whole town's pride, the poor man's bread,
Where, tho' no rent he paid, his cattle fed. (Quoted in Greene 1993,
142)

Leapor's is then a qualified subversion, if it is subversion at all. But in
reading her poem against the grain of conservative histories, we can
remember the human cost which eighteenth-century 'improvement'
and expanding capitalism also wrought. Marxism celebrates the benefits which capitalism brought – increasing agricultural yields certainly
permitted the urban working classes to be fed – while simultaneously
registering its oppressions. And from this perspective we can read
Leapor's final couplet as an incipiently insurrectionary manoeuvre,
with the anonymous, but 'desperate' Diracto as its agent:

Then cease, *Diracto,* stay thy des'prate Hand;
And let the Grove, if not the Parlour, stand.

A woman's perspective

Representations of rural labour are thus transversed by the issues of
class relationships and early capitalist formations. But these issues are
already issues of gender too, as the changing economy shapes and is
in turn shaped by changes in family structure and in definitions of
femininity. The eighteenth century witnessed a general withdrawal of
women, especially middle-class women, from agricultural labour,
partly because proper femininity became synonymous with accom-
plishments such as needlework and musicianship rather than industry and because of growing commercial pressures, new technology
(such as the growing use of the scythe) and the increasingly scientific
nature of modern farming methods (see Shoemaker 1998, 153–7;
Valenze 1995, 48–84). The tension between ideologies of proper femininity and the physicality of rural labour can be read in portraits of
labouring women, in which milkmaids and female reapers are
portrayed as if they were polite ladies. In George Stubbs's paintings
Reapers (1784) and *Haymakers* (1785), for example, individual female
labourers provide statuesque centrepieces, their labour erased in the
aesthetic image of womanhood they proffer to the viewer. And in 1794
A. Pringle wrote: 'It is painful to one ... to behold the beautiful servant
maids of this county toiling in the severe labours of the field. They

drive the harrows, or the ploughs, when they are drawn by three or four horses; nay, it is not uncommon to see, sweating at the dung-cart, a girl, whose elegant features, and delicate, nicely-proportioned limbs, seemingly but ill accord with such rough employment.' (Quoted in Hill 1984, 186.)

Women's labour thus needs to be discussed in its own terms. Indeed their double marginalisation – as labourers and as women – was emphasised as early as 1739 in Mary Collier's poem *The Woman's Labour*. This poem is both an imitation and a rebuke of Duck's *The Thresher's Labour* in which he depicted the female workers as garrulous gossips, ready to slacken from work at the first drop of rain. Collier's poem counters with the argument that women have double the work-load of such men as the threshers. After a day's haymaking, the married woman returns to prepare dinner for her labouring husband, but she must also feed the pigs and attend to the children. During the harvest, children are carried with their mothers to the fields, where they must combine the roles of reaping or gleaning with mothering, feeding and supervising their children. In the second part of the poem, Collier describes her own work of 'charring' (washing, cleaning, brewing) at the houses of the wealthy. She also defends, but does not deny, the charge that women gossip at their work. Instead she celebrates this sociability as an important and necessary part of their tasks, as 'The only Privilege our Sex enjoy' (in Thompson 1989, 17) and compares their talk with the liberty which Duck enjoys (having published an account of his and their work).

Mary Leapor's poem 'Crumble-Hall' might also be read as a response to male representations of female labour. Her extended passage on Ursula appears to mimic the portrayal of labouring women in John Gay's *The Shepherd's Week* (1713). Of Gay's six 'eclogues', three recount the laments of women who have been abandoned by their lovers. In 'Wednesday' Sparabella is so disconsolate for the loss of Bumkinet that she contemplates various methods of suicide until, night coming on, she defers her death until an unlikely tomorrow. In 'Thursday' Hobnelia casts a spell to bring Lubberkin back from the town, but faints when that is fulfilled through her pregnancy ('He vows, he swears, he'll give me a green gown'). And, closest of all to Leapor's Ursula, in 'Tuesday', Marian recounts the ways in which she demonstrated her love for Colin Clout:

> And when at eve returning with thy car,
> Awaiting heard the jingling bells from far;
> Straight on the fire the sooty pot I plac't,
> To warm thy broth I burnt my hands for haste,
> When hungry thou stood'st staring, like an oaf,
> I sliced the luncheon from the barley loaf,
> With crumbled bread I thicken'd well thy mess.
> Ah, love me more, or love thy pottage less! (ll.65–72)

This is close to Ursula's complaint to the unromantic, sleeping Roger, as she reminds him of her loving attentions to him. But though the obvious light-hearted tone is shared by both, the context of the country house makes Ursula's situation the more complex, and potentially sombre. For Ursula, as a kitchen maid at Crumble-Hall, cooks not just, or even primarily for Roger, but for her landlords and employers. While she claims that she cooks solely for him, it is obvious that she also works for a living, a reminder which the poem itself makes when her talking is interrupted by a necessary return to chores: the boiling bran begins to foam and the dishes need to be washed and shone (ll.150–5).

As in the poem itself, the estate owners are conspicuously absent in Ursula's lament, but while they are written out in her account, they are still present in their command and proprietorship. In Landry's reading, the absence of her employers from Ursula's domestic drama is a significant reversal of the traditional country-house poem, and the way in which it erases labour:

> Her putative employers are as tangential to her self-representation as she would be to theirs, if this were a conventional country-house poem. Thus an ironical equivalence is established between property and labor in the country-house domain; each is represented as excluding the other symbolically while remaining materially dependent upon it. (1990, 114)

If we continue to read 'Crumble-Hall' in the context of the country-house tradition, we can interpret Leapor's poem as a radical reworking of the selective and partial insights of that genre. But, as Landry continues, Ursula's complaint also reveals the power of the new ideology of proper domesticity. As women's paid labour was being defined as 'unfeminine', and middle-class housewives hired dairymaids or servants to do the work they once would have performed themselves, the 'proper' sphere for woman is in the home, enjoying 'leisured domesticity'. Thus, as Landry argues, Ursula can be seen to 'trivialize her work (keeping livestock, gardening, cooking, washing-up, house-keeping) by transforming these activities into mere epiphenomena of wifely devotion' (l.115). When Ursula's complaint is interrupted by her return to her chores and the poem's elevated manner of describing the most mundane of rituals (Ursula boiling bran and cleaning dishes is described in elegant heroic couplets), Leapor contains this section within the comedy which characterises 'Crumble-Hall' as a whole. But Leapor never discusses her female servants with the low comedy which is a feature of Gay's work. Marian's complaint quoted above, for example, is abruptly finished with a typically bawdy flourish:

> Thus Marian wail'd, her eyes with tears brimful,
> When Goody Dobbins brought her cow to bull.
> With apron blue to dry her tears she sought,
> Then saw the cow well served, and took a groat. (ll.103–6)

The women workers in *The Shepherd's Week* (with the exception of the harvesters in 'Saturday') are frequently described in lewd terms. This is partly because so many of them are described as dairymaids, stroking the cow's udder (see 'Monday' lines 4 and 78; 'Tuesday' line 11; 'Friday' line 154). Deborah Valenze has written of how milking was viewed as specifically 'feminine' work, because 'gentleness' was thought to be the best approach to extracting milk (1995, 60). Painting in the eighteenth century was more coy: the dairymaid is hardly ever portrayed as actually squeezing the cow's udders (Barrell 1983, 51). The suggestive overtones associated with female dairymaids are also evident in 'Crumble-Hall', but deployed against an aristocratic lady in a classical painting:

> And there (but lately rescu'd from their Fears)
> The Nymph and serious *Ptolemy* appears:
> Their aukward Limbs unwieldy are display'd;
> And, like a Milk-wench, glares the royal Maid. (ll.76–9)

While Leapor quietly satirises her female servants – Ursula's self-delusions and Sophronia's consciousness of place – her poem shows them working while the male servants recline at relative ease. In the comparison between the busy industry of the two women with the albeit uneasy sleep of Colinettus and Roger, we can see a parallel with Collier's response to Duck: Duck's dreams are haunted ('Our labours ev'n in Sleep don't cease'; l.11) but Collier replies 'we have hardly ever *Time to dream*' (l.20). Thus while 'Crumble-Hall' can be seen to expose the ideology of ruling-class self-preservation in the eighteenth century, its quiet feminism reminds us that this is the country house seen from the perspective of a lower-class woman.

The poetry of eighteenth-century labouring women is therefore of especial interest, for in many of their works we can read a combination of incipient class protest and feminism. Labouring women suffered a double discrimination and the interconnections of class and gender in their experiences offer a rebuke to those contemporary feminists and marxists who perpetuate the separation of work and home, economic and sexual relations in their analyses.

Possible critiques of this reading

We cannot invest Leapor's work with the burden of representing her entire class or gender. Her work may appear to give us unmediated access to real experience but we need to remember that hers is a voice produced, like all voices, in a social context which partly, though not exhaustively, determines what she says or thinks. This is especially the case with the eighteenth-century labouring poets, all of whom required the support of patrons or subscribers in order to be heard at all. As Donna Landry cautions in the introduction to her study of labouring women poets: 'Even where a woman of the laboring class attempts her own self-representation, the textual traces of elite literary culture overdetermine the site of "her own" textual production' (1990, 13). This does not mean that we should give up the attempt to read and recuperate the texts of lower-class writers, only that we should be cautious about the claims we make for it.

In rediscovering these labouring voices, we are in danger, not only of reading them to satisfy our own desire for subversive, radical voices, but of permitting them to be fetishised by the industry of scholarship itself. In an essay published two years after the publication of *The Muses of Resistance*, Donna Landry questioned the ways in which her work on labouring-class women had conveniently served her own, professional, ends: 'So there I was, contributing to the commodification of these working-class women writers, making my own career by recovering their exploited labour' (1992, 168). To critics of marxism, this hand-wringing is an easy gesture to make. But it is both not enough and also all that we might do. Commodification of work is something which the individual has little control over, so while we cannot change it, we can at least be self-conscious about it. Meanwhile the poetry of labouring-class women is read and studied by more people than it would otherwise have been, and materialist accounts of their writing will at least recognise the class implications both of their work and of our own.

Notes

1. A substantial part of Thompson's argument is a defence of this bi-polar model from those who accuse him of ignoring the rise of the middle classes in the eighteenth century, a more familiar historical narrative.
2. See Griffin (1995) for the argument that all literary history is thoroughly 'Romanticised', a genealogy of literary value judgements which are influenced by our continuing collusion in Romantic choices.
3. For a marxist critique of Wordsworth's 'Preface', see Sales: '[In the "Preface", r]ural occupations are not hard work, but the best possible linguistic and philosophical training ground' (1983, 68).
4. In 'An Introductory Essay on the Lives and Works of Our Uneducated Poets' (1831), Robert Southey identified John Taylor (the seventeenth-century waterman poet) as the first uneducated poet. But it is only in the eighteenth century that such poets are situated within a discourse of 'natural genius'. In addition to those named, Klaus (1985) includes Henry Frizzle and John Bancks (weaver), who wrote in the 1730s; Greene (1993) refers also to Edward Ward (tavern-keeper) and Jane Holt Wiseman (a domestic servant), both known before Duck's rise (see 103–4); Henry Jones (bricklayer), James Eyre Weeks (shoemaker), Joseph Lewis, and George Smith Green who first published poetry in the 1750s; Constantia Grierson (midwife) and an additional shoemaker poet, John Bennett.
5. See Griffin (1995), *passim* and Rizzo (1991, 329ff.).
6. Offers of support and patronage can also be interpreted with some scepticism: if the poets whom the subscribers supported won fame – as indeed Duck's example suggested they might – then they as literary supporters would stand in reflected glory. And after the tragic death of Chatterton (1770), who poisoned himself with arsenic in a fit of despon-

dency at the age of 17, the wealthy were wary of being seen to let other talented writers suffer. Chatterton's early death quickly took on a mythical quality, making him a symbol of youthful poetic genius neglected by a prosaic world.

7. While eighteenth-century fashionable society thought in terms of the 'peasant' poets, we should remember that this was something of a misnomer: as Shiach notes, these writers were not independent agricultural producers in feudal social relations, but rural labourers, servants, washerwomen and pipemakers (1989, 9).

8. More wrote to Elizabeth Montagu: 'I cannot help troubling you dear Madam with a new production of Lactilla; which I am the more impatient you shou'd see because it betrays totally new Talents, for I think You will agree with me that there is in it, wit, ease and pleasantry; and what sounds quite ridiculous the Poem appears to me to have the tone of good Company, and a gentility that is wonderful in a Milker of Cows, and a feeder of Hogs.' (Quoted in Landry 1990, 130.)

9. For the difficult relationship between Yearsley and More, see also Ferguson 1986. A long section from Yearsley's own narrative is included in Ferguson (1985, 382–6).

10. For contrasting readings of *The Shepherd's Week*, see Greene (1993, 106) and Landry (1990, 2); Landry's is the more obviously marxist reading. Excerpts from Pope and Tickell's *Guardian* essays and Gay's 'Proeme' to *The Shepherd's Week* are included in Loughrey (1984). Philips's poems addressed to children were mocked by Henry Carey in *Namby-Pamby* (1725), from which we derive our current use.

11. Landry (1990, 22) argues that the georgic rose in popularity after 1744, the year of Pope's death.

12. This runs counter to the usual association between the rise of the reading public, particularly novel readers, and the emergence of the middle class in the eighteenth century, identified with the work of Ian Watt (1957).

13. The common kinds of opposition between town and country, and the subsequent idealisations of the countryside are examined by Williams in *The Country and the City* (1973).

14. For the required delicacy of eighteenth-century georgic, see Barrell (1983, 12): 'The poet Joseph Warton apologises for such vulgarity as his own translation of the *Georgics* unavoidably exhibits, which will, he fears, "unconquerably disgust many a delicate reader". His examples include not only such palpable barbarisms as *dung, ashes, horse*, and *cow*, but also *plough, sow*, and *wheat*, which have probably lost forever their power to shock.'

15. See Brown's marxist reading of Pope's *Windsor Forest*, in which, she

argues, Virgil 'must serve as a nationalist and expansionist ideal, and yet sustain an anti-materialist moral standard: he must be the supreme exemplar of Augustan humanism' (1985, 43).

16. A clause added to the poor law legislation in the seventeenth century – first added in 1662, and amended but preserved in 1693 – stipulated that any person born outside the parish could be forcibly removed. A married woman took her settlement from her husband, even if they were living apart, and this meant that many single women were targeted. See Valenze (1995, 20).

17. For further examples of such ambivalences, see Thompson's discussion of eighteenth-century plebeian customs as both conservative and rebellious, rebellious in defence of custom (1993, *passim*) or the particular case of the victory of one Englishman – John Lewis – against Princess Amelia when he sued for lack of access to Richmond Park. Such infrequent victories only served to 'give popular legitimacy to the law and endorsed the rhetoric of constitutionalism upon which the security of landed property was founded' (113).

18. *Upstairs, Downstairs* was a popular television drama series in Britain in the 1970s which focused on the life of an upper-class town-house, with the servants working 'downstairs' and the wealthy owners living 'upstairs'.

19. Fowler (1986) argues that the genre has been defined much too narrowly – usually only the two poems by Jonson and Carew and Marvell's 'Upon Appleton House' are referred to – and includes a much longer list, from which I have included Herrick's poems.

20. Carole Fabricant, in her discussion of the country-house genre, compares its illusions with Karl Mannheim's example of ideology at work (1936), namely the landed proprietor 'whose estate has already become a capitalist undertaking, but who still attempts to explain his relations to his labourers and his own function in the undertaking by means of categories reminiscent of the patriarchal order' (1982, 99–100).

21. Though addressed to the 'Right Honourable Lord Mildmay, Earle of Westmorland', Robert Herrick's poem, 'The Hock-Cart, or Harvest Home' (1648) also makes the bribery of such largesse explicit.

22. 'Myra' was the name Granville used for his poetic mistress and is quoted as such in Pope's *Windsor Forest* (1713, l.298). Mary Leapor worked for a short while as a kitchen maid at Weston Hall, Northamptonshire and perhaps at Edgcote House. There is some debate as to whether Crumble-Hall is a depiction of either.

23. Compare Jane Eyre's similarly snatched moments on the roof of Thornfield and their figuring as a moment of liberation (Brontë 1847; 1966, 140–1).

24. In Landry's reading, this 'ideal' description is revealed as ironic by its culmination, in lines 27–8, in 'a riot of comically conspicuous consumption that wastes resources in order to satisfy human greed' (1990, 109). See also Greene's criticism of Landry's reading (1993, 139–40).

25. This line thus tends to confirm Griffin's argument that '[Leapor's] stance seems resignation and bemused ironic deference rather than resentment and anger' (1996, 195).

26. For the connections between Mandeville's thesis of 'private vices, public benefits' and Pope's *Epistles,* see Brown (1985, 108–27, especially 110). One further complication, which Brown does not discuss, is the satirising of Old Cotta's justification for his meanness in lines 185–6: he defends his lack of hospitality on the grounds that the rich are already crammed and to feed the poor would be to take them from 'providence'.

27. See *Epistle to Burlington* (ll.133–40) and Pope's own note (Rogers 1993, 247, n.133); *Epistle to Burlington* (ll.152–3) and Pope's own note (Rogers 1993, 248, n.153); *Epistle to Bathurst,* Pope's note to l.296 (Rogers 1993, 261).

28. In his discussion of the poem's opening section, Greene argues that: 'its underlying values are not that far removed from the basically conservative view of society advanced in [the country-house] poems' (137). But this is to read nostalgia as inevitably reactionary and falsifying.

29. The Chaunceys tore down Edgcote House and rebuilt it in 1746 (Rizzo 1991, 340 n.9).

30. This poem takes as its ostensible subject the grotto of which Duck was keeper, sympathetically discusses the plight of the poor, and adopts the alias of 'Peter Drake, a fisherman'. William Diaper's *Dryades* also identifies fear of ghosts with vice (see Ross 1970, 83, ll.20–3).

6 'The Muffled Clink of Crystal Touching Mahogany': Jane Austen in the 1990s

> 'It makes me most uncomfortable to see
> An English spinster of the middle class
> Describe the amorous effect of "brass"
> Reveal so frankly and with such sobriety
> The economic basis of society.'
> (Auden 1968, 41)

> '[T]he popular press fluttered readers for three years and more with rumours that Jane Austen's text was not only being readied for television, but was going to feature a *nude* Mr Darcy – as if Austen's economic romance were not more complex, shaded, and, well, more passionate, than mere flesh. If sex were all there were to it, we've seen it before. But when the BBC camera turns its yearning gaze on Britain's Historic Houses, Castles, and Gardens, their vast acres smiling in the sunshine, their sweeping Capability Brown parks, the splendid house presiding over it all, then the blood begins to pump in earnest.' (Copeland 1997, 131)

Among the best-selling authors in Britain in the 1990s was a woman writer whose novels, when first published, had often failed to sell their initially small runs, and two novels had had to be remaindered. Her novels had received few reviews, most of which were short and the only one of any length or consequence was a specially commissioned piece by her publisher. That author was, of course, Jane Austen.[1] Sales figures between then and now can certainly not be correlated directly: editions of novels in the early nineteenth century were typically small because few could afford the price of a novel, and those who could were often unprepared to buy a book which might be read only once. Because novels were held in low esteem, novel-reading being synonymous with frivolity and effeminacy, best sellers were more likely to be Bibles, common prayer books, devotional works, school books, guides and other reference books, 'classics' (books by established and revered authors, such as Shakespeare, Milton, Cowper) and ephemera (cheap almanacs, magazines). The more important publishing figure is thus the number of books sold to the circulating libraries: 351 copies of *Emma* were sold in advance to London booksellers, an indication of its comparative success, while only 36 copies of the second edition of *Mansfield Park* were subscribed in this way (Fergus 1991, 20).

Today you can pay between £1 and £3,000 for a copy of Jane Austen's *Emma*. £3,000 buys a first edition of the novel, re-backed but with contemporary binding in half-leather and with a 'marble boards' cover.[2] £1 buys the same text, but in a paperback edition, published by Wordsworth Classics. Wordsworth editions (only in business since 1987) decided in June 1992 to produce classics without the additional expense of commissioning and printing the traditional apparatus of a classic text: introduction and notes. And because there were no royalties to pay, they could then sell each paperback classic for only £1. The first novel so published – Emily Brontë's *Wuthering Heights* – sold 600,000 copies. Wordsworth Classics now publishes four new titles a month and average sales per title are calculated to be 230,000. In response to this competition, both Penguin and Oxford World's Classics, leading publishers for classic works, brought out cheaper editions of their titles.[3] These cheap editions mean that Jane Austen's fiction is available for most budgets. This does not mean, however, that Jane Austen continues to be read much beyond the middle and upper classes. But for the reasons for the similarity of audiences between then and now, we need to move beyond the cost of the books themselves.

Jane Austen's contemporary popularity is also largely due to the television serialisation and film adaptation of her novels. Thirteen million people are calculated to have watched the final episode of BBC's *Pride and Prejudice*, a record audience for a television costume drama, narrowing the gap between classics and soap operas.[4] In the first two weeks of its run in Britain, *Sense and Sensibility* took £1.8 million at the box-office, while *Emma* took $25 million in its first weekend in the USA. These modern adaptations sell the novels as well as themselves. After the Hollywood film and TV adaptations of *Emma*, *Pride and Prejudice* and *Sense and Sensibility*, the novels were reissued by several publishers. No copyright payment is due to a long-dead author (current legislation specifies that copyright law applies until 75 years after the author's death), but new costs arose. Since these reissues were obviously cashing in on the film adaptations, all wanted tie-in photographs of the actresses playing Austen heroines. Bloomsbury paid Columbia films £60,000 for a cover-shot of Emma Thompson and Kate Winslet as Elinor and Marianne Dashwood; Mandarin paid 'more than' £50,000 for a photograph of Gwyneth Paltrow, the star of Miramax's *Emma*, while Penguin paid £15,000 for one of Kate Beckinsale, Emma in ITV's version. Increased sales of Austen's novels – Bloomsbury sold 150,000 copies of *Sense and Sensibility*, Penguin sold 25,000 copies of *Pride and Prejudice* in just one week – are due both to the adaptations themselves and to the suggestive advertising of these classic cover tie-ins. If evidence were needed, the success of tie-in books supplies it: *The Making of Pride and Prejudice*, for example, sold more than 100,000 copies, outstripping Penguin's reissue of the novel, even with Colin Firth (Darcy) and Jennifer Ehle (Elizabeth Bennet) on the cover. [5]

Like Jane Austen describing 'the amorous effect of "brass"', then, this chapter must consider these hard-core statistics in its reading of the film and TV versions.[6] Information about these adaptations of the novels is not confined to the 'leisure' or 'review' supplements of the broadsheet newspapers, but is also to be found on the home affairs and business sections, even (after the phenomenal success of BBC's *Pride and Prejudice*, for example) in the leader columns. This testifies to the enormous cultural prestige which Jane Austen enjoys, not only as a writer of 'classic novels' which are widely believed to be a necessary part of the school curriculum, but also as a writer who embodies 'Englishness'.[7] And, in the late twentieth century, when service industries such as tourism and entertainment are even bigger business than manufacturing output, when, as the *Guardian* leader writer commented 'we export Austen rather than Austin', the issues of cultural and economic value are more intertwined than ever.[8]

Images of England: the hard sell

Television and film adaptations of classic novels proliferated in Britain in the 1980s and 1990s,[9] but the images of a heritage England are associated primarily with Jane Austen. Raphael Samuel in *Theatres of Memory* (1994) argued that heritage encompasses everything from Viking artefacts to 50s rock memorabilia and is enjoyed by people from all classes. His book is largely a celebration of the way in which post-war British culture has modernised, democratised and expanded our definitions of the past through heritage pursuits and obsessions. But 'heritage England' more popularly suggests the stately homes and gardens and well-crafted artefacts which have become such an essential part of Jane Austen adaptations. This heritage is associated with National Trust landscapes and country houses, Regency muslin dresses, Chippendale furniture and Wedgwood china. But this is an image of country-house culture which satisfies contemporary tastes: there is no room here for the stuffed birds, stags' heads and elephants' feet which were also part of the great estates' ideas of interior design. Samuel historicises this: in the 1950s country houses were seen as moribund, as sepulchres of decay, but in the 1960s, country houses were promoted as the very quintessence of Englishness (1994, 58). Urban dreams of the country were fostered by factors as diverse as central heating (which permitted plants to flourish indoors) and new gardening techniques in container-grown shrubs, so that by the 1980s, garden festivals were created as a key remedy for urban blight (62) and *The Country Diary of an Edwardian Lady* became a world best seller, inspiring a range of objects with flowered borders on everything from matching duvet and curtain sets to kettles (66).

That Jane Austen's popularity might have something to do with romantic images of a pastoral, idyllic England is evident in the kinds of books which are published for the non-specialist reader. Coffee-table books about Jane Austen outnumber those for any other English author. Susan Watkins, for example, in *Jane Austen's Town and Country Style* (1990), writes that the Regency gentry were a 'group of people of unsurpassed elegance and refinement' and that her book will give her readers access to such refinement, insofar as it will allow them 'to wander, to gaze and to gain an almost tactile understanding of this world'. She wants them to imagine 'the muffled clink of crystal touching mahogany'.[10] The concrete link between the fiction and a special kind of England is also evident in the tourist interest in Jane Austen. Chawton House, Austen's home in her final years, receives an average of 30,000 visitors a year. (This figure doubled after the BBC screened its version of *Pride and Prejudice.*) Signposts on A-roads into north-east Hampshire signal 'Jane Austen country'. The BBC adaptation of *Pride and Prejudice* filmed Darcy's estate, 'Pemberley', at Lyme

Park, Cheshire; admissions soared after the television run. Usually Lyme Park would expect 800 visitors per week in off-peak November; in November 1995, 5,500 visitors turned up on the final two days. Lyme Park quickly produced a leaflet for a 'Pemberley trail' showing key shots from the series.[11] Given such statistics, it is not surprising that the English Tourist Board awarded the BBC series one of its top tourism awards, 'England for Excellence'. The BBC series was sold to 15 countries, including Australia, New Zealand, Poland, Israel, Slovenia and all of Scandinavia. On the Arts and Education Network in North America, the series achieved record ratings for that channel of 11.1 million.[12] Visitors to Chawton House, or Lyme Park, are confirmed in the sense that the series' image of England is 'real', rather than a way of seeing. Of course Lyme Park is a 'real' place in a way which Pemberley is not, but one of the consequences of the television dramatisation is to make Pemberley real, to naturalise it as an image of Regency England. This is not a false image, but it is a partial one, and the tendency of the film versions of Jane Austen is to make this particular way of seeing Regency England the 'historical' or representative one.

The film versions of *Emma*, *Sense and Sensibility*, and the television dramatisations of *Persuasion*, *Pride and Prejudice* and *Emma* all share a conscientious attempt to re-create the past in all its detail. Researchers study the details of empire-line dresses and tippets, of frock-coats and straw bonnets. The choreographers of both *Emma* and *Pride and Prejudice* chose the dance 'Mr Beveridge's Maggot', found in *The Apted Book of Country Dancing*. But this attention to detail tends to re-create the past in a pristine condition in which it never existed. Clothes are made from patterns cut from original garments, but the fabric is never worn, recycled or wrinkled. And there is a danger that such 'contrived authenticities', in Samuel's phrase, fetishise the past so that 'authentic' period detail becomes the most important aspect of these versions. Such period details are expected, and even demanded by many viewers who would appear to watch the adaptations as an extension of *Antiques Roadshow*: the makers of the television series of Richardson's *Clarissa* (BBC 1991) received complaints about the inauthenticity of teacup handles, and one viewer of *Middlemarch* (BBC 1994) pointed out that a saddle was twenty years out of date.

Samuel's study of heritage in *Theatres of Memory* includes an attack on those critics who have censured English 'heritage' as a reactionary form of nostalgia (see, for example, Hewison 1987 and Wright 1991). But Samuel himself is severely critical of the period film versions of Dickens, and especially the highly praised *Little Dorrit* (directed by Christine Edzard; 1987). He argues that truthfulness to period and fidelity to the text had been treated as equivalents, and that period authenticities had fetishised the past, rather than re-created the novel (417). Samuels much prefers David Lean's film versions of Dickens in the 1940s, and jokes about how *Great Expectations* (1946) is a film of its time, not ours: 'Satis House, Miss Havisham's mysterious residence, would, of course, be a listed building; possibly on account of the gargoyles classified as Grade I. Pip could hardly set about destroying it, as he does in the closing sequence of David Lean's film. "Watch the dado, darling", it is not difficult to imagine Estella crying out as he moves to rip down the curtain, "and do be careful of the panelling"' (423). Because so much of the culture of that era has been recuperated as fetishised images of an already romanticised past, we are in danger of losing the ability to judge it. We think when we see a lovingly reproduced artefact that we look at what a Georgian lady might have looked upon – but we see differently, because in our context, these artefacts mean very differently indeed. Even the everyday object becomes glamorised as an antique.

That context determines how we view objects is not something which cinematic realism encourages us to consider. Objets d'art, sumptuous rooms and spacious grounds become a major part of these reproductions and, in the camera's loving eye, they compete with the narrative space of the films. This is the film as conspicuous consumption. Roger Michell's dramatisation of *Persuasion* is an exception here: dinner party scenes are shot convincingly darkly, so that candle-light permits faces to be illuminated, but little else.[13] The dinner with Captain Wentworth at Uppercross is shot with close-up frames, so that the film focuses on the characters and their behaviour and feelings, rather than on their surroundings. And throughout the film, the camera is inquisitive, intrusive and probes with melancholy the pallid sadness of Anne Elliott. More typical of the heritage film is the long shot which permits a wide amount of display – shots of the interior of Hartfield in the Hollywood *Emma* and of Norland Park in *Sense and Sensibility*, for example, in which long rooms and high ceilings display conspicuous wealth, such as Norland Park's stairway, 'wallpapered' with paintings. As Andrew Higson has argued: 'The use of long takes and deep focus, and long and medium shots rather than close-ups, produces a restrained aesthetic of display' (Higson 1996, 234). The cinematography of Miramax's *Emma* is especially honeyed, with dappled soft focus lenses and no bad weather at all. (*Sense and Sensibility* and *Persuasion* are at least more accurate about English weather!) And in all the camera-work is pictorialist and the editing unobtrusive, which makes what the camera constructs seemingly 'real'.

Yet representations of wealth need not intrinsically be part of popular conservatism. There is obviously a case to be made for the conspicuous wealth of Norland Park or Hartfield: the first underlines the financial descent which the Dashwood family suffers when they are disinherited from Norland while the second might serve to emphasise Emma's spoilt and privileged upbringing. But the novels' subtle gradations between social and economic ranks are in danger of being lost when everything on screen is so idyllic. In *Sense and Sensibility* the removal of the Dashwoods from Norland Park to Barton Cottage is a plummeting descent down the social ladder, but the Barton Cottage of the film version, with its dramatic setting by the coast and its eggshell blue walls, is a home which estate agents today would sell at a price beyond most viewers' finances, partly because we value such 'unspoilt' country retreats. The screenwriter for *Pride and Prejudice*, Andrew Davies, celebrates the advantages of the camera over the book in, for example, its ability to establish some things quickly, but his illustration of this is in danger of rebounding. Davies argues that the opening shot of Netherfield allows the contrast between Longbourn and Netherfield to be foregrounded, since Longbourn is evidently about twenty times smaller than Netherfield: 'That indicates that the income of the Bennet family is about a twentieth of the income of the guys they hope to marry. And you can convey all of that without any ponderous dialogue' (Birtwistle and Conklin 1995, 3). But Longbourn itself is beyond the incomes of most of the series' spectators. Angela Horn, owner of Luckington Court where the scenes at Longbourn were shot, warned: 'I'd advise anyone contemplating [having their house in a film] to find a separate wing to live in' (25).[14]

That Barton Cottage and Longbourn are in themselves idyllic to contemporary audiences is an indication of how narrow Jane Austen's focus was. While *Emma* might be seen to include the entire range of social gradations, from the dedication of the novel to the Prince Regent to the episode with the gypsies, Jane Austen's focus is primarily that of the 'pseudo-gentry' who, though they did not own landed estates, aspired to the lifestyle and social status of the gentry.[15] They mark their gentility by the things they can afford to buy, but are always financially vulnerable: because their wealth is not in land, loss of income is always potential (perhaps because the breadwinner might die, or ill-judged investments might crash). Gentility might be possible on a competence of £300 to £1000 per annum and so even after their disinheritance the Dashwoods, Austen's poorest principal family, maintain a life of refinement on their £500.[16] This permits them to employ three servants, two women and a boy, with some of the accoutrements of refinement, such as a piano. Not for them a horse and carriage (which requires a competence of at least £800 per annum) nor the expenses of a season in London (which requires upwards of £5,000 per annum). These are the luxuries which will be beyond Elinor and Edward Ferrars: 'neither of them quite enough in love to think that £350 a year would supply them with the comforts of life' (Austen 1906, 312). Compared to Darcy's £10,000 a year, or even Emma's dowry of £1,500 per annum (investing her £30,000 in government bonds of 5%), Edward and Elinor may be poor indeed. But we might need to be reminded at this point that, according to Hobsbawm's calculations, less than 15% of British families in 1800 had an income of more than £50 per annum, and of these only one quarter earned more than £200 per annum (Hobsbawm 1977, 52).

Marxist readings of Jane Austen are thus often as much a matter of reading what the novels exclude or marginalise as what they focus upon. David Aers (1981) argues that Austen's ideology is made extremely vulnerable by its failure to acknowledge the existence of the working class and that Emma's major flaw is her failure to recognise the capitalist dimensions of Tory ideology, a flaw which she also shares with Mr Knightley. Knightley appears to represent a fixed, stable, stratified and coherent social order which is neo-feudal, as, for example, in his criticism of Emma for raising Harriet 'out of' her station. But he fails to see either that this social mobility is the very thing which capitalism makes possible, or that by reinvesting his profits on the land at Donwell Abbey he, like Robert Martin, is a figure of the agrarian capitalist. *Emma* is the only Austen novel to include the poorest classes within its social spectrum, but the episodes in which Emma visits the poor sick family and Harriet is attacked by the gypsies are both briefly sketched and the causal relationship between the wealthiest and the poorest of the neighbourhood is one which is inadmissible to the novel. It never suggests, for example, that we read Emma's snobbery as an inevitable product of her place within English society and while Emma's charity towards the family she visits is ironised by her quick forgetting of them, patrician charity itself is not.[17] Emma's wealth permits her to live untrammelled by material concerns, so that she need only recognise her desires to fulfil them. In Maaja Stewart's discussion of *Emma* (1993), the rural poor and vulnerable, impoverished women (embodied in such figures as Miss Taylor, Jane Fairfax, Harriet Smith and Miss Bates) are equally marginalised by the self-sufficient plenty of Hartfield or Donwell Abbey. But in Stewart's reading this joint marginalisation links them 'in ways that could potentially disturb the novel's dominant celebration of complacent settlement' (138). Indeed, this linking can be read at the level of the text itself. In Chapter 45, Miss Bates's commentary on the news of Jane's being employed by Mrs Smallridge is interwoven with the story of 'Old John', who was clerk to the vicar for 27 years but now, aged and sick, is in need of parish help. And there is a suggestion that the mention of such poverty leads Emma to think of Jane Fairfax: 'There was nothing in all this either to astonish or interest, and it caught Emma's attention only as it united with the subject which already engaged her mind' (Austen 1966, 376). This is not of course to claim that Emma is a potential radical in connecting the rural poor with the precarious social positions of women. As Stewart notes, the connections between the poor and the vulnerability of many of the novel's female characters is undeveloped and '[e]ven as [Emma] absolves Jane Fairfax from the "world's law", she pointedly does not absolve the gypsy woman and "half a dozen children" who frighten Harriet on the high road by "demanding more"' (151). However, reading the novel symptomatically (as in Stewart's discussion) can make what is ostensibly marginalised most significant.[18]

The recent film dramatisations often include shots of the kinds of groups of people which the novels themselves largely ignore. In early shots of Kellynch Hall in the BBC production of *Persuasion* we see labourers in the fields and gardens; servants beat the grass to raise pheasants for the Uppercross shooting party; as the central characters walk on the Cobb at Lyme, women busily fillet fish by the shoreside; in Bath a lamplighter climbs his ladder in one street scene, while Anne gives to a beggar on the doorstep of Mrs Smith's lodgings. In the BBC's *Pride and Prejudice* we see local men drink and cavort in the street outside the Meryton ball and a farrier at work as the Bennet sisters meet with the local militia. The Hollywood *Emma* includes the scenes of Emma's visit to the sick family and the attack by the gypsies, though both appear to feature to endear Emma to us, and at least one critic remarked that the first of these is paralysed by its good intentions. The tendency to people the frames of town and village scenes with extras, including beggars and labourers, is often mocked in the reviews, as a sop to political correctness. But they are of a piece with the shared attempt to portray England in the early nineteenth century more 'realistically' than Austen attempted or even cared to. The ladies trip through mud and horse dung on the way to a London ball in *Sense and Sensibility*, Darcy takes a bath in *Pride and Prejudice*. Such inclusions, added to the naturalistic acting styles and dialogue, and camera-work of regular frames, fixed perspective and eye-level shots, all present the narratives as 'real', supported by the conspicuous 'authenticity' of period detail. Such styles are quite different from earlier costume dramas. In MGM's 1940 film of *Pride and Prejudice* the characters happily exclaim such catchphrases as 'lawks a daisy', 'fiddlesticks' and 'ah, the polka mazurka' and the costumes are updated to the Victorian period because, notoriously, the high-waisted Regency dresses did not flatter Greer Garson (who played Elizabeth Bennet to Laurence Olivier's Darcy). Huge liberties with the text are also taken: Lady Catherine de Bourgh becomes Darcy's benevolent aunt, whose visit to Longbourn is played as high farce (she sits down on a musical box and is squawked at by the family parrot) and whose show-down with Elizabeth is staged only to prove Elizabeth's indifference to Darcy's fortune.

MGM's version of *Pride and Prejudice* is on one level an obviously more 'conservative' text than the 1995 BBC production, nowhere more so than in its sanitisation of the tyrannous Lady Catherine. But its Hollywoodisation of Jane Austen at least entails that its viewers can be under few illusions as to the 'reality' of this representation of Regency England. The film is so conspicuously a representation, at least when viewed in the 1990s. Of course we can also read the recent film versions of Jane Austen as constructions too. *Sense and Sensibility* in particular is shot in such a painterly style that it seems frequently to draw attention to artistic intertexts which foreground its own artfulness. Philip French in his review for *The Observer* wrote: 'Michael Coulter's painterly cinematography evokes from the West Country locations the England of Gainsborough and Stubbs'.[19] The shot in which Marianne gives her mother the letter from Sir John inviting them to take up the tenancy of Barton Cottage evokes Vermeer's painting *The Letter* (1666) in which two women are framed by the perspective window of a doorway, and a subsequent shot in which Edward watches Elinor through the frame of a door, who in turn watches Marianne play the piano through a doorway, also evokes the subdued interiors of Vermeer. Here background is being used expressionistically, rather than referentially.

Both heritage glossiness and ironic undercutting are possible readings in Miramax's *Emma*. It is easy to read this adaptation as Hollywood's fetishisation of an image of England. 'Period' details such as eighteenth-century songs by Handel and John Gay and 'authentic' furniture are lovingly re-created, and acknowledgements are extended to the 'Rare poultry, pig and plant centre' and 'Isis Ceramics'. The final credit of the film is reserved for 'Filmed on location in Dorset and London, England'. But it is a fetishisation rather than a replication, because the re-creation is done to current tastes, while masquerading as 'authenticity'. No respectable lady in Regency England would have worn make-up, but none of the period-film versions show us blemished or pale complexions. *Emma* credits Estée Lauder for its make-up while shooting many of the interior scenes at sunset so that the female characters are bathed in late sunlight and seem more Mediterranean than English. The film's fetishisation is revealed at a number of points. The first credited thanks are given to Giorgio Armani so that, even though most costumes were hired from the London costumiers Cosprop, who specialise in period dress (and were also used for the BBC production of *Pride and Prejudice*) Armani, among the most expensive and chic of contemporary fashion designers, was ultimately preferred for the costumes for Emma/Gwyneth Paltrow. However this ironic undercutting remains only potential, and cinema-going and video-watching practice is usually to ignore the credits beyond the names of the actors. Slightly more overt, if attempting to work subliminally, is the transition from amateur music ensemble to full orchestra when Knightley leads Harriet to the dance floor in the Highbury ball scene. This replicates and exposes the novel as a romance, as evidently a fantasy rather than real. Most of the camera shots have regular frames and a fixed camera perspective so that the eye-level shots are shared with the viewer and the images are then naturalised as 'real'. But there is one camera shot in the film which intervenes in the narrative, rather than merely giving us an ostensibly neutral representation of events and characters. When Mr Knightley complains of having to go to the ball in Highbury, he and Emma are standing in the grounds of Donwell Abbey, a pleasing prospect of fields around. As Knightley says 'I just want to stay here where it's cosy', the camera pans around so that we see the Abbey itself, a rather grand mansion, Palladian in style, for which the adjective 'cosy' seems greatly, and obviously, understated. Here the camera captures something of the tone of narrative irony which is common in Jane Austen's novels though not, admittedly, at the expense of Knightley's conspicuous wealth.

This shot is unusual in the film, though it is truer to the spirit of the novel's narrative. In translating text to film, the camera fulfils the function of the narrator. It directs our attention and has its own 'tone': commonsensical, dispassionate and honest when conveying realism through the conventions of 'unmanipulated' cinematic realism (such as deep-focus photography, long duration sequences with few cut-away shots, a relatively static camera and continuity editing); playful and ironic when experimenting with or deviating from these conventions. But the narrator of *Emma* is not that of classic realism, objective and dispassionate. Rather the narrative voice of Jane Austen's *Emma* shades frequently into that of Emma, allowing us to read Emma ironically at key moments. For example, as Emma anticipates breaking the news to Harriet that Mr Elton has proposed to her, we can see how Emma will reassure herself: 'It was a great consolation ... that Harriet's nature should not be of that superior sort in which the feelings are most acute and retentive ...' (Austen 1985, 156). Through such narrative ironies we can see how Emma's views of others are frequently coloured by her own self-interest. So few scenes take place in Emma's absence, that most of the narrative appears as being from Emma's perspective, through her eyes.[20] This can be seen in the following description of Frank Churchill's decided enthusiasm to hold a ball at the Crown Inn, where the views of Frank and Emma interweave in reported speech (his) and ventriloquised thought (hers):

> Why had not Miss Woodhouse revived the former good old days of the room? – She who could do any thing in Highbury! The want of proper families in the place, and the conviction that none beyond the place and its immediate environs could be tempted to attend, were mentioned; but he was not satisfied. He could not be persuaded that so many good-looking houses as he saw around him, could not furnish

numbers enough for such a meeting; and even when particulars were given and families described, he was still unwilling to admit that the inconvenience of such a mixture would be any thing, or that there would be the smallest difficulty in every body's returning into their proper place the next morning. ... Emma was rather surprized to see the constitution of the Weston prevail so decidedly against the habits of the Churchills. ... Of pride, indeed, there was, perhaps, scarcely enough; his indifference to a confusion of rank, bordered too much on inelegance of mind. He could be no judge, however, of the evil he was holding cheap. It was but an effusion of lively spirits. (209–10)

As the son of Mr Weston, a member of the aspiring gentry, but adopted by his mother's aristocratic family, the Churchills, Frank Churchill is singularly placed both to understand and to want to over-step such discriminations. And in his secret engagement to the impoverished Jane Fairfax he is doubly more relaxed about such class mingling than Emma is prepared to be. Frank here discusses the possibility of a ball with Mr and Mrs Weston and Emma. Of the three, Emma is certainly the most likely to object that there is a lack of suit-able families for a fashionable society in Highbury. And the judge-ment that he is insufficiently proud is more plausibly Emma's than the narrator's, since this judgement is mixed with a determination to think well of him. Added to which, is the fear that to censure him would be to think him 'inelegant', since the criterion of 'elegance' is one which runs throughout Emma's commentaries. (For example, Augusta Elton lacks elegance; 273; and Emma disapproves of her 'studied elegance' of dress; 318.)

In contrast, in the film Emma's snobbery is ultimately underplayed because we judge her almost entirely through her public behaviour.[21] Gwyneth Paltrow catches the little hypocrisies in Emma's manner, her always ever-so-polite responses masking petty jealousies and condescensions. But there are only a couple of scenes in which we engage with a private Emma (when she reads to her diary or discusses her feelings with Mrs Weston) and these are too brief to replace the pervasive interior monologue of the novel. Without an equivalent narrative device, such as might be achieved with edited shots or voice-over, we cannot make the kinds of discrimination which the novel encourages, such as the difference between 'Emma's unap-proved social snobbery and her proper moral aversion to Mrs Elton's loud-mouthed self-approval' (McMaster 1997, 124). Austen's narrative voice is a register which is always potentially shaded. Gary Kelly's analysis of the political implications of her writing is appropriate here, and ideally blends formal and contextual considerations. Literary form in the Romantic period is extremely politicised and Jacobin and anti-Jacobin polemics are expressed in literary reviews, stage plays, history writing and, of course, novels. In analysing Austen's position within this context, Kelly ultimately argues that her narrative method mediates between the opposing political associations of form:

> Apparently she experimented with first-person epistolary form in the 1790s, but finally opted for third-person narration with restricted free indirect discourse, or narrator's representation of the protagonist's inward speech and thought. The effect is to retain narrative authority but allow the reader considerable knowledge of and thus sympathy for the protagonist. Austen's use of this narrative method can be read as a formal homology for a hierarchical yet open social structure, stabilized by inherited authority based on wealth and power but open to individual merit and responsive to individual rights based on it, while avoiding extremes of authoritarianism and individualism. (Kelly 1997, 160–1).

Kelly thus traces the same kind of binary contradictions as Aers and Williams see in the antinomies of bourgeois ideology – at the level of style itself.

In comparison, film's pervasive medium is that of the surface. In her study of the BBC's 1972 serialisation of *Emma* Monica Lauritzen recounts how the researcher, whose special task it was to reproduce Harriet's riddle-book, created 'a beautiful volume decorated with pressed flowers and a variety of pictures', a beautiful book which might plausibly adorn Emma's escritoire, but was inappropriate for Harriet (whose book in the novel is described as 'a thin quarto of hot-pressed paper') and failed to convey the narrator's gentle mocking of Harriet's 'literary pursuit' (Lauritzen 1981, 115–16). As Roger Sales notes, this anecdote illustrates Lauritzen's argument that 'television invariably celebrates elegant surfaces whereas Austen's novels are much more concerned to explore discrepancies between surfaces, particularly conversational ones, and substance' (Sales 1994, 24). For example, the BBC *Pride and Prejudice* makes the distinctions in wealth between the Bingley and Bennet sisters patently clear, but does not allow us to understand the Bingley sisters' extreme condescension as an attempt to shore up their own vulnerable gentility (Mr Bingley, like the Gardiners, was initially a tradesman) because the narrator's positioning of the characters has either been cut from the script or lost in the editing room.

In contrast, Austen's narratives are surprisingly reticent about the kinds of details which the film versions delight in. Ornaments and paintings, dress, interior design and landscaping – none of these are recorded in any specificity in the novels. In reading the novels we do not need to visualise. As Miller argues, in his discussion of the transference of text to film, the mind's eye of the reader can have a completely indeterminate image which doesn't seem incomplete (Miller 1986, *passim*). Film, in contrast, fetishises images, as Virginia Woolf recognised as early as 1926:

> The eye says 'Here is Anna Karenina', a voluptuous lady in black velvet wearing pearls comes before us. But the brain says 'That is no more Anna Karenina than it is Queen Victoria'. For the brain knows Anna almost entirely by the inside of her mind – her charm, her passion, her despair. All the emphasis is laid by the cinema upon her teeth, her pearls, and her velvet.[22]

The sumptuousness of Austen's settings are, of course, implicit in all of her novels, for they are all peopled by gentry families whose aspirations to gentility are measured in conspicuous consumption and the trappings of wealth, whether land, property or the latest fashions. But it is difficult to recuperate this kind of ostentatious wealth when the surrounding apparatus of the film and television series – advertising, reviews, publicity footage, tie-in sales – tie Austen so closely to the false nostalgias of the heritage industry.

Roger Michell's production of *Persuasion* attempts to escape this entrapment in a production which is comparatively dark and melancholy. But since *Persuasion* is the most sombre of all of Austen's novels, it is evidently easier to make a much less glossy film of *Persuasion* than of *Emma*, Austen's sunniest novel, despite the 'presence' of the poor family and the group of gypsies. Anne leaves Kellynch with an unglamorously red nose, a sign that she has been crying; Mary Musgrove's cottage has unplastered walls and both Captain Harville's terraced house in Lyme and Mrs Smith's lodgings in Bath are small, cramped and even dingy. The photographic colour is naturalistically grey, whereas even the poor family which Emma visits in Douglas McGrath's film is illuminated by a shaft of sunlight. Their cottage interior, with its smoky atmosphere but polished table, resembles a living-museum piece rather than a 'realistic' setting.[23] To praise the film version of *Persuasion* for its 'naturalism' is not an intrinsically marxist position. But the Jane Austen versions cannot be taken out of their contemporary culture, a culture which is more likely to give Austen's novels a romantic sheen and so turn an arguably conservative text into a decidedly conservative film. Many of *Persuasion*'s effects are the reverse of marxist practices. In focusing upon individuals, rather than period background, as suggested above, for example, it might be said to exacerbate an existing tension within Jane Austen's novels. For, despite the precision with which incomes, inheritances and real estate are recorded, the tendency of the plots is to lift their heroines out of this world into a world where romance is only a matter of individual feeling and, in the ideology of individualism, love conquers all. This kind of individualism suggests that we are born not into immanent or pre-existing classes or categories (such as class, race, gender, sexuality) but into a self or identity.[24] The cinematography of *Persuasion* certainly heightens the purely emotional register of the story, while also deviating from realist conventions. For Anne's first meeting with Wentworth, for example, the camera zooms quickly to her face and later closes in on her fingers on the cottage chair, both indicating her extreme panic and anxiety. Later, when Anne sees Wentworth pass the coffee-shop in Bath, the intrusive zoom is exacerbated by a sudden artificial silence, breaking off the chatter in the shop and the noise of the street outside. In another film, the close frames of individual faces might suggest an ahistoricising of the narrative in which context is excluded in a focus on temperament, behaviour and character. Because such techniques do not come to us in a predetermined form, once we consider *Persuasion* in the context of the other Jane Austen versions, its pallid naturalism and intense probing of individual characters become liberating gestures. However, the most successful breaks with popular conservatism come in those versions which eschew period detail completely.

Updating Austen

In the 1980s, heritage movies became identified with the productions of Merchant Ivory. Their biggest flop was a film entitled *Jane Austen in*

Manhattan, which suggests that Austen would not translate popularly if transplanted to America. But among the most successful Jane Austen adaptations of the last ten years have been two films which translate her novels into contemporary American settings: Whit Stillman's *Metropolitan* (1989) and Amy Heckerling's *Clueless* (1995). Stillman's movie was made independently from the major Hollywood production companies, and this means that *Metropolitan* was not widely distributed and enjoyed only a low-key success. *Clueless,* in contrast, was directed by Amy Heckerling, who had previously made *Look Who's Talking,* one of the most successful movies of 1989. Her film, backed by Paramount, enjoyed mainstream distribution and commercial success.

Clueless wears its parallels with *Emma* lightly, partly because it appears to have conflated Jane Austen's novel with *Beverly Hills 90210.* Cher (Alicia Silverstone), like Emma, is motherless, spoilt and indulged by her father. Popular at school, she is criticised only by her stepbrother Josh who can see that her befriending of Tai, a gawky unhip girl from the East Coast, is a form of manipulation (playing with her like a Barbie doll, in Josh's description). There are also parallels with Emma's mistaking Elton's interest in her painting for the subject of the painting (Cher's photograph of Tai is pinned inside Elton's locker); Harriet's attack by the gypsies and rescue by Frank Churchill (Tai is almost thrown over a railing by two young men in the shopping mall and is rescued by Christian); Robert Martin's attachment to Harriet (the 'loadie' or 'dope-head' Travis falls in love with Tai); Emma's self-interest in matchmaking (Cher's matching two of her teachers is so that her grades will be higher); Harriet burning mementoes of Elton (Tai burns a towel and cassette tape of special significance); Frank Churchill being not all that he seems (Christian, it is revealed, is gay); Knightley 'rescuing' Harriet from embarrassment at the ball (Josh dances with the left-on-the-shelf Tai); Emma discovering her love for Knightley when Harriet confesses to loving him (as with Cher, Tai and Josh) and Emma's rudeness to Miss Bates (Cher refuses to see any distinction between being a maid from Mexico or from El Salvador). Cher's reformation here is to recognise that she is as 'clueless' (uncool, lost or out of touch) in her failure to know her own feelings as those whom she had patronised. And the voice-over of Cher gives the film the same kind of presence, character and energy as the frequently unreliable narrative voice in the novel.

But *Clueless* works as a significant reinvention of the original text, not only in paralleling the plot details and narrative voice of *Emma,* but also in its choice of setting. Beverly Hills, Los Angeles is an appropriate parallel to the society Jane Austen depicts in that Cher's litigation-lawyer daddy ($500 an hour) can afford to give her a lifestyle where money is of no concern, but money rules. Cher has a masseuse, a personal trainer and a four-wheel drive jeep, with dual air bags and a monster sound system – just for learning to drive in. For such a life, shopping is the solution to all problems and the mall the refuge of the sad or bored. Her wardrobe in *Clueless* is designed by Jean-Paul Gaultier, Calvin Klein, DKNY, Agnes B and many other of the most 'chic', exclusive and expensive dress designers of the 1990s. Cher's first outfit, which we see her assemble virtually on computer, is chosen irrespective of cost. Anatomised her complete outfit costs as follows:

Junior Gaultier tartan jacket	£329
Junior Gaultier matching tartan kilt	£149
Junior Gaultier shrunken-wool knit vest	£109
Calvin Klein fitted T-shirt	£ 12.95
Calvin Klein bra and knicker set	£ 17.50
Hue over the knee socks	£ 9.95
Patrick Cox 'Wannabe' loafers	£120
Prada nylon mini-rucksack	£215
Total cost	£962.40[25]

Tai's gooky style just cannot compete, until Cher takes her in hand, and as Josh mocks, 'improves' her by introducing her to the challenging world of bare-midriff dressing. This is a society where love and money are intertwined (Elton refuses Tai as a girlfriend because of his father's status), where the deaths of young mothers are possible (Cher's mother dies of a 'routine' liposuction operation), appearance is everything and subtle class distinctions are crucial. Dress is the supreme signifier of status, but so too is language. Cher's group speaks a fashionable teenage American-English, sometimes hiply politically correct: a virgin is 'hymenally challenged', no way is 'as if', having a period is 'surfing the crimson wave'. To appear knowledgeable is cool, actually to have that knowledge is not important. Cher's first suggestion for Tai's expanding vocabulary is 'sporadically' which Tai instantly misuses, and which Cher later confuses in claiming to watch 'Sporadicus' (*Spartacus*). Billie Holliday is a man and the *Ren and Stimpy Show* is 'way existential'. (Though there is one finely erudite adjective in 'Monet' which translates as 'from far away it looks ok, but up close it's a way big mess'.) In Austen's fiction, class differences are not only distinct but must appear to be distinct. So in Beverly Hills, status appearance is all: half of the girls at Bronson Alcott High School are having plastic surgery, and when Cher asks 'Would you call me selfish?' and her best friend replies, 'Not to your face', she is sufficiently touched. Both Beverly Hills and Highbury are shown as small societies with pretensions to greatness, teeming with strict forms of etiquette and ludicrous social niceties. *Clueless* portrays a social world which is every bit as narrow as Austen's Highbury, but it wears its narrowness and superficiality unashamedly.

These excellent parallels are never heavy-handed, though there is one playful reference to film adaptations of the classics and the importance they assume. Josh's student girlfriend, Heather, earnest and intellectual, quotes 'To thine own self be true' as a line of Hamlet's. Cher corrects her, but Heather refuses to be corrected: 'I think that I remember *Hamlet* accurately'; Cher: 'Well I remember Mel Gibson accurately and he didn't say that. That Polonius guy did.' In the 1990s, Shakespeare is known through Hollywood adaptations of his plays, and students know Shakespeare's sonnets ('Rough winds do shake the darling buds of May ...') only as a quote from *Cliff's Notes*. High culture in Beverly Hills is used as a status symbol or as an 'investment' (the motivation behind her father's collection of Claes Oldenburg, Henry Moore and Giacometti sculptures to decorate his garden swimming pool). Cher's 'classic' house (complete with neo-classical columns) dates 'all the way back to 1972', an appropriate phrase for a film saturated in 1990s Californian popular culture: from references to the new Christian Slater movie and Snickers to a sound-track which includes REM, David Bowie, Radiohead, the Lightning Seeds, Coolio, the Beastie Boys, the Cranberries et al. And underlying this hip contemporaneity are the references to a comparatively dated and 'high cultural' Jane Austen.

Clueless parallels many of the issues raised in *Emma* in, for example, celebrating the importance of social kindness and puncturing self-opinion, but it does so without fetishising a heritage past. Its success as a film is also due to the way in which it parodies other versions. All of the period adaptations of Jane Austen use the standard technologies to create the illusion of cinematic realism and *Clueless* uses all of these conventions too in order to convince of its own verisimilitude. But it also parodies many of these. For example, all the films use music as an external mood maker, heavily exploited in mass media entertainment. Both *Pride and Prejudice* and *Emma*, for example, amplify a thin amateurish ensemble sound with full orchestra at heightened emotional moments (Knightley's leading Harriet to the dance at the Crown ball; Elizabeth and Darcy's eyes meeting over Georgiana's piano playing). *Clueless* parodies this convention of romantic film-making with ostentatiously saccharine 'mush' music when Christian first appears at the doorway of Cher's classroom, and at the moment of epiphany in which Cher realises she is already in love with Josh, there is both parodic romantic music and a suddenly unrealistically illuminated sky. Ultimately *Clueless* resists the dangers of the period adaptations because it is able to reflect upon its own condition, in distinction from theirs. In its playful use of its 'original' text, *Clueless* is closer to the 'retrochic' which Samuel celebrates than the 'revivalism' which is characteristic of period-costume drama: '[Retrochic] approaches its work in the spirit of the beachcomber, or the snapper-up of unconsidered trifles, rather than that of the antiquarian or the connoisseur collecting gems, treasuring relics and worshipping at time-hallowed shrines' (Samuel 1994, 112). It turns what is old-fashioned into what is up-to-date, it re-invents rather than imitates. And in this way, like Jane Austen, *Clueless* can tell us something about our own period, as well as hers.

Clueless might seem an unlikely choice of film for a marxist critic to celebrate. Its social world is as confined and exclusive as that of Jane Austen's novels. It, like *Emma*, ends with each character having found his or her 'own level' (Tai paired with Travis; Cher with Josh), though enjoying an amicable friendship which appears to transcend their social differences and which inevitably mystifies them. Though its approach to consumer culture, its use of dress and speech as status symbols is ironic, it is also complicit with this culture. And, in contrast to Austen's world, in which feudal and capitalist values are in tension, the world of *Clueless* is a world of triumphant capitalism. Cher's privileged lifestyle is the product of her father's aggressive acquisition of wealth. As in the discussion of *Persuasion*, then, *Clueless* is subversive only insofar as it is read against the more common period-costume treatments of Jane Austen. In transposing Highbury to hip Beverly Hills, *Clueless* exposes some of the purely monetary and capitalist aspects of *Emma* and it does so by moving outside the obsessive concern with period authenticity in the more traditional versions.

Jane Austen: our contemporary?

> 'Jane Austen offers us a vision of English country life that we very much want to have been true.' (Hammond 1993, 83)

> 'Austen is a cultural fetish; loving – or hating – her has typically implied meanings well beyond any encoded in her works.' (Johnson 1997, 212)

In a marxist reading of *Mansfield Park*, Brean Hammond argues that Jane Austen's fiction 'has been remarkably successful in dictating the terms in which it has later been discussed' (1993, 60). Yet, as I suggested above, Austen's fiction is not seen by all commentators as inherently conservative, however conservative Jane Austen herself may have been. The texts themselves can be read symptomatically, or against the grain, to reveal and even to question bourgeois ideology in the particular moment of their inscription. The film versions, in contrast, seem to offer us what we desire of Austen. There is no place here for surprise, or unexpectedness, which a close reading of the novels can always offer. As Lauritzen notes, in her analysis of the 1970 television series of *Emma*: '... the aim of Jane Austen was always to puncture the kind of complacent acceptance of appearances that the serial tends to invite from its audience' (1981, 116). Lauritzen's argument is open to the charge of condescension towards television spectators, as if they passively consume an ideological message already enclosed in the film. But the popularity of the adaptations is surely because they embody, in Blake's words, 'the lineaments of gratified desire'.

In this respect, the 1990s fashioning of Jane Austen is little different from the ways in which the cult of Jane Austen has been created and sustained since the later Victorian period. Austen's 'classic' status was not ensured until the last third of the century, when her great-nephew, the Reverend James Edward Austen-Leigh, published *A Memoir of Jane Austen* (1870). This portrayed Austen as the quintessentially domestic lady, a paragon of propriety and good sense (those particularly English qualities) and nostalgically placed her within a romantically pre-Industrial society: 'before express trains, sewing machines and photograph books' (see Sales 1994, 33 and Johnson 1997, *passim*). In turn-of-the-century studies by Constance Hill (*Jane Austen: Her Homes and Haunts*, 1901) and others, the stately homes and gardens and hand-crafted artefacts associated with her particular brand of Regency were foregrounded. There is more than a fortuitous link between this fashioning and the foundation of The National Trust (1895) and the heightened nostalgia for country life that developed almost simultaneously. In the First World War, Jane Austen was prescribed reading for soldiers suffering from post-traumatic stress (Kent 1989, 59), a surprisingly factual basis for Kipling's story of the artilleryman who reads Austen to escape into an extra-historical world far removed from the Great War ('The Janeites'; 1924). Thus in the early twentieth century, Austen is already being pressed into service as a national icon. Jane Austen societies have flourished since 1940 (when the first society was founded) and today stretch from Bath to Denmark, appreciating and commemorating Austen and her novels in all her and their lovingly precise details. And, in her bicentenary year (1975) Austen joined Dickens and Shakespeare in being commemorated in the UK with a series of postage stamps, signifying that she has 'arrived' indeed, as a writer whose novels have acquired considerable cultural prestige.

The relations between the 'Janeites' or non-professional appreciators of Austen and her academic critics have scarcely been collaborative, and tend to be deeply mistrustful.[26] In this divisive climate, any readings of Austen or her fiction which threaten her legacy are treated with hysteria. Two obvious examples of such readings are Eve Kosofsky Sedgwick's article, 'Jane Austen and the Masturbating Girl' (1991) and Terry Castle's review of a new edition of Jane Austen's letters (1995) in which she argued that we might now read the letters in the context of the recently recovered diaries of her lesbian contemporary, Anne Lister, and traced the passionate and sensuous elements of her letters to her sister Cassandra. Castle's article, predictably, caused a real stir in the tabloids and many of the broadsheets as headlines shocked those accustomed to associating Austen with English 'heritage'. (The headline in *The Sun* was 'Austen a lesbo'.)

Many of the 1990s adaptations do attempt to create a more radical Jane Austen in which the snobberies and condescensions of early nineteenth-century England are foregrounded. In the television films of *Persuasion* and *Pride and Prejudice* the aristocratic figures of the Dowager Lady Catherine Dalrymple and Lady Catherine de Bourgh are portrayed as oppressive and ridiculous. Lady Dalrymple wears white face powder which makes her look antiquated and cantankerous and her house in Bath is so heavily swathed in rich fabrics that the shaft of light through the curtained window looks as much like dust as sunlight. Lady de Bourgh wears a hat decorated with a dead bird, a visual echo of the great oil painting in her sitting room at Rosings and an oblique suggestion of her predatory nature.

In addition, these adaptations of Jane Austen often foreground the feminist potential within the texts. In *Sense and Sensibility*, for example, an added scene has Elinor explain to the young Margaret, in a direct and modern idiom, why they are being disinherited of Norland Park: 'Houses go from father to son, dearest – not from father to daughter. It is the law'. It also adds a conversation between Elinor and Edward in which the plight of the idle eldest son and that of middle- and upper-class ladies is contrasted: Edward notes that their circumstances are the same, but Elinor argues 'except that you will inherit your fortune; we cannot even earn ours'. And while this chapter has already considered the ways in which the film adaptations commodify the past, fetishising images of wealth and pre-industrial, rural beauty, the adaptations also commodify the male body. Many of the visitors to Lyme Park enquired if they could see the pond where Darcy/Colin Firth swam, which might suggest that they were as interested in him as they were in the country house itself. ('Darcy's wet shirt draws visitors' was one newspaper headline.)[27] In the 1990s, it is sex, as much as money, which sells; and the male body, as much as objets d'art, which is commodified. Roger Sales suggests that the cheesecake poses of dashing male heroes on the tie-in covers foreground the importance of the dandy-figure in Jane Austen's fiction (1994, 26).

Among the reasons cited for the popularity of Jane Austen adaptations (five period film versions in 1995–6) is that their popularity among women is made possible by changes within the film and television industries, with more female movie executives and producers; and that they provide challenging roles for actresses of all ages. The films' popularity among women might also be fruitfully studied in conjunction with cultural theories on romance fiction and film. Christine Geraghty's study of television soap operas in the 1980s might apply to the popularity of the film versions of Austen too: in both genres there is a division between public and private spheres, and women's centrality is based on their control of the emotional arena. Geraghty argues that there are important characteristics which the romance novel, the women's film and prime-time soaps share: 'all three genres seek to enable their readers to imagine an ideal world in which values traditionally associated with women are given space and expression and in which there is some model of the way in which relationships, particularly those between men and women, could be differently organised on women's terms' (1991, 116). In Janice Radway's analysis of popular romance fiction (1987), its popularity is interpreted as symptomatic of stresses elsewhere, a sign, for example, of women's need for time and privacy. And in her study of the Gainsborough melodramas of the 1940s, Pam Cook defends their popularity against those who dismiss costume drama as lightweight, feminine, obsessed with mere decoration and display, and as lacking the seriousness of real history (Cook 1996).[28]

There are other ways in which these adaptations foreground aspects of Austen's fiction which have been overlooked by Janeites and academic specialists alike. Roger Sales suggests, for example, that all of these versions illustrate the theatrical nature of Austen's fiction. The BBC adaptation of *Pride and Prejudice* suggests some melodrama in its obvious portrayal of the Bingley sisters as ugly sisters to Jane and Elizabeth's Cinderellas. And the ITV adaptation of *Emma* foregrounds the ways in which Emma's fantasies of power and influence through matchmaking are predicated on popular romances: as soon as Emma thinks of matching Mr Elton with Harriet, she is already imagining their wedding day, humorously embodied for us in a daydreaming, point-of-view shot, in which the couple perform for her. But the obvious fictionality of these scenes are both quickly subsumed by the overwhelming 'historicity' or 'realism' of the productions as a whole.

Thus despite these developments of the fiction, it remains difficult to recuperate the films from the accusation of popular conservatism because of the way in which they powerfully combine realist aesthetics with prevailing images of heritage England. This is something of a lost opportunity, for the conflation of our voyeurism and vicarious snooping on the houses and lifestyles of the wealthiest estates in England with that of Austen's own characters might fruitfully have been developed. Domestic tourism to English country houses became increasingly popular in the Romantic period, partly as a consequence of the war with France which made continental travel difficult, partly as a result of the rise of the picturesque. Improved roads (funded by turnpike levies), better sprung carriages and more commodious coaching inns also played a part. Thus social tourism arose as a national, patriotic and aesthetic pursuit, a way in which English ladies and gentlemen could learn to appreciate and in turn themselves embody 'refinement'. And, unlike the expensive Grand Tour to Italy, country-house visiting was open to the 'respectable' middle classes, who would be admitted by the housekeeper and would tip her accordingly. Ian Ousby, in his book on early tourism, argues that this accommodation between the aristocracy and the middle classes acted as a social cohesive, so that Englishmen in the 1790s or in 1848, the years of revolutionary ferment in France, were content to become tourists rather than revolutionaries (1990, 91).

This is a history in which we are still embedded. Part of the story of the late twentieth century's popular affection for country-house culture is the willingness of the car-owning middle classes to pay to visit country estates (Hewison 1987, 56–68). In 1960, Evelyn Waugh wrote a new preface for *Brideshead Revisited* (1945) in which he admitted that he had misjudged the future of the country houses, believing that they would fall into dereliction. By the 1970s, maintaining these estates was perceived to be the responsibility of the nation, rather than of their private owners. Peter Mandler (1997), in his survey of changing attitudes to the country estates, argues that from the 1970s the aristocracy ceased to pose a threat to middle-class aspirations and so their properties were viewed indulgently. In the 1990s estates can expect to win lottery grants, backed by the government agency English Heritage, and offer a wide range of commercial tourist activities, from golf courses to wildlife parks, model railways to housing and office parks. These are late twentieth-century economic strategies but the selling of these estates as tourist attractions is often solidly based on their eighteenth-century or Regency credentials. Stephen Daniels notes that in 1989 the stockbrokers Capel-Cure Myers advertised their investment plans using Capability Brown's maps and contracts for landscaping country houses (Daniels 1993, 106). In the 1990s, more than 16 million people were estimated to visit country seats in England (Ousby 1990, 59). The apparently 'democratic' openness of the country estates to visitors can be seen to encourage the same kind of political quietism as Ousby remarks of eighteenth-century tourism.[29]

The BBC adaptation of *Pride and Prejudice* suggested the complicity between Elizabeth Bennet's and our pleasure in the prospect of Pemberley, when the first sudden sight of the house, radiant in the sunlight, is presented. Here Andrew Davies's script foregrounds that Elizabeth's desire for Darcy is also inextricably linked with desire for his property. The novel certainly suggests this: 'They were all of them warm in their admiration; and at that moment she felt that to be mistress of Pemberley might be something!' (Austen 1972, 267). But its suggestion is oblique, deflected by the characteristic irony of the narrative voice. In the television series, the romance which property itself extends is made explicit in the following conversation between Elizabeth and her aunt and uncle Gardiner:

> Mrs Gardiner: I think one would be willing to put up with a good deal to be mistress of Pemberley. How do you like the house, Lizzie?
>
> Elizabeth: Very well. I don't think I've ever seen a place so happily situated. I like it ... (*pause*) ... very well indeed. ...
>
> Mr Gardiner: Pity then its owner should be such a proud and disagreeable man.
>
> Elizabeth: Yes, a great pity. (*She laughs*)
>
> Mrs Gardiner: Perhaps the beauty of the house renders its owner a little less repulsive, Lizzie.
>
> Elizabeth: Yes, perhaps. (*Pause. She laughs.*) Perhaps a very little.

Austen's description of Darcy's house is characteristically succinct. But from the few details that are given, Pemberley would appear to be quite different from Lyme Park, where this episode was shot for the BBC production. In the novel's description, the naturalness of the situation is emphasised: ' ... in front, a stream of some natural importance was swelled into greater, but without any artificial appearance. Its banks were neither formal nor falsely adorned. Elizabeth was delighted. She had never seen a place for which nature had done more, or where natural beauty had been so little counteracted by an awkward taste' (Austen 1972, 267). Lyme Park's neo-classical style (it was built around 1725 by Giacomi Leoni) is of a quite different order. The disjuncture between the baroque style of Lyme and the picturesque romanticism of Pemberley's front reveals that this is a vision which speaks to *our* desire.[30]

Similarly, in *Emma* Donwell Abbey and its grounds are presented as an idyllic vision of England. This is nowhere so apparent than in the description of Donwell's Abbey-Mill Farm:

> It was a sweet view – sweet to the eye and the mind. English verdure,
> English culture, English comfort, seen under a sun bright, without
> being oppressive. ... It might be safely viewed with all its appendages
> of prosperity and beauty, its rich pastures, spreading flocks, orchard
> in blossom, and light column of smoke ascending. (1985, 355)

This pastoral paradise is a place where the orchard is in bloom, even
though the trip to Donwell Abbey takes place in the strawberry season
of the middle of June. But neither apple blossom nor burning fires
(the 'light column of smoke') nor lambing ('spreading flocks') are
associated with June. John Sutherland considers this passage as one
of the anomalies of nineteenth-century fiction, only to solve it,
persuasively, as a view of the place where Robert Martin lives seen
through Emma's imagining of Harriet's response. That, whatever the
season – spring, early summer, midsummer (21 June) or autumn –
Harriet is 'safe' from Martin's charms (1996, 14–19). Certainly this
passage suggests that the houses where prospective suitors live are
metonymic signs of their owners: Pemberley for Darcy; Donwell
Abbey for Knightley; Abbey-Mill Farm for Robert Martin. But it also
suggests a paradisal idyll, where bud and blossom are simultaneous in
an image of amplitude and plenty. Robert Martin lives at Abbey-Mill
Farm, but Mr Knightley owns it, and it is Knightley who, the novel
teaches us, Emma thinks of as a husband, if unconsciously. That
Emma is in love with Donwell Abbey (of which the farm is a part) as
well as with its owner is evident in her response to a possible marriage
between Knightley and Jane Fairfax: ' ... she could not at all endure the
idea of Jane Fairfax at Donwell Abbey. A Mrs Knightley for them all to
give way to! – No – Mr Knightley must never marry. Little Henry must
remain the heir of Donwell' (236).

In their readings of *Emma*, Lionel Trilling sees a vision of England
as a pastoral idyll, Raymond Williams a portrayal of a rapidly changing modern society. Both are persuasive interpretations, but neither
are portrayed by the film versions. Their realistic conventions are too
complicit with contemporary heritage culture to be overt about the
ways in which this way of seeing is a fantasy; their attempts to portray
the rapid changes of this society in the interests of historical authenticity only serve to reinforce this complicity.

Possible critiques of this reading

The reading outlined in this chapter might be defined as a somewhat hybridised cultural materialist/cultural studies approach. In its interest in the popular, the argument implicitly legitimises contemporary and populist formations: principally Hollywood film and mainstream television. And inasmuch as it communicates the seriousness of 'trivial' and 'ephemeral' forms, it is an approach which can draw upon cultural studies. But its argument is also that Jane Austen – a 'high' canonical figure – cannot be discussed outside of the frame of contemporary responses to her work and the ways in which our contemporary culture fashions her as an iconic figure. In its interest in the way in which Austen infiltrates our culture – through tourism, memorabilia, postage stamps and the popular media – this chapter is cultural materialist (a theory discussed in John Brannigan's book of this series, although it is also in significant ways a marxist theory). In the 1990s Jane Austen television adaptations were reviewed in *The Sun* (the British tabloid most associated with the conservative working classes) and the exclusive fashion designer Donna Karan named her 1996 winter menswear collection 'Stretch and Sensibility'.[31] The long history of discussing Austen as a writer who transcends historical contexts began in the 1870s. But, as Sales warns, we are in danger of replicating this error if we fail to consider Austen as transcending *representations* of her historical context which circulate in our own culture (Sales 1994, 26–7).

Both these theories are rooted in marxism, nowhere more so than in their eclectic use of marxist thinkers such as Williams, Bourdieu and Althusser. Their theories of ideology underpin much of the discussion here: from the claim that Austen universalises particular interests to the questioning of realism as an ideology of the visible. Marxist theories are deeply divided in their responses to popular culture: between the scepticism of Adorno and the optimistic faith of Bloch, the celebration of philistine pleasures by Beech and Roberts and the defence of aestheticism by Andrew Bowie, for example. Jane Austen is a significant choice here because she is, peculiarly, a best-selling, 'populist' author while also highly canonical. (Austen was one of the few writers to be admitted to Leavis's 'great tradition' and Chapman's 1923 edition of her novels was the first scholarly edition of any English novelist, male or female.[32]) There is certainly a self-congratulatory element to the way in which Jane Austen adaptations are used as easy signifiers of cultural respectability. Catherine Bennett, in a newspaper article entitled 'Hype and heritage', complains of this when she mistrusts the proud boasts of *Pride and Prejudice* delivered in a speech by the BBC's controller, John Birt: 'It was clear, from John Birt's boasts in "Extending Choice", that each classic serial is a stately, triumphant flagship meant to excuse any number of Noel's House Parties.'[33] Implicit in Bennett's criticism is the suggestion that Jane Austen is every bit as populist as *Noel's House Party*, cited here as representative of trashy television which panders to the lowest common denominator in audience tastes. But we can also read from this that Jane Austen adaptations defy the kinds of 'high'/'low' cultural divisions which tend to be the ways in which we discuss canonical and popular literature respectively. They defy this binary opposition by uniting the contrasting terms. Cultural studies has recuperated the pursuits and entertainments of the working classes as worthy of study and celebration. But what of middle-brow tastes with which Jane Austen is associated? The Jane Austen adaptations are unlikely to be much discussed by either cultural studies practitioners or Adornians. The first are more likely to see Austen as an archetypal figure of the canonicity which has condescended to and excluded the kinds of culture they reclaim. High cultural Adornians will disdain the popularising of the fiction as equivalent to a kind of 'dumbing down', a hollowing out of high culture for the demands of the entertainment industry.

Ideally we ought to attempt to transgress these oppositions, to articulate the ways in which these versions both misrepresent and illuminate Austen's texts, so as to escape the kinds of immediate responses generated by the opposition of 'high'/'low' culture. Added to this, we should remember that texts, including cinematic realism, are never inherently 'ideological' or 'oppositional' but are so only in relation to their context(s). One of these contexts is the current disjuncture between the academy and 'lay' interest in Jane Austen. Roger Sales warns that critics of Jane Austen ought not to condescend towards those who enjoy Austen outside of the academy:

> Popular modern texts are relevant to the academic study of Austen since readers construct an idea of the author, and therefore of her works and their historical period, from the materials that are readily available within a particular culture at a particular time. It would be very arrogant indeed to assume that all those who teach or study

Austen are necessarily exempt from, rather than implicated in, this cultural process. (Sales 1994, 26)

Ultimately this chapter might be accused of being more 'high Adornian' than 'critical populist'. While novels, films and television series are treated as equivalent, since all are discussed as representations, I have finally suggested that film is more conformist to ideological norms, which texts can continue to resist in offering greater possibilities for critical readings. Realist cinema must be studied as among the most popular and potentially powerful media in the 1990s, but this same popularity means that few spectators are likely to read, say, *Sense and Sensibility* as a construction modelled on Gainsborough, Stubbs and Vermeer, painters unlikely to be known by the majority of those attending the multiplex cinemas. Such considerations remain within marxist concerns, for the audiences attending 'art-house' cinema are more likely to recognise such intertextual references. They are also more likely to be middle-class professionals with a university education.

Notes

1. The largest single edition of an Austen novel was *Emma* (1816), although its 2,000 copies failed to sell out. Established novelists in the early nineteenth century might expect editions of 2,000 to 3,000. The specially commissioned review was written by Sir Walter Scott, on Murray's urging. See Jan Fergus (1991, 25, and *passim*). The second edition of *Emma* (159) and the first edition of *Northanger Abbey and Persuasion* (171) were remaindered. That there was no collected edition of her novels until 1882 suggests that her writing enjoyed comparatively little initial success.
2. *The Observer*, 21/01/96, Business section, 17.
3. Peter Lennon, 'Classics for borassics', *The Guardian*, 15/08/95, G2T, 10. Penguin also introduced a series of 60 pence classics comprising extracts and short pieces which was extremely successful.
4. Andrew Culf, 'Millions attend Darcy wedding', *The Guardian*, 31/10/95, 5.
5. Richard Brooks, '"Emma" cover girls set for battle of the bookshelves', *The Observer*, 15/09/96.
6. The dramatisations are: BBC (co-financed by WGBH, America and Millésime Productions, France) *Persuasion* (1995) directed by Roger

Michell; BBC (co-financed by Arts and Entertainment Network, USA) *Pride and Prejudice*, directed by Simon Langton (1995); Paramount *Clueless* (1995), directed by Amy Heckerling; Columbia Tri-Star *Sense and Sensibility*, directed by Ang Lee (1995); Miramax *Emma* (1996), directed by Douglas McGrath; ITV (co-financed by Arts and Entertainment Network, USA) *Emma* (1996), directed by Diarmuid Lawrence.

7. Sales (1994) discusses an article concerning the donation of books to the former Soviet Union in *The Times* (20/01/92). The article, entitled 'Emma goes East', singles out Austen as the representative of a particular kind of Englishness. 'It then seeks to establish contrasts, to which all readers will subscribe, between Austen's rural English gentility and the grim realities of life in the former Soviet states. The idea of *Emma* being a novel about provincial boredom, familiar enough in academic criticism, which may therefore have something in common with the Russian literary tradition, is not canvassed' (13).

8. 'Austin' is a British manufacturer of cars. *The Guardian*, 31/10/95, 14.

9. Recent television adaptations have included Eliot, *Middlemarch*; Dickens, *Our Mutual Friend*; Hardy, *Far from the Madding Crowd*; Conrad, *Nostromo*; Defoe, *Moll Flanders*; Swift, *Gulliver's Travels*; Fielding, *Tom Jones* and Thackeray, *Vanity Fair*. Film versions have included Hardy, *Jude*; James, *Portrait of a Lady* and *The Wings of the Dove*; and Conrad's *The Secret Agent*.

10. I have taken these quotations from Sales (1994, 19–20). The publication details for Hawkins's book are as follows: London: Thames and Hudson, 1990 (quotations from p.84). Other coffee-table titles cited by Sales include Marghanita Laski, *Jane Austen and Her World* (1969); Maggie Lane, *Jane Austen's England* (1989); Nigel Nicolson, *The World of Jane Austen* (1991), which mainly discusses Regency architecture. There are also countless Jane Austen cookbooks and souvenir gifts.

11. David Ward, 'Darcy's wet shirt draws visitors', *The Guardian*, 07/11/95, 10.

12. Andrew Culf, *The Guardian*, 13/03/96, Home Affairs, 9.

13. Compare the reluctance of the photographer on the BBC production of *Pride and Prejudice* to shoot the dinner scenes 'authentically': 'If you have a glorious room with a hundred actors in costume and make-up, and I lit it so you couldn't see them, I think no one would be happy, even if the lighting were authentic' (Birtwistle and Conklin 1995, 84).

14. The same might be said of the differences in dress between the Bingley and Bennet sisters and between the dances at Meryton and Netherfield. For the series' attempt to foreground these differences, see Birtwistle and Conklin (1995, 6–7 and 36).

15. The term 'pseudo-gentry' is taken from David Spring (1983, 60).
16. Copeland defines 'competence' as 'that amount of money that it takes to live "genteelly"', calculated as a yearly income (1995, 10).
17. Emma's responses to both the poor family and the gypsies is ironised by the narrator when her interest in these episodes is subsumed into self-interest: both serve as romantic vignettes which will further her matchmaking (see 112 and 322).
18. For other marxist readings of Jane Austen, see Williams (1973), Lovell (1977), Thompson (1988), Tobin (1988), Hammond (1993) and Said (1994).
19. *The Observer*, 25/2/96, Rev., 11.
20. There are only two exceptions: when Knightley and Mrs Weston discuss the friendship between Emma and Harriet in Chapter 5 and Knightley's watching Frank tease Jane with the word 'Dixon' in Chapter 41, a male perspective which is extremely rare in Jane Austen's fiction.
21. Emma's snobbery towards the Coles and Robert Martin is also under-played. In the novel, for example, Emma's matchmaking of Elton and Harriet is hatched in an attempt to dissuade Harriet from Robert Martin. In the film, Emma is determined to match them from the very first, so that her matchmaking is foregrounded rather than her snobbery.
22. V. Woolf, 'The Movies and Reality' in *New Republic*, XLVII (4 August 1926), 309. Quoted in Gittings et al. (1990, 19).
23. Compare Samuel on *Little Dorrit*: 'Film requires a different aesthetic from conservation, and *Little Dorrit* illustrates some of the difficulties in attempting to marry the two. The sets, so lovingly reconstructed, take on a life of their own. The period costume, with its high arm-holes, turns the actors and actresses into clothes-hangers. ... The beautiful copperware makes even the Clennam kitchen cosy; the simple table in the Dorrit garret, even if intended to signify poverty, cannot fail to look like a period piece' (1994, 410).
24. See Mary Poovey (1984), for example: '... romantic love purports to be completely "outside" ideology. It claims to be an inexplicable, irre-sistible, and possibly biological attraction that, in choosing its object, flouts the hierarchy, the priorities, and the inequalities of class society. Romantic love seems to defy self-interest and calculation as completely as it ignores income and rank; as a consequence, if it articulates (or can be educated to articulate) an essentially unselfish, generous urge toward another person, it may serve as an agent of moral reform ... But it is crucial to recognise that the moral regeneration ideally promised by romantic love is as individual and as private as its agent. In fact, the fundamental assumption of romantic love – and the reason it is so

compatible with bourgeois society – is that the personal can be kept separate from the social, that one's "self" can be fulfilled in spite of – and in isolation from – the demands of the marketplace' (236). In *Emma*, this is also true of friendship: Emma refuses to recognise the power and class relations which exist between her and Miss Taylor-Mrs Weston, and reads their relationship instead as one of purely intimate relations. Whereas, as Poovey argues in her later book (1989), the nineteenth-century governess – as both substitute mother and paid worker – occupies an ideologically charged position.

25. Susan Corrigan, 'Pretty and Vacant', *The Observer*, 15/10/95, 6.
26. Johnson (1993 and 1997) discusses the resistance to imposing 'theory' upon Austen's texts.
27. David Ward, *The Guardian*, 07/11/95, 10.
28. Other defences of popular culture by feminist cultural critics include Walkerdine on girls' comics (1984), Light on Daphne du Maurier (1984), Jones on Mills and Boon (1986) and Tasker on crime fiction (1991). Many of these are problematic from a marxist perspective however. Morag Shiach's argument here is important: 'it seems that, for feminist critics, all roads within cultural studies lead to consumption, pleasure and femininity, with only brief detours via hegemony, production and class' (in Storey 1994, 337).
29. Woburn Abbey, the nearest country estate to where I live and work, charges £7.50 per adult for admittance, with £3.50 additional car-parking fee.
30. See Harris (1985, 35).
31. *The Times*, 18/9/96, 16.
32. This last point is taken from Johnson (1997, 218) who adds that: '... as reviewers were quick to note, he treated Austen's novels with a scrupulousness customarily reserved for classical authors'.
33. *The Guardian*, 22/9/95, G2T, 2.

7 A Portrait of Modern Times: Reading *The Picture of Dorian Gray* (1891)

> 'Lord Henry came over and examined the picture. It was certainly a wonderful work of art, and a wonderful likeness as well. "My dear fellow, I congratulate you most warmly," he said. "It is the finest portrait of modern times".' (Wilde, *The Picture of Dorian Gray*, 24)

> '... a telegram from Paris arrived: "Stop all proofs. Wilde." He arrived by cab with a last-minute correction. He had given a picture-framer in [*Dorian Gray*] the name Ashton. It would not do. "Ashton is a gentleman's name. And I've given it to a tradesman. It must be changed to Hubbard. Hubbard particularly smells of the tradesman."'
> (Ellmann 1988, 304)

Wilde: socialist or aesthete?

The Picture of Dorian Gray (1891) is prefaced by a series of aphorisms which present, we might think, an inauspicious opening for a marxist approach to the novel. This preface reads as a veritable manifesto of aestheticism, evident in such arguments as 'The artist is the creator of beautiful things'; 'The critic is he who can translate into another manner or a new material his impression of beautiful things'; 'Those who find ugly meanings in beautiful things are corrupt without being charming. This is a fault' and, finally, 'All art is quite useless' (Wilde 1981, xxiii, xxiv). In these lines we see Wilde the aesthete, the follower of Walter Pater, whose writings had inspired British Aestheticism, a movement which celebrated art as the supreme human achievement and which argued that since art existed solely for the sake of its own beauty, it could not be judged in moral, practical or political terms, but ought instead to be appreciated by purely aesthetic criteria. Art gives individual pleasure, rather than a moral message; its beauty is subjective rather than social, sensual rather than utilitarian, amoral rather than didactic. In Pater's most influential work, *Studies in the History of the Renaissance* (1873) he writes: 'For art comes to you proposing frankly to give nothing but the highest quality to your moments as they pass, and simply for those moments' sake' and 'Art ... is always striving to be independent of the mere intelligence, to become a matter of pure perception, to get rid of its responsibilities to its subject or material' (Pater 1986, 153). Such arguments appear to deny or at least counter in advance a materialist interpretation, in which art is inevitably social and is to be interpreted within that context.

Yet there are significant links between Wilde's novel and his social-ist essay, 'The Soul of Man under Socialism', first published in *The Fortnightly Review* in February 1891. The most 'material', though not, perhaps, the most significant, link is one line from the pamphlet which Wilde incorporated at the last minute into the preface of his novel: 'The artist can express everything.'[1] *The Picture of Dorian Gray* had first been published in the American periodical, *Lippincott's Monthly Magazine*, in June 1890. 'The Soul of Man under Socialism' followed seven months later and, as Regenia Gagnier has argued, was in part a defensive reaction to the vilification which the magazine version of *Dorian Gray* had suffered. 'The Soul of Man under Socialism' is hardly an orthodox socialist piece, as its rather paradoxical title suggests. Indeed, socialism's claim to value here is simply because it will lead to individualism. But the essay's defence of individualism, as a right which those who labour in factories are denied, is an important part of a Romantic marxism which more orthodox varieties have excluded as intrinsically 'bourgeois'. (In the preface to the English edition of *The Condition of the Working Class in England*, 1892, for example, Engels disparaged Wilde's socialism in the image of a chic socialism which 'has actually donned evening dress and lounges lazily on drawing-room *causeuses*'; Engels 1969, 34.) The links between Wilde's aestheticism and his socialism are evident in his fastidious rejection of poverty as ugliness: 'Under Socialism ... [t]here will be no people living in fetid dens and fetid rags, and bringing up unhealthy, hunger-pinched children in the midst of impossible and absolutely repulsive surroundings' (Wilde 1954a, 20). But, despite the ostensible hauteur of Wilde's style, we can easily juxtapose Wilde's socialism with that of William Morris, who also attacked the industrial squalor of Victorian

England and attempted to bring artistic beauty to those working people whose environment stood as the very antithesis of aestheticism. The following excerpt from Morris's pamphlet, 'How I Became a Socialist' (1894), illustrates something of this proximity:

> Surely anyone who professes to think that the question of art and cultivation must go before that of the knife and fork (and there are some who do propose that) does not understand what art means, or how that its root must have a soil of a thriving and unanxious life. Yet it must be remembered that civilization has reduced the workman to such a skinny and pitiful existence, that he scarcely knows how to frame a desire for any life much better than that which he now endures perforce. It is the province of art to set the true ideal of a full and reasonable life before him, a life to which the perception and creation of beauty, the enjoyment of real pleasure that is, shall be felt to be as necessary to man as his daily bread, and that no man, and no set of men, can be deprived of this except by mere opposition, which should be resisted to the utmost. (Morris 1962, 37)

In a recent essay, Terry Eagleton celebrated the 1890s as a period in which 'subjectivity and social transformation consort together' and defended Wilde from the charge of pursuing an apolitical 'art for art's sake' (in Ledger and McCracken 1995, 20).[2] In 'The Soul of Man under Socialism', art is celebrated as the most intense form of individualism so that, when everyone is realised as an individual, everyone will be an artist. Here Wilde is closer to other marxist theorists as diverse as Adorno, Bloch, Benjamin and Jameson, in imagining the utopian dimension of art, than we might at first presume.

This is not to say, of course, that Wilde is a marxist literary theorist or that his writings can resolve the kinds of political debates which remain contentious even at the turn of the twenty-first century. And it would certainly be wrong to suggest that marxist literary readings begin by sketching the class or other political interests of the author. Lukács (writing on Sir Walter Scott), Lenin (on Tolstoy), Macherey (on Balzac) are just three of the many marxist critics who have ignored the status of the author in their readings. But the links between aestheticism and socialism which we find in Wilde's critical essays are also explored in his fictional works. This chapter, then, attempts a materialist reading of *The Picture of Dorian Gray*, in examining the novel both through marxist concerns and through a consideration of the context of Britain in the *fin de siècle* period, a concern which is of course itself 'marxist'. In his last published work, *De Profundis* (published posthumously in 1905), Wilde wrote: 'I was a man who stood in symbolic relations to the art and culture of my age' (Wilde 1954a, 151). Whatever its Paterian aesthetics, Wilde's life and work tell us much of the culture of his age, in its widest sense.

The commodity world of *Dorian Gray*

> 'Fired by [Oscar Wilde's] fervid words, men and women hurled their mahogany into the streets and ransacked the curio-shops for the furniture of Annish days. Dados arose upon every wall, sunflowers and the feathers of peacocks curved in every corner, tea grew quite cold while the guests were praising the Willow Pattern of its cup.'
> (Max Beerbohm; quoted in Holbrook Jackson 1988, 210)

> Lady Bracknell: 'Do you smoke?'
> Jack: 'Well, yes, I must admit I smoke.'
> Lady Bracknell: 'I am glad to hear it. A man should always have an occupation of some kind.' (Wilde, *The Importance of Being Earnest*, 1954b, 266)

The world of *Dorian Gray* is a world of two spheres. Principally there is the aristocratic sphere which Lord Henry Wotton and Dorian enjoy, a world of luncheon and shooting parties, a leisurely world of at-homes and visits. In the world of London's West End, fashionable Mayfair, Dorian and Wotton behave and dress as upper-class dilet-tantes, as dandies. Their conspicuous leisure and finery constitute a cultivated pose which only the wealthiest gentlemen could afford. Middle-class wives and daughters in the nineteenth century came to enjoy something of this lifestyle. As the totems of their husbands' and fathers' wealth, the largesse of their clothes and hospitality, and the number of their servants, all testify to the wealth which their families enjoy. Lady Bertram, reclining on her sofa with her pug, in Jane Austen's *Mansfield Park* (1814), is one such example. But this leisure and glamour is won (or 'earned') only through the industriousness of their fathers and husbands: Lord Bertram spends much of the novel visiting his sugar plantations in the West Indies. Thus the dandy's ostentatious privilege, in which smoking passes as an occupation, is not only beyond the means of the working classes, but an affront to the middle-class virtues of thrift, industry, earnestness and responsibility. And, whereas the Regency dandy at least shared the middle classes' social aspirations (the most notorious Regency dandy was Beau Brummell, the son of a valet), the decadent dandy of the 1890s had always been a gentleman. His flippancy, caprice, ostentatious dress, eccentricity, public display and languorous ennui are all the more shocking to the values of a predominantly bourgeois society.

It is this middle-class world that is absent in *Dorian Gray*. Indeed, Regenia Gagnier argues that the outrage which the novel aroused was largely due to the absence of normative middle-class values and settings (see 1987, Chapter 2). Instead, the second world of *Dorian Gray* is that of the working classes of London, the world of the Vanes' shabby home in Euston Road, the seedy world of the drug-dealers and prostitutes by London's docks, the world of the East End through which Dorian wanders in a dark night of the soul (88). Dorian's environment is the antithesis of this world, an antithesis marked in the structuring of the chapters (as in the containment of the Vanes' home within Chapter 5 or of the seedy quayside dens in Chapter 16), and in the juxtaposed contrast of the two worlds as Dorian walks through, and out of, the night:

> He remembered wandering through dimly-lit streets, past gaunt black-shadowed archways and evil-looking houses. Women with hoarse voices and harsh laughter had called after him. Drunkards had reeled by cursing, and chattering to themselves like monstrous apes. He had seen grotesque children huddled upon doorsteps, and heard shrieks and oaths from gloomy courts.
>
> As the dawn was just breaking he found himself close to Covent Garden. The darkness lifted, and, flushed with faint fires, the sky hollowed itself into a perfect pearl. Huge carts filled with nodding lilies rumbled slowly down the polished empty street. The air was heavy with the perfume of the flowers, and their beauty seemed to bring him an anodyne for his pain. (Wilde 1981, 88)

Later, Dorian can only whisper the address of the opium dens he seeks, a place beyond the hansom driver whose hesitation that the place is 'too far' suggests a moral distance which is even greater than the hour's drive. The driver's agreement, however, can be bought with a sovereign (184).

This lower-class world is one which few of the novel's readers would have experienced, though they could read of it in novels, radical tracts, government blue books, pornography and the many reforming works of the Victorian era. Social reporting flourished between 1840 and 1860, including the investigations of the London poor by Henry Mayhew, first for *The Morning Chronicle* (1849–50) and later expanded for his book *London Labour and the London Poor* (1861–2).[3] In the decade before *Dorian Gray* there had been Richard Rowe's *Life in the London Streets or Struggles for Daily Bread* (1881); Walter Besant's popular *All Sorts and Conditions of Men* and Andrew Mearns's best-selling *The Bitter Cry of Outcast London* (both in 1883); the *Pall Mall Gazette*'s survey of working-class districts which showed that one in four Londoners lived in abject poverty (1885) and Charles Booth began *Life and Labour of the People in London*, a major examination of the nature and causes of poverty which was published in 17 volumes between 1889 and 1903. When General William Booth published his arguments for social reform, their title and manner were both constructed as imitations of Stanley's journeys into 'darkest Africa' – *In Darkest England and the Way out* (1890). But this suggests a segregation or unfamiliarity between classes which was quickly punctured by Charles Booth's continuing studies. His first volume (1889) concentrated solely on the East End of London. The second volume (1891), against his own expectations, demonstrated that almost a third of the entire population of London lived on or below the poverty line and that the poor were scattered throughout the city, even in the same neighbourhoods as the middle and upper classes. Dorian's encounters with 'low-life' characters may therefore not have been as uncommon as the reviewers liked to think.

Wilde's portrayal of the underclasses of Victorian London is closer to Henry Mayhew than to Charles Booth, insofar as Booth's interpretations were consistently filtered through middle-class values, so that any deviation from these was perceived as immorality or delinquency. Mayhew, in comparison, was able to gain the confidences of the working-class people he questioned, despite class differences, and discussed their own cultural values without condescension (see Thompson and Yeo 1973, 97–100). For E.P. Thompson, this was possible because of Mayhew's 'bohemian irreverence' (55).[4] Here is a glimpse of one of the ways in which the socialist and the aesthete may be linked in Wilde's writings, as the diffidence which the bohemian/dandy enjoys also allows him to judge the poor beyond the moralism of the bourgeois. Dorian's infatuation with Sybil Vane is untroubled by her plebeian origins, his eventual repudiation of her nothing to do with the huge difference in their social ranks. Dorian's fastidious description of the theatre where he sees Sybil perform exemplifies this difference, both in the setting described and in the manner of its telling:

> I found myself seated in the horrid little private box, with a vulgar drop-scene staring me in the face. I looked out from behind the curtain, and surveyed the house. It was a tawdry affair, all Cupids and cornucopias, like a third-rate wedding-cake. The gallery and pit were fairly full, but the two rows of dingy stalls were quite empty, and there was hardly a person in what I suppose they called the dress-circle. Women went about with oranges and ginger-beer, and there was a terrible consumption of nuts going on. (49)

This theatre is not designed to accommodate such spectators as Dorian (there is only one box and the 'dingy' stalls and dress-circle are quite empty) and its 'vulgar' decorations – like a 'third-rate wedding-cake', complete with kitsch cupids and cornucopias – match the tastes of the 'vulgar' in the gallery and pit (the cheaper seats in any nineteenth-century theatre). Dorian is already distanced from the rest of the audience in his private box, but his condescending description of the theatre serves to distance him from them yet further. (For example in the circumlocutionary phrase – 'what I suppose they called the dress-circle' – and the clinical tone of 'a terrible consumption of nuts'.) Yet it is this setting which increases the romance of Sybil for Dorian. His desire for her is only enhanced by the tawdriness of her surroundings, as, in his adoring eyes, she transforms the theatre and all its spectators (81). Moreover, this passage suggests that the pose of the dandy is as dependent upon defining itself in relation to that which it disdains, as it is aloof from it.[5]

Despite the absence of the middle class in the novel – whether in the form of its setting, characters or the values expressed by those characters – *Dorian Gray* is still a novel of the bourgeois era. This is nowhere more evident than in its portrayal of a commodity culture. In his study *The Commodity Culture of Victorian England* (1991) Thomas Richards argues that nineteenth-century capitalism came to dominate England not just economically, but semiotically too, for accompanying its economic mode of exchange, was a corresponding mode of representation which was also specifically capitalist: that of the spectacle. Richards bases his argument on studies of Victorian advertising, from the Great Exhibition of 1851 to the use of the 'seaside girl' to sell everything from toiletries to Beecham's pills. Thus, Richards writes: 'In the short space of time between the Great Exhibition of 1851 and the First World War, the commodity became and has remained the one subject of mass culture, the centerpiece of everyday life, the focal point of all representation, the dead center of the modern world' (Richards 1991, 1).

Something of this context inevitably imbues *The Picture of Dorian Gray*. The world which Dorian inhabits is an opulent world of beautiful things, but they are curiously disembodied by their descriptions: the Louis-Quatorze clock (44), 'an oval glass framed in ivory Cupids' (90); 'old Sèvres china', 'olive-satin curtains, with ... shimmering blue lining' (92); the bathroom 'onyx-paved', the elaborate dressing-gown made of 'silk-embroidered cashmere wool' (93); the screen 'an old one, of gilt Spanish leather, stamped and wrought with a rather florid Louis-Quatorze pattern' (94). Dorian hides opium in 'a large Florentine cabinet, made out of ebony, and inlaid with ivory and blue lapis', in 'a small Chinese box of black and gold-dust lacquer, elaborately wrought, the sides patterned with curved waves, and the silken cords hung with round crystals and tasselled in plaited metal threads' (183). These things are defined by their expensiveness, labelled in terms which suggest their price, or exchange value. In this way, *The Picture of Dorian Gray* writes of these objects just as a sales catalogue might, as if these objects are on display, attempting to entrance all or any spectators/consumers. As antiques, these *objets d'art* are seemingly removed from the tawdriness of the market: they are not priced according to labour costs or the costs of raw materials or the mode of production. This commodity culture is thus one of 'rarefied consumerism' (Brantlinger 1996, 193), a consumerism of the wealthy. Exemplary of this conspicuously aristocratic consumerism is Dorian's collection in Chapter 11: perfumes, musical instruments, jewels, embroideries and tapestries, textiles and ecclesiastical vestments – all are meticulously collected over years, as attempts to forget his crimes, but also to protect his name. In this society, wealth covers a multitude of sins. As the narrator comments: 'Society, civilized society at least, is never very ready to believe anything to the detriment of those who are both rich and fascinating' or, in Wotton's quip, 'Even the cardinal virtues cannot atone for half-cold *entrées*' (142). But antiques do not escape market forces, just because they are not mass-produced. They also partake of fashion, the perpetually new, for their price is determined by what is considered to be 'chic'. Pre-industrial artefacts, or those of other, exotic, non-industrial countries, become a means of distinguishing the taste of the upper classes from the mass products bought by others. Thus, even though collecting such *objets d'art* might seem, as Brantlinger argues, to resist the 'bourgeois life-style of materialist consumption and conformity', it is still, ironically, an 'attempt to create *an authentic style in consumption* uncontaminated by the marketplace' (193; my emphasis).[6] In capitalist societies, contamination by the market is almost inevitable, an inevitability that questions the possibility of 'authenticity'. The tawdry mercantilism of Victorian Britain infects even those who ostensibly disclaim it. For example, one of the most powerful ways in which advertising works is to blur the boundary between our needs and wants. This indistinction is parodied in the following facetious defence of Dorian's spendthrift ways: 'There was a rather heavy bill, for a chased silver Louis-Quinze toilet-set, that he had not yet had the courage to send on to his guardians, who were extremely old-fashioned people and did not realize that we live in an age when unnecessary things are our only necessities' (93).

The rise of aestheticism in the late nineteenth century might also be interpreted as a response to capitalist culture, as an attempt to resist the commodification of art. In a commodity culture, art is that which has market value, and can be sold like any other thing. William Morris's designs began as an ideal restoration of craft and handiwork, as a protest against mechanisation and the indignity of factory labour. We now recognise Morris designs on everything from shopping bags to notelets.[7] But as early as the 1880s, Morris and Co. had become the supplier of furnishings to the new artistic middle class who bought a recognisable style, a 'look', an 'alternative' aesthetic which itself was caught within the dynamics of fashion. Indeed, as Fiona MacCarthy argues in her biography of Morris, only a degree of commercial success could allow him to do the work he wanted in the way he chose to do it (MacCarthy 1994, 171 and 412). Not only was art a product which was priced and sold according to the market, but it could also *sell*. In 1886 Millais, one of the founders of the Pre-Raphaelite Brotherhood, allowed his painting 'Bubbles' – of a little boy blowing bubbles – to be used as a poster to advertise Pears' soap (see Corelli 1998, 80 and Gagnier 1987, 55). And the serialisation of novels – in magazines, newspapers, reviews, or separately published 'numbers' – led to these texts being surrounded by advertising. The Parisian *feuilleton* in which a serialised novel ran along the bottom half of the front page of the newspaper illustrated this clearly. Gissing's *New Grub Street* (1891) was just one anguished response to this kind of contamination: the struggling artist Edwin Reardon dies of a neglected cold following the financial failure of his writing and desertion by his wife while the unscrupulous Jasper Milvain, an opportunistic journalist, is rewarded with commercial success and marriage to Edwin's widow.[8]

That literature is increasingly becoming a trade like any other is reflected in *The Picture of Dorian Gray* too. Sir Henry Wotton quips that American novels have become a form of 'dry-goods' (38), and advises Basil that revealing his passion for Dorian will be good business practice: 'Poets are not so scrupulous as you are. They know how useful passion is for publication. Nowadays a broken heart will run to many editions' (11). That literature has become a commodity like any other is reflected in the apparently casual description of one of Dorian's books. After Basil's death, Dorian randomly picks a book from his shelves: 'It was Gautier's "Émaux et Camées", Charpentier's Japanese-paper edition, with the Jacquemart etching. The binding was of citron-green leather, with a design of gilt trellis-work and dotted pomegranates' (163). This volume included Gautier's famous poem 'L'art' in which art is acclaimed as the supreme and sole value. Here however Gautier's volume is described as a material object, a beautiful artefact which however 'aesthetic' its appearance, is also evaluated as any other piece of china or fabric might be. There's a suggestion in this description that its value resides in its difference from the mass-produced paperbacks, cheap reprints of the classics, 'yellow-backs' and dime novels which were quickly becoming the standard forms of late Victorian literary production.[9] Later Dorian's absorption by his 'yellow book' is signalled by the nine large-paper copies, first edition, bound in nine different colours to reflect his changing moods (126–7). The conspicuous opulence of all of these books is the very antithesis of the popular, cheap books which Matthew Arnold described as 'hideous and ignoble of aspect, like the tawdry novels which flare in the bookshelves of our railway stations, and which seem designed, as so much else that is produced for the use of our middle-class seems designed, for people with a low standard of life' (quoted in Williams 1965, 190). The distinction between Dorian's edition of Gautier and the pulp fiction of the late nineteenth century must be signalled in its very materiality, not merely in its content.

Arnold's description is a further reminder that it is the middle classes which are defined as 'philistine' in the late Victorian period as definitions of art and culture attempt to separate themselves from incipient commercialism. In *Dorian Gray*, Lord Henry Wotton is the very epitome of the dandy who disdains all things bourgeois – morals, taste, manners. Yet his own behaviour is revealingly that of the bargainer too. Late for his meeting with Dorian in Chapter 4, he explains: 'I went to look after a piece of old brocade in Wardour Street, and had to bargain for hours for it. Nowadays people know the price of everything and the value of nothing' (46). But there is a double irony in this last sentence: Lord Henry sneers at those who are particular over prices (in marxist terms, exchange values), caring little for 'value' (or use values), while he himself 'spends' hours bargaining the price down. And Wilde himself was to 'recycle' this quip as a definition of the cynic in *Lady Windermere's Fan* (1892), thus getting double value from what quickly become its own form of 'commodity'.[10] Within *Dorian Gray* there are several passages which suggest that Wilde was aware of the potential commodification of thought and speech itself: for example, in Lord Henry's complaint that information is overpriced: '"... the mind of the thoroughly well-informed man is a dreadful thing. It is like a bric-a-brac shop, all monsters and dust, with everything priced above its proper value"' (12). And Lord Henry's conversational sally at a lunch party is described as if it were tangible, so that a witticism becomes a thing: 'He played with the idea, and grew wilful; tossed it into the air and transformed it; let it escape and recaptured it; made it iridescent with fancy, and winged it with paradox' (41). Many of Lord Henry's witty aphorisms rely upon a grubby mercantilism which he part-parodies, part-reproduces: good resolutions 'are simply cheques that men draw on a bank where they have no account' (100) and Lord Henry can be confident that Basil wasn't murdered because he was 'very popular and always wore a Waterbury watch' (212) – a very common gentleman's watch, in other words, too cheap to be 'worth' murdering someone for. Sir Henry's quip proves incorrect, of course, for Dorian has murdered Basil, for motives quite different than mercenary. But it is also prescient of Dorian's own death. In the novel's closing sentence Dorian, dead, is so hideously disfigured, 'withered, wrinkled and loathsome', that only by examining the rings on his fingers, can the servants recognise it is

Dorian Gray (224). This is one of the many occasions in which Dorian himself is figured as an *objet d'art*. Thus, for all its dilettantish settings and characters, *The Picture of Dorian Gray* is a portrait of the commodity culture of late Victorian Britain, as it is of its eponymous hero.

This argument – that apparent aristocratic disdain for the market and its middle-class connotations merely masks its own collusion in the system – is suggested by Walter Benjamin in his study of the *flâneur*. The *flâneur* is the conspicuously leisured gentleman of Paris (or London), whose casual city strolling is permitted by the arcades: those glass-covered shopping walks which are the forerunners of our twentieth-century department stores and shopping malls. The *flâneur* resists modernity in the shape of hectic city pace and mechanisation, for his leisurely pace is a protest against such forces. (Benjamin writes of the rather comic fashion of 1840 for Parisien *flâneurs* to stroll at the pace of their turtles, walked by them on a leash.) The *flâneur* resists industriousness and specialisation (of profession). But, as the crowd surges around him, the *flâneur*, in Benjamin's study, is also a type of the commodity (Benjamin 1997, 55).[11] Later, the belief that city crowds permit crime to remain hidden, anonymous, will perversely make the *flâneur* 'useful' in fashioning him as the possible detective. This 'accredits' his idleness: 'He only seems to be indolent, for behind this indolence there is the watchfulness of an observer who does not take his eyes off a miscreant' (41). Thus even the *flâneur* cannot escape absorption by capitalism, with its ethos of productivity and profiteering. Because the city is the *flâneur*'s home, he is merely incorporated into its own values: 'To him the shiny, enamelled signs of businesses are at least as good a wall ornament as an oil painting is to a bourgeois in his salon' (37). Despite his apparent indifference and apartness, idling where others rush in haste, lounging while others work industriously, the *flâneur* becomes the prototype of the modern consumer. Similarly, Benjamin argues that the dandy is formed out of the capitalist system, originating in the stock markets of England, where the trader needed to combine quick reaction with apparent facial sangfroid (96). Here the dandy is literally the product of capitalism.[12]

Thus there is a kind of ostensible paradox which is evident in both Benjamin's studies of the *flâneur* and the dandy and in *The Picture of Dorian Gray*. His very turn away from mercantilism, the bourgeois values of the market, is the facet which links the dilettante hero with that same context:

The late-Victorian dandy in Wilde's works and in his practice is the human equivalent of aestheticism in art; he is the man removed from life, a living protest against vulgarity and means-end living. He provides a commentary on a society he despises, in the form of wit at its expense; indeed this is his major form of participation in that society. (Gagnier 1987, 8)

The image of the dandy thus comes to stand as the image of art itself, appropriate for a figure who turned himself into a living symbol, an art work. His aloofness from bourgeois society is the very means by which he can question it, just as, in some marxist theories, the art work achieves its particular power as a critique of capitalism only through its apparent freedom from such questions. Already I am alluding to Theodor Adorno, who defended the autonomy of literature. In *Aesthetic Theory*, for example, Adorno argues:

Art is social, not merely by virtue of its process of production, in which at any given moment the dialectic of productive forces and productive relations is at work, not even only in the social origins of its contents and raw materials. Rather it becomes social by virtue of its oppositional position to society itself, a position it can occupy only by defining itself as autonomous. (Adorno 1984, 321)

But, as the echoes of this paragraph already suggest, we have not yet finished with the possible echoes of marxist concerns in *Dorian Gray*. For this metaphor – the dandy as autonomous work of art – is literalised in the narrative's central and most famous trope: Dorian's Faustian pact to become a work of art. Thus far I have sketched *The Picture of Dorian Gray* against a late-Victorian context – of the social spheres of the aristocracy and the poor, of advertising, commodities and consumerism, Benjamin's marxist analyses of the *flâneur* and the dandy. But the major trope of *Dorian Gray*, in which Dorian's ageing and the scars of his sinfulness are displaced onto the portrait while Dorian himself retains his youthful and innocent looks, can also be read as a metaphorical enactment of the marxist theory of commodity fetishism.

Commodity fetishism

Marx's theory of commodity fetishism is most explicitly addressed in a section of *Capital*, 'The Fetishism of the Commodity and its Secret' (the fourth section of Chapter 1), in which his theory is linked with gothic tropes of magic and spiritualism. Indeed, in the opening paragraph of the chapter he associates the commodity with the nineteenth-century fad of 'table-turning'. This is a suggestive link for a marxist reading of that gothic novel, *The Picture of Dorian Gray*. Marx adapts the term 'fetish' from its anthropological definition as an object believed to procure for its owner the services of a spirit lodged within it, an object regarded with irrational reverence. Etymologically, 'fetish' is derived from the Portuguese *feitico* meaning magic, a name subsequently given by Portuguese traders to the cult objects of West Africa. (See the *Chambers Dictionary* entry for 'fetish'.) Later Freud would adopt this term to describe the spurious, surrogate object of desire, an object of obsessive fixation. Marx's adoption of the term is linked with all of these uses. In his theory too, the commodity becomes the object of our fixation, an object which we endow with a mystical charm.

An object's use value is intrinsic, as a thing that by its properties satisfies our wants or needs whatever they might be. Its exchange value is constituted in its relationship with other objects, it is that which permits objects to be interchangeable. When labour itself becomes one of these interchangeable variables – a product like any other – the system of exchange value has achieved an autonomy from use values, and the object's origins in human labour are obscured. Many of Marx's arguments here seem to anticipate the era of the spectacle, the world of advertising and exhibition, in which commodities are endowed with a mystery, an aura which only serves to sell them. Partly this 'aura' is a consequence of their detachment from the material processes of production: when we look at the commodity we see, not the labour and materials which were required to manufacture or craft it, but the thing-in-itself, as if it had an existence independent of its production. When commodities become so detached from their producers, they 'appear as independent beings endowed with life, and entering into a relation both with one another and the human race' (Marx 1995, 43). Endowed with life in this way, such products seem to have a 'social relation' with each other, which is in ironic contrast to the producers – often factory 'hands' – whose being is objectified and whose relationship to one another resembles that of things.

> [T]he relation of the producers to the sum total of their own labour is presented to them as a social relation, existing not between themselves, but between the products of their labour. ... [T]heir own social action takes the form of the action of objects, which rule the producers instead of being ruled by them. (Marx 1995, 43, 46)

Marx's theory here has a visual parallel in the cartoons of the French artist, Grandville, such as his image of clothes behaving like their owners ('Fashionable people represented in public by their accoutrements'; 1844, reprinted in Buck-Morss 1993, 100).

We have already encountered an aspect of commodity fetishism in the discussion of Dorian's collecting, which forms most of Chapter 11 in the novel. Dorian's collections are each introduced casually: 'He knew that the senses, no less than the soul, have their spiritual mysteries to reveal. And so he would now study perfumes ...' (Wilde 1981, 133); 'At another time he devoted himself to music ...' (134); 'On one occasion he took up the study of jewels ...' (135); 'Then he turned his attention to embroideries ...' (137) and so on. His collections are framed within this chapter by descriptions of the influence the 'yellow book' has had upon him, commonly considered to be a conflation of Pater's *Renaissance* and Huysmans's *A Rebours* (1884). In Huysmans's novel its aristocratic hero, Des Esseintes, is determined to overcome his boredom by the refinement and unusualness of his tastes and sensations. Collecting and dilettantism are thus intimately connected, since for both Dorian and Des Esseintes, collecting is partly a way of passing the time while simultaneously marking one's sensitivity and good taste, the same qualities which distinguish the dilettante from the crowd. But their collecting is also fetishistic. It certainly consists in an excessive attachment to commodities, excessive insofar as it is beyond both their use and exchange value. And this kind of fetishism is not exclusive to the upper classes. In Henry James's novel, *The Spoils of Poynton* (1897), for example, the middle-class Mrs Gereth identifies her whole life with objects in her home: 'the things in the house .... were our religion, they were our life, they were *us*' (James 1987, 53).[13] This was what William Morris called the 'Tyranny of Things', epitomised in the rise of magazines which responded to the passion of collecting, such as *The Studio* (1893) and *The Connoisseur*

(1901). For some social historians, the desire of the collector represents an attempt to resist an industrial culture in which mass-
produced objects become disposable and gratuitous. But this very
attempt to resist commodification repeats the fetishistic gesture, as
the collected object is even further displaced from its production.[14]
Thus, as Susan Stewart suggests, the collection becomes the paradigmatic mode of commodity fetishism:

> ... collected objects are not the result of the serial operation of labor
> upon the material environment. Rather, they present the seriality of
> an animate world; their production appears to be self-motivated and
> self-realized. If they are "made", it is by a process that seems to invent
> itself for the pleasure of the acquirer ... an illusion of a relation
> between things takes the place of a social relation. (Stewart 1993, 165)

The reverse of this is that Dorian himself is objectified: he is judged by
the 'gorgeous splendour of his mode of life' (141) and his corpse is
ultimately identifiable only by his rings (224).

Beyond the notorious collections of Chapter 11, and the glitter of
objets d'art throughout the novel, there is also a very obvious parallel
with commodity fetishism in the central motif of *Dorian Gray*. When
Dorian wishes for a life like that of his portrait – unchanging, eternal,
absolute – the portrait is anthropomorphised. As it takes on the
features of Dorian's changing, ageing face, the portrait becoming a
'living' thing, so Dorian becomes an artefact. But this reversal is anticipated, long before the consequences of Dorian's Faustian pact are
recognised, when Dorian's desire for the object becomes a form of
jealousy, a desire to *be* the object:

> [Dorian]   'Appreciate it? I am in love with it, Basil. It is part of
>   myself. I feel that.'
> [Hallward]   'Well, as soon as you are dry, you shall be varnished,
>   and framed and sent home.' (27)[15]

Dorian's first recognition that the words he uttered in Basil's drawing-
room were performative (since his wish was literalised) does not
occur until Chapter 7 (90). Here, having returned after his callous
rejection of Sybil, Dorian realises the consequences of his wish,
because the portrait has altered. Now there is an expression of cruelty
in the portrait's mouth, disfigured by his cruelty and its consequences

(Sybil's suicide). The rejection of Sybil itself signifies a reified world in which Dorian has been unable to distinguish between social and object relations. His love for Sybil depended upon the artificiality of her roles: he could love the actress but not the real woman. But even before this sign that the portrait is 'alive', there have already been glimpses of Dorian's own objectification. As Sybil lay crouching, sobbing on the ground before him, Dorian's cruelty and superciliousness towards Sybil were already evident as 'his *chiselled* lips curled in exquisite disdain' (88). Much later, Dorian recalls a love-letter sent to him by an ardent lover: 'The world is changed because you are made of ivory and gold' (220).

Dorian's 'objectification' is also symbolic of the pose of the dandy. Regenia Gagnier argues: 'The late-Victorian dandy, however, unlike Brummell and D'Orsay, had no patrons, so he needed a product. He produced himself. The commodification, or commercial exploitation, of the dandiacal self ... amounts to the reinscription of art into life' (Gagnier 1987, 8). We might remember that Wilde's flamboyant costume, the signifier by which we recognise his decadence and eccentricity, was part of the commercial contract with his sponsors, D'Oyly Carte, when he toured America in 1882. The dandy confused art and life, at the cost of reducing life to art. But the novel *Dorian Gray* might be read as an exposure of such objectification, as a revisionist turn upon Paterian aesthetics. Pater's theories served only to collapse the distinction between art and life, as life was turned into a work of art. This is mimicked in the fate of Dorian Gray, while the novel itself, in contrast, suggests that the static eternity of the art work is not something to be envied. In *Culture and Society* Raymond Williams discusses Pater's aesthetics in a way which is suggestive of *The Picture of Dorian Gray* and which might stand as a kind of marxist reading of the novel, even if unknowingly:

> [Pater's] relation to art is such that he seems genuinely unable to distinguish between the condition of a work of art – a made thing, containing within itself an achieved stillness – and the condition of any life, which is not made but making, and which can only in phantasy be detached from a continuous process and a whole condition. Pater's kind of sensibility thus reduces a general and active proposition to what is, in effect, its negation. Art for art's sake is a reasonable maxim for the artist, when creating, and for the spectator when the work is being communicated; at such times, it is no more than a defi-

> nition of attention. The negative element is the phantasy – usually explicable – that a man can himself become, can confuse himself with, a made work. (Williams 1963, 171)

The confusion between art and life is one which must be judged ethically, according to a marxist perspective. But Wilde's novel has already problematised such pure aestheticism for us: Dorian's wish that he live immutably, unchanging as an art work becomes a means by which he can escape the reality of his own actions, the consequences of his own crimes. And while Dorian achieves a life of unageing beauty, the portrait continues to remind him that there are no actions which do not have consequences, that there is no way in which we can live 'outside of' the real. Even an attempt to evade responsibility, is a kind of irresponsibility.

Wilde's critical writings are characterised by their celebration of artificiality, of what Wilde paradoxically argued were the profundities of superficialities and trivialities. In 'The Decay of Lying' (1889), for example, artifice is preferred over authenticity; insincerity and frivolity over sincerity; personality over character; pose over commitment and reality is seen to mimic art: 'Where, if not from the Impressionists, do we get those wonderful brown fogs that come creeping down our streets, blurring the gas-lamps and changing the houses into monstrous shadows?' (Wilde 1954a, 78). In the dialogue form of the essay, Cyril – in quasi-marxist fashion – argues that 'Art expresses the temper of its age, the spirit of the time, the moral and social conditions that surround it, and under whose influence it is produced'. But Vivian – who is traditionally seen as articulating Wilde's own views – sharply disagrees: 'Certainly not! Art never expresses anything but itself' (80). Thus the aphorisms of the preface to *Dorian Gray* are seen by many critics to be closer to Wilde's own aestheticism than the rather moralistic narrative of the novel itself. And yet the plot of *Dorian Gray* appears rather to test the limits of aesthetic autonomy: this picture is more 'real' than its original, while the 'real' Dorian Gray lives the life of an aesthetic ideal, detached from the quotidian, unchanging. In Dorian's tragedy we might read the consequences of the disjunction between art and life. In destroying both himself and the portrait, Dorian, as Regenia Gagnier has suggested, comes to recognise the inevitability of their interrelationship (Gagnier 1987, 8).

From the first page of the novel, there is a deliberate blurring of the 'natural' and the 'artificial':

From the corner of the divan of Persian saddlebags on which he was lying, smoking, as was his custom, innumerable cigarettes, Lord Henry Wotton could just catch the gleam of the honey-sweet and honey-coloured blossoms of a laburnum, whose tremulous branches seemed hardly able to bear the burden of a beauty so flame-like as theirs; and now and then the fantastic shadows of birds in flight flitted across the long tussore-silk curtains that were stretched in front of the huge window, producing a kind of momentary Japanese effect, and making him think of those pallid jade-faced painters of Tokio who, through the medium of an art that is necessarily immobile, seek to convey the sense of swiftness and motion. (1)

Here the shadow of the (real, living) birds on the (artificial, inanimate) curtains can be mistaken for the artistry of Japanese engravings. And, as John Sutherland has remarked in his book of nineteenth-century literary conundrums, the flowers of the novel's first sentence release their perfumes impossibly or 'unnaturally' at the same time (Sutherland 1996, 196–8). Later, Dorian takes the infamous yellow book from a reading stand, which looks like 'the work of some strange Egyptian bees that wrought in silver' (125).[16] In *A Rebours*, Des Esseintes is similarly fascinated by the boundary between that which is artificial and that which is natural. He fashions a tortoise whose shell is encrusted with gold and precious jewels. But, like *Dorian Gray*, even in this quintessentially 'decadent' work, there is a moral: Des Esseintes's tortoise dies as soon as its fashioning is completed (Huysmans 1959, 53–62).[17]

These kinds of blurring allow both novels, and especially *Dorian Gray*, to suggest a moral, perhaps something like Williams's comment on Pater above, and to resist the kind of complacency incipient in any form of moralism. The one line which is common to both *The Picture of Dorian Gray* and 'The Soul of Man under Socialism' is 'the artist can express everything', a phrase which we might apply not just to content but to perspectives and stances too. The ironies and interpretative possibilities of Wilde's novel certainly demonstrate this. We need think only of the interpretative conundrum raised by the preface alone: its polemicising absolutes, so assured and seemingly definitive, are crossed by contrary impulses in the novel itself, and by its original title when published in the *Fortnightly Review*, 'Dogmas for the Use of the Aged'. This title suggests that the aphorisms of the preface might be read ironically. Yet Wilde also wrote publicly to the *St James's*

Gazette that he feared the novel was too moralistic, in his judgement, an artistic error (see Kohl, 167).

This ostensible contradiction – between the preface and the narrative – is interesting from a marxist perspective, since it parallels many of the debates within marxist literary theories. We might expect, as suggested above, that the Paterian aesthetics of the preface are opposed to a materialist theory. But defences of literary decadence and aestheticism often discuss their oppositionality to bourgeois culture, in a way which is analogous to Adorno's defence of the necessary autonomy of literature. In a recent debate in *The New Left Review*, the schisms within marxist approaches to art were re-examined. Beech and Roberts questioned the ways in which 'autonomy' is read, arguing that the Romantic conception of autonomy is misread by modernists and later Victorians as a form of isolation and that this misreading has been compounded by the ways in which the 'new aesthetics' on the Left in the 1990s have misread Adorno (Beech and Roberts 1996). Art's necessary autonomy from the means-ends utilitarianism of capitalism has become a celebration of marginalisation and social estrangement.[18] But Wilde's novel suggests that this kind of total separation is never possible, and that, however we might celebrate or deny it, the interrelationships between art and life, the artificial and the real, will continue, irrespective of our judgements on them.

The Picture of Dorian Gray inevitably not only reflects, but reflects on, its own context. And in doing so, it can have something to tell us about our own, too. But the novel is also ultimately not a socio-historical record, nor a political tract. And its freedom from these modes permits it to be inconsistent, even contradictory. For example, there is the tension between the preface and the narrative. The preface argues: 'There is no such thing as a moral or an immoral book' (xxiii), yet Dorian's 'yellow book' is later described as 'poisonous' (125, 146, 218). The preface declares finally 'All art is useless', and is later echoed by Lord Henry's assertion that 'Art has no influence upon action' (218), but Sybil's acting, the 'yellow book' and the portrait are all forms of art which make a very material difference to Dorian's life. As we have seen, the novel exalts aestheticism as a principle, while at the same time exposing the materiality of that principle. It appears to be ambiguous towards the commodity culture it both satirises and celebrates. In Gagnier's words: 'Wilde insisted on the "moral" of the story, ... that an exclusive preoccupation with the physical and material surfaces of life would result in the attrition of human creativity. But simultaneously his prose insisted on ornate description of material conditions and an obsession with physical beauty' (Gagnier 1987, 56). The novel is conspicuously 'literary' with its allusions to and influences from French symbolism and its refined references to high art, yet its own plot borrows extensively from such popular forms as the gothic tale (Dorian's nightmarish visions of white fingers creeping through the curtains, for example, 131; or the portrait's spectral haunting of Dorian), the fantastic story (principally in the convention of the magic portrait), melodrama and the penny dreadful (the avenging brother, still pursuing Dorian after eighteen years, his face pressed against the conservatory window).[19] But it is in its very inconsistencies that the novel is able to hold seemingly contrary motifs in suspension: pose and commitment, irony and deadly seriousness, artificiality and sincerity. And it is in these inconsistencies that it may have most to tell us.

In the late twentieth century, poststructuralist and postmodernist theories have both called truth claims into question, so that conviction itself has no claim to truth. Yet conviction is the one thing which marxism cannot abandon, without becoming a merely playful theoretical approach. Within philosophical postmodernism and post-marxism some theorists, most notably Laclau and Mouffe, have attempted to enable conviction while simultaneously weakening claims to absolute truth. What makes it possible to have convictions or to act within conviction in a world which is made up of competing truths which are all equally coherent within their discursive formations (or ideological world-views)? Post-marxism suggests this is possible only by establishing provisional and strategic positions, while its critics claim that this urges us to pay only lip-service to provisionality in order to hold on even more tenaciously to our conviction, our claim to truth. This is a theoretical debate which is unresolved – within pure theory. But fictive writing permits contraries to exist simultaneously within the one frame. As Wilde quipped, 'A Truth in art is that whose contradictory is also true ...' ('The Truth of Masks' 1885; in 1994, 1173). In this way literary texts can escape the impasse, a frivolous manoeuvre for a serious topic.[20]

Possible critiques of this reading

This reading suggests that it is only when bringing marxist thinking on commodity fetishism to the novel that we can see the novel's potential for a materialist reading and, indeed, the novel's foregrounding of some of the tensions in the idea of 'art for art's sake'. Even in the act of celebrating such a principle, pure aestheticism always turns out to have a relation with the real, the commodity, the object.

However, this reading is open to several critiques. For example, it completely omits the implications of the novel's homosexual motifs, not least of which is the way the novel became a very material artefact in Wilde's trial in 1895, during which substantial extracts from the novel were read aloud as 'proof' of his sexuality. Such considerations are not inadmissible from a marxist perspective. Regenia Gagnier, for example, argues that homosexuality was an affront, not just to Victorian morality, but Victorian economics too, in that the gay man or woman resists (sexual) 'productivity'.[21] Homosexuality is not a form of classlessness, as class identity does not exclude sexuality. These categories are thoroughly implicated in any individual. But the importance of sexuality as a mode of subversion in late Victorian Britain extends beyond the economic sphere too, and here classical marxist analyses have been unable to theorise the ways in which homosexuality might constitute a kind of classless grouping. Possible encounters between Dorian and rent-boys in the London docks would add to this analysis. Considerations of gender might also develop further some of the points raised in this reading. For example, Dorian as a commodity is also feminised, since woman is the exemplary figure for consumerism, both consumer and commodity. Regenia Gagnier suggests some of the links between the dandy and the late Victorian woman in *Idylls of the Marketplace* (1987).

Similarly, this reading fails to address the novel's genre, other than in a rather fleeting reference to the ways in which the novel – like most novels – mixes 'high' and 'low' genres. However, *The Picture of Dorian Gray* could be discussed in terms of the marxist debates concerning realism. This is a novel which certainly foregrounds issues of representation: Dorian's 'true' portrait becomes a kind of inverted mimesis, in which Dorian's human ageing and spiritual disfigurement are represented in his portrait. And this portrait might be contrasted with the photograph, that popular and democratic medium which posed a threat to painting's pretensions to mimesis, indeed to painting's pretensions. (There is one fleeting reference to the 17 or 18 photographs of Dorian which Lord Henry owns; 44.) The mechanical reproduction of photography opposed the 'aura' of the painting, that cultic significance of art which Pater struggled to reclaim. Here a marxist approach to the novel might situate it within the theories of Pater and Benjamin, since Benjamin's discussion of aura is figured in the motif of *Dorian Gray* too: 'To perceive the aura of an object we look at means to invest it with the ability to look at us in return' (Benjamin 1992, 184). A significant irony of *Dorian Gray* is that the issue of mimesis is explored through anti-mimetic, gothic tropes. In 'The Decay of Lying', we might remember, Vivien complains that Stevenson's *Dr Jekyll and Mr Hyde* is too lifelike, too realistic to be believed: 'the transformation of Dr Jekyll reads dangerously like an experiment out of the *Lancet*' (Wilde 1954, 61). Increasingly too, marxist analyses are conducted under the gothic motif of spectrality, in which the ontological certainties of classical marxism are shown to be haunted by that which disturbs such easy absolutes. Postmodernism questions classical marxism as a form of 'enlighten-ment' thinking in which depth is hierarchically elevated above surface. But recent work has retrieved a gothic marxism – commodity fetishism, for example, is the uncanny spiritualisation of the commodity, and in reification the relationship between people becomes a thing, a 'phantom objectivity'. And marxism itself is seen as that knowledge which haunts capitalism, ghosting it from within. Here a 'post-marxist' reading might discuss the ways in which the 'picture' of Dorian – both portrait and novel – is a critical haunting: not simply mimetic but a critical reflection. (For readings of Marx and Benjamin as 'gothic marxists' see Derrida 1993 and Cohen 1995 and the following chapter on post-marxism.)

In contrast, from a more orthodox marxist perspective, it could be argued that the reading outlined in this chapter is rather fanciful, remaining happily disengaged from the kinds of ill effects and even oppression which it claims to anatomise. This critique is pre-empted in Eagleton's play on Wilde, *Saint Oscar*, in which the union striker, Wallace, mocks Wilde's privileged dandy: 'The dandy as dialectical materialist; I don't think the dockworkers have thought of that one. Well, it's certainly an original strategy: just lie in bed all day sipping absinthe and be your own communist society' (Eagleton 1989, 24).

Notes

1. The preface to *Dorian Gray* was first published in *Fortnightly Review* (1 March 1891). The same periodical had published 'The Soul of Man under Socialism' one month previously.

2. Eagleton's essay is, like much of his recent writing, also an attack on contemporary postmodernisms, for their occlusion of political praxis in the delight of free play, subjectivities and pure textuality. In his play, *Saint Oscar*, Eagleton suggests that Wilde was a socialist *because* he was so deeply an individualist (Eagleton 1989, 24). For contrasting views of the relationship between Wilde and socialism see Thomas (1965) and D'Amico (1967).

3. Other writers on poverty in England include George Godwin, George Augustus Sala (*Gaslight and Daylight, with Some London Scenes they Shine upon*, 1872), James Greenwood (*Seven Curses of London*), Friedrich Engels (*The Condition of the Working Class in England*, 1845; trans. 1885).

4. Thompson argued that: 'The glorious irreverent statements of the patterers, street sellers, and Irish, which are his best-known writings, are material which only a man at odds with the usual moralisms and hypocrisies could have gathered' (Thompson and Yeo 1973, 50). Eileen Yeo's introduction to the same volume explicitly contrasts Mayhew and Booth.

5. We might compare Gustave Doré's etchings of London (1872) which contrasted the poor and wealthy of the city in terms of darkness and light.

6. This last quotation is from Rosalind Williams, *Dream Worlds: Mass Consumption in Late Nineteenth Century France* (1982), as quoted by Brantlinger. Compare also Adorno: '... in Wilde's *Dorian Gray* ... the interiors of a chic aestheticism resemble smart antique shops and auction halls and thus the commercial world Wilde ostensibly disdained' (1997, 16).

7. Samuel (1994, 80 n.35): 'Sanderson, the wallpaper manufacturer, began to print coordinating William Morris designs on fabrics and wallpapers in 1965.'

8. See Buck-Morss (1993, 136ff.) on, for example, the studio workshops of the dramatist Eugène Scribe and novelist Alexandre Dumas in which poorly paid apprentices wrote much of the copy: 'Dumas boasted of producing four hundred novels and thirty-five dramas in twenty years, in a process that "permitted 8,160 persons to earn a livelihood"' (138).

9. 'Yellow-backs' were so-called because of their glossy colour covers and advertising. *Lloyd's Weekly* reached a million-copy sale for the first time

in Britain in the 1890s (Hobsbawm 1987, 53). For the cheap reprints of classics, see Hobsbawm (1987, 371, n.8).

10. Jerusha McCormack argues that: 'It is hard to say anything original about *The Picture of Dorian Gray*, largely because there is so little that is original in it' (in Raby 1997, 110). She lists as possible sources: *Dr Jekyll and Mr Hyde*, Poe, Balzac, Bulwer-Lytton, Disraeli, the French decadents, Suetonius, Walpole, Gibbons, Goethe, Radcliffe, Maturin, Tennyson, Arnold, Pater, D.G. Rossetti, Symonds, Hawthorne, Louisa May Alcott and the journalist George Augustus Sala.

11. Benjamin (1997, 55): 'If the soul of the commodity which Marx occasionally mentions in jest existed, it would be the most empathetic ever encountered in the realm of souls, for it would have to see in everyone the buyer in whose hand and house it wants to nestle. Empathy is the nature of the intoxication to which the flâneur abandons himself in the crowd.'

12. Compare Chris Jenks's discussion of the *flâneur* (1995) as a figure who both resists and inverts the nihilism of urban experience, whose gaze is not one of supercilious disregard for the crowd, but a potentially ironic gaze which is his mode of engagement too.

13. A more recent example is George Perec's *Les choses* (1965). See Levin (1996, 71–2): '*Les choses* depicted a young married couple, Sylvie and Jerome, living in a state of almost total absorption in a kind of netherworld of commodities, things, objets d'art ... Sylvie-and-Jerome only wafted from object to object, almost unnoticed, merging with the system of objects. Their relationships were quite literally "reified".'

14. Benjamin's analyses of collecting – in his studies of Edward Fuchs, of the Parisian arcades, and of himself as bibliophile – consider both these aspects. See also McLaughlin (1995, 'On Benjamin's "Collector"').

15. See also the following exchange: '[Lord Henry] " ... which Dorian? The one who is pouring out tea for us, or the one in the picture?" ... [Basil] "I shall stay with the real Dorian" ... "Is it the real Dorian?" cried the original of the portrait [i.e. Dorian] ... "Am I really like that?"' (29).

16. Compare the following passage from Huysmans's *A Rebours*: 'Nature, he used to say, has had her day; she has finally and utterly exhausted the patience of sensitive observers by the revolting uniformity of her landscapes and skyscapes. After all, what platitudinous limitations she imposes, like a tradesman specializing in a single line of business; what petty-minded restrictions, like a shopkeeper stocking one article to the exclusion of all others; what a monotonous store of meadows and trees, what a commonplace display of mountains and seas! In fact, there is not a single one of her inventions, deemed so subtle and sublime, that human ingenuity cannot manufacture ... the time has surely come for artifice to take her place wherever possible.' (Huysmans 1959, 36).

17. I am grateful to Ruth Robbins for pointing out this parallel.
18. Bell-Villada makes a similar argument in regard to the perversion of Kant and Schiller's specifically enlightenment form of aesthetics in his recent book (1998). Bell-Villada's target of criticism, however, is the New Critics and deconstructionists of American literary theory, while Beech and Roberts criticise, from within a leftist perspective, the philosophic writings of Jay Bernstein, Andrew Bowie and Peter Osborne and the literary theories of Fredric Jameson, Terry Eagleton and Mike Sprinker.
19. Cf. Bowlby (1985, 154): '... the Wildean aesthete continually making and remaking artistic poses and identities, as in *The Picture of Dorian Gray* (1890), reveals the profound connection at this time between the values and images of "pure" art and those of fashion'.
20. Cohen argues in this way in her discussion of the figurative language of Marx's *The Eighteenth Brumaire* (Cohen 1995, 248).
21. Gagnier (1987, 4): 'The British aesthetes' critique of purposiveness, productivity, and Nature was related to homosexuality and what amounted to a social revolution in domestic options.'

Part III

Marxism for the Twenty-first Century

Beyond 2000: Alternative Futures

'All forms of radical politics need the future, just as all conservative
politics require the past.' (Young 1990, 112)

In 1983, Raymond Williams published a work which attempted to
assess the state of contemporary and future capitalism and to imagine
the possibilities of socialism for the twenty-first century. He considered how the small-scale collective and co-operative organisations of
the 1970s and 1980s might be expanded; how the domestic work of
cooking, housekeeping, caring for children and the elderly ought to be
considered as a form of 'employment'; how democracy might be
deepened by electoral reform, proportional representation and a
more complex system of possible recall of political delegates; how
media and advertising ought to be controlled and monopolisation
resisted, the means of cultural production and transmission owned in
a trust free of political interference, for example. Williams's 'resources
of hope' include not just traditional socialism, but the participation of
environmentalists, feminists, peace movements and other emancipatory social groups. Williams's work was entitled *Towards 2000*. By the
time this book is published, we will be living on the eve of 2000, and
most of Williams's ideal forms of socialism will be no nearer realisation. While Britain's 'New Labour' has instigated a number of consti-
tutional changes (devolution, reform of the House of Lords, a partial
enquiry into proportional representation), none of these have proved
to be as radical as Williams's proposals. 'Beyond 2000', then, suggests
that we need to imagine a future more distant than that of Williams's
hope.

Widespread disaffection and disappointment with 'New Labour'
from the Left however may well be the means to regenerate debates
about democratic socialism in this country. *Marxism Today*, for
example, which folded in December 1991, re-formed for a special issue

in November 1998 in order to challenge the limited vision of Blair's New Labour. With the global capitalist economy in disarray following successive 'crashes' in 1998, even those free-marketeers who once espoused the continual liberalisation of the economy – such as George Soros, Jeffrey Sachs and Paul Krugman – have called for government controls and intervention. And New Labour has yet to suggest anything as radical as these former apologists for neo-liberalism. Martin Jacques, Eric Hobsbawm and Stuart Hall all write in the special issue of *Marxism Today* of how New Labour has surrendered to the idea of a global free market which cannot be controlled or tamed and in which growing inequality can only be mollified, not reversed. New Labour is failing to seize the opportunity of the present. (1998 is the first time since 1947 that most countries of what is now known as the European Union have been ruled simultaneously by centre-Left governments.)

Marxism Today throughout the 1980s urged Labour to modernise its project, to embrace the technologies of modern media and communications, for example. But in 1998 *Marxism Today* found New Labour's publicity campaigns and press releases as hollow and superficially glossy as the traditional 'Old Left'. Stuart Hall criticised 'the constant hype about "hard choices" coupled with the consistent refusal to make them' (in Jacques 1998, 13). New Labour does appear to be obsessed purely with electability. Blair's policies are presented as if they will please everyone, whether City businessmen, middle-class families or the homeless. But policies which are 'all-things-to-all-men' are not properly political, for politics involves making decisions and distinctions, deciding priorities which will always discriminate against some constituency. Thus when Tony Blair and such Labour think-tanks as Demos (founded 1992) argue that their politics are 'non-ideological', and in abandoning abstract principles are adjusting the 'world as it should be' to the 'realities' of the world as it is, this, as Timothy Bewes has argued, is tantamount to abandoning the symbolic aspirations of politics itself (1997, *passim*). Bewes's definition of politics is that it 'reaches for the impossible as a matter of principle, a gesture of faith in the realm of *possibility* that is couched within the unknowable' (5). Insofar as Blair's vision is non-contentious, it is thus apolitical.

Here I may seem to be a considerable distance away from literary and cultural study. What have such debates got to do with how we might read Shakespeare, Irvine Welsh or the films of Quentin

Tarantino? Many are convinced of the appropriateness of marxist literary and cultural theories for eighteenth- and nineteenth-century culture, those cultures which were formed through and embedded within the formation, development and entrenchment of modern industrial capitalism. The theoretical work of Marx and Engels, Gramsci and Lukács contains obvious relevance for such studies. But to apply marxist approaches only to literature and culture of these periods is to use marxism as a historical rather than a political tool. It is to make marxism 'safe', in stripping it of its contemporary resonances. If marxism is to be more than an interpretative procedure, it must continue to be relevant to the ways in which we live and attempt to create change. Thus the contemporary relevance of marxist critiques of capitalism is a question which we must also answer. Although this final section of the book is not concerned specifically with reading literature, in arguing for the importance of marxism today, it is also defending marxist literary and cultural theories as contemporary critical practices.

The narrowing of political ambition apparent in the Blair project suggests significant parallels with contemporary philosophy and theory too. Radical philosophy, under poststructuralist paradigms, has put the truth-claims of knowledge under scrutiny. This is the challenge which postmodern and post-marxist theories pose to marxism today, explored in the following chapter. But we also need to ask questions of the political effectivity of such postmodernisms. If, as Derrida implies in *The Other Heading* (1992), politics is only possible *despite* deconstruction, for example, we will need to preserve a strategic difference between such philosophy and politics. This is the claim Bewes makes, in arguing that politics is incapable of functioning with metaphysical irreproachability (210) and that politics is 'both *inaccurate* and *indispensable*' (211; original emphasis). I have therefore largely followed Bewes's arguments in staging these final debates in terms of an opposition between philosophy and politics. This book ends with a pessimism of the intellect, optimism of the will, split into two chapters in which first the theoretical challenges to contemporary marxism are sketched, then the 'wilful' refusal to abandon marxism's aspirations in the face of a world which still needs them.

8 The Challenge of Post-marxism

'I am a "post-marxist" only in the sense that I recognize the necessity to move beyond orthodox marxism, beyond the notion of marxism guaranteed by the laws of history. But I still operate somewhere within what I understand to be the discursive limits of a marxist position. ... So "post" means, for me, going on thinking on the ground of a set of *established problems*, a problematic. It doesn't mean deserting that terrain but rather, using it as one's *reference point*.' (Hall, in Morley and Chen 1996, 148–9)

'To set the historical limits of Marxism is to reestablish a living dialogue with that tradition, to endow it with a certain contemporaneity against the *timelessness* that its orthodox defenders attribute to it. In this sense, "post-Marxism" is not an "ex-Marxism", for it entails an active involvement in its history and in the discussion of its categories.' (Laclau, in Docherty 1993, 339)

'Socialism as the unification of history – the idea has frightened a lot of people, for whom totalization and totalitarianism are but different words for the same thing (although they have worried rather less about the totalizing force holding together the de-totalized forms of capital accumulation).' (Osborne 1995, 34–5)

This chapter turns to the most recent, and aggressive, debates under the rubric of marxism, those which concern post-marxism as a postmodern political theory. In Chapter 3, postmodernism was considered as an important mode in our current understandings of modernism and realism but, in concentrating only on the work of Jameson, the discussion of postmodernism there was considerably simplified. For postmodernism itself is an issue of debate and conflicting interpretation. There are many definitions of postmodernism, though we might bracket these under the conflicting terms of the postmodern *condition* as opposed to the postmodern *period*. For Jameson and Baudrillard (marxist theorists not usually seen as theoretical allies), postmodernism is the cultural formation of the late twentieth century, and is thus thoroughly historical. For Lyotard and Docherty, the postmodern is a condition which can be traced in countless antecedents. Indeed Docherty's forthcoming work reads the postmodern in eighteenth-century philosophy such as the writings of Hutcheson and Hume.[1] Lyotard refuses the idea of linear temporal progression in the concept of 'post'. The prefix 'post-' does not simply describe a time 'after' since the post*modern* is already part *of* the modern. Lyotard repudiates linear chronology in describing the 'postmodern' because chronology is itself 'modern', part of that thinking which postmodernity questions. Whereas modernity confidently believes in the possibility of new beginnings, postmodernity knows that the past can never be surpassed in this way, it can only be repressed or forgotten. Thus Lyotard and Docherty discuss the postmodern as a 'procedure in "ana-"', that prefix which suggests 'back – up – again'.[2]

For Docherty (1993), theoretical postmodernism can be traced in the work of Adorno and Horkheimer, particularly in *Dialectic of Enlightenment* (1944). The emancipatory claims of the Enlightenment – that man would be freed from the irrationalities and tyrannies of superstition, for example – are shown as substituting the very tyrannies they sought to eradicate with that of their own. Rationality and the will-to-knowledge become the new tyrannies, empowering only those who 'know' and dominating those things and people who do not conform to the principles of utility and computation. This was a narrow form of rationality which could not engage with anything other than itself and reduced all things to its own terms. This, in Adorno's terms, was the self-fulfilling rationale of 'identity thinking'. Docherty paraphrases this argument: 'the Subject would be reduced to an engagement with and a confirmation of its own rational processes rather than being committed to an engagement with the material alterity of an objective world' (1993, 8). As a result of postmodernism's early theorisation in the work of Adorno and Horkheimer, Docherty argues that 'the issue of the postmodern is also – tangentially, at least – an issue of Marxism' (3). It is also because of 'the particular intimacy of the relation between the aesthetic and the political under the rubric of the postmodern', explored by postmodern theorists such as Lyotard and Jameson, irrespective of their conflicting definitions of the postmodern itself (3).

These debates map onto the challenge which post-marxism poses to marxism. What is the relationship between post-marxism and marxism? Does post-marxism constitute a movement away from or even an erasure of marxist paradigms, theories, aspirations? Or a continuation of these? Does it supplement or supersede marxism as a theoretical practice? The responses to Laclau and Mouffe's *Hegemony and Socialist Strategy* (1985), taken as an exemplary work of post-marxism, illustrate the extent of this debate. For many marxist theorists, the post-marxism of Laclau and Mouffe is a form of 'ex-' or 'anti-Marxism' (see, for example, Geras 1987 and 1988; Jameson makes the same point concerning Tafuri and Lyotard in 1992a, 61), while from the Derridean perspective of Landry and MacLean (1991), the traces of marxism are all too visible in what they define as only putatively 'post'-marxist. Michèle Barrett, whose own work might be defined as marxist-feminist or materialist-feminist, also criticises the tendency of Laclau and Mouffe's work to remain within marxist paradigms, while celebrating the ways in which their theory confronts the flaws in marxist thinking (1991, 74–8). Barrett's approach to post-marxism is thus to think of it as the paradoxical expression of both continuity and transcendence (a 'paradoxical dualism' which she borrows from Charles Jencks's characterisation of the relationship between postmodernism and modernism: see Barrett 1991, 80).

Obviously, the way in which we think of post-marxism will be determined by our understanding of 'marxism' itself. And since there has been a plurality of marxisms, this allows for much dissension. The narrower our understanding of 'marxism', the easier it will be for us to discover 'post-marxisms'. Thus if we read marxism as a strict tradition, any apparent questioning of that tradition can then be read as 'post-marxist'. For example, green movements, in questioning the fundamentalist marxist goal of 'the mastery of nature', would then constitute a form of post-marxism. Rudolph Bahro, André Gorz and Cohn-Bendit are all notable activists who effected this transition from 'red to green' from the late 60s onwards. The same might also be said of British cultural studies in their turn to the problems of generational differences and to studies of the school as an institutional state apparatus in their studies of subcultures, or of feminist and postcolonial theories, in opposing the patriarchal or eurocentric bias of much marxist work, including Marx's. (Sim's anthology of post-marxist writings includes a section specifically on feminist interventions; 1998.)

But since the marxist tradition itself is marked by challenges and revisions, to characterise marxism in this way is to apply a narrowly theological reading to what is an extremely diverse and self-reflective theoretical practice. It is to 'vulgarise' marxism itself. Properly speaking we would need to call these 'post-marxisms', 'post-one-hegemonic-version-of-marxism'![3]

However, post-marxism under the aegis of various poststructuralisms, including the philosophical postmodernism of Lyotard, does present a challenge to marxism as a theoretical way of knowing, not least because it questions the very possibility of knowing. As the brief discussion of Adorno and Horkheimer above indicates, philosophical postmodernism questions the status of theory itself, not only as a mode of knowledge which confidently attempts to secure foundations and rules, but as a claim to knowledge itself. How can we legitimate our claims to know? Poststructuralist challenges to empiricism have long taught us to distrust claims of science, of objectivity and neutrality and the imperialistic power which they wield. Because our knowledge of the world is always formed discursively (that is contextually, historically), we can tell ourselves narratives about the world, but not claim to know the world definitively. Thus the narrative form of all knowledge is recognised (although the debate has been particularly explicit, and provocative, in historiography). Thomas Docherty summarises this turn as: 'Rather than knowing the stable essence of a thing, we begin to tell the story of the event of judging it ... The postmodern prefers the event of knowing to the fact of knowledge, so to speak' (Docherty 1993, 25). Postmodernity thus chooses 'pragmatic usefulness' over claims to 'Truth' (36) and, in aesthetics, the question becomes not 'What is beautiful?' but 'What can be said to be art (and literature)?' (see Lyotard in Docherty 1993, 41). For this reason too, the postmodern resists definition.[4] The Enlightenment's claim to know and its confident belief in progress are rejected as imperialising discourses which only empower the Subject who knows. And because marxism is seen to be implicated in the Enlightenment project, with its political aspirations to better conditions for all, and its conviction that its own function is crucial in the realisation of these, it is rejected with all other 'metanarratives'. The metanarrative organises historical moments teleologically, in terms of the projected revelation of meaning: for example, the eighteenth-century *encyclopédistes* believed that their knowledge would free humanity from superstition through enlightenment leading to universal knowledge; free-market capitalism believes that the creation of wealth will free mankind from poverty through technological breakthroughs and the working of its own system. To a postmodernism incredulous of grand narratives, marxism seems to offer the most glaring 'metanarrative' of all, in its orthodox assumption that marxism will free the proletariat from bondage by means of revolution.

Such a 'grand narrative', raised to the principle of a science, is true of many thinkers within the marxist tradition. Marxist theorists of the Second International, such as Karl Kautsky and the even more determinist Plekhanov, predicted with all the confidence of their theoretical 'science' that socialism was inevitable: the ineluctable laws of history decreed that the destiny of the working class was to assume power in the interests of the whole of society and these laws operated irrespective of national characteristics or uneven economic development. In *Hegemony and Socialist Strategy* (1985), this 'vulgar' marxism is used as the standard against which conflicting or revisionist marxisms are compared. Laclau and Mouffe trace in such theorist-activists as Luxemburg, Bernstein, Sorel and Gramsci successive attempts to counter the economic determinism, classism and essentialism which they characterise as typical of marxism as a theoretical tradition. Each sought ways to integrate cultural, political and ideological formations into marxist analyses of the working class.[5] But for Laclau and Mouffe, their attempts ultimately collapsed, as in each case theoretical allegiance to the tradition of marxism pulled their thinking back within its imperialising orbit.

Few contemporary marxist theories would argue with Laclau and Mouffe's criticism of economic determinism or Second International marxism. Indeed, many of their criticisms of fundamentalist marxism mirror the attempts of 'Western' marxism (as sketched by Perry Anderson) and, in particular, of marxist aesthetics to escape the reductionism of Soviet marxism and its pretence of 'actually existing socialism'. Raymond Williams, in an interview collected in *Politics and Letters* repudiated the complacency of those Communist parties who knew 'what the next epoch of human history held in store' (1981, 311). Laclau and Mouffe's book is more provocative when they apply Lacanian and Derridean philosophy to the analysis of society itself, so that the economic is in danger of disappearing altogether. Ultimately the 'revisionist' marxists are seen to fail because Laclau and Mouffe's suspicion of 'economism' entails that they reject *any* economic analysis.[6] But once political endeavour is judged in isolation from institutional and economic structures, indeed from capitalism, then it is arguable how 'marxist' their approach can be.

Gregor McLennan (1996) has summarised post-marxist critiques as identifying the four 'sins' of marxism as those of reductionism, functionalism, essentialism and universalism. Marxist approaches have been reductive in that they have 'reduced' the complexity of the social to an analysis of the working class (the associated sin of 'classism') or the economic mode of production. Marxist 'functionalism' has been a reversal of this, in accounting for a part in terms of the whole. Thus marxist approaches have, for example, accounted for the working class in terms of their structural position within capitalism; they have 'essentialised' society by arguing that economic structures are central to the ways in which we live and work. And they have made their theories 'universal' in believing that they are unconditionally 'true'. There are a number of ways in which we might counter these accusations. Firstly, the portrayal of 'marxism' here is identical to those anti-marxists who know little of the tradition of marxist theory, other than the failures of Russia, China and other 'marxist' states to embody this tradition. Thus the marxism which is being transformed is a highly schematic and simplified marxism. Indeed, rather ironically, it might be said to be an 'essentialised' or even 'reductive' view of marxism. Marxist theoretical positions and judgements are frequently read by post-marxists as absolute and necessitarian logics. For example, Laclau and Mouffe characterise marxism as a theory which binds social classes to a sense of 'class-belonging' by virtue of their structural position within capitalism. But no marxist thinker – outside of the most determinant theories of, say, the Second International – held that 'class-belonging' was automatic in this way. Thus Laclau and Mouffe's categorisation of marxism seems to replicate the travestied portrayals so typical of anti-marxist arguments.

Secondly, there are strong arguments as to why we need to continue to retain aspects of 'essentialism' or 'reductionism'. This is the argument which McLennan outlines in his response to Michèle Barrett's book, *The Politics of Truth* (Barrett 1991; McLennan 1996). If we are to study and attempt to explain society at all, McLennan argues, many of these theoretical strategies will need to be retained. Post-marxism may be of value as an attempt to rethink marxism within the context of contemporary philosophy, but for sociologists and political activists, super-subtle nuances of thought and argument are inhibiting rather than enabling. McLennan's argument is that these theories are ways of 'making sense' and should be understood as 'imaginings' rather than 'representations' (65).[7] Those theories which are characterised as *a priori* or absolute by post-marxism, such as the structural importance of the economy, are laws which have the greatest power to explain the world as it is. They are not equivalent to dogma which are forever closed to discussion or challenge, but provide explanatory and predictive models, despite their limits. In defending marxism from post-marxist critique, Rustin similarly argues that: 'The specific and situation nature of social knowledge should lead to a proper humility in the face of uncertainty, not to the renunciation of understanding as the ground of political practice' (Rustin 1988, 168).

By contrast, Laclau and Mouffe's theories do not provide conceptual tools with which we might analyse long-term or global social formations or study subjects and practices within a context of economic structures. Like McLennan, Nicos Mouzelis, in his response to *Hegemony and Socialist Strategy* (Mouzelis 1988), also rejects the logic that marxism's 'holistic' approach entails a form of theoretical totalitarianism: 'At its best, a holistic framework merely proposes an anti-atomist strategy of investigation: it attempts to provide conceptual tools that guard against the study of economic, political and cultural phenomena in a compartmentalized, contextless or *ad hoc* manner' (123). Here the case of universal human rights is instructive. All people, of whatever age, gender, sexual preference, race or class, have basic rights which, however obvious it may be to list them (freedom from oppression, right to education, food, shelter), testify to the necessity of 'universal' standards. Organisations such as Amnesty International, the 'Truth Commission' in South Africa and Human Rights Watch would not exist otherwise. McLennan also notes that these critiques of marxism are not at all new, that attacks on the 'metaphysical' nature of marxism have existed as long as marxism itself.

A third, and related response, is that post-marxism itself is not immune from accusations of 'essentialism'. Post-marxism privileges contingency, difference, non-fixity. In place of the fundamentalist theory of economic determinism which post-marxism rejects, is enshrined an equally one-dimensional theory of ideological determination, since classes are constituted entirely through discursive activity, with no necessary reference to objectively given conditions.[8] The emphasis upon contingency also prohibits post-marxism from considering the structural frameworks that have to be taken into account in devising political action. Laclau and Mouffe, for example, propose a 'radical' politics which addresses cultural and political changes in contemporary society, but which ignores those capitalist formations (such as divisions of labour and the production of surplus value) which are still with us. The post-capitalist society does not exist.

Despite these criticisms of post-marxism, it is important for marxist theorists to engage with, and even learn from, the challenge of post-marxism. Post-marxism challenges marxism antagonistically, but it is also a paradigm which marxists today must think through. It is both an opponent to be countered *and* a legitimate critique from which we can learn. To ignore post-marxism would merely compound the suspicion, already held by anti-marxists, that marxist thinking is 'closed' and rather complacently convinced of its own immutability. Laclau and Mouffe's work is also an opportunity for marxism: we need ways in which we can think of the relations between class and other social groupings. This need is a theoretical one – in order to prevent the kind of closure which resists the validity of other work – but it is also a political one. Today we need to form coalitions and activist groups which will be non-exclusive. We cannot allow the experiences of all disadvantaged groups to be arranged into some kind of hierarchical chain, in which both theory and praxis threaten to repeat the inequalities of the system. In short, we need ways in which we can conceptualise both difference and equality, not within the logic of antagonism but of simultaneity. Thus to argue, as some marxists have done, that Laclau and Mouffe's work is purely theoretical is to ignore the ways in which it parallels political attempts to realign political groupings, the ways in which, for example, the 'Old Left' in 1990s Britain was beginning to forge alliances with feminism and environmentalism. In short, their work is of more interest to us than the rather arcane academic project of rubbing marxism up against poststructuralist theory.

The politics of poststructuralism

Poststructuralism, in questioning the received thinking of Western logic, has long considered itself to be intrinsically political. But reading a text in such a way as to dismantle its complacent claims to truth, to resurrect the traces which the rhetoric tries so hard to repress, is hardly the kind of exciting call to barricades with which marxism has long been associated. Derrida has stated that deconstruction should interfere 'with solid structures, "material" institutions, and not only with discourses or signifying representations' (1987, 19). But it is difficult to see how even his much-anticipated engagement with Marx, *Specters of Marx* (1994) lives up to this claim.[9] While Derrida himself has been active in many political campaigns – that of retaining philosophy as a school subject, criticising nuclear armament, supporting East European 'dissidents' and Nelson Mandela among other activists – his philosophical work continues the kind of theoretical manoeuvres which are not accessible to political activism. Partly this is a matter of the difficulty of his theory, a criticism which might, of course, be equally applied to many marxist theories and to Derrida's most 'effective' political work, to which I will now turn. For in Laclau and Mouffe's writings we can see an attempt to deploy Derrideanism (and Lacanianism) in such a way as to enrich political theory.

In *Hegemony and Socialist Strategy* Laclau and Mouffe conceptualise society as an 'open' space, not as an ensemble bound by necessary laws. This conceptualisation leads them to the provocative claim that '"Society" is not a valid object of discourse' (1985, 111).[10] Since we can only know the social formation discursively (that is, we have no access to a social totality in itself, or its 'existence', other than through the historical and linguistic contexts in which we come to think of it), we cannot assume that its meaning can be transparently read. Thus while traditional marxism claims to know society 'in its naked existence' (Laclau and Mouffe 1987, 84), post-marxists argue that existence will always be articulated within discourse, which is the horizon of experience. These poststructuralist concepts have given rise to much misunderstanding in the debates concerning their work. For example, Norman Geras conflates discourse with language, and thus charges Laclau and Mouffe with reducing all material practices to ideas. But this is to misunderstand that poststructuralism uses the concept of discourse to denote any thing or practice which creates meaning, which is not to say that reality can be reduced to discourse. Extra-discursivity exists but we can only know it within the horizon of discursivity. Jameson, in *The Political Unconscious*, maintains this distinction in the formulation: 'that history is *not* a text, not a narrative, master or otherwise, but that, as an absent cause, it is inaccessible to us except in textual form, and that our approach to it and to the Real itself necessarily passes through its prior textualization, its narrativization in the political unconscious' (1983, 35).

Laclau and Mouffe's example is that of the earthquake which is a 'natural phenomenon' or an 'act of God', depending on whether the discursive formation is scientific or religious. (Both meanings are equally 'true' insofar as they are held with equal conviction by those who interpret in these ways.) These arguments have important consequences for the ways in which Laclau and Mouffe discuss identity and group affiliation. Like the social structure, identity escapes fixity as its meaning is also determined within a variety of discursive formations. Identity originates in multiple sources, and can thus be said to be 'overdetermined' and 'fluid', its meaning never closed. Gramsci, for example, recognised that the political centrality of the working class was partly historical, contingent. In order to achieve social change, the working class needed to articulate a plurality of struggles and democratic demands and in this very articulation, its own identity would be transformed.[11] To this extent, Gramsci's theory anticipated their own. But Gramsci's discussion of the status of the working class remained ambiguous, because this articulatory role was conceived as assigned to the working class by the economic base. Thus Gramsci's theory embodied a contradiction: the centrality of the working class was both contingent and necessary. And, because of the 'necessary' correspondence between social class and economic base, the hegemonic group was still identified only in terms of class. Gramsci's residual 'classism' also entailed that the social formation would be viewed as structured around a single, hegemonic centre, co-ordinated around the centre of class. For Laclau and Mouffe, there is no necessary correspondence between the working class and socialism (though this does not suggest, as many marxists have argued, that there is a 'necessary non-correspondence' between class and economic positioning).

Laclau and Mouffe's recognition of contingency means that political action is thought of and historicised as strategic. There is no universal panacea, no one 'big solution' which can solve all the world's problems at a stroke. Rather, there are 'articulatory practices' which can connect and unify different elements, under certain conditions.[12] This connection is not absolute, since it will not be possible at all times. It is neither necessary nor determined. But at strategic moments it will be possible. Theoretically, this is an attempt to think in such a way as to avoid such polarities as agency and structure, or subjectivity and subjection, the contingent and the necessary, relational and autonomous identity, contextualisation and independence of context, universality and particularity. Those who accuse Laclau and Mouffe of simply inverting marxist categories, and thus replicating the very errors of absolutism which they denounce, argue that their post-marxism privileges the first of each of these binary oppositions (a criticism made by arguments from marxist and poststructuralist positions alike).[13] Since *Hegemony and Socialist Strategy* however, Laclau has implicitly replied to such accusations by emphasising the ways in which post-marxism not only opposes the marxist logic of prioritisation but the logic of opposition itself. Thus, later work re-emphasises the Derridean aspect of their thinking, the way in which the logic of supplementarity (both one *and* the other) is crucial to their reconception of politics. Many of Laclau's subsequent lectures and articles (collected in *Emancipations* 1996) overtly denounce the 'self-defeating' hypotheses of 'pure particularism'. To essentialise particularism is to forget that the principle of particularism might authorise the rights to self-determination of all sorts of reactionary groups (those who deny the Holocaust, for example), that recognising only difference led to apartheid, that no identity can be formed without recourse to some form of general principle or indeed, without a context.[14]

Laclau's lecture 'Universalism, Particularism and the Question of Identity' (reprinted in Laclau 1996) is a good illustration of his most recent work. Here he characterises traditional attempts to reconcile universality with particularity as theological: Christianity inaugurated a tradition of 'incarnation' by a privileged agent of history whose particularity was the expression of a universality transcending it. In the marxist tradition, the incarnation of Jesus Christ was replaced by that of the working class which, in both Marx and Lukács, became the possible incarnation of a 'universal class' which could usher in revolution. But the logic of incarnation was also disrupted as the source of universal guarantor became reason (in place of the omniscience of God), that which was intrinsic to rather than transcendent of the particular body of the working class. Thus the working class as the privileged agent of revolution became a class in which the distinction between universality and particularity was no longer applicable. Universality found itself embodied in a particularity – but a particularity which was white, male, Eurocentric. Thus such an incarnation was indistinguishable from colonisation, by which the claims of the (very particular) imperialising class were made universal, commonplace.[15] This Laclau terms 'the universalization of its own particularism' (24). Because the guarantor of universality is intrinsic to society (rather than extrinsic, as in Christian theology), a privileging of those who are viewed to be incarnations of the universal (the proletariat) is inevitable.[16] Laclau's reconceptualisation of marxism is to argue that constellations of particular actors or groups can actualise the universal at any moment – a contingent, non-necessary and only temporary incarnation. And for this possibility to remain open, we require a universal that is horizon, rather than a concrete content, so that no one particularity could ever completely appropriate it. We need, in Laclau's terms, to make the asymmetry between the universal and the particular permanent. Here, in Laclau's final summing up of his lecture, we see his attempt to escape a polarised thinking which would ultimately return us to forms of domination:

> The universal is incommensurable with the particular, but cannot, however, exist without the latter. How is this relation possible? My answer is that this paradox cannot be solved, but that its non-solution is the very precondition of democracy. The solution of the paradox would imply that a particular body had been found, which would be the *true* body of the universal. But in that case, the universal would have found its necessary location, and democracy would be impossible. If democracy is possible, it is because the universal has no necessary body and no necessary content; different groups, instead, compete between themselves to temporarily give to their particularisms a function of universal representation. (35)

In this way, Laclau attempts to think beyond the impasse of much postmodern theory, such as its excessive celebration of pure particularism or its total rejection of a theoretical ground, because he recognises that such 'vulgar' postmodernism merely inverts the very metanarratives it aims to counter. Laclau's theory remains marxist insofar as its theoretical aspiration remains one of praxis, or practical political efficacy.[17] Baudrillard, for example, is criticised for his theory that, with the absence of foundation, there is an implosion of all meaning and the entry into a world of 'simulation'. While Laclau concedes that a universal ground is theoretically 'impossible', it is also, he argues, still necessary (Laclau 1996, 59). Instead, it becomes an empty place which can be partially filled in a number of ways, which is his own definition of the political.[18]

Unlike other ('vulgar') postmodernist thinkers, Laclau and Mouffe do not subsume the diversity of marxist thinking – from Stalinist varieties to the most nuanced attempts to think through causality – under the one rubric. Marxist responses to postmodernism equally need to remember that there are as many varieties of postmodernism as there are of marxism. Postmodernism can be liberal, conservative, radical, even apolitical. It can be used as a method to analyse cultural texts in a narrow and depoliticised fashion; it can occlude social division and institutional power; but it can also foreground exclusions in dominant narratives and practices or highlight how social groups are formed within relations of inequality. Judith Butler, for example, has used postmodernism to deconstruct gendered representations.[19] It is thus not particularly helpful for marxist critiques of postmodernism, such as that of Eagleton in *The Illusions of Postmodernism* (1996), to caricature or unify what is a very complex phenomenon.[20] In their article on Bloch and the radical educator Paulo Freire, Giroux and McLaren address various forms of postmodernism and argue that some of these forms might be appropriated for marxist practice. Their article largely draws upon a distinction which Teresa Ebert argued between a politically effective 'resistance postmodernism' and 'ludic postmodernism', described by her as a 'cognitivism and an immanent critique that reduces politics to rhetoric and history to textuality and in the end cannot provide the basis for a transformative social practice' (1991, 293). While ludic postmodernism criticises the hierarchical binary oppositions of logocentric or phallogocentric discourse, it rarely goes further than this; resistance postmodernism, in contrast, recognises that difference is more than textual, that difference is situated in social conflict and struggle and thus challenges these hierarchies politically. Giroux and McLaren do not discuss Laclau and Mouffe's work but there are similarities between their redefinition of foundationalism and Laclau's defence of a universal ground:

> We argue ... that foundational referents, when viewed as contingent, such as the discourse of justice and freedom, do not predetermine strategies or specific social or cultural practices. Rather, those foundationally contingent referents delimit the arena in which these provisional strategies may be undertaken without recourse to any transcendental justification or guarantees for exact knowledge of the

outcome or consequences of specific actions. Foundationally contingent referents are important but only in the context of legitimating and enabling *particular* actions that need to be evaluated in the contextual specificity of their occurrence. We argue that the discourse of rights and freedom can be unifying without dominating and for this reason constitutes a 'metadiscourse' rather than a totalizing 'master discourse'. (Giroux and McLaren 1997, 155)

For Laclau and Mouffe, Giroux and McLaren, 'post-marxist' positions attempt to enable conviction while simultaneously weakening claims to an absolute truth. While this is a narrowing of conviction, it is not an abandonment of it. In Laclau and Mouffe's 'post-marxism', then, the jettisoning of grand narratives does not also entail repudiating ideas of progress, of possible emancipation. And for this reason, we ought to keep the debate between marxisms and postmodernisms open.

Ultimately, if most defensively, Laclau and Mouffe's insistence that their work is post-*marxist* must be accepted because to designate them as 'anti-' or 'ex-'marxists would be to close the definition of 'marxism' and thus to characterise it as a dogma. In an essay entitled 'Politics and the Limits of Modernity', Laclau argued: 'Most frequently, the ultimate act of servility and faith in the unity of Marxism is to abandon it completely; but this serves only to maintain the myth of its coherence and unity' (1988, 76–7). Today 'marxism' is being defined as much by so-called 'post-marxism' as by the traditions of its thinking over the past 150 years. But of all theories, marxism was always-already open-ended: Marx envisaged the supersession of his own thinking. It is our misfortune today that so much of Marx's theory is still applicable, because it indicates that the effects of capitalism remain and that the voices of anti-capitalism are more necessary than ever.

Notes

1. See Docherty (1996, 98): ' ... the question of the postmodern arises whenever a culture begins explicitly to consider itself historically, and whenever as a result it begins to consider the levels of its own modernity. Such moments would include the turning of the seventeenth century, when writers and artists began to deal seriously with the new

configurations of the post-Copernican world, or the period of "Enlightenment" in the eighteenth century when the epistemological progresses that mathematical procedures had enabled had also the effect that the culture was able to consider earlier moments as "backward", and hence it was able to think itself "modern".'

2. See Lyotard's 'Note on the Meaning of "Post-"' in Docherty (1993, 47–50; 50): 'the "post-" of "postmodern" does not signify a movement of *comeback, flashback*, or *feedback* – that is, not a movement of repetition but a procedure in "ana-": a procedure of analysis, anamnesis, anagogy, and anamorphosis that elaborates an "initial forgetting".'

3. Stanley Aronowitz makes this point in Prendergast (1995, 339, n.31).

4. Ihab Hassan categorises the differences between modernism and postmodernism, but this opposition is itself seen as a modernist tendency: see Docherty (1993, 144–56).

5. For each, the unity of the working class was not intrinsic but in need of formation: for Luxemburg working-class unity would be achieved through revolutionary action, for Bernstein, through participation in political (social democratic) parties, for Sorel, only through and in the moment of opposition to the capitalist class (a definition which, Laclau and Mouffe concede, was equally true of fascist and nationalist movements).

6. For example, Laclau and Mouffe praise Luxemburg's analysis of the mass strike as a working-class unity formed through symbolic means (the petition for higher wages becomes symbolic of a revolutionary desire to change the system itself and these symbolic unifying practices help to unite a working class which is more usually highly diverse). This unity is formed through a strategic, contingent, momentary and thus 'open' coalition of groups whose opposition to the system is equivalent, but not identical. But the more obviously 'economist' points of Luxemburg's argument are ignored (the working class is also unified by its structural situation within capitalism, that is, by shared experiences of oppression, perhaps a lack of autonomy or interest at work and so on). See Geras (1987). Geras's criticisms of their work are, however, more problematic than the responses of Mouzelis (1988), Rustin (1988) and McLennan (1996) because he wrongly accuses Laclau and Mouffe of conflating 'discursive' with 'thought' and argues in such vitriolic terms that it is difficult to be persuaded by his anger.

7. That theoretical 'sins' such as 'essentialism' are strategic requirements for political practice has also been debated by feminism. See, for example, D. Fuss, *Essentially Speaking* (1989).

8. Landry and MacLean's Derridean critique of Laclau and Mouffe also argues that they reverse and thereby merely mimic marxist errors (1991, *passim*).

9. For criticisms of Derrideanism from marxist perspectives, see Eagleton's review of Michael Ryan (1982) in Eagleton (1986, 79–89) and Schulte-Sasse's foreword to Bürger (1984).

10. The title of the article which later came to be incorporated within *Hegemony and Socialist Strategy* was even more provocative: 'The Impossibility of Society' (1983), especially since it echoed Margaret Thatcher's infamous remark that 'there is no such thing as society'.

11. Laclau and Mouffe define 'articulation' as 'any practice establishing a relation among elements such that their identity is modified as a result of the articulatory practice' (1985, 105).

12. Rustin (1988) argues that there are connections here between Habermas's theory of communicative action and theirs of constituting the social through discursive practice (172). Laclau himself, however, has categorised Habermas's theory as necessarily transcending all particularism in the drive to consensus (1996, viii).

13. See, for example, Eagleton (1997, 25): ' Marxists are supposed to be "doctrinaire" thinkers, yet recognize that there can be no authentic socialism without the rich heritage of enlightened bourgeois liberalism. Postmodernists are self-declared devotees of pluralism, mutability, open-endedness, yet are constantly to be caught demonizing humanism, liberalism, the Enlightenment, the centered subject, and the rest.'

14. See Laclau (1996, 27): 'I cannot assert a differential identity without distinguishing it from a context, and, in the process of making the distinction, I am asserting the context at the same time.'

15. Here Laclau's thinking links with contemporary postcolonial theory. For example: ' ... a system of oppression (that is of closure) can be combated in two different ways – either by an operation of inversion which performs a new closure, or by negating in that system its universal dimension: the principle of closure as such' (33) and calls for 'a systematic decentring of the West' (34).

16. Laclau adds that when a gap developed between the 'universal character' of the tasks of the working class and the 'particularity of its concrete demands', this gap was then open to a succession of substitutions: the Party (e.g. the Bolsheviks) replaced the class, the autocrat (e.g. Stalin) the Party and so on (25). Laclau concedes that such a history was never part of Marx's prophecies, but the argument controversially implies that Soviet-style communism was an inevitable outcome of marxist theory.

17. In this I disagree with Bewes (1997, 209–10).

18. See, for example, Laclau (1996, 6): 'The universal is certainly empty, and can only be filled in different contexts by concrete particulars. But, at the same time, it is absolutely essential for any kind of *political* interac-

tion, for if the latter took place without universal reference, there would be no political interaction at all: we would only have either a complementarity of differences which would be totally non-antagonistic, or a totally antagonistic one, one where differences entirely lack any commensurability, and whose only possible resolution is the mutual destruction of the adversaries.'

19. For a discussion of Laclau and Mouffe's influence on Butler's work, and a critique of the way in which all erase social labour in their theories, see Hennessy (1996).

20. Eagleton is sufficiently self-reflexive to anticipate these charges in his preface but, despite the validity of his argument there (that it is the 'commonplace' uses of postmodernism which his book addresses), the book is still weakened by its refusal to engage with specific theorists.

9 Utopian Orientations

Brecht: 'If you deem all of this utopian, I beg you to reflect on the reasons which render it utopian.' (Quoted in Suvin 1997, 136)

'A crucial task of socialist thought in the new century is to thwart that foreclosure of historical imagination ...' (Mulhern 1998, 115)

As I write this conclusion, in the autumn of 1998, the world economy is attempting to recover from the financial crashes of the Asian markets and many people in the former Soviet Union can barely survive because, as Russia makes the transition to a market economy, the shops are empty and workers are not being paid. That we have reached the 'end of history' with the 'triumph of capitalism', as Fukuyama has argued, is thus far from apparent. Given continuing turbulences in the world markets, in former communist countries and the nationalist aggression in numerous territories (the dispossession and murder of Albanians by Serbian forces and of Kurds by Turkish forces, armed with weaponry sold to them by Britain's defence indus-try, for example), the twenty-first century does not appear any more auspicious than the twentieth century. In his eagerly awaited response to marxism, *Specters of Marx* (1994), Derrida continually reminds us of such facts:

> Instead of singing the advent of the ideal of liberal democracy and the capitalist market in the euphoria of the end of history, instead of cele-brating the 'end of all ideologies' and the end of the great emancipa-tory discourses, let us never neglect this obvious macroscopic fact, made up of innumerable singular sites of suffering: no degree of progress allows one to ignore that never before, in absolute figures, never have so many men, women, and children been subjugated, starved, or exterminated on the Earth. (Derrida 1994, 53)

In November 1998 a Wall Street hedge fund (the 'Long-Term Capital

Management Fund') teetered on the brink of bankruptcy after gambling over 250 times its capital base, but this capital 'mismanagement' was saved by a rescue package of $3.5 billion, largely funded from US Federal Reserves. Simultaneously, the worst flood in Central America for 200 years engulfed Nicaragua, El Salvador, Guatemala and Honduras. With at least 11,000 dead and millions homeless, the West has so far managed only a $100 million rescue package. It is this kind of obscenity which Derrida's book acknowledges.

Derrida's full-length study of Marx came at a time when to study Marx at all seemed 'out of joint' and thus his book is as much a meditation on the question of spectrality and inheritance as it is a book 'about' marxism.[1] But Derrida's injunction is that today, more than ever, we should be true to the 'spirit' of Marx, that his inheritance, like all inheritances, is 'never a given, it is always a task' (54). Derrida's pervasive trope of spectrality is suggestive for a discussion of contemporary marxism. We are living in a time of advanced, global capitalism and our cultures are pervaded by a sense of political powerlessness and disillusionment. And a concomitant part of our scepticism is that marxism has little to offer us. Marxists are affected by this disillusionment too, as in Samuel's narrowing definition of marxist goals: 'Whenever I feel gloomy about politics, I think of Marx's 11th thesis on Feuerbach – the philosophers have only interpreted the world; the point is to change it – and then think also that one can have consolation from reversing it – if we can't actually change the world, the least we can do is to understand it' (in Thompson 1960, 148). At the very least then, marxism is a critical 'haunting' of capitalism, a knowledge of its contradictions and structural inequalities. To argue in this way is also to suggest that marxism's strength lies in its purely theoretical status and thus to go against the central tenet of marxist commitment: the necessity of theory *and* practice. And it might seem then rather like a form of that utopianism denounced as bad faith by marxists since Marx and Engels's critique of utopian socialism.[2] A common marxist critique of utopianism is that it effectively prevents utopia by deflecting attention from the already existing conditions for change, or that it risks becoming little more than a condemnation of the actual in the light of the impossible. However, Bloch's distinction between 'abstract' and 'concrete' utopias permitted a specific form of utopianism to be retained for marxism. For Bloch the distinction between abstract utopia and concrete utopia is the difference between wishful and wilful thinking, between compensatory and anticipatory thinking, between desire and hope. Marxism's traditional suspicion of utopianism was that, content merely to imagine a better world, it would fail to create one. Bloch's defence of (concrete) utopianism was that to imagine or dream an alternative world might propel one. Rather than thinking of utopia as a place, we should consider it as an aspiration towards the 'not yet' or, in Darko Suvin's terms, an 'orientation toward a better place somewhere in front of the orienter' (Suvin 1997, 131).[3]

These are considerably more modest claims for marxism than many of its previous practitioners would have professed. Partly these limited ambitions are already sufficient for those who work within cultural studies. While we have always been confident that the kinds of questions we ask are the most challenging and even central to our disciplines – what is the relation between culture and society? does cultural value exist and if so in what? what is the relation between my study and the lives of others outside of the academy? – we have never thought that asking such questions might effect a revolution. But the history of communist regimes in this century has also taught us that some of the most ambitious and confident marxisms have also been the most managerial, the most tyrannical and the most brutal. The best kinds of marxism today are open to allegiances and dialogues, to corrections and lessons. Feminist, black, gay and green movements have all taught marxism something of its own past. But this willingness to correct marxism's mistakes, to acknowledge past and current wrongs, does not mean that marxism gives up certain dogmatisms. There are still fundamental goals which are non-negotiable and, contrary to current philosophical fashion, marxism still holds that if convictions are not to be mere performances and postures, there need to be claims to truth, and choices which are value-based. Thus marxism needs to be both certain and open to persuasion. And in this, as in other things, marxism as a complete tradition might do well to mimic the strategies and commitments of its cultural practitioners. Stuart Hall's analogy of teaching practice, for example, is one which gestures beyond the classroom:

> You have to be sure about a position in order to teach a class, but you have to be open-ended enough to know that you are going to change your mind by the time you teach it next week. As a strategy, that means holding enough ground to be able to think a position but always putting it in a way which has a horizon toward open-ended theorization. (In Morley and Chen 1996, 150)

A classroom is not a political parliament, or a city-square in the midst of revolution. But the very fact that the stakes seem to be lower in the field of cultural study than they might be in a culture in political turmoil also makes it an important crucible in which we can keep 'political work alive in an age of shrinking possibilities' (Grossberg 1992, 18).

Notes

1. For marxist responses to Derrida's book, compare Eagleton's scathing review (1995b), with Jameson's more sympathetic response, a synthetic treatment of 'opposing' viewpoints which is characteristic of Jameson's work (1995). See also Soper, Fletcher and Callinicos (all 1996). Soper's clearly argued and balanced review is the one I'd recommend.
2. See Levitas (1997, 68–70) for Marx and Engels's praise of utopian socialism too.
3. Suvin here adapts a phrase from Robert Musil's *The Man Without Qualities*: 'A utopia ... is not a goal but an orientation'.

Appendix

Thomas Carew (1594–1639), 'To Saxham'

Though frost, and snow, lockt from mine eyes
That beautie which without dore lyes:
Thy gardens, orchards, walkes, that so
I might not all thy pleasures know;
Yet (Saxham) thou within thy gate,   5
Art of thy selfe so delicate;
So full of native sweets, that blesse
Thy roofe with inward happinesse;
As neither from, nor to thy store
Winter takes ought, or Spring addes more.   10
The cold and frozen ayre had sterv'd
Much poore, if not by thee preserv'd;
Whose prayers have made thy Table blest
With plenty, far above the rest.
The season hardly did afford   15
Course cates unto thy neighbours board,
Yet thou hadst daintyes, as the skie
Had only been thy Volarie;
Or else the birds, fearing the snow
Might to another deluge grow: 20
The Pheasant, Partiridge, and the Larke,
Flew to thy house, as to the Arke.
The willing Oxe, of himselfe came
Home to the slaughter, with the Lambe,
And every beast did thither bring   25
Himselfe, to be an offering.
The scalie herd, more pleasure tooke
Bath'd in thy dish, then in the brooke:
Water, Earth, Ayre, did all conspire,
To pay their tributes to thy fire,   30
Whose cherishing flames themselves divide

Through every roome, where they deride
The night, and cold abroad; whilst they
Like suns within, keepe endlesse day.
Those chearfull beames send forth their light,   35
To all that wander in the night,
And seeme to becken from aloofe,
The weary Pilgrim to thy roofe;
Where if refresh't, he will away,
Hee's fairly welcome, or if stay   40
Farre more, which he shall hearty find,
Both from the Master, and the Hinde.
The strangers welcome, each man there
Stamp'd on his chearfull brow, doth weare;
Nor doth this welcome, or his cheere   45
Grow lesse, 'cause he staies longer here.
Ther's none observes (much lesse repines)
How often this man sups or dines.
Thou hast no Porter at the doore
T'examine, or keep back the poore;   50
Nor locks, nor bolts; thy gates have bin
Made onely to let strangers in;
Untaught to shut, they doe not feare
To stand wide open all the yeare;
Carelesse who enters, for they know,   55
Thou never didst deserve a foe;
And as for theeves, thy bountie's such,
They cannot steale, thou giv'st so much.

Mary Leapor, 'Crumble-Hall' (1751)
Poems upon Several Occasions, Volume II, London: J. Roberts,
1951, pp. 111–22

When Friends or Fortune frown on *Mira*'s Lay,
Or gloomy Vapours hide the Lamp of Day;
With low'ring Forehead, and with aching Limbs,
Oppress'd with Head-ach, and eternal Whims,
Sad *Mira* vows to quit the darling Crime:
Yet takes her Farewel, and repents, in Rhyme.

But see (more charming than *Armida*'s Wiles)
The Sun returns, and *Artemisia* smiles:

Then in a trice the Resolutions fly;
And who so frolick as the Muse and I? 10
We sing once more, obedient to her Call;
Once more we sing; and 'tis of *Crumble-Hall*;
That *Crumble-Hall,* whose hospitable Door
Has fed the Stranger, and reliev'd the Poor;
Whose *Gothic* Towers, and whose rusty Spires,
Were known of old to Knights, and hungry Squires.
There powder'd Beef, and Warden-Pies, were found;
And Pudden dwelt within her spacious Bound:
Pork, Peas, and Bacon (good old *English* Fare!),
With tainted Ven'son, and with hunted Hare: 20
With humming Beer her Vats were wont to flow,
And ruddy *Nectar* in her Vaults to glow.
Here came the Wights, who battled for Renown,
The sable Frier, and the russet Clown:
The loaded Tables sent a sav'ry Gale,
And the brown Bowls were crown'd with simp'ring Ale;
While the Guests ravag'd on the smoking Store,
Till their stretch'd Girdles would contain no more.

Of this rude Palace might a Poet sing
From cold *December* to returning Spring; 30
Tell how the Building spreads on either Hand,
And two grim Giants o'er the Portals stand;
Whose grisled Beards are neither comb'd nor shorn,
But look severe, and horribly adorn.

Then step within – there stands a goodly Row
Of oaken Pillars – where a gallant Show
Of mimic Pears and carv'd Pomgranates twine,
With the plump Clusters of the spreading Vine.
Strange Forms above, present themselves to View;
Some Mouths that grin, some smile, and some that spew. 40
Here a soft Maid or Infant seems to cry:
Here stares a Tyrant, with distorted Eye:
The Roof – no *Cyclops* e'er could reach so high:
Not *Polypheme,* tho' form'd for dreadful Harms,
The Top could measure with extended Arms.
Here the pleas'd Spider plants her peaceful Loom:
Here weaves secure, nor dreads the hated Broom.
But at the Head (and furbish'd once a Year)

The Heralds mystic Compliments appear:
Round the fierce Dragon *Honi Soit* twines,   50
And Royal *Edward* o'er the Chimney shines.

Safely the Mice through yon dark Passage run,
Where the dim Windows ne'er admit the Sun.
Along each Wall the Stranger blindly feels;
And (trembling) dreads a Spectre at his Heels.

The sav'ry Kitchen much Attention calls:
Westphalia Hams adorn the sable Walls:
The Fires blaze; the greasy Pavements fry;
And steaming Odours from the Kettles fly.

See! yon brown Parlour on the Left appears,   60
For nothing famous, but its leathern Chairs,
Whose shining Nails like polish'd Armour glow,
And the dull Clock beats audible and slow.
But on the Right we spy a Room more fair:
The Form – 'tis neither long, nor round, nor square;
The Walls how lofty, and the Floor how wide,
We leave for learned *Quadrus* to decide.
Gay *China* Bowls o'er the broad Chimney shine,
Whose long Description would be too sublime:
And much might of the Tapestry be sung: 70
But we're content to say, The Parlour's hung.

We count the Stairs, and to the Right ascend,
Where on the Walls the gorgeous Colours blend.
There doughty *George* bestrides the goodly Steed;
The Dragon's slaughter'd, and the Virgin freed:
And there (but lately rescu'd from their Fears)
The Nymph and serious *Ptolemy* appears:
Their aukward Limbs unwieldy are display'd;
And, like a Milk-wench, glares the royal Maid.

From hence we turn to more familiar Rooms;   80
Whose Hangings ne'er were wrought in *Grecian* Looms:
Yet the soft Stools, and eke the lazy Chair,
To Sleep invite the Weary, and the Fair,

Shall we proceed? – Yes, if you'll break the Wall:

If not, return, and tread once more the Hall.
Up ten Stone Steps now please to drag your Toes,
And a brick Passage will succeed to those.
Here the strong Doors were aptly fram'd to hold
Sir *Wary's* Person, and Sir *Wary's* Gold.
Here *Biron* sleeps, with Books encircled round;   90
And him you'd guess a Student most profound.
Not so – in Form the dusty Volumes stand:
There's few that wear the Mark of *Biron*'s Hand.

Would you go farther? – Stay a little then:
Back thro' the Passage – down the Steps again;
Thro' yon dark Room – Be careful how you tread
Up these steep Stairs – or you may break your Head.
These Rooms are furnish'd amiably, and full:
Old Shoes, and Sheep-ticks bred in Stacks of Wool;
Grey *Dobbin*'s Gears, and Drenching-Horns enow;   100
Wheel-spokes – the Irons of a tatter'd Plough.

No farther – Yes, a little higher, pray:
At yon small Door you'll find the Beams of Day,
While the hot Leads return the scorching Ray.
Here a gay Prospect meets the ravish'd Eye:
Meads, Fields, and Groves, in beauteous Order lie.
From hence the Muse precipitant is hurl'd,
And drags down *Mira* to the nether World.

Thus far the Palace – Yet there still remain
Unsung the Gardens, and the menial Train.   110
Its Groves anon – its People first we sing:
Hear, *Artemisia*, hear the Song we bring.
Sophronia first in Verse shall learn to chime,
And keep her Station, tho' in *Mira*'s Rhyme;
Sophronia sage! whose learned Knuckles know
To form round Cheese-cakes of the pliant Dough;
To bruise the Curd, and thro' her Fingers squeeze
Ambrosial butter with the temper'd Cheese:
Sweet Tarts and Pudden, too, her Skill declare;
And the soft Jellies, hid from baneful Air.   120

O'er the warm Kettles, and the sav'ry Steams,
Grave *Colinettus* of his Oxen dreams:

Then, starting, anxious for his new-mown Hay,
Runs headlong out to view the doubtful Day:
But Dinner calls with more prevailing Charms;
And surly *Grusso* in his aukward Arms
Bears the tall Jugg, and turns a glaring Eye,
As tho' he fear'd some Insurrection nigh
From the fierce Crew, that gaping stand a-dry.

O'er-stuff'd with Beef; with Cabbage much too full,   130
And Dumpling too (fit Emblem of his Skull!)
With Mouth wide open, but with closing Eyes
Unwieldy *Roger* on the Table lies.
His able Lungs discharge a rattling Sound:
Prince barks, *Spot* howls, and the tall roofs rebound.
Him *Urs'la* views; and, with dejected Eyes,
"Ah! *Roger,* Ah!" the mournful Maiden cries:
"Is wretched *Urs'la* then your Care no more,
"That, while I sigh, thus you can sleep and snore?
"Ingrateful *Roger*! wilt thou leave me now?   140
"For you these Furrows mark my fading Brow:
"For you my Pigs resign their Morning Due:
"My hungry Chickens lose their Meat for you:
"And, was it not, Ah! was it not for thee,
"No goodly Pottage would be dress'd by me.
"For thee these Hands wind up the whirling Jack,
"Or place the Spit across the sloping Rack.
"I baste the Mutton with a chearful Heart,
"Because I know my *Roger* will have Part."

Thus she – But now her Dish-kettle began   150
To boil and blubber with the foaming Bran.
The greasy Apron round her Hips she ties,
And to each Plate the scalding Clout applies:
The purging Bath each glowing Dish refines,
And once again the polish'd Pewter shines.

Now to those Meads let frolick Fancy rove,
Where o'er yon Waters nods a pendent Grove;
In whose clear Waves the pictur'd Boughs are seen,
With fairer Blossoms, and a brighter Green.
Soft flow'ry Banks the speading Lakes divide: 160
Sharp-pointed Flags adorn each tender Side.

See! the pleas'd Swans along the Surface play;
Where yon cool Willows meet the scorching Ray,
When fierce *Orion* gives too warm a Day.

But, hark! what Scream the wond'ring Ear invades!
The *Dryads* howling for their threaten'd Shades:
Round the dear Grove each Nymph distracted flies
(Tho' not discover'd but with Poet's Eyes):
And shall those Shades, where *Philomela*'s Strain
Has oft to Slumber lull'd the hapless Swain;   170
Where Turtles us'd to clap their silken Wings;
Whose rev'rend Oaks have known a hundred Springs;
Shall these ignobly from their Roots be torn,
And perish shameful, as the abject Thorn;
While the slow Carr bears off their aged Limbs,
To clear the Way for Slopes,and modern Whims;
Where banish'd Nature leaves a barren Gloom,
And aukward Art supplies the vacant Room?
Yet (or the Muse for Vengeance calls in vain)
The injur'd Nymphs shall haunt the ravag'd Plain: 180
Strange Sounds and Forms shall teaze the gloomy Green;
And Fairy-Elves by *Urs'la* shall be seen:
Their new-built Parlour shall with Echoes ring:
And in their Hall shall doleful Crickets sing.

Then cease, *Diracto,* stay thy desp'rate Hand;
And let the Grove, it not the Parlour, stand.

Annotated Bibliography

Adorno, Bloch, Lukács, Brecht, Benjamin, *Aesthetics and Politics*. London: Verso, 1980.

This includes key writings on such issues as realism and modernism, commitment in art, marxist writing and interpretative practices. It illustrates the extent of debate between these theorists, with several of the essays responding to each other. Introductions to each of the five theorists, written collaboratively by Rodney Livingstone, Perry Anderson and Francis Mulhern, situate the essays in their contexts and foreground the implications of the debates. A final essay by Fredric Jameson considers these debates in the light of late twentieth-century culture and politics. This is an excellent place to start and, in its combination of early debates and later reflections, is an extremely valuable collection.

Barrell, John, *Poetry, Language and Politics*. Manchester: Manchester University Press, 1988.

This is exemplary of the best kinds of marxist readings, in successfully linking theoretical analysis, political commitment and close reading practices. Barrell reads sonnets by Shakespeare and Milton, Wordsworth's 'Tintern Abbey', the poetry of Thomson and Clare and, in a chapter co-written with Harriet Guest, Pope's 'Epistle to Bathurst'. Here his commitment to marxist concerns does not entail universalist or grand claims, but a detailed attention to the poetry and its contexts so as to achieve an ostensibly paradoxical 'marxist New Criticism'.

Brantlinger, Patrick, *Fictions of State: Culture and Credit in Britain, 1694–1994*. Ithaca and London: Cornell University Press, 1996.

Brantlinger's study might be taken as both characteristic and exemplary of the 'new economic criticism', which while not always theologically 'marxist', is certainly inspired by marxism's linking of the cultural and the economic. Brantlinger explores both narrative and money as social forms of representation in suggestive readings of a wide range of texts (from Swift to Martin Amis). But he also considers the linkages between Britain's imperial formation and narrative and financial credit. This book represents an exciting synthesis of a wide cultural history with marxist, poststructuralist and postcolonial theories.

Brown, Laura, *Ends of Empire: Women and Ideology in Early Eighteenth-Century English Literature*. Ithaca and London: Cornell University Press, 1993.

Brown's book is exemplary of the kinds of hybrid theoretical approaches increasingly practised today: a kind of marxist-feminist-postcolonial theory. Her argument is that in the early eighteenth century the image of woman was crucial not only to literary culture, but to a growing mercantile capitalist ideology. Studies of Aphra Behn's *Oroonoko* and of Defoe and Swift illustrate how imperialist ideology utilises the threat of the commodification and consumerism of woman.

Eagleton, Terry, *Walter Benjamin: or Towards a Revolutionary Criticism*. London: Verso, 1981.

This book is ostensibly divided into two sections: the first, a study of Benjamin's major tropes and concerns, the second, 'Towards a Revolutionary Criticism', a study of marxist possibilities today. But the book is written more in the spirit of Benjamin than that of critical study, and thus embraces a range of issues – the (absence of) comedy in marxism, contemporary feminism, the politics of deconstruction, the commodity as cultural object – in essays which reflect upon each other and refuse predeterminations.

Eagleton, Terry, *The Eagleton Reader*. ed. Stephen Regan. Oxford: Blackwell, 1998.

This anthology reproduces work from throughout Eagleton's career, and thus demonstrates something of the shifts in British marxist theories in the last thirty years, from early work inspired largely by Williams, through the structuralist marxism of the 1970s and early 1980s to the critiques of postmodernism and the exploration of Irish postcoloniality of the 1990s. The writings include theoretical reflections as well as particular readings of literary texts. Regan's introduction and notes to each essay provide a useful commentary on Eagleton's work, if not a particularly critical one.

Eagleton, Terry and Milne, Drew, eds. *Marxist Literary Theory: a reader*. Oxford: Blackwell, 1996

Both this and Mulhern's (see below) are good places to start, as their anthologised essays reflect the diversity of marxist approaches to literature.

Eagleton's and Milne's anthology has the broader historical range: from seminal extracts from Marx and Engels to Callinicos's polemic against post-modernism (1989). Excerpts from theorists now seen as problematically 'vulgar' marxists (such as Caudwell and Goldmann) can be usefully contrasted with later structuralist marxisms, and marxist-feminist and post-colonial approaches illustrate the increasingly hybrid nature of marxist theories.

Felski, Rita, *Beyond Feminist Aesthetics: feminist literature and social change.* UK: Hutchinson Radius, 1989.

Felski's book is a powerful argument for the necessity of materialist femi-nisms. It is also a sustained polemic against those feminisms which inter-pret literature in isolation from the social conditions of gender constructions and of literary production, fetishising ahistorical definitions of 'femininity' or 'subversive' literary form. Thus while Felski reads in particular novels of confession and self-development by women writers, the book is also a compelling defence of realism against charges of its intrinsic conservatism.

Jameson, Fredric, *The Political Unconscious: Narrative as a Socially Symbolic Act.* (1981) London: Routledge, 1983.

Here Jameson reads a succession of writers – Balzac, Gissing and Conrad – according to the interpretative procedures outlined in two theoretical chap-ters. His major theses argue that interpretation is always a political act, our access to 'History' or to the 'Real' always through its prior textualisation, or narrativisation in the political unconscious, and that narratives employ 'strategies of containment' in order to so depict the Real. Ideology is read as necessary illusion, and this permits Jameson to close with an epilogue on the utopian possibilities of even the most 'dominant' ideologies. While this book's difficulty makes it one of the least accessible of those recommended here, Jameson does combine theory with particularised readings of the novels and develops an impressively original argument out of a synthesis of a range of theoretical perspectives.

Milner, Andrew, *Literature, Culture and Society.* London: UCL Press, 1996.

Milner presents a convincing case for the centrality of literary studies and counters the tendency to increasingly semiotic analysis in the cultural studies project. He explains in a highly accessible form diverse approaches to textual analysis, from hermeneutics to postmodernism, and outlines his own preferred approach – that of a sociology of literature in which the tech-nologies of mechanical production and the social relations of commodification remain key issues. *Paradise Lost, Frankenstein* and *Blade Runner* are used as illustrative case-studies of the theoretical arguments.

Morley, David, and Chen, Kuan-Hsing, eds. *Stuart Hall: Critical Dialogues in Cultural Studies.* London: Routledge, 1996.

This volume collects key essays by and about Stuart Hall and new interviews with Hall in dialogue with Kuan-Hsing Chen. It raises such issues as the relationship between cultural studies and marxism, postmodern political and cultural formations (largely under the rubric of Hall's 'New Times' work), the development of cultural studies as an international and postcolonial phenomenon and Stuart Hall's engagement with questions of 'race', identity and ethnicity.

Mulhern, Francis, *Contemporary Marxist literary criticism.* Harlow, Essex: Longman, 1992.

Mulhern's anthology is an important supplement to that of Eagleton and Milne, as its more limited focus permits the inclusion of more contemporary and specialised topics: issues of gender (Cora Kaplan) and empire (Said) are included, as are discussions of popular culture (Bennett and Denning), the avant-garde (Bürger) and film theory (Stephen Heath). Mulhern's introduction situates these readings within a discussion of the evolution of marxist literary criticism and reviews the state of marxist theory in the early 1990s.

Williams, Raymond, *The Country and the City.* London: Hogarth Press, 1973.

In focusing upon literary representations of the country and the city, this book explores the connections between literature, politics and history. It puts our nostalgia for the countryside under scrutiny, for example, but also understands this as part of a history and celebrates the values of rural life and labour, as ideals which are necessary to modernity. Williams's use of 'structures of feeling' as mediations between representations and 'lived experience' is developed here, but so too is a way of looking at literature as a distinct mode, with its own ways of working.

Williams, Raymond, *Marxism and Literature.* Oxford: Oxford University Press, 1977.

This is the first book in which Williams explicitly identified his practice with marxism, but its value is primarily its ability to discuss complex and subtle theories clearly. In the first section there is a focus on the historical development of the key terms culture, language, literature and ideology; in the second Williams questions and redefines key marxist concepts such as 'base and superstructure' and 'determination', and elaborates his most influential theory – of the 'dominant, residual and emergent' ideologies of society; in the final section Williams turns to literature as a material practice (the social character of signs, notations and conventions, for example) and concludes with the questions of commitment and creative practice.

Williams, Raymond, *Politics and Letters: Interviews with New Left Review*. London: Verso, 1981.

Through the mode of interviews, this book allows us to see both the divergences between marxist perspectives (between Williams and his interviewers from the *New Left Review*) and Williams's own revisions of his earlier work. There are substantial interviews on each of his published books, as well as biographical and political discussions, and all are highly accessible and lively.

Wood, Ellen Meiksins, and Bellamy, John, eds. *In Defense of History: Marxism and the Postmodern Agenda*. New York: Monthly Review Press, 1997.

While none of the essays in this collection engage with specifically literary or cultural issues, it is useful for anyone interested in the continuing viability of marxism as a theoretical practice. It challenges the political defeatism and repudiation of marxist analysis currently popular in many forms of postmodernism and thus is a useful corrective to anyone thinking that marxist thinking has disappeared.

Bibliography

Abercrombie, N., Hill, S. and Turner, B. *The Dominant Ideology Thesis.* Hemel Hempstead: Allen and Unwin, 1980.

Adorno, Bloch, Lukács, Brecht and Benjamin. *Aesthetics and Politics.* London: Verso, 1980.

Adorno, Theodor W. *Prisms.* Trans. Samuel and Shierry Weber. London: Neville Spearman, 1967.

— *Philsophy of Modern Music.* (1949) Trans. Anne Mitchell and Wesley Bloomster. New York: Seabury Press, 1973a.

— *Negative Dialectics.* (1966) Trans. E.B. Ashton. New York: Continuum, 1973b.

— 'Culture Industry Reconsidered'. *New German Critique* 6 (Fall 1975): 12–19.

— 'Trying to understand *Endgame*'. Trans. Michael T. Jones. *New German Critique* 26 (1982): 119–50.

— *Aesthetic Theory.* Trans. Christian Lenhardt. London: Routledge and Kegan Paul, 1984.

— *The Culture Industry: selected essays on mass culture*, ed. J.M. Bernstein. London: Routledge, 1991a.

— *Notes on Literature I* (1958) Trans. Shierry Weber Nicholsen. New York: Columbia University Press, 1991b.

— and Horkheimer, Max. *Dialectic of Enlightenment.* (1944) Trans. John Cumming. London: Verso, 1979.

Aers, David. 'Community and Morality: Towards Reading Jane Austen'. In *Romanticism and Ideology*, eds. David Aers, Jonathan Cook and David Punter. London: Routledge, 1981. 118–36.

Althusser, Louis. *Reading Capital.* Trans. Ben Brewster. London: Verso, 1979.

— *Essays on Ideology.* London: Verso, 1984.

— *For Marx.* (1965) Trans. Ben Brewster. London: Verso, 1990.

Anderson, Benedict. *Imagined Communities.* London: Verso, 1991.

Anderson, Perry. *Considerations on Western Marxism.* London: Verso, 1979.

— *Arguments within English Marxism.* London: Verso, 1980.

— *A Zone of Engagement.* London: Verso, 1992.

Ang, Ien. *Watching Dallas: Soap Opera and the melodramatic imagination.* London: Methuen, 1985.

Armstrong, Isobel. 'And beauty? A dialogue: debating Adorno's Aesthetic Theory'. *Textual Practice* 12: 2 (Summer 1998): 269–89.

Auden, W.H. *Collected Longer Poems.* London: Faber and Faber, 1968.

Austen, Jane. *Sense and Sensibility.* (1811) London: J.M. Dent, 1906.

— *Pride and Prejudice.* (1813) Harmondsworth: Penguin, 1972.

— *Emma.* (1816) Harmondsworth: Penguin, 1966.

Bannet, Eve Tavor. *Postcultural Theory: Critical Theory after the Marxist Paradigm.* New York: Paragon House, 1993.

Barker, Francis et al. *Literature, Society and the Sociology of Literature.* Essex: University of Essex, 1977.

— Coombes, John, Hulme, Peter, Mercer, Colin and Musselwhite, David, eds. *1848: The Sociology of Literature.* Essex, U.K.: University of Essex, 1978.

— Hulme, Peter, Iversen, Margaret and Loxley, Diana, eds. *Literature, Politics and Theory: Papers from the Essex Conference, 1976–84.* London: Methuen, 1986.

Barker, Martin. *Comics: Ideology, power and the critics.* Manchester: Manchester University Press, 1989.

Barrell, John. *The dark side of the landscape: The rural poor in English painting, 1730–1840.* Cambridge: Cambridge University Press, 1983.

— *Poetry, language and politics.* Manchester: Manchester University Press, 1988.

Barrett, Michèle. *The Politics of Truth: from Marx to Foucault.* Oxford: Polity Press, 1991.

Baudrillard, Jean. *The Evil Demon of Images.* Trans. P. Patton and P. Foss. Annandale: Power Institute, 1987.

Beech, Dave and Roberts, John. 'Spectres of the Aesthetic'. *New Left Review* 218 (July-August 1996): 102–27.

— 'A Defence of Philistines'. *New Left Review* 227 (January–February 1998): 45–71.

Bell-Villada, Gene H. *Art for Art's sake and literary life: How politics and markets helped shape the ideology and culture of aestheticism, 1790–1990.* Lincoln and London: University of Nebraska Press, 1998.

Belsey, Catherine. *Critical Practice.* London: Routledge, 1980.

Benjamin, Walter. *Understanding Brecht.* (1966) Trans. Anna Bostock. London: New Left Books, 1977.

— *Illuminations.* Trans. Harry Zohn. London: Fontana, 1992.

— *Charles Baudelaire: A Lyric Poet in the Era of High Capitalism.* (1955–71) Trans. Harry Zohn. London: Verso, 1997. (1st English translation 1973.)

— 'Central Park'. Trans. Lloyd Spencer. *New German Critique* 34 (Winter 1985): 32–58.

Bennett, Tony. *Formalism and Marxism*. London: Methuen, 1979.

— et al. *Culture, Ideology and Social Process: a reader*. Milton Keynes: Open University Press, 1981.

— *Outside Literature*. London: Routledge, 1990.

— 'Putting Policy into cultural studies'. In Grossberg 1992: 23–37.

Berger, John. *Ways of Seeing*. Harmondsworth: Penguin, 1972.

Bermingham, Ann and Brewer, John, eds. *The Consumption of Culture, 1600–1800: Image, Object, Text*. London: Routledge, 1995.

Bernstein, J.M. 'Against Voluptuous Bodies: Of Satiation without Happiness'. *New Left Review* 223 (September/October 1997): 89–104.

Bewes, Timothy. *Cynicism and Postmodernity*. London: Verso, 1997.

Bhabha, Homi. K. *The Location of Culture*. London: Routledge, 1994.

Birtwistle, Sue and Conklin, Susie. *The Making of Pride and Prejudice*. Harmondsworth: Penguin BBC Books, 1995.

Bloomfield, J. ed. *Papers on Class, Hegemony and Party*. London: Lawrence and Wishart, 1977.

Bottomore, Tom, et al., eds. *A Dictionary of Marxist Thought*. Oxford: Blackwell, 1991.

Bourdieu, Pierre. *Distinction: A Social Critique of the Judgment of Taste*. Trans. Richard Nice. Cambridge, Massachusetts: Harvard University Press, 1984.

— *Language and Symbolic Power*. Cambridge: Polity Press, 1991.

— *The Field of Cultural Production: Essays on Art and Literature*. Cambridge, U.K.: Polity Press, 1993.

Bowie, Andrew. 'Confessions of a "New Aesthetc": A Response to the "New Philistines"'. *New Left Review* 223 (September/October 1997): 105–26.

Bowlby, Rachel. *Just Looking: Consumer Culture in Dreiser, Gissing and Zola*. London: Methuen, 1985.

Brannigan, John. *New Historicism and Cultural Materialism*. Basingstoke: Macmillan, 1998.

Brantlinger, Patrick. *Crusoe's Footprints: Cultural Studies in Britain and America*. London: Routledge, 1990.

— *Fictions of State: Culture and Credit in Britain, 1694–1994*. Ithaca and London: Cornell University Press, 1996.

Brecht, Bertolt. *Messingkauf Dialogues*. Trans. John Willett. London: Methuen, 1977.

— *Brecht on Theatre: The development of an aesthetic*. (1957–64) Trans. John Willett. London: Methuen, 1990.

Brewer, John. *The Pleasures of the Imagination: English Culture in the Eighteenth Century*. London: HarperCollins, 1997.

Bronte, Charlotte. *Jane Eyre*. (1847) Harmondsworth: Penguin, 1966.

Brooks, Chris and Faulkner, Peter, eds. *The White Man's Burden: An anthology of British Poetry of the Empire*. Exeter: University of Exeter Press, 1996.

Brown, Laura. *Alexander Pope*. Oxford: Basil Blackwell, 1985.

— *Women and Ideology in Early Eighteenth-Century English Literature*. Ithaca and London: Cornell University Press, 1993.

Buck-Morss, Susan. *The Dialectics of Seeing: Walter Benjamin and the Arcades Project*. (1989) Cambridge, Massachusetts: MIT Press, 1993.

Bull, Malcolm. 'The Ecstasy of Philistinism'. *New Left Review* 219 (September / October 1996): 22–41.

Bürger, Peter. *Theory of the Avant-garde*. Trans. Michael Shaw, foreword Jochen Schulte-Sasse. Minneapolis: University of Minnesota, 1984.

Butler, Marilyn. *Jane Austen and the war of Ideas*. (1975) Oxford: Clarendon Press, 1990.

Byron, Lord. *Don Juan*. (1819–24) Harmondsworth: Penguin, 1982.

Callinicos, Alex. *Against Postmodernism: A Marxist Critique*. Oxford: Polity Press, 1989.

— 'Messianic Ruminations'. *Radical Philosophy* 75 (Jan/Feb 1996): 37–41.

Caudwell, Christopher. *Illusion and Reality: A Study of the Sources of Poetry*. (1937) London: Lawrence and Wishart, 1946.

CCCS (Centre for Contemporary Cultural Studies). *Resistance through Rituals: Youth Subcultures in Post-War Britain*. London: Hutchinson, 1976.

— *Women Take Issue: Aspects of Women's Subordination*. London: Hutchinson, 1978.

Chambers, Ian, Clarke, John, Connell, Ian, Curti, Lidia, Hall, Stuart and Jefferson, Tony. 'Marxism and Culture'. *Screen* 18:4 (Winter 1977–8): 101–19.

Churchill, Caryl. *Plays: Volume Two (Softcops, Top Girls, Fen, Serious Money)*. London: Methuen, 1990.

Cohen, Margaret. *Profane Illumination: Walter Benjamin and the Paris of Surrealist Revolution*. London: University of California Press, 1995.

Connor, Steven. *Postmodernist Culture: An Introduction to Theories of the Contemporary*. Oxford: Basil Blackwell, 1989.

— *Theory and Cultural Value*. Oxford: Basil Blackwell, 1992.

Conrad, Joseph. *Nostromo* (1904). Harmondsworth: Penguin, 1963.

Cook, Pam. 'Neither Here nor There: National Identity in Gainsborough Costume Drama'. In Higson, ed. 1996: 51–65.

Coole, Diana. 'Is class a difference that makes a difference?'. *Radical Philosophy* 77 (May/June 1996): 17–25.

Copeland, Edward. *Women Writing About Money: Women's Fiction in England, 1790–1820*. Cambridge: Cambridge University Press, 1995.

— 'Money'. In Copeland and McMaster, eds. 1997: 131–48.

— and McMaster, Juliet, eds. *The Cambridge Companion to Jane Austen*. Cambridge: Cambridge University Press, 1997.

Corredor, Eva L. *Lukács After Communism: Interviews with Contemporary Intellectuals*. London: Duke University Press, 1997.

Cosgrove, Denis and Daniels, Stephen, eds. *The iconography of landscape: Essays on the symbolic representation, design and use of past environments*. Cambridge: Cambridge University Press, 1988.

Coward, Rosalind and Ellis, John. *Language and Materialism: Developments in semiology and the theory of the subject*. London: Routledge, 1977a.

Coward, Rosalind. 'Class, "Culture" and the Social Formation'. *Screen* 18: 1 (Spring 1977b): 75–105.

Craig, David. *Marxists on Literature: an anthology*. Harmondsworth: Penguin, 1975.

D'Amico, Masolino. 'Oscar Wilde Between Socialism and Aestheticism'. *English Miscellany* 8 (1967): 111–39.

Daniel, Jamie Owen and Moylan, Tom, eds. *Not Yet: Reconsidering Ernst Bloch*. London: Verso, 1997.

Daniel, Stephen. *Fields of Vision: Landscape Imagery and National Identity in England and the United States*. Princeton, New Jersey: Princeton University Press, 1993.

Davies, Ioan. *Cultural Studies and Beyond: Fragments of Empire*. London: Routledge, 1995.

Debord, Guy. *The Society of the Spectacle*. (1967) Trans. Donald Nicholson-Smith. New York: Zone Books, 1994.

Denning, Michael. *Mechanic Accents: Dime Novels and Working-Class Culture in America*. London: Verso, 1987.

Dentith, Simon. *Bakhtinian Thought: An introductory reader*. London: Routledge, 1995.

Derrida, Jacques. *The Truth in Painting*. Trans. Geoffrey Bennington and Ian McLeod. Chicago: University of Chicago Press, 1987.

— 'Call It a Day for Democracy'. In *The Other Heading: Reflections on Today's Europe*. Trans. Pascale-Anne Brault and Michael B. Naas. Bloomington and Indianapolis: Indiana University Press, 1992.

— *Specters of Marx: The State of the Debt, the Work of Mourning, and the New International*. Trans. Peggy Kamuf. London: Routledge, 1994.

Dollimore, Jonathan and Sinfield, Alan, eds. *Political Shakespeare*. Manchester: Manchester University Press, 1985. (Second edition with additional chapters, 1994).

Drain, Richard, ed. *Twentieth-Century Theatre: a sourcebook*. London: Routledge, 1995.

Duckworth, Alistair. *The Improvement of the Estate: A Study of Jane Austen's Novels*. Baltimore: Johns Hopkins, 1971.

During, Simon, ed. *The Cultural Studies Reader*. London: Routledge, 1993.

Dworkin, Dennis. *Cultural Marxism in Postwar Britain: History, the New*

Left, and the Origins of Cultural Studies. London: Duke University Press, 1997.

Eagleton, Terry. *Criticism and Ideology.* London: New Left Books, 1976a.

— *Marxism and Literary Criticism.* London: Methuen, 1976b.

— 'Text, Ideology, Realism'. In *Literature and Society: Selected Papers from the English Institute, 1978*, ed. E. Said. London: Johns Hopkins University Press, 1980.

— *Walter Benjamin: or Towards a Revolutionary Criticism.* London: Verso, 1981.

— *The Rape of Clarissa: Writing, Sexuality, and the Class-Struggle in Samuel Richardson.* Oxford: Blackwell, 1982.

— *Literary Theory: An Introduction.* Oxford: Blackwell, 1983.

— *Against the Grain: Essays 1975–1985.* London: Verso, 1986.

— 'Nationalism: Irony and Commitment'. *Field Day Pamphlet.* Derry: Field Day, 1988.

— *Saint Oscar.* Derry: Field Day, 1989.

— *The Ideology of the Aesthetic.* Oxford: Blackwell, 1990a.

— ed. *Raymond Williams: Critical Perspectives.* Boston: Northeastern University Press, 1990b.

— *Ideology: an introduction.* London: Verso, 1991.

— ed. *Ideology.* Harlow, Essex: Longman, 1994.

— *Heathcliff and the Great Hunger: Studies in Irish Culture.* London: Verso, 1995a.

— 'Marxism without Marxism': Review of *Specters of Marx* by Jacques Derrida. *Radical Philosophy* 73 (1995b): 35–7. (Reprinted in Regan 1998.)

— *The Illusions of Postmodernism.* Oxford: Blackwell, 1996.

— 'Where Do Postmodernists Come From?'.In Wood and Foster, eds. 1997: 17–25.

— Jameson, Fredric, and Said, Edward. *Nationalism, Colonialism and Literature.* (1988) Minneapolis: University of Minnesota Press, 1992.

— and Milne, Drew, eds. *Marxist Literary Theory: a reader.* Oxford: Blackwell, 1996.

Easthope, Anthony. *Literary into Cultural Studies.* London: Routledge, 1991.

Ebert, Teresa. 'Writing in the Political: Resistance (Post) Modernism'. *Legal Studies Forum* 15: 4 (1991): 291–303.

Ellmann, Richard. *Oscar Wilde.* Harmondsworth: Penguin, 1988.

Emerson, Caryl. *The First Hundred Years of Mikhail Bakhtin.* Princeton, New Jersey: Princeton University Press, 1997.

Engels, Friedrich. *The Condition of the Working Class in England.* London: Granada, 1969.

Fabricant, Carole. *Swift's Landscape.* Baltimore: Johns Hopkins University Press, 1982.

— 'The Literature of Domestic Tourism and the Public Consumption of Private Property'. In *The New Eighteenth Century: Theory, Politics, English Literature*, eds. Felicity Nussbaum and Laura Brown. London: Routledge, 1987: 254–75.

Fausset, Hugh l'Anson, ed. *Minor Poets of the Eighteenth Century: Parnell, Green, Dyer and Anne, Countess of Winchelsea*. London: J.M. Dent, 1930.

Febvre, Lucien and Martin, Henri-Jean. *The Coming of the Book*. (1958) London: Verso, 1997.

Felski, Rita. *Beyond feminist aesthetics: feminist literature and social change*. UK: Hutchinson Radius, 1989.

Feltes, Norman. *Modes of Production of Victorian Novels*. Chicago: University of Chicago Press, 1986.

— *Literary Capital and the late Victorian Novel*. Madison: University of Wisconsin Press, 1993.

Fergus, Jan. *Jane Austen: A Literary Life*. Basingstoke: Macmillan, 1991.

Ferguson, Moira. *First Feminists: British Women Writers, 1578–1799*. Bloomington: Indiana University Press, 1985.

— 'Resistance and Power in the Life and Writing of Ann Yearsley'. *The Eighteenth Century: Theory and Interpretation* 27 (1986): 247–68.

Fiske, John. 'British cultural studies and television' (1987). In Storey, ed. 1996: 115–46.

— *Understanding Popular Culture*. Boston: Unwin Hyman, 1989.

Fletcher, John. 'Marx the uncanny?'. *Radical Philosophy* 75 (Jan/Feb 1996): 31–7.

Forgacs, David. 'Gramsci and the British Left'. *New Left Review* 176 (July–August 1989): 70–88.

— 'Marxist literary theories'. In *Modern Literary Theory: a comparative introduction*, eds. Ann Jefferson and David Robey. London: Batsford, 1986.

Fowler, Alistair. 'Country House Poems: The Politics of a Genre'. *The Seventeenth Century* 1: 1 (1986): 1–14.

Fried, Albert and Elman, Richard, eds. *Charles Booth's London: A Portrait of the Poor at the Turn of the Century drawn from his 'Life and Labour of the People in London'*. Harmondsworth: Pelican, 1971. (With a preface by Raymond Williams.)

Frith, Simon and John Savage. 'Pearls and swine: the intellectuals and the mass media'. *New Left Review* 198 (1992): 107–16.

Frow, John. *Marxism and Literary History*. (1986) Oxford: Basil Blackwell, 1988.

— *Cultural Studies and Cultural Value*. Oxford: Clarendon Press, 1995.

Fukuyama, Francis. *The End of History and the Last Man*. New York: The Free Press, 1992.

Fuss, Diana. *Essentially speaking: feminism, nature and difference*. New York: Routledge, 1989.

Gable, Robin, ed. *Resources of Hope: Culture, Democracy, Socialism*. London: Verso, 1989.

Gagnier, Regenia. *Idylls of the Marketplace: Oscar Wilde and the Victorian Public*. Aldershot: Scolar Press, 1987.

— 'Is market society the *fin* of history?' In Ledger and McCracken 1995: 290–310.

— 'Wilde and the Victorians'. In Raby 1997: 18–33.

Geraghty, Christine. *Women and Soap Opera*. Cambridge: Polity Press, 1991.

— 'Reflections on History in Teaching Cultural Studies'. *Cultural Studies* 10: 2 (1996): 345–53.

Geras, Norman. 'Post-Marxism?'. *New Left Review* 163 (1987): 40–82.

— 'Ex-Marxism Without Substance: Being a Real Reply to Laclau and Mouffe'. *New Left Review* 169 (May/June 1988): 34–62.

Gibbons, Luke. *Transformations in Irish Culture*. Cork: Cork University Press, 1996.

Gilroy, Paul. *Small Acts: Thoughts on the Politics of Black Cultures*. London: Serpents Tail, 1993.

Girouard, Mark. *Life in the English Country House: A Social and Architectural History*. Harmondsworth: Penguin, 1980.

Giroux, Henry A. and McLaren, Peter. 'Paulo Freire, Postmodernism, and the Utopian Imagination: A Blochian Reading'. In Daniel and Moylan 1997: 138–62.

Gittings, Robert, Selby, Keith, and Wensley, Chris. *Screening the Novel: The Theory and Practice of Literary Dramatization*. Basingstoke: Macmillan, 1990.

Golby, J.M., ed. *Culture and Society in Britain, 1850–1890: A Source Book of Contemporary Writings*. Oxford: Oxford University Press, 1988.

Goldmann, Lucien. *The Dialectics of Liberation*, ed. D. Cooper. Harmondsworth: Penguin, 1969.

Goodridge, John. *Rural Life in Eighteenth-Century English Poetry*. Cambridge: Cambridge University Press, 1995.

Gorz, Andre. *Farewell to the Working Class*. Trans. M. Sonenscher. London: Pluto, 1982.

Gramsci, Antonio. *Selections from Prison Notebooks*. London: Lawrence and Wishart, 1971.

Greene, Richard. *Mary Leapor; A Study in Eighteenth-Century Women's Poetry*. Oxford: Clarendon Press, 1993.

Griffin, Dustin. *Literary Patronage in England, 1650–1800*. Cambridge: Cambridge University Press, 1996.

Griffin, Robert J. *Wordsworth's Pope: A Study in Literary Historiography*. Cambridge: Cambridge University Press, 1995.

Grossberg, Larry. *We Gotta Get Out of This Place: Popular Conservatism and Postmodern Culture*. New York: Routledge, 1992.

— and Nelson, C., eds. *Marxism and the Interpretation of Culture*. Basingstoke: Macmillan, 1988.

—, Nelson, Cary and Treichler, Paula, eds. *Cultural Studies*. London: Routledge, 1992.

Hall, Gary. '"It's a thin line between love and hate": why cultural studies is so "naff"'. In Hall and Wortham. 1996: 25–46.

Hall, Gary, and Wortham, Simon, eds. 'Authorizing culture'. *Angelaki* 2: 2. Oxford: Anthony Rowe, 1996.

Hall, Stuart. 'Authoritarian Populism: A Reply to Jessop et al.'. *New Left Review* 151 (1985): 115–25.

— *The Hard Road to Renewal: Thatcherism and the Crisis of the Left*. London: Verso, 1988.

—, Hobson, Dorothy, Lowe, Andrew and Willis, Paul, eds. *Culture, Media, Language: Working Papers in Cultural Studies, 1972–79*. (1980) London: Routledge, 1992.

— and Jacques, Martin, eds. *The Politics of Thatcherism*. London: Lawrence and Wishart, 1983.

— eds. *New Times: The Changing Face of Politics in the 1990s*. London: Lawrence and Wishart, 1989.

Hammond, Brean. 'The Political Unconscious in *Mansfield Park*'. In *Mansfield Park*, ed. Nigel Wood (1993): 56–90.

Harris, David. *From Class Struggle to the Politics of Pleasure: The Effects of Gramscianism on Cultural Studies*. London: Routledge, 1992.

Harris, John. *The Design of the English Country House, 1620–1920*. London: Trefoil Books, 1985.

Harrison, J.C. *Late Victorian Britain, 1875–1901*. Glasgow: Fontana, 1990.

Harrison, Tony. *Selected Poems*. Harmondsworth: Penguin, 1984.

— *V*. Newcastle upon Tyne: Bloodaxe, 1985.

Hawkes, David. *Ideology*. London: Routledge, 1996.

Hebdige, Dick. *Subculture: The Meaning of Style*. London: Methuen, 1979.

— 'Hiding in the light: youth surveillance and display', in *Hiding in the Light: Images and Things*. London: Routledge, 1989: 17–37.

Hennessy, Rosemary. 'Queer Theory, Left Politics'. In Makdisi et al. 1996: 214–42.

Hewison, Robert. *The Heritage Industry: Britain in a Climate of Decline*. London: Methuen, 1987.

Higson, Andrew. 'Re-presenting the National Past: Nostalgia and Pastiche in the Heritage Film'. In Lester Friedman, ed. *Fires Were Started: British*

Cinema and Thatcherism. Minneapolis, Minnesota: University of Minnesota Press, 1993: 109–29.

— 'The Heritage Film and British Cinema'. In *Dissolving Views: Key Writings on British Cinema*, ed. Andrew Higson. London: Cassell, 1996: 232–48.

Hill, Bridget. *Eighteenth-Century Women: An Anthology*. London: George Allen and Unwin, 1984.

Hill, John. *Sex, Class and Realism: British Cinema 1956–63*. London: British Film Institute, 1986.

Hobsbawm, E.J. *The Age of Revolution: Europe, 1789–1848*. (1962) London: Abacus, 1977.

— *The Age of Empire, 1875–1914*. London: Weidenfeld and Nicolson, 1987.

Hobson, Dorothy. *Crossroads: The Drama of a Soap Opera*. London: Methuen, 1982.

Hoggart, Richard. *The Uses of Literacy*. (1957) Harmondsworth: Pelican, 1958.

— *Speaking to Each Other, vol.2: About Literature*. Oxford: Oxford University Press, 1970.

Huysmans, J.K. *Against Nature*. (1884) Trans. Robert Baldick. Harmondsworth: Penguin, 1959.

Jackson, Holbrook. *The 1890s*. (1913) London: The Cresset Press, 1988.

Jackson, Leonard. *The Dematerialisation of Karl Marx: Literature and Marxist Theory*. London: Longman, 1994.

Jacques, Martin, ed. *Marxism Today* (November–December 1998).

James, Henry. *The Spoils of Poynton*. 1897. Harmondsworth: Penguin, 1987.

Jameson, Fredric. *Marxism and Form: Twentieth-Century Dialectical Theories of Literature*. (1971) Princeton, NJ: Princeton University Press, 1974.

— 'Reification and Utopia in Mass Culture'. *Social Text* 1 (Winter 1979): 130–48. (Also reprinted in Jameson 1992b.)

— *The Political Unconscious: Narrative as a Socially Symbolic Act*. (1981) London: Routledge, 1983.

— *The Ideologies of Theory: Essays 1971–1986, Vol.II The Syntax of History*. Routledge, 1988.

— *Postmodernism; or, The Cultural Logic of Late Capitalism*. (1991) London: Verso, 1992a.

— *Signatures of the Visible*. London: Routledge, 1992b.

— *The Seeds of Time*. New York: Columbia University Press, 1994.

— 'Marx's Purloined Letter'. *New Left Review* 109 (1995): 75–109.

— *Late Marxism*. (1990) London: Verso, 1996.

Jarvis, Simon. *Adorno: A Critical Introduction*. Cambridge: Polity Press, 1998.

Jenks, Chris. 'Watching your step: The history and practice of the flâneur'. In *Visual Culture*, ed. Chris Jenks. London: Routledge, 1995: 142–60.

Jessop, B., Bennett, K., Bromley, S. and Ling, T. 'Authoritarian Populism: Two Nations and Thatcherism'. *New Left Review* 147 (1984): 32–60.

— 'Thatcherism and the Politics of Hegemony: A Reply to Stuart Hall'. *New Left Review* 165 (1985): 87–101.

— 'Popular Capitalism, Flexible Accumulation and Left Strategy'. *New Left Review* 165 (1987): 104–22.

Jessop, B., Bennett, K. and Bromley, S. 'Farewell to Thatcherism?'. *New Left Review* 179 (1990): 81–102.

Johnson, Claudia. 'Gender, Theory and Jane Austen Culture'. In *Mansfield Park*, ed. Nigel Wood (1993): 91–120.

— 'Austen cults and cultures'. In Copeland and McMaster, eds. 1997: 211–26.

Jones, Ann Rosalind. 'Mills and Boon meets feminism'. In *The Progress of Romance: The politics of popular fiction*, ed. Jean Radford. London: Routledge and Kegan Paul, 1986: 195–220.

Jones, Paul. 'The myth of "Raymond Hoggart"'. (1994) *Cultural Studies* 8:3 (October 1994): 394–416.

Jones, Vivien, ed. *Women in the eighteenth century: constructions of femininity*. London: Routledge, 1990.

Kelly, Gary. 'Religion and politics'. In Copeland and McMaster. 1997: 149–69.

Khanin, Dmitry. 'Will aesthetics be the last stronghold of Marxism?'. *Philosophy and Literature* 16 (1992): 266–78.

Klaus, II. Gustav. *The Literature of Labour: Two Hundred Years of Working-class Writing*. Brighton: Harvester, 1985.

Kohl, Norbert. *Oscar Wilde: The Works of a Conformist Rebel*. Trans. David Henry Wilson. Cambridge: Cambridge University Press, 1989.

Laclau, Ernesto. *Politics and Ideology in Marxist Theory: Capitalism, Fascism, Populism*. London: New Left Books, 1977.

— 'The Impossibility of Society'. *Canadian Journal of Political and Social Theory* 7:1–2 (1983).

— 'Post-Marxism without Apologies'. *New Left Review* 166 (1987): 79–106.

— 'Politics and the Limits of Modernity'. In Ross, ed. 1988: 63–82.

— *Emancipation(s)*. London: Verso, 1996.

—, and Mouffe, Chantal. *Hegemony and Socialist Strategy: Towards a Radical Democratic Politics*. London: Verso, 1985.

Landry, Donna. *The Muses of Resistance: Laboring-class women's poetry in Britain, 1739–1796*. Cambridge: Cambridge University Press, 1990.

— 'Commodity Feminism'. In *The Profession of Eighteenth-Century Literature: Reflections on an Institution*, ed. Leo Damrosch. Madison: University of Wisconsin Press, 1992: 154–74.

—, and MacLean, Gerald. 'Rereading Laclau and Mouffe'. *Rethinking MARXISM* 4: 4 (Winter 1991): 41–60.

Lauritzen, Monica. *Jane Austen's Emma on Television: A Study of a BBC Classic Serial.* Goteborg: Acta Universitatis Gothoburgensis, 1981.

Leavis, F.R. *The Great Tradition.* 1948. Harmondsworth: Pelican, 1972.

Ledger, Sally and McCracken, Scott, eds. *Cultural Politics at the fin de siècle.* Cambridge: Cambridge University Press, 1995.

Levin, Charles. *Jean Baudrillard: a study in cultural metaphysics.* Hemel Hempstead: Harvester Wheatsheaf, 1996.

Levin, Thomas V. 'For the Record: Adorno on Music in the Age of its Technological Reproducibility'. *October* 55 (Winter 1990): 23–64.

Levinson, Marjorie. *Wordsworth's Great Period Poems.* Cambridge: Cambridge University Press, 1986.

Levitas, Ruth. 'Educated Hope: Ernst Bloch on Abstract and Concrete Utopia'. In Daniel and Moylan. 1997: 65–79.

Leys, C. 'Still a Question of Hegemony'. *New Left Review* 181 (1990): 119–28.

Light, Alison. '"Returning to Manderley" – romance fiction, female sexuality and class'. *Feminist Review* 16 (April 1984): 7–25.

Loughrey, Bryan. *The Pastoral Mode: A Casebook.* Basingstoke: Macmillan, 1984.

Lovell, Terry. 'Jane Austen and Gentry Society'. In *Literature, Society and the Sociology of Literature: Proceedings of the Conference Held at the University of Essex, July 1976.* University of Essex, 1977, 118–32.

— *Pictures of Reality: Aesthetics, politics and pleasure.* London: British Film Institute, 1980.

— *Consuming Fiction.* London: Verso, 1987.

Lucas, John. *England and Englishness: Ideas of Nationhood in English Poetry, 1688–1900.* London: Hogarth, 1991.

Lukács, Georg. *The Historical Novel.* (1937) Trans. Hannah and Stanley Mitchell. London: Merlin, 1962.

— 'Narrate or Describe?' in *Writer and Critic.* Trans. Arthur Kahn. London: Merlin Press, 1970: 110–48.

— *History and Class Consciousness: Studies in Marxist Dialectics.* (1922) Trans. Rodney Livingstone. London: Merlin Press, 1971 (with Lukács's Preface to the 1967 edition).

MacCabe, Colin. *James Joyce and the Revolution of the Word.* Basingstoke: Macmillan, 1979.

MacCarthey, Fiona. *William Morris: A Life for Our Time.* London: Faber and Faber, 1994.

Macherey, Pierre. *A Theory of Literary Production.* (1966) Trans. Geoffrey Wall. London: Routledge and Kegan Paul, 1978.

— *The Object of Literature.* (1990) Trans. David Macey. Cambridge: Cambridge University Press, 1995.

— 'An Interview with Pierre Macherey', *Red Letters* 5 (Summer 1977): 3–9.

Magnus, Bernd and Cullenberg, Stephen, eds. *Whither Marxism?: Global Crises in International Perspective.* New York and London: Routledge, 1995.

Makdisi, Saree, Casarino, Cesare and Karl, Rebecca E., eds. *Marxism Beyond Marxism.* London: Routledge, 1996.

Mandler, Peter. *The Rise of the English Country House.* New Haven and London: Yale University Press, 1997.

Marcuse, Herbert. 'The Affirmative Character of Culture'. In *Negations: Essays in Critical Theory.* London: Free Association Books, 1988: 88–133.

Marx, Karl. *Grundrisse: Foundations of the Critique of Political Economy.* Trans. Martin Nicolaus. Harmondsworth: Pelican, 1973.

— *Capital: An abridged edition,* ed. David McLellan. Oxford: Oxford University Press, 1995.

Marx, Karl and Engels, Frederick. *Selected Correspondence.* Trans. I. Lasker. Moscow: Progress Publishers, 1965.

— *The German Ideology.* London: Lawrence and Wishart, 1970.

— *Marx and Engels: Basic Writings on Politics and Philosophy.* London: Fontana, 1984.

— *Selected Works in One Volume.* London: Lawrence and Wishart, 1991.

McCracken, Scott. *Pulp: Reading Popular Fiction.* Manchester: Manchester University Press, 1998.

McGann, Jerome. *The Romantic Ideology.* Chicago: University of Chicago Press, 1983.

McGuigan, Jim. *Culture and The Public Sphere.* London: Routledge, 1996.

McLaughlin, Kevin. *Writing in Parts. Imitation and Exchange in Nineteenth-Century Literature.* Stanford, California: Stanford University Press, 1995.

McLellan, David. *Ideology.* Milton Keynes: Open University Press, 1986.

McLennan, Gregor. 'Post-Marxism and the "Four Sins" of Modernist Theorizing'. *New Left Review.* 218 (July/August 1996): 53–74.

McMaster, Julict. 'Class'. In Copeland and McMaster, eds. 1997: 115–30.

McRobbie, Angela. 'Settling Accounts with Subcultures: A Feminist Critique'. *Screen Education* 34 (Spring, 1980): 37–49. [Reprinted in Bennett et al. 1981.]

Miller, Jonathan. *Subsequent Performances.* London: Faber and Faber, 1986.

Milne, Drew. Review of Macherey, *The Object of Literature. Textual Practice* 10:1 (Spring 1996): 201–207.

Milner, Andrew. *Cultural Materialism.* Melbourne, Australia: Melbourne University Press, 1993.

— *Literature, culture and society.* London: UCL Press, 1996.

Minihan, Janet. *The Nationalization of Culture: The Development of State Subsidies to the Arts in Great Britain*. London: Hamish Hamilton, 1977.

Moers, Ellen. *The Dandy: Brummell to Beerbohm*. London: Secker and Warburg, 1960.

Moi, Toril. *Sexual/Textual Politics: Feminist Literary Theory*. London: Methuen, 1985.

Montagu, Lady Mary Wortley. *Essays and Poems and Simplicity, a Comedy*, ed. Robert Halsband and Isobel Grundy. Oxford: Clarendon Press, 1993.

Morley, David. *Television, Audiences and Cultural Studies*. London: Routledge, 1992.

— and Chen, Kuan-Hsing, eds. *Stuart Hall: Critical Dialogues in Cultural Studies*. London: Routledge, 1996.

Morris, Meaghan. 'Things to do with shopping centres'. (1987) In During, ed. 1993: 295–319.

— 'Banality in cultural studies'. (1988) In Storey, ed. 1996: 147–67.

Morris, William. *News from Nowhere and Selected Writings and Designs*. Harmondsworth: Penguin, 1962.

Mouzelis, Nicos. 'Marxism or Post-Marxism?'. *New Left Review* 167 (January/February 1988): 107–123.

Mulhern, Francis, ed. *Contemporary Marxist Literary Criticism*. London: Longman, 1992.

— 'A welfare culture?: Hoggart and Williams in the fifties'. *Radical Philosophy* 77 (May–June 1996): 26–37.

— *The Present Lasts a Long Time: Essays in Cultural Politics*. Cork: Cork University Press, 1998.

Mulvey, Laura. 'Visual pleasure and narrative cinema'. *Screen* 16:3 (Autumn 1975): 6–18.

— 'Afterthoughts on "Visual pleasure and narrative cinema" inspired by *Duel in the Sun*'. In *Psychoanalysis and Cinema*, ed. E. Ann Kaplan. London: Routledge, 1990: 24–35.

Neuburg, Victor E. *Popular Literature: A History and Guide*. Harmondsworth: Pelican, 1977.

Nicholsen, Shierry Weber. *Exact Imagination, Late Work: On Adorno's Aesthetics*. Cambridge: MIT Press, 1997.

Nussbaum, Felicity. *The Autobiographical Subject: Gender and Ideology in Eighteenth-Century England*. Baltimore: Johns Hopkins University Press, 1995.

Osborne, Peter. *The Politics of Time: Modernity and Avant-garde*. London: Verso, 1995.

Ousby, Ian. *The Englishman's England: Taste, travel and the rise of tourism*. Cambridge: Cambridge University Press, 1990.

Parfitt, George. *English Poetry of the Seventeenth Century*. London: Longman, 1992.

Pater, Walter. *The Renaissance: Studies in Art and Poetry*. (1873) Oxford: Oxford World's Classics, 1986.

Pêcheux, Michel. *Language, Semantics and Ideology*. London: Macmillan, 1982.

Pittock, Murray G.H. *Spectrum of Decadence: The Literature of the 1890s*. London: Routledge, 1993.

Poovey, Mary. *The Proper Lady and the Woman Writer: Ideology as Style in the Works of Mary Wollstonecraft, Mary Shelley and Jane Austen*. Chicago: University of Chicago Press, 1984.

— *Uneven Developments: The Ideological Work of Gender in Mid-Victorian England*. London: Virago, 1989.

Porter, Roy. *English Society in the Eighteenth Century*. Harmondsworth: Penguin, 1982.

Prendergast, Christopher, ed. *Cultural Materialism: On Raymond Williams*. London: University of Minnesota Press, 1995.

Raby, Peter, ed. *The Cambridge Companion to Oscar Wilde*. Cambridge: Cambridge University Press, 1997.

Radway, Janice. *Reading the Romance: Women, patriarchy, and popular literature*. (1984) Chapel Hill: North Carolina University Press, 1987.

Regan, Stephen, ed. *The Eagleton Reader*. Oxford: Blackwell, 1998.

Rice, Philip and Waugh, Patricia. *Modern Literary Theory: A Reader*. London: Edward Arnold, 1992.

Richards, Thomas. *The Commodity Culture of Victorian Britain: Advertising and Spectacle, 1851–1914*. London: Verso, 1991.

Rizzo, Betty. 'Mary Leapor: An Anxiety for Influence'. *The Age of Johnson*. 4 (1991): 313–43.

Roberts, Andrew. *Psychoanalysis and Literature*. Basingstoke: Macmillan, forthcoming.

Rogers, Pat, ed. *Alexander Pope: The Oxford Authors*. Oxford: Oxford University Press, 1993.

Root, Jane. *Open the Box*. London: Comedia, 1986.

Rose, Mark. *Authors and Owners: The Invention of Copyright*. Cambridge, Massachusetts: Harvard University Press, 1993.

Ross, Andrew, ed. *Universal Abandon? The Politics of Postmodernism*. Minneapolis: University of Minnesota Press, 1988.

Ross, Angus, ed. *Poetry of the Augustan Age*. London: Longman, 1970.

Rowbotham, Sheila. 'Dear Dr Marx: A Letter from a Socialist Feminist'. In *The Communist Manifesto Now: Socialist Register 1998*, ed. Leo Panitch and Colin Leys. Rendlesham, Suffolk: Merlin Press, 1998: 1–17.

Rustin, Michael. 'Absolute Voluntarism: Critique of a Post-Marxist Concept of Hegemony'. *New German Critique* 43 (1988): 146–73.

Ryan, Michael. *Marxism and Deconstruction: A Critical Articulation*. Baltimore: Johns Hopkins University Press, 1982.

Ryle, Martin. 'Long live literature? English Literature, Radical Criticism and Cultural Studies'. *Radical Philosophy* 67 (Summer 1988): 21–7.

Said, Edward W. *Musical Elaborations*. London: Vintage, 1992.

— *Culture and Imperialism*. London: Vintage, 1994.

Sales, Roger. *English Literature in History, 1780–1830: Pastoral and Politics*. London: Routledge, 1983.

— *Jane Austen and Representations of Regency England*. London: Routledge, 1994.

Sambrook, James, ed. *The Seasons and the Castle of Indolence, by James Thomson*. Oxford: Clarendon Press, 1972.

Samuel, Raphael. *Theatres of Memory, Vol I: Past and Present in Contemporary Culture*. London: Verso, 1994.

Saunders, David. *Authorship and Copyright*. London: Routledge, 1992.

Schwarz, Bill. 'Popular Culture: The Long March'. *Cultural Studies* 3:2 (1989): 250–5.

— 'Where is cultural studies?'. *Cultural Studies* 8:3 (October 1994): 377–93.

Scott, Joan. '"La Querelle des Femmes" in the late Twentieth Century'. *New Left Review* 226 (November–December 1997): 3–19.

Scott, Walter. *Waverley*. (1814) London: J.M. Dent, 1906.

Sedgwick, Eve Kosofsky. 'Jane Austen and the Masturbating Girl'. *Critical Inquiry* 17 (1991): 818–37.

Shawe-Taylor, Desmond. *Dramatic Art: Theatrical Paintings from the Garrick Club*. London: Dulwich Picture Gallery, 1997.

Shiach, Morag. *Discourse on Popular Culture: Class, Gender and History in Cultural Analysis, 1730 to the Present*. Oxford: Polity Press, 1989.

Shoemaker, Robert B. *Gender in English Society, 1650–1850: The Emergence of Separate Spheres?* London: Longman, 1998.

Sim, Stuart. *Georg Lukács*. Hemel Hempstead: Harvester Wheatsheaf, 1994.

— ed. *Post-marxism*, Edinburgh: Edinburgh University Press, 1998.

Simpson, David, ed. *Subject to History: Ideology, Class, Gender*. Ithaca and London: Cornell University Press, 1991.

Sinfield, Alan. *Alfred Tennyson*. Oxford: Basil Blackwell, 1986.

— *Faultlines: Cultural Materialism and the Politics of Dissident Reading*. Oxford: Oxford University Press, 1992.

Sivanandan, A. *Communities of Resistance: Writings on Black Struggles for Socialism*. London: Verso, 1990.

Slater, Don. 'Photography and Modern Vision; The spectacle of "natural magic"'. In *Visual Culture*, ed. Chris Jenks. London: Routledge, 1995: 218–37.

Soper, Kate. 'The limits of hauntology'. *Radical Philosophy* 75 (January/February 1996): 26–31.

Spring, David. 'Interpreters of Jane Austen's Social World: Literary Critics and Historians'. In *Jane Austen; New Perspectives*, ed. Janet Todd. New York: Homes and Meier, 1983: 59–72.

Sprinker, Michael. *Imaginary Relations: Aesthetics and Ideology in the Theory of Historical Materialism.* London; Verso, 1987.

— *History and Ideology in Proust: 'A la recherche du temps perdu' and the Third French Republic.* (1994) London: Verso, 1998.

Stallybrass, Peter and White, Allon. *The Politics and Poetics of Transgression.* London: Methuen, 1986.

Steedman, Carolyn. 'A Weekend with Elektra'. *Literature and History.* 6:1 (Spring 1997): 17–42.

Steele, Tom. *The Emergence of Cultural Studies 1945–65: Cultural Politics, Adult Education and the English Question.* London: Lawrence and Wishart, 1997.

Stewart, Maaja A. *Domestic Realities and Imperial Fictions: Jane Austen's Novels in Eighteenth-Century Contexts.* Athens, Georgia and London: University of Georgia Press, 1993.

Stewart, Susan. *On Longing: Narratives of the Miniature, the Gigantic, the Souvenir, the Collection.* (1984) Durham, NC, and London: Duke University Press, 1993.

Storey, John, ed. *Cultural Theory and Popular Culture.* Hemel Hempstead: Harvester Wheatsheaf, 1994.

— ed. *What is Cultural Studies?: A Reader.* London: Arnold, 1996.

Sutherland, John. *Is Heathcliff a Murderer?: Puzzles in Nineteenth-Century Fiction.* Oxford: Oxford University Press, 1996.

Suvin, Darko. 'Locus, Horizon, and Orientation: The Concept of Possible Worlds as a Key to Utopian Studies'. In Daniel and Moylan, eds. 1997: 122–37.

Tasker, Yvonne. *Feminist Crime Writing: The politics of genre.* Sheffield: Pavic, 1991.

Thomas, J.D. '"The Soul of Man Under Socialism": An essay in Context'. *Rice University Studies* 51:1 (Winter 1965): 83–95.

Thompson, E.P. 'Socialist Humanism: An Epistle to the Philistines'. *New Reasoner* 1 (Summer 1957): 105–43.

Thompson, Edward P., ed. *Out of Apathy.* London: Stevens and Sons, 1960.

— *The Making of the English Working Class.* Harmondsworth: Penguin, 1968.

— *William Morris: Romantic to Revolutionary.* (1955) London: Merlin Press, 1977 (revised ed.).

— *The Poverty of Theory.* London: Merlin, 1978.

— *Customs in Common.* (1991) Harmondsworth: Penguin, 1993.

— and Sugden, Marian, eds. *Two eighteenth century poems: The Thresher's Labour and The Woman's Labour.* London: Merlin, 1989.

— and Yeo, Eileen, eds. *The Unknown Mayhew: Selections from the 'Morning Chronicle', 1849–50.* Harmondsworth: Pelican, 1973.

Thompson, James. *Between Self and the World: the Novels of Jane Austen.* University Park, Penn.: Penn State University Press, 1988.

Tobin, Mary-Elizabeth Fowkes. 'Aiding Impoverished Gentlewomen: Power and Class in *Emma'*. *Criticism* 30 (Fall 1988): 413–30.

Tuchman, Gaye and Fortin, Nina E. *Edging Women Out: Victorian Novelists, Publishers and Social Change.* London: Routledge, 1989.

Turner, Cheryl. *Living by the Pen: Women Writers in the Eighteenth Century.* London: Routledge, 1994.

Turner, Graeme. *British Cultural Studies.* London: Unwin Hyman, 1990.

Valenze, Deborah. *The First Industrial Woman.* Oxford: Oxford University Press, 1995.

Vološinov, V.N. *Marxism and the Philosophy of Language.* Trans. Ladislav Matejka and I.R. Titunik. Cambridge, Mass.: Harvard University Press, 1986.

Walkerdine, Valerie. 'Some day my prince will come: young girls and the preparation for adolescent sexuality'. In *Gender and Genderation,* ed. Angela McRobbie and Mica Nava. London: Macmillan, 1984: 162–84.

Watt, Ian. *The Rise of the Novel: Studies in Defoe, Richardson and Fielding.* (1957) Harmondsworth: Penguin, 1963.

Wilde, Oscar. *Selected Essays and Poems.* Harmondsworth: Penguin, 1954a.

— *Plays.* Harmondsworth: Penguin, 1954b.

— *The Picture of Dorian Gray.* 1891. Oxford: World's Classics, 1981.

— *The Complete Works of Oscar Wilde,* ed. Merlin Holland. Glasgow: Harper Collins, 1994.

Williams, Raymond. *Culture and Society, 1780–1950.* (1958) Harmondsworth: Penguin, 1963.

— *The Long Revolution.* (1961) Harmondsworth: Pelican, 1965.

— *The English Novel from Dickens to Lawrence.* London: Chatto and Windus, 1971.

— *The Country and the City.* London: Hogarth Press, 1973.

— *Marxism and Literature.* Oxford: Oxford University Press, 1977.

— *Problems in Materialism and Culture: Selected Essays.* London: Verso, 1980.

— *Politics and Letters: Interviews with New Left Review.* London: Verso, 1981.

— *Keywords: A vocabulary of culture and society.* London: Fontana, 1983a.

— *Towards 2000.* London: Chatto and Windus, 1983b.

— *What I Came to Say*. London: Hutchinson Radius, 1989a.

— *Resources of Hope: Culture, Democracy, Socialism*, ed. Robin Gable. London: Verso, 1989b.

— *The Politics of Modernism*. (1989) London: Verso, 1996.

Williams, Rosalind. *Dream Worlds: Mass Consumption in Late Nineteenth-Century France*. Berkeley and Los Angeles: University of California Press, 1982.

Wolff, Janet. *The Social Production of Art*. Basingstoke: Macmillan, 1993.

Wood, Ellen Meiksins. 'What is the "postmodern" agenda?'. In Wood and Foster, eds. 1997: 1–16.

— and Bellamy, John, eds. *In Defense of History: Marxism and the Postmodern Agenda*. New York: Monthly Review Press, 1997.

Wood, Nigel, ed. *Mansfield Park*. Buckingham, U.K.: Open University Press, 1993.

Wright, Patrick. *On Living in an Old Country: The National Past in Contemporary Britain*. London: Verso, 1991.

Wu, Chin-tao. 'Embracing the Enterprise Culture: Art Institutions since the 1980s'. *New Left Review* 230 (July–August 1998): 28–57.

Young, Robert. *White Mythologies: Writing History and the West*. London: Routledge, 1990.

— 'The Dialectics of Cultural Criticism'. In Hall and Wortham, eds. 1996: 9–24.

Žižek, Slavoj. *The Sublime Object of Ideology*. London: Verso, 1989.

— ed. *Mapping Ideology*. London: Verso, 1994.

Index